INDIGENOUS MOVEMENTS, SELF-REPRESENTATION, AND THE STATE IN LATIN AMERICA

Indigenous Movements, Self-Representation, and the State in Latin America

Edited by Kay B. Warren & Jean E. Jackson

University of Texas Press
Austin

Requests for permission to reproduce material from this work should
be sent to Permissions, University of Texas Press, P.O. Box 7819,
Austin, TX 78713-7819.

⊗ The paper used in this book meets the minimum requirements of
ANSI/NISO Z39.48-1992 (R1997) (Permanence of Paper).

Library of Congress Cataloging-in-Publication Data
Indigenous movements, self-representation, and the state in Latin
America / edited by Kay B. Warren and Jean E. Jackson.
    p.   cm.
Includes bibliographical references and index.
    ISBN 0-292-79138-0 (cloth : alk. paper)—ISBN 0-292-79141-0 (pbk. :
alk. paper)
    1. Indians—Politics and government.   2. Indians—Government
relations.   3. Indians, Treatment of—Latin America.   4. Indian
activists—Latin America.   5. Self-determination, National—Latin
America.   6. Latin America—Race relations.   7. Latin America—
Social policy.   8. Latin America—Politics and government.
I. Warren, Kay B., 1947–   II. Jackson, Jean E. (Jean Elizabeth),
1943–
    E65 .I475 2002
    323.1′198—dc21

                                                    2002005056

CONTENTS

ACKNOWLEDGMENTS

On behalf of all contributors to this volume we want to acknowledge the generous encouragement received in Colombia, Guatemala, and Brazil from anthropologist, political science, and linguist colleagues and from the indigenous communities and organizations that gave so generously of their time and helped the research in so many ways. Along with our contributors, David Maybury-Lewis, Bruce Mannheim, Deborah Yashar, and Wendy Weiss provided valuable commentaries during a preliminary conference in January 1999, which was generously funded by the David Rockefeller Center for Latin American Studies at Harvard University. The DRCLAS staff offered valuable logistical support for the meetings. We are grateful to the Office of the Dean of Humanities, Arts, and Social Sciences at the Massachusetts Institute of Technology for additional financial support. Bret Gustafson served as a skillful organizer and insightful rapporteur during and after the conference, and Kara McClellan deserves recognition for exceptionally competent and resourceful support during the manuscript preparation, and Tim Smith was an expert proofreader. Lynn Stephen and Ana Alonso, who reviewed the manuscript for the University of Texas Press, offered excellent comments and useful suggestions for revision. We deeply appreciate their candor and intellectual engagement with the essays. We are grateful to our editors at UT Press, Theresa May, Leslie Tingle, and Jan McInroy, for all their efforts on our behalf.

One aspect of the collaborative process has brought special pleasure: our engagement with indigenous movements in very different parts of Latin America—the Guatemalan highlands and the Amazonian lowlands. As we exchanged drafts of the introduction and reviewed the essays of other contributors, we were rewarded with fresh insights on issues old and new. We hope the introduction conveys this spirit of comparative discovery. Our special thanks to Loy Carrington and Louis Kampf for encouragement throughout this project.

INDIGENOUS MOVEMENTS, SELF-REPRESENTATION, AND THE STATE IN LATIN AMERICA

1. INTRODUCTION

Studying Indigenous Activism in Latin America

Kay B. Warren and Jean E. Jackson

This volume examines the cross-currents of change that lie behind the growing indigenous activism in Latin America.[1] Conventional portrayals often stereotype indigenous groups as either victims or survivors of state violence. This impulse—regularly felt and acted upon by well-meaning supporters, anthropologists, human rights groups, and indigenous activists themselves—is understandable, given the chronic violence and political instability that have plagued Latin America over the last fifty years. Political scientist Crawford Young (1976, 1993) exemplified the victim/survivor view when he initially concluded that Latin American indigenous people had suffered from such severe fragmentation and economic and cultural deprivation that they would be unable to mobilize nationalist movements as have ethnic minorities in other parts of the world. Other authors, despite their investigations into indigenous resistance and rebellion in the past, nonetheless predicted a future of inevitable disintegration and assimilation (e.g., Kicza 1993).

As Alcida Ramos, Víctor Montejo, and Kay Warren argue in this volume, many social scientists, in fact, missed the dramatic shifts in activism that began in the 1960s and 1970s.[2] Those decades marked an early wave of transnational organizing as indigenous groups used international forums, human rights law, and international conventions to press for their goals. Many groups were involved in complex projects of self-affirmation, organizing to build their own constituencies and influence wider politics. They were actively confronting the issue of fragmentation by arguing that culture is an important resource and making a wide variety of demands to overcome political marginalization and poverty (Bonfil Batalla 1982; Van Cott 1994a, 2000). In the process, indigenous groups generated bilingual spokespeople and in some cases consolidated new elites. To neglect the diverse early movements in which indigenous communities were involved is to miss important transformations in Latin American political life.[3]

More recently, the mass media—newspapers, television, documentaries, and the internet—have contributed to a growing public awareness of indigenous activism. Readers have been exposed to mesmerizing photos of indigenous representatives at international environmental meetings, like the 1992 United Nations–sponsored environmental summit held in Rio de Janeiro, but hear little of their activism outside public conferences or the substance of what they have to say. Coverage has chronicled Mayan involvements in Guatemala's war and peace process, focusing on the excavation of clandestine cemeteries that bear witness to the violence directed at rural families. Yet the images have been fleeting. Just as quickly, the attention skips to indigenous vigilante attacks on their neighbors who support the Zapatista rebels in Mexico and the betrayal of indigenous activists in Ecuador's 2000 coup, only to return to Guatemala with the exposé of the Central Intelligence Agency's involvement in the military's human rights abuses during their civil war. With the announcement in 2000 of a plan to pump over a billion dollars of U.S. foreign aid into Colombia, earlier stories of the government's ceding of regional autonomy to indigenous groups have been displaced by coverage of the drug war, rightist paramilitaries, and the mounting territorial power of leftist insurgents. In March 2001 photos appeared of the familiar masked face of *subcomandante* Marcos, who toured the countryside by bus with other Zapatista leaders to catalyze public support en route to Mexico City, where they pressured the new government of President Vicente Fox to halt repression and negotiate zones of indigenous self-government.

Although internet coverage by specialized newsgroups offers fuller details for regional experts and human rights fundraisers, few journalists have the mandate from their editors to produce sustained analysis of social movements that bridges the moments of intense media attention (see Allen and Seaton 1999). Rarely does coverage probe the ways indigenous groups use the media with increasing expertise to celebrate their culture across communities and to present their case for self-determination to the court of public opinion. To fill the void and communicate their own views, indigenous groups now fund-raise, circulate newsletters, and organize international conferences via the internet. Not surprisingly, there remains a striking digital divide between groups that have the resources to mobilize in these ways and others who find that getting together for pan-community meetings is a major challenge, given the lack of basic telephone service and the prolonged river travel required in many tropical forest regions.

INDIGENOUS CRITICS AND THE DILEMMAS
OF ENGAGED ANTHROPOLOGY

The challenge for the anthropology of social movements is to document indigenous activism more fully than other observers can. From the outset such a project poses important analytical and ethical dilemmas, among them the politics of anthropological field research and the dilemmas of representing the cultural continuity that indigenous movements assert in the face of so much evidence to the contrary.

Indigenous intellectuals, based in their own countries and occasionally working in the United States as academics, have become vocal critics and transnational colleagues. They represent a wider group of men and women who have gained entrance into national universities and the professions in growing numbers since the 1970s. These observers provide sophisticated analyses of the foreign presence and the effects of economic development in Latin America, concerns they actively voice to wider audiences (Palomino Flores 1986; Raxché 1989, 1995; Sam Colop 1990, 1991; Montejo and Akab' 1992; Cojtí Cuxil 1994, 1997; Krenak 1996; Vasco 1997; Montejo 1999; Zapeta 1999). In some cases, these intellectuals have created their own research centers, publishing houses, and transnational networks. They are activists as well as scholars.

On many fronts, activist-intellectuals are criticizing foreign research practices which for the last eighty years have used passive "native" informants as sources of data for foreign scholars' analyses, frequently destined for what are perceived as esoteric debates in the foreign academy (Montejo and Akab' 1992; Montejo 1993; Warren 1998). They are certainly correct that only a tiny percentage of research is translated and repatriated to the communities that serve as the "objects" and "subjects" of anthropological investigation. Although there are wonderful exceptions, few foreign investigators spend substantial amounts of time working with indigenous researchers and students, enabling them to gain access to the analytical skills routinely taught at national and foreign universities (for example, OKMA 1993). Still fewer foreigners coordinate their projects with the agendas set by indigenous groups. For all researchers, work on indigenous movements increasingly involves submitting one's own fieldwork and writings to critical scrutiny from the people being studied.

The politicization of research has resulted in many awkward moments as foreign scholars have found their findings and motives being questioned in public forums in Latin America and the United States (Sam Colop 1991). Yet, as the moral contract for research has been rewritten, the possibilities for collaboration with new generations of indigenous activists have opened up (Campbell et al. 1993; Fischer and Brown 1996; Instituto de Lingüística 1997).[4]

The scholars in this volume have pursued different modes of engagement in part due to their contrasting subject positions as insiders or outsiders, indigenous or not, and as fellow citizens with indigenous nationals or not. We have varied our involvements, depending on the issues faced by the individuals with whom we work, and have made distinctive personal choices at different times in our lives. Many of us have found ways to combine our scholarly writing with other kinds of activism. As is evident from a brief accounting of the activities of the contributors to this volume, there are diverse possibilities for engagement.

Colombia—a weak state aptly termed a "façade democracy," which has been plagued by internal violence, the drug trade, and ecological destruction—legislated a new constitution in 1991 that assigns self-administration to the diverse indigenous groups which inhabit their traditional territories (known as *resguardos*). In aggregate, they make up approximately 1.6 percent of the national population. Joanne Rappaport, an anthropologist and professor at Georgetown University who has worked in the country since 1973, has followed the complicated implications of constitutional reforms in practice (Rappaport 1996) and continues to work closely with local and national public intellectuals. She served as a Fulbright scholar in Colombia in 1999, holding university seminars with Nasa (Páez) and Guambiano students who represent the next generation of indigenous intellectuals. Both she and David Gow, who works as a professor at the Elliot School of International Affairs and focuses his research on community development, have been involved in Colombian earthquake relief and rebuilding efforts. They have been active in stateside endeavors to expose human rights abuses and change U.S. foreign policy in Colombia.

Jean Jackson, a professor of anthropology at MIT, has worked in Colombia since 1968, initially among Tukanoans in the Vaupés region. More recently she has looked at the articulation between local organizing efforts and the National Indigenous Organization of Colombia (ONIC). Some of her translated writing has been used by regional indigenous groups in workshops on organizing. She has also participated in efforts to organize opposition to U.S. policy favoring a military solution to ending guerrilla narcotrafficking in Colombia's protracted civil war and to inform concerned citizens about the indigenous communities caught in the crossfire.

For the contributors who work with Guatemala's Mayan majority, the 1978–1985 counterinsurgency war and subsequent indigenous resurgence through the Pan-Mayan movement have been watersheds for engaged research. Anthropologist Víctor Montejo, a Jakaltek-Maya who was forced to flee Guatemala during the war, has pursued a binational activist career. He currently works in Guatemala on democratic reforms and the promotion of indigenous leadership, writes on Mayan culture and politics for the Guatemalan press, publishes his work in Jakaltek, Spanish, and English, and teaches at the University of California at Davis as a professor of Native American Studies. Over the last thirty years, he has written widely on Mayan experiences of state violence and exile (Montejo and Akab' 1992; Montejo 1993, 1999).

Kay Warren, a professor of anthropology at Harvard, has worked closely with rural and urban Mayan intellectuals in Guatemala since 1970 and collaborated on conferences and publications for Mayan forums throughout the 1990s. She developed a field methodology that involves ongoing Mayan critique of her research findings as a central aspect of ethnographic research and writing before publication. The Mayan press Editorial Cholsamaj is publishing a Spanish translation of her recent book on the Pan-Mayan movement (1998) which will incorporate commentaries written by young Mayan and non-Mayan scholars on their readings of the work.

To work as an anthropologist in Brazil has long meant to be directly engaged in the human rights struggles allied with dispersed indigenous groups that make up 0.2 percent of the national population and have been subject to forced and sometimes violent displacement from their territories by national "development" efforts. Alcida Ramos, a Brazilian anthropologist and professor at the University of Brasília, has worked for decades with Yanomami communities. Through newspaper articles and academic writings (1998), she has established herself as a public critic of government policy and the violence against indigenous communities.

Terence Turner, a professor of anthropology at Cornell,[5] is famed for the Kayapó media project that he began in 1990. Taking advantage of Turner's technical training in video production, the Kayapó have learned to videotape and edit documentaries for their own purposes. Their videographers have recorded cultural performances for their communities' enjoyment and deployed video cameras—where they knew they would be filmed by the international press—in demonstrations against the government's expansion of hydroelectric dams to their region (Turner 1992).

Laura Graham, an anthropological linguist at the University of Iowa who has worked in Brazil since 1981, has directed the Xavante Education Fund, which provides funds for higher education. She has also worked as a consultant on wildlife management for the World Wildlife Fund and on health and education projects for the United Nations International Children's Emergency Fund (UNICEF). Graham also participated in organizing opposition to a development project on the Araguaia-Tocantins River.

Through the experiences of these anthropologists, one can trace the changing tenor of indigenous advocacy in Latin America, from an earlier paradigm where activism meant self-appointed foreigners speaking on behalf of groups, to the repositioning occasioned by the growing recognition that many groups have generated their own spokespeople and agendas for engaging the state and international nongovernment organizations (NGOs). There are still situations where the old-style advocacy is important, especially in the case of isolated groups—such as the Brazilian and Venezuelan Yanomami, the Brazilian Waiãpi, and the Ecuadorian Huaorani—which face genocidal incursions by gold and oil prospectors, massive land clearing by nonindigenous peasants, and other development efforts.[6] But one sees an ever-growing range of groups who represent themselves and tactically choose their own collaborators in public arenas, political forums, and state bureaucracies.

The authors in this collection deal with the analytical and ethical dilemma of revealing the inventive character of identity in different ways because the circumstances of ethnic formations and cultural practices they study are so varied. The essays are designed to illustrate important dimensions of activism in Colombia, Guatemala, and Brazil and to raise questions for other parts of Latin America. Indigenous groups in these countries share a longer history of organizing; hence the movements are relatively mature when compared to those of Venezuela, Peru, Chile, and Argentina.[7] We chose these countries because they reveal a variety of state responses to multiculturalism and illustrate a range of demographic situations, cultural practices, political tactics, and involvements with movements on the left.[8] They also demonstrate the recurrent tensions that arise from the distinctive political struggles pursued by national and local leaders with their different constituencies and contrasting agendas.

A little more than a decade ago, Greg Urban and Joel Sherzer edited the first volume on indigenous movements and the state in Latin America

(1991). A considerable body of literature on new social movements, including Latin American indigenous movements, has appeared in the interim, providing us with the opportunity to pursue the politics of these movements' self-representation.[9] In this volume, we have focused our efforts to produce two essays on each of a narrower field of countries to provide a fuller portrayal of their cultural politics and to illustrate how different framings of the issues reveal distinctive aspects of the interface between national and local politics. The introductory and final essays offer historical and comparative observations on indigenous organizing in a variety of countries.

Colombia, Guatemala, and Brazil experienced the democratic opening that occurred in Latin America during the 1980s and 1990s. Indigenous movements in these countries have made the claims that Donna Lee Van Cott considers to be characteristic of indigenous mobilizing in general: self-determination and autonomy, with an emphasis on cultural distinctiveness; political reforms that involve a restructuring of the state; territorial rights and access to natural resources, including control over economic development; and reforms of military and police powers over indigenous peoples (1994a: 12).

Emerging activism has begun to undermine the earlier overly sharp contrast that anthropologists made between highland and lowland groups — the former being shaped by their intimate contact with the colonial process and forced submission to colonial labor policies and institutions over time, and the latter (for those who were not annihilated) maintaining a tenuous independence of state politics and a modified version of their precontact culture due to their dispersed isolation and techno-economies that did not produce surpluses that states could tap. The twenty-first century is marked by the political self-consciousness of highland and lowland groups and the ways they have organized to intervene in policies that affect them.[10] This period of neoliberal integration, we hope, represents the final blow to persistent neo-evolutionary contrasts that have treated some indigenous groups as if they were passive survivors of another age, existing outside historical time and agency (Wolf 1982; Urban and Sherzer 1991).

Finding new colleagues and new ways of positioning themselves in wider fields of engaged research has made anthropologists more aware of the implications of their research for broader audiences. In this situation, another dilemma faced by anthropologists working on indigenous movements is that our methods are to a certain extent "deconstructive" — albeit in a social scientific sense. Ethnographic studies demonstrate that identities which appear enduring often have a more recent genesis than many would expect and that collective advocacy for self-determination often involves tenuous coalitions and complex groupings. As anthropologists, we seek to do justice to the intricate social fields of people's lived experience. In this instance, we seek to show how complex the on-the-ground situation is for communities organizing for their local needs and wider goals. Researchers examine crosscutting identities—among them gender, class, religion, language, place, and political affiliation—to demonstrate the richness of social life and to show how partial ethnic (or any other) claims are, given that other identifications routinely make counterclaims on people's interests and loyalties.

Anthropologists have struggled to represent the strategic essentialism of indigenous leaders who are busy creating the possibility of unification across historical cleavages and linguistic, cultural, and economic differences. "Essentialism" refers to discourses of enduring commonalties— common ethnic roots and historical pasts, cultural essences, and experiences that are seen as naturally binding people together.[11] Essences can be defined in terms of a transcendent spirituality, ties to place, common descent, physical differences, cultural practices, shared language, and common histories of suffering.[12] Discourses of racial difference and inferiority are another form of essentialism, and their virulence in Latin America reminds us that essentialism can be coercively imposed by the state as well as deployed by indigenous groups as a form of resistance to demeaning political imaginaries and policies.

A recent essentialist tactic has involved the borrowing of anthropological terminology, particularly the "culture" concept. It is not uncommon to see indigenous groups forging their sense of identity around the organizing idea of a coherent and bounded common culture. In many countries, indigenous communities must legally establish their legitimacy through the rhetoric of cultural continuity in order to gain official recognition, protection, and access to resources including their lands. Ironically, the notion of uniformly shared culture rooted in a particular place has been abandoned by the discipline of anthropology. Instead, anthropologists favor studies that engage multiple interacting identities, globalized flows of culture and people, and conflicting views and subject positions in contemporary society (Clifford 1988; Rosaldo 1989; Fox 1991; Gupta and Ferguson 1992; Appadurai 1996; Kearney 1996).

Yet critics of indigenous movements who question their legitimacy by pointing to signs of cultural hybridity often miss the point, because groups inevitably mix strategic essentialism with other lines of argument to legitimize their existence (Guha and Spivak 1988; Gupta 1998; Warren 1998; Fischer 1999). For anthropologists, the issue is not proving or disproving a particular essentialized view of culture but rather examining the ways essences are constructed in practice and disputed in political rhetoric. As activists have pointed out, there is an inherent polyvalence and ongoing selectivity in the markers of identity that indigenous groups single out for themselves. For instance, a woman's hand-woven blouse in Guatemala incorporates emblems of ancient Mayan cosmology and markers of her place in a woman's life cycle. It also signals the community from which the woman hails. During the counterinsurgency war, however, politicized women used Mayan dress rather than Western tops and skirts to reaffirm their cultural existence and thus to communicate their resistance to genocidal violence. Currently, upscale professional women amass collections of beautifully crafted woven blouses from different Mayan communities to mark their class mobility, visually illustrating the continual refashioning of indigenous self-presentation and their transcendence of place in the rural landscape (Urban and Sherzer 1991; Hendrickson 1995; Otzoy 1996). Graham (in this volume) refers to such deliberate appropriation of a symbol to build on its meaning as "second-order indexicality."[13]

The politics of interethnic inclusion and exclusion is striking for its diverse and changeable outcomes. For instance, it is not uncommon to see indigenous "separatists" unexpectedly join mainstream political parties to press for cultural rights or sponsor intercultural curriculum reforms in the public schools (Esquit Choy and Gálvez Borrell 1997). Consequently, it would be a mistake to freeze groups in formulaic sorts of essentialism or activism. Many indigenous groups and development institutions use the rhetoric of "culture," "a culture," "intercultural," and "multicultural," so the issue is to trace the circulation and usage of these terms while not assuming consensus or stability about their meanings and politics.

The issue of "authenticity" is closely related to debates about essentialism. Whether contemporary indigenous culture is authentic has preoccupied many of the critics of these movements. One line of argument points to the evident cultural hybridity of communities since the colonial period, when many were forced to adopt Christianity and other colonial-era practices that local communities reworked and made their own. In the present, the process of cultural synthesis has been intensified once again by the eager consumption of transnational organizing tactics, popular culture, and new technology, alongside reborn indigenous ritual, by some indigenous youth and bicultural leaders. This collage of cultural practices is used by some observers to argue that the emerging indigenous leadership on the national level is illegitimate. Mario Roberto Morales (1998) asserts that indigenous culture has become a commodity promoted by entrepreneurial leaders in Guatemala to take advantage of a historical moment when the tourist industry and international funders are fascinated by the exotic.[14]

One response to critics like Morales is to point out that anthropology, with its current more dynamic notion of culture, sees no absolute standard of authenticity. Rather, our focus is on the authenticators—on the authorities in indigenous communities and the experts beyond who determine what is deemed authentic at any one time. That authorities have changed from the days of community governance by tribal leaders or ritual elders to new kinds of leaders in local and national affairs is a crucial part of this history. For instance, in an attempt to create authentic modernized forms of their languages in Guatemala and Mexico, indigenous linguists (often with advanced training and university degrees in linguistics) are creating neologisms for modern technology and constitutional politics and are working to purge indigenous languages of loanwords from Spanish.[15] Whether local communities will incorporate these changes into everyday speech, as their advocates hope, is an open question and the subject of ongoing research. Our analytic strategy would focus on the production and consumption of authenticity rather than on the elaboration of criteria for an objective standard (see Jackson 1989, 1995). To these concerns, we would add the intense cultural debates between indigenous movements and their national societies over the commodification of their culture in tourism and national folklore exhibition and performance. At issue are the immense profits generated by these businesses for urban entrepreneurs that rarely trickle down to benefit the local communities which serve as the source of the cultural forms.

It would seem that anthropological analysis both supports indigenous movements' claims of discrimination and complicates the central goal of many movements to achieve recognition through the unproblematic cultural continuity of current practices. The focus on official recognition by many movements is the result of the legal leverage that the 1989 International Labor Organization's Indigenous and Tribal Peoples Convention 169 and other international legal agreements have given to indigenous groups,[16] a strategy that has been widely disseminated in regional indigenous meetings throughout the Americas. This is one of several ways in which indigenous activism has reached out globally to challenge the coercive power of the state. For groups that have faced extreme pressures to assimilate national urban culture, one important rhetorical move centers on "renewal"—that is, on the assertion of a common past which has been suppressed and fragmented by European colonialism and the emergence of modern liberal states. In this view, cultural revitalization reunites the past with the present as a political force.[17]

In these circumstances, the anthropology of indigenous organizing becomes the study of the choices that people in different settings make in the ongoing process of their own identity formation. Clearly these are not unencumbered choices; rather they are contingent on wider political and economic pressures as well as on local history. Communities with indigenous roots find themselves in very different demographic situations. In some countries, such as Brazil and Venezuela, they are dispersed microminorities with divergent pasts, social organizations, languages, and beliefs. In other cases, such as Guatemala, Bolivia, and Ecuador, they form a substantial proportion of the national population, arguably the majority, and some populations are in a position to argue for a common history, cosmology, and genealogy of languages. As is clear from these essays, there are many models for self-identification and unity. Cultural and linguistic diversity as a strength and a source of common interests is advanced in many ways—from the common goal of challenging histories of marginalization to the idea of biodiversity.[18]

From the onset, then, certain presuppositions should be clear across the case studies offered in this volume. First, the "indigenous" in our title is itself, of course, a historical product of European colonialism that masks enormous variations in history, culture, community, and relations with those who are considered nonindigenous.[19] As a result of this diversity, we can expect that the peoples identifying themselves as indigenous will pursue a variety of struggles and accommodations in different parts of the Americas. Even when activism is phrased in terms of being a people (as opposed to class, religion, or political affiliation), the definition of belonging—the terms of inclusion and exclusion developed by these communities in their practice of self-identification—is variable and often situational.

Second, "movements" rarely emerge in the singular and most often come in the highly contested plural. Rarely are indigenous movements as standardized in vision or coherent in organization as their supporters suggest. Their heterogeneity may be an asset in some situations and a liability in others. Some are community or regionally based, while others—fluent in the transnational language of cultural rights—still manage to maintain local, often weaker, ties. Some are long-standing; others ephemeral. Some movements incorporate class politics; others resist this fram-

ɪ movements defy political scientists' attempts to categorize them typologies, such as "resource focused" or "culturally focused" ɪn et al. 1996), because they clearly do both and because culture itself is an important internal resource—one, in many instances, relevant for attracting international funding at this historical moment (Melucci 1989; Alvarez et al. 1998; Warren 1998).

Many situations depicted in this volume involve the interplay of local leaders and their communities with pan-community activists who operate primarily in national affairs. To the extent that these movements have been generated across the post–Cold War political transition, some activists may have long histories of Marxist organizing or histories of seeking a third way outside the grammar of insurgent-counterinsurgency politics. The Cold War is an important backdrop for understanding national politics, but it is insufficient to explain the development and current dilemmas of indigenous organizing.

Third, "self-representation" is double sided. Analysts need to examine the ways communities represent social life and the media, politics, and hermeneutics of self-knowledge which they create for their own consumption and for negotiations with regional and transnational others. Yet the alternative significance of representation is relevant as well—that is, the dynamic question of who represents whom, who collaborates with whom, and how this dimension of representation is debated in ongoing politics.

In this moment of transnationalism, the state remains a crucial focus of indigenous activism because state politics continues to mediate the impact of global political and economic change on local communities. Despite economic globalization, it does not make sense to dismiss the state as irrelevant. Given the way states continue to repress indigenous communities, such generalizations fail to capture the crosscurrents of change in late capitalism. Each case study in this volume questions monolithic images of the state by revealing the inner workings and discursive practices of its heterogeneous institutions. The national state has not withered in the face of economic neoliberalism, multistate trading blocs such as the North American Free Trade Agreement (NAFTA), and suprastate structures such as the International Monetary Fund (IMF), World Bank, European Community, or multinational corporations. The continuing importance of "national security" concerns to Latin American states, even in the face of multistate economic blocs such as NAFTA, belies the assumption that states with weakened sovereignty will weakly react to internal challenges to their hegemony. Yet it is vital to be aware of the concessions that states are making to international commerce in order to stay in business and important to question the models of decentralized federalism that Latin American states are promulgating in response to cost-cutting measures mandated by foreign lenders such as the IMF. Indigenous struggles for greater autonomy are enacted within the pressured context of global capitalism, which makes the nexus of state and transnational affairs an important backdrop to the histories of activism in this volume (see Yashar n.d.).

GLOBAL TRANSFORMATIONS AND INDIGENOUS ORGANIZING

Ever since the conquest, indigenous communities in Latin America have been contesting the dominant ideology of the sixteenth-century European colonizers and the institutionalized exploitation and oppression it legitimized. As leftist and labor movements suffered continuing repression during the 1970s and 1980s, however, mobilizing switched to the new discourses of collective rights and cultural diversity. Working with International Labor Organization (ILO) and United Nations templates for indigenous rights, indigenous movements strove to create political space for groups to make claims on the basis of being a distinct "people" rather than as an ethnic group or minority. In sixteen Latin American countries,[20] constitutional reforms have challenged the dominant imaginary of the nation by redefining the legal status of indigenous communities and transforming the meanings of citizenship. While territorial rights continue to be a focus of struggle, activists speak of other, newly formulated demands, such as the right to use their own languages in public affairs, to read about their own cultures and histories in schools and the media, and to have decision-making powers over how they are to be represented. Activists have sought new opportunities, as distinct peoples rather than as marginalized minorities, to confront institutionalized discrimination and prejudice.

The pan-American discourses that emerged to celebrate indigenous otherness often stress a nonmaterialist and spiritual relation to the land, consensual decision-making, a holistic environmentalist perspective, and a reestablishment of harmony in the social and physical worlds. Implicit in these values is a critique of occidental forms of authority, desires to control and commodify nature, and the sovereign nation-state model with its accompanying power to define democracy, citizenship, penal codes, jurisdiction, and legitimate violence (see Assies 2000: 3–22; Van Cott 2000). The new indigenous rhetoric engages the "modern" state in terms of its political, legal, and moral dimensions, with the terms of engagement in constant revision due to the embryonic nature of indigenous discourses of "difference" and the racist discrimination that is still hegemonic in many quarters (see Wade 1997). Although the symbolic reach of these movements has often exceeded their policy impact, activists and their allies have contributed in significant ways to discussions of how the state itself needed to be restructured. In cases such as Colombia and Mexico, where questions about government legitimacy have fueled calls for democratic reform, observers have advanced the truly remarkable argument that indigenous people's highly participatory norms for decision-making have the potential to help achieve democratization throughout the country (Van Cott 2000; Nash 2001).

How these struggles play out varies from country to country. The history and successes of indigenous movements have varied. For example, in Mexico the San Andrés peace accords[21] did not produce the constitutional reforms that might have emerged, but it is significant that claims pertaining to many cultural and political domains in addition to land titles were negotiated, as was the case for the Guatemalan peace accords (Programa de Desarrollo de los Pueblos Mayas 1995; Cojtí Cuxil 1996b; Warren 1998; Plant 1999). A surprising success story is Venezuela's new constitution, legislated after lengthy battles, which provides consociational[22] participation of indigenous groups at the federal level.

This volume argues in support of juxtaposing rich ethnographic case studies to promote contrasts and comparisons across political systems. We are particularly interested in the tensions of multiculturalism and democracy in the post–Cold War era. The goal is to highlight diverse responses to current global transformations in economics, politics, and communications while not marginalizing the locally practiced social forms and meanings that mediate the impact of these transformations on community life. The local and global have complex relations, given that communities continually incorporate and rework global forms. The ethnographic project is to specify how this cultural reweaving occurs in particular circumstances and the consequences of these cultural dynamics for local power structures, divisions of labor, and engagements with the wider world. The synthetic reworking of wider influences by communities is reflected in patterns of intergroup cooperation and conflict, histories of colonial intrusion, and waves of globalization.

The case studies in this volume trace the ways in which indigenous activism responds to (1) global pressures of economic integration,[23] (2) liberal democratic reforms generated by the international community's focus on rights,[24] (3) state politics in response to the continued erosion of national sovereignty, and (4) diverse locally generated issues and social formations. Key questions emerge in these essays: To what extent is the turn to new forms of activism due to the increasing gap between the rich and poor[25] and the erosion of land bases as national governments have been pressured by international lenders to cut governmental services and subsidies and promote free market economies? How do activists react to political pressures from the United Nations to promote liberal democracy and to extend political and civil rights to individual citizens?

Global economic integration has brought with it yet another wave of free market social ideology that foregrounds the individual as the economic agent, bearer of rights and obligations, and owner of property, while in many cases indigenous groups are arguing in favor of collective rights and communal forms of cultural expression and control over resources.[26] As one would expect, what stands as communal and how the micropolitics of authority over resources play out within communities are extraordinarily variable.[27] The slippage between "the individual" in liberal democratic discourse and "the communal" in indigenous claims is negotiated by some groups in a way that asserts the incommensurability of their own and the wider cultural systems (see Gow and Rappaport, this volume).

There may be no compelling reason for groups to translate their cosmologies or social practices into the Westernized language of the mainstream, though many groups routinely prepare bilingual representatives to mediate wider politics and represent the groups in national and international forums. As in the case of the Kayapó of Brazil, their common goal is greater territorial autonomy and self-administration, which states resist because these demands directly challenge state authority and the state-centric grammar of contemporary politics (McClure 1997). State sovereignty has also been eroded by the communications revolution, which has created new international opportunities such as the development of transnational electronic networks of indigenous activists who share strategies and agendas across borders and their international allies, among them NGOs, which make other resources and kinds of leverage available (see Nelson 1999: 245–282).

How indigenous leaders represent themselves and how audiences react to their presentations in national forums reveal the complicated layering of meaning and politics in intercultural communication, especially when the cultural systems are incommensurate. Laura Graham's essay deals with the double binds faced by indigenous leaders as they deploy cultural signs in national forums in Brazil and Venezuela. If indigenous leaders choose to speak in the national language in these settings, they are open to accusations of inauthenticity, of being puppets of nonindigenous activists. However, if they speak in their own language, given the incommensurability of cultures, many such signs will be untranslatable. Indigenous translators routinely erase the ways Xavante speech patterns represent a radically non-Western vision of social and political realities, anticipating that the audience will not understand them. Her analysis offers a framework for understanding the linguistic dilemmas of speaking and being heard in situations where the performance of a radical non-Western vision is required if the speaker is to be granted the authority to represent an indigenous community's position. Graham's chapter and Turner's chapter on the Kayapó ritual of reconciliation demonstrate how every speech act sends nonreferential, social information, even when no referential information is received by some of the audience.[28]

Graham's essay also explores the advisability of an indigenous self-representation strategy that employs an ecologically informed lexicon utilizing Western concepts like biodiversity, so that basic goals such as recuperation of land or funding for locally initiated development projects can appeal rather than repel, as her example of Xavante requests for tractors illustrates. It is as much a reflection on their audience as on the values of the speakers that many indigenous organizations campaigning for land rights in lowland South America argue from an environmentalist perspective.[29]

Other indigenous groups have chosen to translate their efforts directly into the language of state politics in order to press for the reform of state institutions such as the school system and the courts. The recent focus of activism on constitutional reforms in many Latin American countries raises the issue of the impact of state discipline on distinctive cultural systems. Indeed, there is often no neat way in which the terminologies and norms of Western legal systems and the conventions and values central to indigenous practices can be mapped onto each other. "Customary law" and "indigenous language" educational programs are constructions subject to political maneuver in a complex field of social relations (Gustafson 2001).

States' recognition of customary law or implementation of educational programs in local languages can bring a cascade of other changes—including moves to standardize community practices and decentralize decision-making—which have wide ramifications for communities that have long been marginalized. Anthropologists face important choices in how they interpret the actions of international funders, states, and indigenous leaders when they involve creating standardized representations of heterogeneous local practices (Sánchez 1992; Sieder 1997). Formalizing the power of customary law and standardizing spoken language for textbooks can be seen as a grassroots triumph in the struggle to create a multicultural state or, alternatively, as a hierarchical process of forcing diverse local communities into alignment through the discipline of state power. Clearly this situation complicates the distinction of working within or outside the system, because multiple "systems" are at play, as is evident in many of this volume's case studies. The trick for anthropological analysis is to find a way of mirroring the process we are attempting to study—to pursue multiple lines of interpretation to see if they yield insights into the highly situational and dynamic process of indigenous organizing, rather than to prematurely classify the outcome of these changes as either one of structural autonomy or one of subordination to the dictates of the wider system (Centro de Estudios de la Cultura Maya 1994; Esquit Choy and Ochoa García 1995; Esquit and García 1998).

Gow and Rappaport's essay illustrates the multiple systems in which indigenous leaders participate and the ways in which knowledge and thought are appropriated from the wider society and hybridized to create new categories of indigenous identity and thought. Their materials illustrate in rich detail how indigenous movements are changing in response to a new generation of bilingual leaders, some with university educations. They argue that characterizations of indigenous representatives as members of bounded ethnic groups who interact with peers from other groups or with state representatives need to be expanded to include what they term a pan-community "inside." Following Paul Gilroy (1987), this sphere of operation is tangibly experienced by the actors themselves, who now define themselves collectively as native Colombians—an identity distinct from their identification with specific indigenous communities. Such a process, like the united voice which indigenous citizens of a nation-state hope to achieve through pan-indigenous organizing in Guatemala, Mexico, and Brazil, emerges out of lengthy and oftentimes unresolved conflicts inside this "inside."

The indigenous leaders in Gow and Rappaport's examples attempt to decolonize knowledge by creating novel hybrid categories of thought and, in so doing, to decolonize representation itself, taking it out of the hands of nonindigenous scholars and those indigenous players who go along with such scholars' characterizations. This contrasts with the leaders at the national level that Jackson discusses, who for the most part rely on Western discourse. In both situations, political discourses from the dominant society continue to intrude in the *Realpolitik* of collective decision-making, however, because so many interested parties with complex and varied agendas participate. The theme of the "conflicts inside this inside" created through the process of indigenous groups who are redefining themselves as they seek to contest the power of the wider society and to heighten their own spheres of autonomy resonates throughout the volume. Central to the chapters by Montejo, Warren, and Turner are discussions of the contested positionings of groups *within* the various organizations involved in indigenous political decision-making.

Víctor Montejo's essay builds on the themes of pan-community identity and on the conflicts that indigenous leaders like himself must face within the movement for self-reaffirmation. He compares the two prevailing forms of Mayan leadership following the signing of the Guatemalan peace accords and provides, in addition to a scholarly analysis, political recommendations for his own people. Analytically, he points out the different histories, positions, and strengths of the two main strands in the Mayan movement, the leftist *populares* and the culturally based *mayanistas*. Because he is a Maya from the community of Jacaltenango who writes in his own community language as well as in Spanish and English, his work is further anchored in the specificity of his natal language and home community. His goal is to craft the strongest possible Mayan political front, to allow all of Guatemala's indigenous people to speak with as powerful a voice as possible. Although the Maya represent a majority in the country, a great deal of both the formal governmental machinery and the informal, backroom deal-making sector remains in the hands of a small minority of privileged nonindigenous (Ladino) politicians. Montejo offers advice about the most effective ways to incorporate the Mayan worldview into leaders' political strategizing, in order to empower the leaders and promote a strong foundation for the nationwide Mayan identity that must emerge.

Central to the analytic genre that Montejo creates for the message of Mayanness is his decision to depart from standard scholarly convention and stress his own unique perspective and spirituality as a Jakaltek-Maya. This perspective exemplifies what Lila Abu-Lughod (1986) has termed the status of being a "halfie," with a subjectivity that is both "native" and "anthropologist." In this case, Montejo is a "halfie" in two senses: as an anthropologist and a Mayan intellectual; and, "inside the inside," as a Jakaltek, a speaker of a minority Mayan language, and a Maya in the transcendent sense he works to establish on a national scale. Montejo employs this multiple vision in a dynamic fashion, shifting, combining, or, temporarily, completely embracing one of his subjectivities. As he says, by being an insider he can envision several ways to contribute to forging a unifying self-representation of the Mayan people that draws on the complex linguistic diversity and adequately encompasses the wide variety of Mayas found in the country today.

In practice, Latin American states have supported constitutional and judicial reform efforts that give indigenous communities the conditional right to settle their own internal affairs, so long as the basic law of the land is not violated. As is evident, anthropologists have important choices in how they interpret these changes. On the one hand, we can emphasize the ways in which the application of customary law in criminal cases and internal governance gives real substance to the official recognition of indigenous groups and how this conceptualization carries with it implicit if not explicit notions of dignity and parity with other sectors. The manner in which customary law plays out in the wider judicial system is one domain in which self-representation in both senses of the term makes a difference, for on it rest the quality and extent of state recognition, valorization, and protection of cultural distinctiveness. Success here provides a form of insurance that a community's other demands (for example, to control its own natural resources) will be taken seriously (see Van Cott 2000).

On the other hand, localized power to adjudicate disputes between indigenous parties has appeared at various times in Latin American history from the colonial period to the present. When disputes have involved indigenous and nonindigenous parties, however, the national legal system has almost inevitably taken precedence, revealing the basic hierarchy rather than parity of the legal systems. Guatemalan indigenous activists in the 1970s rejected older forms of legal and religious separatism in closed corporate communities as fostering their own subordination rather than giving them greater autonomy (Warren 1978, 1998). For them, the issue was challenging wider structural hierarchies in an interethnic world, including a court system that was subject to political manipulation by the dominant ethnic group. Nevertheless, since 1990 the activists operating at the national level have promoted customary law in national affairs to create a sphere of administrative autonomy which mirrors, if only in miniature, the dream of a federalist political system with regional autonomy for indigenous communities. Given an electoral system which has largely been unresponsive to indigenous concerns, tactics for organizing are fluid and heterogeneous, pressing for change in interethnic affairs and seeking realms for wider self-administration at the same time.

By contrast, in Colombia the establishment of a Constitutional Court that privileges the exercise of customary law whenever possible has resulted in jurisdiction and accumulated case law on indigenous rights far more extensive than elsewhere in Latin America. The formal support of local juridical systems seeks to reduce case backlogs, eliminate extrainstitutional conflict resolution and violence, and formally recognize the legitimacy and effectiveness of local institutions that are often perceived as more legitimate than state courts (Van Cott 2000: 74, 112, 113–116). This case raises important issues for the rest of Latin America, where the courts are often corrupt and unable to act independently to carry out the rule of law in rural affairs, whether it be in land disputes, theft, or interpersonal violence. These conflicts frequently soar after civil wars, when the demobilization of guerrillas, soldiers, and police is accompanied by rising rates of organized criminal violence in the wider society.

In many countries, debates about the recognition of customary law have opened up spaces for indigenous citizens to rethink the state in its entirety and to contest the parameters of all political institutions. If a nation's citizens are so diverse, what does citizenship consist of? What other demands can indigenous groups advance in these newly created domains of participation? In this sense we can say that the notion of "identity politics" must include the identity of the state as well, and needs to be seen as a far-reaching element of Latin America's democratic transition.

Note, however, that the interface between local decision-making and state law is extremely unstable, in part because both sides are continually constructing and negotiating spheres of authority. Attempts by the state explicitly to recognize and explain the nature of customary law illustrate the dangers of over-codification and decontextualization (see Assies 2000: 19). Conversely, the risk that indigenous communities run when trying to articulate their rights derives from an underlying worry that in so doing they concede some of their autonomy to outside authorities.[30]

In many realms, governments have complicated stakes in "representing" indigenous communities to their constituents and to international markets.[31] Governmental policy and media representations are often complex and ambivalent, partaking of the attractively different (mysterious, alluring, exotic) and the repulsively different (dirty, stupid, lazy) virtually at the same time. Images often slip easily between idealized and deprecating judgments. The ambivalence of national authorities is evident in the theatrical celebration of the indigenous past in high nationalist ritual and the tourist industry yet the failure to see contemporary communities as modern protagonists and citizens. When indigenous groups break the mold of these conventional representations—by joining the market economy and, for example, building a casino with hundreds of hotel rooms—they are often seen as illegitimately discarding their indigenousness and hence are no longer entitled to occupy the "savage slot" that the nonindigenous "mainstream" has created for them (see Trouillot 1991).

This ambivalence has powerful implications for national responses to activism and for the political imaginaries that nonindigenous groups evoke to justify their preference for monocultural government policies. In Guatemala, the military and Ladino elites have a long history of tactically deploying images of "the rebellious Indian" who may at any moment rise up against Ladinos (the country's term for non-Indians) and whites (Montejo 1987; Smith 1990; Sam Colop 1991; Hale 1996; Warren 1998). These fears have been used to justify preemptive violence and to inflame nonindigenous resistance to reforms that would reconfigure power relations (see Warren, this volume).

In Brazil, government agents' sense of their role is shaped by notions of "the savage innocent" who needs state paternalism because Indians cannot represent themselves to the wider system (Ramos 1998). This imagery reveals much more about nonindigenous identity and the modes of control perpetuated through nationalist culture and state bureaucracies than it does about the capacities of the country's indigenous peoples. Inevitably, this imagery is used by a variety of individuals and institutions to reproduce older patterns of racist discourse that naturalize indigenous inferiority and nonindigenous superiority. Mainstream nationalism is frequently hispanicized in a way that robs indigenous communities of an independent voice in crafting public culture. It is telling that this imagery, with its deep historical roots, has survived the post–Cold War transition to democracy in Latin America.

In turn, indigenous responses are often ambivalent and fluid. Mapuche activists in Chile may brilliantly employ official discourse on democracy and justice while simultaneously making it clear that negotiating in these terms by no means implies acceptance of the discourse (see Briones n.d.). The same could be said of the elder Pan-Mayanist leaders in Guatemala, who formally agree with the "women in development" initiatives promoted by the U.S. Agency for International Development (AID) but, once off stage, openly oppose women's education and involvements outside the home because of the idealized role they construct for women as the promoters of Mayan language and culture across generations. Activists' behavior can elicit impressions of savvy strategizing, innocence, contempt, resistance, complicity, or genuine perplexity that rapidly appear and disappear—all behavior difficult to characterize in categorical terms. Rarely are activists totally opposed (save for rhetorical purposes) or totally coopted.

One way of understanding indigenous movements is to see them as a postnationalist phenomenon (Geertz 2000).[32] Their increasingly public face reveals what nationalist rhetoric has obscured since the nineteenth century in Latin America: that nation and national culture are not coterminous with the state (see Gellner 1983; Hobsbawm 1990; Anderson 1991). Rather, Latin American countries are homes to communities with diverse family forms, religious beliefs, judicial processes, and modes of cultural expression. For every nationalist narrative of *mestizaje* (the biological and cultural blending of Europeans, indigenous groups, and enslaved Africans over the conquest and colonial period), there are other histories of communities resisting the state-sponsored implementation of such ideologies (Hale 1994; Howe 1998) and histories of indigenous ethnogenesis (Stern 1987; Smith 1990; Mallon 1996; Hill 1997). Our mistake, perhaps, has been to see ethnogenesis as a distant one-time affair rather than—as Mayan cosmology would have it—as the ongoing result of violent disjunctures through which the world is clarified, only to give birth to other moments of rupture (Warren 1998).[33]

Since the end of the Cold War, the "efflorescence" (Hale 1996, 1997) of a politicized indigenous identity has caused anthropologists to move definitively past the community-studies tradition that had guided earlier research toward multisited considerations of social movements, state politics, and globalization. Just as African-American and Latino Studies programs in the United States have generated a reconsideration of white identity, so Indigenous Studies programs are provoking a reconsideration of mestizo identity in Latin America. One interesting trend is the ethnification of identities and literatures that shunned cultural identity in favor of class issues in the past. One can read this post-Marxist project as an attempt to resituate research on inequality after the Cold War and the apparent eclipse of revolutionary socialism as the major opposition to the status quo of continuing inequality.[34]

On the one hand, in Guatemala urban Ladinos in the intelligentsia are beginning to talk about their own *ladinidad* (Ladino ethnicity), though whether this will become a personally compelling identity movement is not clear. On the other hand, historians and anthropologists are contributing to a reappraisal of bipolar constructions of indigenous vs. nonindigenous identities and of the demonization of Ladinos as anti-indigenous racists (Warren 2002b; see Ramírez n.d. for a Colombian example). At issue for these analysts is the Ladino underclass, whose members are often as exploited and marginalized as impoverished Mayan peasants and wage laborers. Poor Ladinos are further marginalized when analyses of inequality focus on anti-indigenous racism as if Ladinos were a homogeneous block of privileged mestizos. The emerging argument is a fascinating one: that Ladino ethnogenesis has had its own neglected history (Smith 1990) and that the focus on the antagonism between indigenous and Ladino ethnic groups has obscured the reality that poor Ladinos may be of recent indigenous background, a sociological fact that families suppress for a variety of reasons (see Warren 2002b).

The focus on polarized antagonisms ignores the transcendent power of nonindigenous, non-Ladino elites—endogamous lineages of Guatemalans claiming pure European descent who have controlled the country's basic religious, commercial, and political institutions since the sixteenth century (Casaús Arzú 1992; González Ponciano n.d.). Researchers are now turning their attention to ideologies of white superiority and Ladino inferiority that have informed interethnic relations from behind the scenes. The opening of these identities to further analysis reminds us that ethnic identities are highly relational and that specific identities do not have an existence autonomous from the history of interethnic relations. The question remains how these Guatemalan scholars will respond to indigenous activists for whom nonindigenous racism is a continuing, everyday issue at work and in their communities.

The essays in this volume ask: what do the dilemmas of self-representation reveal about the fields of power relations in which indigenous movements operate? In Colombia, Guatemala, and Brazil, the social history of cultural difference and current inter/intragroup relations raises specific issues for indigenous activism. Movements create and appropriate an array of self-representations for their own expressive reasons, educational efforts, and political goals. They also deal with legal authorities, foreign funders, human rights groups, anthropologists, and business interests. These essays provide illustrations of the genres and media that politicized indigenous groups use for self-representation. They highlight the ways in which social relations and power structures influence the production and circulation of self-knowledge.

Terence Turner examines the ironies of intersecting national and indigenous power structures in the Kayapó case, when representatives of the Brazilian government's National Indian Foundation (FUNAI) visited a Kayapó community to participate in a Kayapó ritual of reconciliation involving rival leaders, one of whom was a national as well as local figure in indigenous politics. Uncomprehending of the community's language, the government official did not realize that he was being ridiculed by his hosts as he gave his paternalistic blessing to the process.

Given the national and local scope of this leadership, it is hard to see the event as merely an instance of James Scott's (1985) "weapons of the weak." In fact, although there are multiple "hidden transcripts" (Scott 1990) being enacted in this ritual, it is clear that a major aspect of the dispute centers on a succession to power, negotiated through the distinctly Kayapó discourse of masculinity and only obliquely derived from the dilemmas of contact with national culture.

Without the intimate knowledge of Kayapó hermeneutics, one would miss the richness of this event, which stubbornly resists conventional categories of political analysis. The moment of reconciliation, however, directly addresses wider politics by representing and negotiating local disputes over who represents whom to the state and international donors. That a Kayapó videographer filmed the ritual for internal consumption and edited it to achieve political agendas of his own as well as to express indigenous aesthetics for an audience of dispersed communities illustrates the savvy appropriation of expressive forms for local concerns.

As a result of the focus on agency and diverse kinds of power, these essays take the form of studies in the micropolitics of national and local disputes with various sorts of international leverage.[35] Rather than discussing power in structural terms as a simple function of social hierarchy, the case studies look at the ironies of multiculturalism and power.

One such irony is the way the indigenous embrace of multiculturalism turns out to be quite compatible with neoliberalism, peculiar though such a notion initially appears to many progressive and left-leaning individuals, indigenous and nonindigenous alike. Neoliberal tenets such as decentralization and political and ethnic pluralism permit indigenous communities to strike their own bargains with national and international corporations and NGOs, bypassing paternalistic regional and state agencies. Examples from North America illustrate possible models, the most striking example, perhaps, being the corporation created by the Inuit in Alaska that manages the land on which oil pipelines stretch from the distant northern fields to pumping stations on the shore or farther south in Canada (also see Hale 1999).

Of course, governments and NGOs have their own reasons for promoting decentralization in the name of democratic reform. For NGOs funded by major international donors, such as the northern Europeans, the issue has been to sidestep the corrupt and inefficient national government bureaucracies in order to channel aid to local communities for democratic reconstruction efforts after the civil wars of the 1980s. Conservative governments have been eager to decentralize, because doing so allows them to trim budgets for rural services and to undercut pancommunity political organizing that is characteristically critical of their politics. In the Guatemalan case, the net effect of these trends has been to weaken grassroots opposition groups.

As is clear in Kay Warren's essay in this volume, the defeat of the national Guatemalan indigenous rights referendum in 1999 was due in part to the difficulty that the grassroots left experienced in repositioning itself as a potent electoral force after the 1996 peace accords, the failure of Pan-Mayanism to forge a unified urban-rural mass movement, and the strong pull of localism in Mayan identity that has made indigenous mobilizing in electoral politics very difficult above the municipal level. As Warren shows, indigenous discourses of pan-community activism have a longer history; yet many critics of indigenous politics argue that community identity is the only authentic arena for Mayan politics. Decentralization—embraced in the 1990s by Mayan activists even as it was being imposed by the state and foreign donors—is only part of the story, as this analysis shows by examining the practice of democracy in rural communities and the savvy use of the media by Mayan critics such as Estuardo Zapeta to mobilize opposition to the referendum.

Warren's case study examines the varying meanings of pan-community Mayanism during its development and the way this transcendent identity responds to indigenous communities' historical engagement with neo-colonialism, decades of political repression during the counterinsurgency war, and discourses of modernity that deny the achievement in the 1980s and 1990s of a Mayan voice in urban as well as rural political culture. This is an example of a movement that has balanced a separatist impulse and dreams of a distinctive Mayan nation with the creation of hundreds of Pan-Mayanist groups dealing with a range of cultural and political issues. Mandated, perhaps cynically, by the congress rather than by the movement, the referendum sent Pan-Mayanists back to the drawing boards to imagine ways of working within an electoral system which had humiliated Mayas in the past for attempting to organize their own party.

These essays also point to numerous ways in which our analytical language needs to be problematized, either because we lack words to convey a concept adequately or because the words we employ are loaded with misleading evaluative connotations. At issue is how easily classificatory labels, necessary for scholarship, bureaucratic administration, jurisprudence, diplomacy, and a host of other functions, become reified and hinder comprehension. The state dissolves as a monolithic entity when its inner workings are brought to light, as indigenous groups in Colombia, Guatemala, and Brazil have been quick to understand as they have promoted indigenist[36] and, more recently, pluralist policies.

Jean Jackson's essay demonstrates that, while we must not think of the state as irrelevant in these days of transnationalism, neither should we reify it. Her Colombian case illustrates how interpersonal conflicts between indigenous activists and officials representing state agencies in charge of dealing with the nation's indigenous communities are—along with built-in institutional conflicts—sources of disagreement, incomprehension, and stalemate. Negotiations between indigenous leaders and the state are, after all, negotiations between people, so that local histories, micropolitics, personalities, and shifts in alliances between various state agencies are intertwined with the larger structural forces that affect the outcome of a conflict. The essay shows how discourses of ethnic and cultural difference feed into a politics of knowledge in situations in which different parties to a conflict at the national level employ such knowledge strategically to evaluate one another's standing with respect to moral bearing, unchallengeable authority, and uncontestably authentic cultural difference.

Alcida Ramos, as an internationally recognized expert on the role of the state in determining the current situation of Brazil's indigenous peoples, adds another dimension to the consideration of the state with an overview of what she sees as the telling clash between the subjectivities of foreign anthropologists and those of indigenous movements. Ramos condemns some foreign anthropologists for failing to appreciate the contingent, flexible, and opportunist dimensions of indigenous leaders in their involvements with national society, and for neglecting the deeper history of the impact of international human rights and indigenous rights conventions beginning in the 1940s that have provided indigenous groups with room to maneuver in dealing with state systems. International law and larger forces, such as globalization and the rise of NGOs, have contributed to the liberalism that now characterizes many Latin American countries' official policies toward their indigenous populations. Her analysis makes an apt comparison between Brazilian and Colombian policies toward their indigenous populations. Unlike Bolivia and Ecuador, Colombia and Brazil have small percentages of Indians, who occupy a larger portion of the national imaginary than the demographics might seem to warrant. In both countries indigenous populations were considered to be wards of the state, although some Colombian highland populations worked themselves free of this characterization much earlier, with the land repossessions and organized resistance beginning early in the twentieth century. And both countries moved from an indigenist, assimilationist set of policies toward their Indians to more liberal, pluralistic policies. However, there are marked differences in how legislat/ proposed and enacted (or voted down) in the two countries / tory, including the new reforms each country signed into be/ ample being Colombia's legislation during the 1970s and 1980s estab... ing collective and unalienable indigenous titles to land.

CONCLUSIONS

Indigenous representation and self-representation are our topics. We ask a basic set of ethnographic questions. Who is entitled to represent indigenous populations? Who makes the decisions about who is entitled? What are the various ways in which indigenous peoples are represented in their own and in others' political imaginaries? What conflicts arise in the course of fashioning such representations? The essays in this volume illustrate many of the issues, dilemmas, and ironies that arise in polyethnic polities. The case studies address the realities of asymmetrical power relations and the ways in which indigenous communities and their representatives deploy Western constructions of subjectivity, alterity, and authentic versus counterfeit identity as well as how they manipulate bureaucratic structures and the mass media. Each study provides examples of indigenous alliance-building with other indigenous groups or nonindigenous organizations such as environmentalist, human rights, and development-focused NGOs and examines the implications for those leaders who serve as bridges to other social fields. Each asks how such alliances attempt to link local concerns with the current preoccupations of broader publics.[37]

In this volume's analyses, the *indigenous movement*—a classic example of a new social movement at one level of abstraction—dissolves into widely diverse and divergent sets of goals, discourses, and strategies; factions emerge that espouse a broad array of notions about how ethnic identity is constituted, what principles should underlie organization efforts, and what strategies provide the highest probability of success. While we celebrate grassroots organizing and counterhegemonic successes, we must not forget, as Néstor García Canclini (1995: 475) points out, that power sediments itself in all social institutions and agents. While indigenous movements may successfully subvert the traditional *personalismo* of party politics, they may also successfully invoke "tradition" to render certain sectors invisible as they authorize the power of others.

The supposedly homogeneous nature of indigenous communities— their solidity seemingly so apparent from a distance—also dissolves when seen up close. A Colombian *resguardo* turns out to be ethnically diversified, and the jurisdiction of the *cabildo* (the local authoritative council) stretches across territories to include members who have emigrated from their traditional lands. Self-other oppositions, drawn both by activists in their oratory and by anthropologists in their ethnography, turn out to be anything but fixed. Rather, interaction occurs in social fields where alliances shift, definitions are reworked, entities are renamed, and authority is rethought. The same can be said for processes seen as bringing people in the hinterland into modernity's fold. It often turns out that the available models of these processes are strikingly incomplete, in part because they are overly simple (speaking in terms of communities, peasants, and families without concern for the real-world heterogeneity of these categories) and in part because they rest on linear and chronologically staged assumptions about social and economic change.

As anthropological critiques of political science and economistic models of development so often point out, *meaning* is ignored in such models or reduced to little more than background noise that explains discrepancies between the data and the model. Meanings are always problematic in some ways: their production and control usually involve struggles taking place on fields with discursive, spatial, material, symbolic, and power dimensions (see Comaroff and Comaroff 1992; Warren 1992). Symbols utilized in indigenous representation and self-representation have a kind of polymorphous perversity to them; they are portmanteaux for other symbols, or, chameleonlike, they take on and shed meanings in quick succession. Most striking, perhaps, is the ill-advised and often harmful assumption that indigenousness and modernity are mutually exclusive— modernity the essence of change, indigenousness the essence of atemporal continuity.

The essays in this volume call on researchers in various ways to problematize the notion of "culture." One approach involves examining political culture—the ways in which indigenous movements, like all social movements, challenge the boundaries of cultural and political representation and social practice (Alvarez et al. 1998: 8). We suggest that—rather than seeing culture as a distinct set of discourses and practices all too often contrasted with, say, political economy—we should understand it as a dimension of all institutions, "a set of *material* practices which constitute meanings, values and subjectivities" (Jordan and Weedon 1995: 8, as cited in Alvarez et al. 1998: 3). Finally, we examine the varied ways in which this concept is appropriated by indigenous communities. As a result of the dynamic Bahktinian process of appropriation, the diverse meanings and roles the culture concept takes on can resist elements of its

Western ideological underpinnings, becoming a subaltern political tool as Gow and Rapport demonstrate in this volume.[38] However, it would be a mistake to ignore the ways in which the international community's use of "culture," "peoples," "rights," and "democracy" has compelled indigenous groups to repackage their concerns and identities for access to wider audiences and resources. Gender issues are an arena where the tensions between international development discourse and local expectations collide.

These studies reveal new roles and liberal political ironies for anthropologists, national and foreign; in one example in this volume, they are found to be providing expert testimony for both sides of a legal suit. The essays provide instances in which anthropological theory is enlisted to shore up the state's arguments during disputes; is used to buttress claims of authority to define who is and is not indigenous; and is seen to be so profoundly enmeshed in a Western worldview that it is incommensurate with a particular indigenous pueblo's cosmovision.

Finally, the essays reveal occasions, some of them spectacular, on which indigenous leaders display creative engagement, adaptive flexibility, political acuity, nimble positioning, humor, and profound understanding of the requirements of leadership, especially in hostile surroundings. This particular meaning of "representation" needs to be acknowledged as very much to the point, for clearly the individuals and collectivities depicted in this volume represent the possibility of arriving at a community's collective vision of its goals, despite at times protracted struggle, inspiring in turn a tenacious and ultimately successful will to prevail against the enormous odds in achieving it.

Notes

1. The conventions for the usage of "indigenous" and "Indian" in Latin America are not uniform. Gow and Rappaport and Warren avoid the term "Indian" in their chapters because of its pejorative connotations where they work. Its cognates in Spanish and Portuguese remain highly derogatory, despite its appearance in some scholarship and despite efforts by some indigenous intellectuals to appropriate it in a manner similar to the way in which "black" was appropriated by African-Americans in the United States during the 1960s (see, for example, the Peruvian publication *Pueblo Indio: Vocero del Consejo Indio de Sud América*). Jackson chooses "indigenous" except when a noun must be used; "indigene" is, unfortunately, not really English, and she finds "native" (see Gow and Rappaport, this volume) equally problematic. Many English-speaking Native Americans continue to use "Indian."

2. See also Starn (1991); Montejo and Akab' (1992); Ramos (1998); Warren (1998); Assies et al. (2000); Muehlebach (2001).
3. See especially Escobar and Alvarez (1992); Yashar (1996, 1998); Alvarez et al. (1998).
4. Although it has a long tradition in North American research, collaboration on publications of traditional indigenous lore (usually myths) is, for the most part, recent in South America. Two examples are Berta Ribeiro's work with two Desanas of the Brazilian Northwest Amazon (Kumu and Kenhíri 1980) and Robin Wright's work with Arawak speakers of the Aiari River region (Cornelio et al. 1999).
5. In 1990–1991 Turner was chair of the American Anthropological Association Special Commission to Investigate the Situation of the Brazilian Yanomami (see Graham, this volume).
6. See Turner (1993); Gallois (1996); Ramos (1998). Cultural Survival (1993) provides a variety of examples of advocacy work.
7. Hence we present no discussion of countries with "autonomous regions," like Nicaragua. We have no southern cone representation. Nor do we provide sustained comparison of the most similar countries—for example, Colombia, Bolivia, and Ecuador are all Andean countries with tropical lowlands. Another line of comparison would be Ecuador, Bolivia, and Guatemala, all of which contain a large proportion of highland indigenous agriculturalists. We hope this volume will spur other in-depth comparative efforts in Central and South America, the United States (including Hawai'i), and Canada.
8. In the process of producing this collection, we considered other countries as well, including Mexico, Bolivia, the United States, and Canada. In the end, we decided that a richer consideration of fewer cases would be better than shorter studies of many cases. In this sense, any collection is arbitrary and open ended, limited by resources and the economics of publishing.
9. See, for example, the following studies, some of which appeared before 1991: Young (1976, 1993); Slater (1984); Díaz Polanco (1991); Urban and Sherzer (1991); Escobar and Alvarez (1992); Morris and Mueller (1992); Ribadeneira (1993); Van Cott (1994b, 2000); Calderón (1995); Foweraker (1995); García Canclini (1995); González Casanova and Roitman Rosenmann (1996); Jelin and Hershberg (1996); McAdam et al. (1996); Sánchez (1996); Chalmers et al. (1997); Gómez (1997); Wade (1997); Alvarez et al. (1998); Assies et al. (2000).
10. This is not to deny the very significant techno-environmental differences that affect the dynamics producing self-consciousness. For example, in the immense *resguardos* of the Colombian Amazon, populations are small and dispersed, and ownership of land per se is not a problem. In these areas, indigenous self-representation with respect to territorial claims stresses the need to preserve biodiversity, and self-consciousness will develop around the idea of indigenous guardians of nature. In contrast, as the main problem in highland areas continues to be landlessness, Andean communities will continue to see

themselves as claimants regarding arable land. Exceptions to the highland/ tropical forest lowland contrast include the Wayúu (Guajiro) of Colombia, Mapuche of Argentina and Chile, Guaraní of Paraguay and Bolivia, and groups of the Chaco regions of Uruguay and Argentina (see Reed 1995, 1997; Carrasco and Briones 1996).

11. Some scholarship on indigenous movements in the 1980s espoused essentialist or instrumentalist (that is, stressing the manipulation of identity features) approaches. Poststructuralist approaches appearing in the 1990s stressed the discursive constitution of identities (see Wade 1997).

12. They are often asserted as foundational realities. In the United States, essentialisms tend to be biologically grounded, as in the case of gender, race, and sexuality. But this is not a universal pattern.

13. "The process by which signs take on novel indexical meanings in new contexts" (Graham, this volume); a graphic example is the artist Andy Warhol's appropriation of Campbell Soup cans.

14. See Warren (1998) for a critical reading of his work. Discussing the way in which the Hawai'ian chiefs appropriated "those aspects of the dominant system that constituted a cultural form more resistant to political conquest even as it incorporated certain cultural practices and institutions of that dominant system itself" (such as far-sweeping changes in the family and gender order), Sally Merry suggests that indigenous movements' appropriation of occidental notions of authentic tradition can be seen as an example of this strategy rather than of cooptation (1998: 602–603).

15. Interesting Colombian and Guatemalan examples of construction of neologisms were the attempts to translate their constitutions into major indigenous languages to educate indigenous citizens about the reforms (see Rojas 1997). Edward Said (1978) terms this "auto-orientalization"; Ramos develops a related concept in her notion of the "hyperreal Indian" (1998: 267–283).

16. For example, the Draft United Nations Declaration on the Rights of Indigenous Peoples and the Draft Inter-American Declaration on the Rights of Indigenous Peoples (see Ramos, this volume; also Muehlebach 2001).

17. A key feature of these efforts has been a stress on these communities' *inherent* rights, based upon a community's claim to have been in a location before anyone else. In general, they have avoided the earlier appeals based on minority rights because of the assimilationist implications of such appeals by liberal states. The inherent rights argument strengthens claims to autonomy and self-determination.

18. Maintaining a region's plant and animal species—its biodiversity—has been championed by scientists, environmentalists, governments, and NGOs for the areas inhabited by indigenous groups that are vulnerable to rapid destruction produced by misguided development projects (see Grueso et al. 1998: 196–197).

19. A substantial literature is to be found on just what "indigenous" means. To

some degree, western hemisphere groups do not present the thorny problems found elsewhere in the world because there is a consensus that indigenous people belong to autochthonous, pre-Columbian communities. Several definitions employ the criteria of preexistence, nondominance, cultural difference (i.e., being only partly integrated into the dominant national state), and self-identification and note that colonization and invasion play a significant role in constituting indigenous peoples.

Many would agree that definitions enlisting such characteristics as statelessness or nonindustrial mode of production should be avoided, as they perpetuate the stereotype of a people frozen in tradition. Such criteria also suggest that once a community is a player in "modernity"—for example, by setting up a casino—it somehow ceases being indigenous.

The Colombian government has consistently ruled that the higher the degree of a community's acculturation, the less protection the government will offer for ethnic and cultural identity. The objective of withholding protection, one magistrate claimed, is "to stimulate indigenous peoples to continue upholding their species and culture" (Sánchez 2000: 226). The term "species" is telling. This reasoning follows a long tradition; Christian Gros documents a 1963 court decision that in effect ruled that as the inhabitants of the Yaguara *resguardo* had successfully made the effort to educate themselves to the point of being able to use laws in their favor, the court no longer considered them to be indigenous and hence prohibited them from benefiting from those laws (2000: 206–204). Ramos (1998) documents similar decisions in Brazil.

20. Argentina, Bolivia, Brazil, Chile, Colombia, Costa Rica, Dominican Republic, Ecuador, Guatemala, Mexico, Nicaragua, Panama, Paraguay, Peru, Uruguay, Venezuela (see Van Cott 2000).

21. The 1996 Accords on Indigenous Rights and Culture, negotiated between the Zapatista Army of National Liberation and the Mexican government, recognize the existence of political subjects called *pueblos índios* and give conceptual validation to the terms "self-determination" and "autonomy" (Stephen 1997: 75).

22. Consociation, a mechanism for institutionalizing legal pluralism, comes in two forms: direct and indirect. Direct consociation allows "indigenous peoples to govern themselves, within a certain territory and to a specified extent, according to their own political and legal customs." Indirect consociation involves "the drawing of administrative borders in such a way that an indigenous people constitutes the majority within a certain administrative unit so that it can realize a degree of self-government within the current structures of public government" (Assies 2000: 17).

23. The reforms we are witnessing throughout Latin America involve the transformation of the relations between the state, civil society, and the economy and are greatly influenced by the fiscal crisis, structural adjustment policies, and the move to neoliberalism. As was happening in the United States prior

to 9/11, the goal is a "lean" government whose declining role is assumed by voluntary organizations and NGOs, which, in this capacity, can evolve into para-state institutions. The neoliberal project in part relies on a cultural project, which is concerned with packaging these reforms in a palatable manner through appeals to solidarity and a celebration of civil society (see Nash 2001; Stephen 2001; Warren 2002b).

24. Although this volume does not comprehensively address the issue of the role of the international indigenous peoples' movement or, more broadly, the role of international trends and events in shaping the evolution of indigenous organizations, the symbolic and concrete links with one another and with the global indigenous movement are substantial (see Brysk 1994). Cross-border diffusion is visibly influential, although its precise documentation can be difficult. In addition to discussions and advice surrounding the formal development of a set of indigenous constitutional rights and the ratification of various international covenants (see Ramos, this volume), there are innumerable exchanges that result in more informal transformations. Hirsch provides an example of such transnational processes in her analysis of how the Argentine Guaraní responded to their Bolivian counterparts in complex ways, learning new styles and strategies and learning new meanings about being Guaraní in the present and in the past (2000). Wade discusses how shamanism often works interactively in the construction of indigenous identity as part of a much broader national and at times international cultural space (1997: 94; also see Taussig 1987). And Van Cott provides a nonindigenous example: the awareness of the Venezuelan public and politicians during the 1990s that the country's existing indigenous laws meant that it was "backward" in the eyes of its neighbors—a difficult image for a society with a marked affection for all things modern—helped produce a constitution in 1999 surprisingly favorable to the nation's indigenous communities (Van Cott n.d.).

25. Despite democratic transitions, neoliberal "openings" that do away with protective tariffs and similar legislation have resulted in an economic worsening for a majority of people, including most Latin American indigenous peoples, who continue to be "the poorest, sickest, most abused and most defenseless members of their societies" (Brysk 1994: 47). With some spectacular exceptions, the situation Brysk described in 1994 remains: ". . . foreign debt inspired uncontrolled colonization of Indian territories in rain forest regions, guerrilla movements and drug traffickers contested indigenous areas, and militaries shifted their mission to border and conflict zones disproportionately inhabited by tribal peoples" (1994: 32). Overexploitation of forest resources, ecologically unwise hydroelectric projects, and increased exploitation of subsoil resources on much vaster scales have been stepped up in many areas, posing new threats (see Grueso et al. 1998 for a Colombian example). The potential destabilization of local forms of governance of communal lands produced by the liberalization of land markets is another example.

26. An especially interesting case is the struggle for indigenous intellectual property rights, often seen as collectively owned. Examples include hybrid corn varieties, sacred ritual knowledge, and expertise in botanical pharmaceuticals. See Greaves (1994) and Brush and Stabinski (1996).

27. Even though eleven Latin American states have recognized some form of collective ownership of territory—but not always subsoil rights (note that Brazil recognizes only the right to collective use of land, which remains the property of the state)—Western jurisprudence has consistently displayed ambivalence toward collective rights (see, for example, Rosen 1997). Western law supports the interests of the individual rather than the collectivity and attempts to apply to all citizens uniformly. Although scholars such as Rodolfo Stavenhagen maintain that collective rights are necessary for the full realization of individual rights (cited in Assies et al. 2000: 302), indigenous activists' insistence on group rights and, ideally, custom-tailored values and institutions derived from local *usos y costumbres* (uses and customs) nonetheless flies in the face of many of the foundational assumptions of liberal positivist law concerned with land ownership.

Hence the actual implementation of collective rights turns out to be an extremely complex issue. The ambivalence is in part because the concepts underpinning the nature of those rights are unfamiliar and in part because a collective right to territory is the fundamental premise of self-determination and is thus often perceived as threatening state sovereignty in some way. Note that indigenous people want "territory" to be understood very broadly; in addition to land and the natural resources on it, they see it as a fundamental and multidimensional space within which a community can work out its own social, economic, political, juridical, and cultural values and practices (see Grueso et al. 1998: 208; Assies 2000: 16).

28. They also illustrate Jean Franco's point that the power to interpret and the active appropriation and invention of language are crucial tools (1998: 278).

29. See Redford (1990); Peluso (1993); Conklin and Graham (1995); Slater (1996); Stevens (1997).

30. See Sánchez (2000: 224) on witches, the disabled, and twins.

31. One prominent example of the high stakes perceived by governments is their difficulty with the word "peoples." "People" fits into the traditional notion of a nation coterminous with a state in which all individuals have equal rights. "Peoples" suggests membership in a potentially rival collectivity which demands recognition of certain rights to which members are exclusively entitled. The Draft U.N. Declaration on the Rights of Indigenous Peoples was unacceptable to many potential signatories because "peoples" suggested self-determination with no specified limits, hypothetically permitting secession. Due to the explosive connotations of the term, "populations" is often substituted. The ILO Convention 169 on Indigenous and Tribal Peoples inserted a disclaimer concerning potential rights derived from international

law. While some radical indigenous nationalists speak in terms of separatism (Cojtí Cuxil 1991; Montejo, this volume), most indigenous organizations interpret self-determination as permitting a dramatic increase in their representation in the political system: "there will never be a Mexico without us" (see Stephen 1997: 93). Ramos (this volume) discusses the unbreachable semantic hurdles this term has generated.

32. We prefer this term to the more general "postcolonial" because it indicates that a kind of nationalism continues to be important, but one which no longer partakes of the unitary, exclusive qualities so many nationalists have struggled to define and claim for the particular nation they were championing. Lynn Stephen's phrase "imagined communities in the plural" (personal communication, 2000) suggests a polity consisting of local nationalisms embedded, Russian-egg fashion, in the larger nation, one of whose defining characteristics is its tolerance and celebration of precisely this diversity, including a pluralistic legal system (see also Mallon 1995).

33. In certain respects the question of how to theorize ethnogenesis returns us to the questions of how to define and utilize the concepts of culture and authenticity. Clearly, all cultures continuously change. Some members will be in favor of the changes, others opposed, and sometimes no one wants the changes that occur. The issue of authenticity can arise when a dominant society becomes concerned about some aspects of its own authenticity. A great deal of literature exists on why such collective malaise should have developed in the West—see Baudrillard (1999), for instance. Attempts are then made to imbue certain subordinate groups with different degrees of authenticity based on their differing degrees of proximity to the hegemonic (but insecure) mainstream (see Deloria 1998; Hale 1999).

When this happens, individuals and institutions in the subaltern communities who come to understand the symbolic capital that derives from performing authentic identities run the risk of being perceived as no longer truly living their identity. Rather than appearing to be an unself-conscious habitus (Bourdieu 1977), their actions seem to be a purposeful exploitation of this capital to achieve moral and political ends. Apart from this process, however (and an extensive literature exists on its implications for anthropological theory and practice), we can say that the antecedents to ethnogenesis occur with regularity, with few scholars remarking on this process in the abstract. A nice illustration of the building blocks of ethnogenesis is the case of indigenous women contesting a tradition that excludes them from participation in political decision-making and by so doing vindicating their role in processes of ethnic reorganization (Assies 2000: 18). As Peter Wade has put it, cultural continuity can appear as the mode of cultural change (1997).

Of course, when a lot is at stake, self-representations that signal authenticity are politicized and contested by competing or opposed interests. The way in which certain entitlements contained in collective land rights are overturned in specific cases, at present in Chile (Mapuche) and Colombia (U'wa), depends in part on the outcome of struggles over just what indigenous identity consists of—are *these* people truly authentic? Even basic issues like demography depend on how indigenous people become demographic categories in the first place, often through an extremely politicized struggle about representation with many sectors attempting to influence the census categories and the counting. The best evidence of this is the wide range of estimates of a given country's indigenous population.

In many cases, alternative demographic estimates index political allegiances. Moreover, in Guatemala, the shift in the national consensus about the proportions of indigenous citizens in the population and anti-indigenous violence during the counterinsurgency war reflected the successful consolidation of opposition voices and their strategic ties with the international human rights community. The transformation from a view of the indigenous population as hundreds of dispersed and distinctive local communities to an aggregate of 63 percent of the national population has had wide political and economic ramifications (see Tzian 1994; Ball et al. 1999; Comisión para Esclarecimiento Histórico 1999).

Another way to contest indigenous claims is to challenge the authenticity of their citizenship. For example, Argentine Toba run a risk not of no longer being seen as "authentic" Indians but of being seen as Bolivian-oriented Indians (see Hirsch n.d.).

34. See Díaz Polanco (1997).

35. In this we are answering Abu-Lughod's call for "ethnographies of the particular" (1993), willing to forgo generalizations and models in favor of scrutinizing how individuals are in fact sites of multiple subjectivities.

36. Note that "indigenist" has two well-established, potentially confusing, meanings. The first, most often used in reference to the policies of a state toward its indigenous peoples, indicates an integrationist position; this is particularly the case in the Spanish and Portuguese cognates. The second meaning refers to any individuals (Indian or non-Indian) or institutions in favor of indigenous rights.

37. Deloria discusses specific North American Indians who also played "bridge" roles (such as Ely S. Parker, Ella Deloria, Francis LaFlesche, and D'Arcy McNickle) and the ways in which they represented a troubling challenge to conventional notions of Indians and Indianness in the nineteenth and twentieth centuries, representing a hybridity in some ways analogous to the kinds discussed by authors in this volume. Looking at non-Indians who desired to cross over and partake of Indianness in the twentieth century, Deloria notes that "Indianized quests for authenticity rested upon a contradictory foundation. In order to be authentic, Indians had to be located outside modern American societal boundaries. Because they were outside those boundaries, however, it became more difficult to get at them, to lay claim to the charac-

teristics Indians had come to represent"; and that at times "the very presence of a modern person contaminated the authenticity of the primitive" (1998: 115). Also see Berkhofer (1978).
38. See Friedman (1994). For interesting discussions of these issues in U.S. settings, see Haley and Wilcoxon (1999); and Field (1999).

References

Abu-Lughod, Lila. 1986. *Veiled Sentiments: Honor and Poetry in a Bedouin Society.* Berkeley: University of California Press.
———. 1993. Introduction. In *Writing Women's Worlds: Bedouin Stories,* 1–44. Berkeley: University of California Press.
Albó, Xavier. 1987. From MNRistas to Kataristas to Katari. In Steven J. Stern, ed., *Resistance, Rebellion, and Consciousness in the Andean Peasant World, 18th to 20th Centuries,* 379–419. Madison: University of Wisconsin Press.
Allen, Tim, and Jean Seaton. 1999. *The Media of Conflict: War Reporting and Representations of Ethnic Violence.* London: ZED Books.
Alvarez, Sonia E., Evelina Dagnino, and Arturo Escobar, eds. 1998. *Cultures of Politics/Politics of Cultures: Re-visioning Latin American Social Movements.* Boulder: Westview Press.
Anderson, Benedict. 1991. *Imagined Communities: Reflections on the Origin and Spread of Nationalism.* London: Verso.
Appadurai, Arjun. 1996. *Modernity at Large: Cultural Dimensions of Globalization.* Minneapolis: University of Minnesota Press.
Assies, Willem. 2000. Indigenous Peoples and Reform of the State in Latin America. In Willem Assies, Gemma van der Haar, and André Hoekema, eds., *The Challenge of Diversity: Indigenous Peoples and Reform of the State in Latin America,* 3–22. Amsterdam: Thela Thesis.
Assies, Willem, Gemma van der Haar, and André Hoekema, 2000. Diversity as a Challenge: A Note on the Dilemmas of Diversity. In Willem Assies, Gemma van der Haar, and André Hoekema, eds., *The Challenge of Diversity: Indigenous Peoples and Reform of the State in Latin America,* 295–313. Amsterdam: Thela Thesis.
Ball, Patrick, Paul Kobrak, and Herbert Spirer. 1999. *State Violence in Guatemala, 1960–1996: A Quantitative Reflection.* Washington, D.C.: American Association for the Advancement of Science.
Baudrillard, Jean. 1999. *Simulacra and Simulation.* Trans. Sheila Faria Glaser. Ann Arbor: University of Michigan Press.
Berkhofer, Robert F. 1978. *The White Man's Indian: Images of the American Indian from Columbus to the Present.* New York: Alfred A. Knopf.
Bonfil Batalla, Guillermo, et al. 1982. *America Latina: Etnodesarrollo y etnocidio.* San José, Costa Rica: FLACSO.
Bourdieu, Pierre. 1977. *Outline of a Theory of Practice.* Trans. Richard Nice. Cambridge: Cambridge University Press.
Briones, Claudia. 2000. The Politics of Indigenous Re-presentation: Mapuche

Views on State Law and Juridical Pluralism. Paper presented at the American Anthropological Association Annual Meeting, San Francisco, November.

Brown, Michael. 1993. Facing the State, Facing the World: Amazonia's Native Leaders and the New Politics of Identity. *L'Homme* 33 (2–4): 307–326.

Brush, Stephen, and D. Stabinski, eds. 1996. *Valuing Local Knowledge: Indigenous Peoples and Intellectual Property Rights.* New York: Island Press.

Brysk, Alison. 1994. Acting Globally: Indian Rights and International Politics in Latin America. In Donna Lee Van Cott, ed., *Indigenous Peoples and Democracy in Latin America*, 29–51. New York: St. Martin's.

Calderón, Fernando. 1995. *Movimientos sociales y política.* Mexico City: Siglo XXI.

Campbell, Howard, et al., eds. 1993. *Zapotec Struggles: Histories, Politics, and Representations from Juchitán, Oaxaca.* Washington, D.C.: Smithsonian Institution Press.

Carrasco, Morita, and Claudia Briones. 1996. *"La tierra que nos quitaron": Reclamos indígenas en Argentina.* Copenhagen: International Work Group for Indigenous Affairs.

Casaús Arzú, Marta Elena. 1992. *Guatemala: Linaje y racismo.* San José: FLACSO.

Centro de Estudios de la Cultura Maya (CECMA). 1994. *Derecho indígena: Sistema jurídico de los pueblos originarios de América.* Guatemala City: Serviprensa Centroamericana.

Chalmers, Douglas, et al., eds. 1997. *The New Politics of Inequality in Latin America: Rethinking Participation and Representation.* Oxford: Oxford University Press.

Clifford, James. 1988. *The Predicament of Culture: Twentieth-Century Ethnography, Literature, and Art.* Cambridge, Mass.: Harvard University Press.

Clifton, James A. 1990. Introduction: Memoir, Exegesis. In *The Invented Indian: Cultural Fictions & Government Policies*, 1–28. New Brunswick: Transaction.

Cojtí Cuxil, Demetrio. 1991. *Configuración del pensamiento político del pueblo maya.* Quetzaltenango, Guatemala: Asociación de Escritores Mayances de Guatemala.

———. 1994. *Políticas para la reivindicación de los mayas de hoy.* Guatemala City: Editorial Cholsamaj.

———. 1996a. Estudio evaluativo del cumplimiento del acuerdo sobre identidad y derechos de los pueblos indígenas. In Carlos Aldana, ed., *Acuerdos de paz: Efectos, lecciones y perspectivas*, 51–90. Debate 34. Guatemala City: FLACSO.

———. 1996b. The Politics of Mayan Revindication. In Edward Fischer and R. McKenna Brown, eds., *Maya Cultural Activism in Guatemala*, 19–50. Austin: University of Texas Press.

———(Waqi' Q'anil). 1997. *Ri Maya' Moloj Pa Iximulew: El movimiento maya.* Guatemala City: Editorial Cholsamaj.

Comaroff, John, and Jean Comaroff. 1992. *Ethnography and the Historical Imagination.* Boulder: Westview Press.

Comisión para Esclarecimiento Histórico (CEH). 1999. *Guatemala: Memoria de silencio.* Washington, D.C.: American Association for the Advancement of Science. http://hrdata.aaas.org/ceh/.

Conklin, Beth, and Laura R. Graham. 1995. The Shifting Middle Ground: Amazonian Indians and Eco-Politics. *American Anthropologist* 97 (4): 695–710.

Cornelio, José Marcellino, Ricardo Fontes, Manuel da Silva, Marcos da Silva, Luís Manuel, Inocêncio da Silva, and Maria da Silva. 1999. *Waferinaipe Ianheke: A sabedoria dos nossos antepassados: Histórias dos Hohodene e dos Walipere-Dakenai do rio Aiari*. São Gabriel da Cachoeira: Associação das Comunidades Indígenas do Rio Aiari.

Cultural Survival. 1993. *State of the Peoples: A Global Human Rights Report on Societies in Danger*. Boston: Beacon Press.

Deloria, Philip J. 1998. *Playing Indian*. New Haven: Yale University Press.

Díaz Polanco, Héctor. 1991. *Autonomía regional: La autodeterminación de los pueblos indios*. Mexico City: Siglo Veintiuno Editores.

———. 1997. *Indigenous Peoples in Latin America: The Quest for Self-Determination*. Trans. Lucía Rayas. Boulder: Westview Press.

Escobar, Arturo, and Sonia E. Alvarez, eds. 1992. *The Making of Social Movements in Latin America*. Boulder: Westview Press.

Esquit, Edgar, and Iván García. 1998. *El derecho consuetudinario, la reforma judicial y la implementación de los acuerdos de paz*. Debate 44. Guatemala: FLACSO.

Esquit Choy, Alberto, and Victor Gálvez Borrell. 1997. *The Mayan Movement Today: Issues of Indigenous Culture and Development in Guatemala*. Guatemala City: FLACSO.

Esquit Choy, Edgar, and Carlos Ochoa García, eds. 1995. *Yiqalil q'anej kunimaaj tzij niman tzij; El respeto a la palabra: El orden jurídico del pueblo maya*. Guatemala City: CECMA.

Field, Les. 1994. Who Are the Indians? Reconceptualizing Indigenous Identity, Resistance, and the Role of Social Science in Latin America. *Latin American Research Review* 29 (3): 237–248.

———. 1999. Complicities and Collaborations: Anthropologists and the "Unacknowledged Tribes" of California. *Current Anthropology* 40 (2): 193–209.

Fischer, Edward. 1999. Cultural Logic and Maya Identity: Rethinking Constructivism and Essentialism. *Current Anthropology* 40 (4): 1–61.

Fischer, Edward, and R. McKenna Brown, eds. 1996. *Maya Cultural Activism in Guatemala*. Austin: University of Texas Press.

Foweraker, Joe. 1995. *Theorizing Social Movements*. London/Boulder, Colo.: Pluto Press.

Fox, Richard, ed. 1991. *Recapturing Culture: Working in the Present*. Santa Fe: SAR Press.

Franco, Jean. 1998. Defrocking the Vatican: Feminism's Secular Project. In Sonia E. Alvarez, Evelina Dagnino, and Arturo Escobar, eds., *Cultures of Politics/Politics of Cultures: Re-visioning Latin American Social Movements*, 278–289. Boulder: Westview Press.

Friedman, Jonathan. 1994. *Cultural Identity and Global Process*. London: Sage.

Gallois, Dominique. 1996. Controle territorial e diversificação do extrativismo na Area Indígena Waiãpi. In *Povos indígenas no Brasil, 1991–1995*, 263–271. São Paulo: Instituto Socioambiental.

García Canclini, Néstor. 1995. *Hybrid Cultures*. Minneapolis: University of Minneapolis Press.

Geertz, Clifford. 2000. Indonesia: Starting Over. *New York Review of Books*, May 11.

Gellner, Ernest. 1983. *Nations and Nationalism*. Ithaca: Cornell University Press.

Gilroy, Paul. 1987. *There Ain't No Black in the Union Jack: The Cultural Politics of Race and Nation.* Chicago: University of Chicago Press.

Gómez, Magdalena, coord. 1997 *Derecho indígena.* Mexico City: Instituto Nacional Indigenista Interamericano.

González Casanova, Pablo, and Marcos Roitman Rosenmann, coords. 1996. *Democracia y estado multiétnico en América Latina.* Mexico City: UNAM/La Jornada.

González Ponciano, Jorge Ramón. n.d. Whiteness and the Indian-Ladino Dichotomy in Post-War Guatemala. Unpublished MS.

Graham, Laura R. 1995. *Performing Dreams: Discourses of Immortality among the Xavante of Central Brazil.* Austin: University of Texas Press.

Greaves, Tom, ed. 1994. *Intellectual Property Rights for Indigenous Peoples: A Source Book.* Oklahoma City: Society for Applied Anthropology.

Gros, Christian. 1991. *Colombia indígena: Identidad cultural y cambio social.* Bogotá: Fondo Editorial CEREC.

———. 2000. *Políticas de la etnicidad: Identidad, estado y modernidad.* Bogotá: Instituto Colombiano de Antropología e Historia.

Grueso, Libia, Carlos Rosero, and Arturo Escobar. 1998. The Process of Black Community Organizing in the Southern Pacific Coast Region of Colombia. In Sonia E. Alvarez, Evelina Dagnino, and Arturo Escobar, eds., *Cultures of Politics/Politics of Cultures: Re-visioning Latin American Social Movements,* 196–219. Boulder: Westview Press.

Guha, Ranajit, and Gayatri Chakravorty Spivak, eds. 1988. *Selected Subaltern Studies.* New York: Oxford University Press.

Gupta, Akhil. 1998. *Postcolonial Developments: Agriculture in the Making of Modern India.* Durham: Duke University Press.

Gupta, Akhil, and James Ferguson. 1992. Beyond "Culture": Space, Identity and the Politics of Difference. *Cultural Anthropology* 7: 6–23.

Gustafson, Bret. 2002. Native Languages and Hybrid States: A Political Ethnography of Guarani Engagements with Bilingual Education Reform in Bolivia, 1989–1999. Diss., Harvard University, Department of Anthropology.

Hale, Charles. 1994a. Between Che Guevara and the Pachamama: Mestizos, Indians, and Identity Politics in the Anti-Quincentenary Campaign. *Critique of Anthropology* 14: 9–39.

———. 1994b. *Resistance and Contradiction: Miskitu Indians and the Nicaraguan State, 1894–1987.* Palo Alto: Stanford University Press.

———. 1996. Mestizaje, Hybridity and the Cultural Politics of Difference in Post-revolutionary Central America. *Journal of Latin American Anthropology* 2 (1): 34–61.

———. 1997. Cultural Politics of Identity in Latin America. *Annual Reviews of Anthropology* 26: 567–590.

———. 1999. Does Multiculturalism Menace?: Governance, Cultural Rights and the Eclipse of "Official Mestizaje" in Central America. Paper given at American Anthropological Association 98th Annual Meetings, Chicago.

Haley, Brian D., and Larry R. Wilcoxon. 1999. Anthropology and the Making of Chumash Tradition. *Current Anthropology* 38 (5): 761–794.

Hendrickson, Carol. 1995. *Weaving Identities: Construction of Dress and Self in a Highland Guatemalan Town.* Austin: University of Texas Press.

Hill, Jonathan, ed. 1988. *Rethinking History and Myth: Indigenous South American Perspectives on the Past.* Urbana and Chicago: University of Illinois Press.

———, ed. 1997. *Ethnogenesis in the Americas.* Iowa City: University of Iowa Press.

Hirsch, Silvia María. 2000. Inventing the Generic Guaraní: Pan-Indianism and Politics among the Guaraní Indians of Northwest Argentina. American Anthropological Association Meetings, San Francisco, November.

Hobsbawm, Eric. 1990. *Nations and Nationalism since 1780.* Cambridge: Cambridge University Press.

Howe, James. 1998. *A People Who Would Not Kneel: Panama, the United States, and the San Blas Kuna.* Washington, D.C.: Smithsonian Institution Press.

Instituto de Lingüística. 1997. *Primer congreso de estudios mayas.* Vols. 2 and 3. *Cultura de Guatemala.* Guatemala City: Universidad de Rafael Landívar and Editorial Cholsamaj.

Jackson, Jean E. 1989. Is There a Way to Talk about Making Culture without Making Enemies? *Dialectical Anthropology* 14 (2): 127–144. Reprinted in Fernando Santos Granero, ed., *Globalización y cambio en la Amazonía indígena,* 439–472. Quito, Ecuador: FLACSO, Biblioteca Abya-Yala, 1996.

———. 1995. Culture, Genuine and Spurious: The Politics of Indianness in the Vaupés, Colombia. *American Ethnologist* 22 (1): 3–27.

———. 1999. The Politics of Ethnographic Practice in the Colombian Vaupés. *Identities: Global Studies in Culture and Power* 6 (2–3): 281–317.

Jelin, Elizabeth, and Eric Hershberg, eds. 1996. *Constructing Democracy: Human Rights, Citizenship, and Society in Latin America.* Boulder: Westview Press.

Jordan, Glenn, and Chris Weedon. 1995. *Cultural Politics: Class, Gender, Race and the Postmodern World.* Oxford: Blackwell.

Kearney, Michael. 1996. *Reconceptualizing the Peasantry: Anthropology in Global Perspective.* Boulder: Westview Press.

Kearney, Michael, and Stefano Varese. 1995. Latin America's Indigenous Peoples: Changing Identities and Forms of Resistance. In S. Halebsky and R. Harris, eds., *Capital, Power and Inequality in Latin America.* Boulder: Westview Press.

Kicza, John. 1993. *The Indian in Latin American History: Resistance, Resilience, and Acculturation.* Wilmington, Del.: Scholarly Resources.

Krenak, Ailton, ed. 1996. *Nucleus of Indian Culture/Indian Research Center.* São Paulo: Núcleo de Cultural Indígena.

Kumu, Umúsin Panlõn, and Tolamãn Kenhíri. 1980. *Antes o mundo não existia: A mitologia heróica dos índios Desâna.* São Paulo: Libraria Cultura Editora.

Mallon, Florencia E. 1995. *Peasant and Nation: The Making of Postcolonial Mexico and Peru.* Berkeley: University of California Press.

———. 1996. Constructing Mestizaje in Latin America: Authenticity, Marginality, and Gender in the Claiming of Ethnic Identities. *Journal of Latin American Anthropology* 2 (1): 170–181.

McAdam, Doug, John D. McCarthy, and Mayer N. Zald, eds. 1996. *Comparative Perspectives on Social Movements: Political Opportunities, Mobilizing Structures, and Cultural Framings.* New York: Cambridge University Press.

McClure, Kirstie. 1997. Taking Liberties in Foucault's Triangle: Sovereignty, Discipline, Governmentality, and the Subject of Rights. In Austin Sarat and Thomas R. Kearnes, eds., *Identities, Politics, and Rights,* 149–194. Ann Arbor: University of Michigan Press.

Melucci, Alberto. 1989. *Nomads of the Present: Social Movements and Individual Needs in Contemporary Society.* Edited by John Keane and Paul Mier. London: Hutchinson Radius.

Merry, Sally Engle. 1998. Law, Culture, and Cultural Appropriation. *Yale Journal of Law & the Humanities* 10 (2): 575–603.

Montejo, Víctor. 1987. *Testimony: Death of a Guatemalan Village.* Willimantic, Conn.: Curbstone Press.

———. 1993. In the Name of the Pot, the Sun, the Broken Spear, the Rock, the Stick, the Idol, Ad Infinitum & Ad Nauseam: An Exposé of Anglo Anthropologists' Obsessions with the Invention of Mayan Gods. *Red Pencil Review: A Journal of Native American Studies* 9 (1) (Spring): 12–16.

———. 1999. *Voices from Exile: Violence and Survival in Modern Maya History.* Norman: University of Oklahoma Press.

Montejo, Víctor, and Q'anil Akab'. 1992. *Brevísima relación testimonial de la continua destrucción del Mayab' (Guatemala).* Providence, R.I.: Maya Scholars Network.

Morales, Mario Roberto. 1998. *La articulación de las diferencias o el síndrome de Maximón.* Guatemala City: FLACSO.

Morin, Françoise, ed. 1988. *Indianidad, etnocidio, indigenismo en América Latina.* Mexico City: Instituto Indigenista Intramericano, Centre d'Etudes Mexicaines et Centraméricaines.

Morris, A., and Carol McClurg Mueller, eds. 1992. *Frontiers of Social Movement Theory.* New Haven: Yale University Press.

Muehlebach, Andrea. 2001. "Making Place" at the United Nations: Indigenous Cultural Politics and the U.N. Working Group on Indigenous Politics. *Cultural Anthropology* 16 (3): 415–448.

Nash, June C. 2001. *Mayan Visions: The Quest for Autonomy in an Age of Globalization.* New York: Routledge.

Nelson, Diane. 1996. Maya Hackers and the Cyberspatialized Nation-State: Modernity, Ethnostalgia, and a Lizard Queen in Guatemala. *Cultural Anthropology* 11 (3): 287–308.

———. 1999. *The Finger in the Wound: Body Politics in Quincentennial Guatemala.* Berkeley: University of California Press.

OKMA (Oxlajuuj Keej Mayab' Ajtz'iib') [Ajpub', Ixkem, Lolmay, Nik'te', Pakal, Saqijix, and Waykan]. 1993. *Maya' Chii': Idiomas mayas de Guatemala.* Guatemala City: Editorial Cholsamaj.

Otzoy, Irma, 1996. *Maya' B'anikil Maya' Tzyaqb'al: Identidad y vestuario maya.* Guatemala City: Editorial Cholsamaj.

Palomino Flores, Salvador. 1986. Del indigenismo a la indianidad. *Pueblo Indio: Vocero del Consejo Indio de Sud América* 8: 52–58.

Peluso, Daniela. 1993. Conservation and Indigenismo. *Hemisphere* (Winter/Spring): 6–8.

Plant, Roger. 1999. Indigenous Identity and Rights in the Guatemalan Peace Process. In Cynthia Arnson, ed., *Comparative Peace Processes in Latin America,* 319–338. Washington, D.C.: Woodrow Wilson Center.

Price, David. 1989. *Before the Bulldozer: The Nambiquara Indians and the World Bank.* Cabin John, Md.: Steven Locks Press.

Programa de Desarrollo de los Pueblos Mayas. 1995. *Acuerdo sobre identidad y derechos de los pueblos indígenas y documentos de apoyo para su comprensión.* Guatemala City: Editorial Cholsamaj.

Ramírez, María Clemencia. n.d. The Politics of Identity and Cultural Difference in the Putumayo: Claiming Special Indigenous Rights in Colombia's Amazon. In David Maybury-Lewis, ed., *Identities in Conflict: Indigenous Peoples and Latin American States.* Cambridge, Mass.: DRCLAS.

Ramos, Alcida Rita. 1998. *Indigenism: Ethnic Politics in Brazil.* Madison: University of Wisconsin Press.

Rappaport, Joanne. 1994. *Cumbe Reborn: An Andean Ethnography of History.* Chicago: University of Chicago Press.

———. 1996. *The Politics of Memory: Native Historical Interpretation in the Colombian Andes.* New York: Cambridge University Press.

Raxché, Demetrio Rodríguez Guaján. 1989. *Cultura maya y políticas de desarrollo.* Guatemala City: COCADI.

———. 1995. *Las ONGs y las relaciones interétnicas.* Guatemala City: Editorial Cholsamaj.

Redford, Kent H. 1990. The Ecologically Noble Savage. *Orion Nature Quarterly* 9 (3): 27–29.

Reed, Richard. 1995. *Prophets of Agroforestry: Guaraní Communities and Commercial Gathering.* Austin: University of Texas Press.

———. 1997. *Forest Dwellers, Forest Protectors: Indigenous Models for International Development.* Boston: Allyn and Bacon.

Ribadeneira, Juan Carlos, ed. 1993. *Derecho, pueblos indígenas y reforma del estado.* Quito: Biblioteca Abya-Yala.

Rojas Curieux, Tulio. 1997. La traducción de la Constitución de la República de Colombia a lenguas indígenas. In Ministerio de Justicia y del Derecho, ed., *"Del olvido surgimos para traer nuevas esperanzas": La jurisdicción especial indígena,* 229–244. Bogotá: Ministerio de Justicia y del Derecho/Ministerio del Interior, Dirección General de Asuntos Indígenas.

Rosaldo, Renato. 1989. *Culture and Truth: The Remaking of Social Analysis.* Boston: Beacon Press.

Rosen, Lawrence. 1997. Indigenous Peoples in International Law. *Yale Law Journal* 107 (1): 227–259.

Said, Edward W. 1978. *Orientalism.* New York: Pantheon.

Sam Colop, Enrique. 1990. Foreign Scholars and Mayans: What Are the Issues? In Marilyn Moors, coord., *Guatemala Scholars Network News* (February): 2. Washington, D.C.: GSN.

———. 1991. *Jub'aqtun Omay Kuchum K'aslemal: Cinco siglos de encubrimiento.* Seminario Permanente de Estudios Mayas, Cuaderno No. 1. Guatemala City: Editorial Cholsamaj.

Sánchez, Enrique, comp. 1996. *Derechos de los pueblos indígenas en las constituciones de América Latina.* Bogotá: Disloque Editores.

Sánchez, Esther. 1992. *Antropología jurídica: Normas formales, costumbres legales en Colombia.* Bogotá: Sociedad Antropológica de Colombia/Comité Internacional para el Desarrollo de los Pueblos.

———. 1997. Conflicto entre la jurisdicción especial indígena y la jurisdicción ordinaria (enfoque antropológico). In Ministerio de Justicia y del Derecho/ Dirección General de Asuntos Indígenas, ed., *"Del olvido surgimos para traer nuevas esperanzas": La jurisdicción especial indígena*, 287–292. Bogotá: Ministerio de Justicia y del Derecho/Ministerio del Interior, Dirección General de Asuntos Indígenas.

Sánchez Botero, Esther. 2000. The Tutela-System as a Means of Transforming the Relations between the State and the Indigenous Peoples of Colombia. In Willem Assies, Gemma van der Haar, and André Hoekema, eds., *The Challenge of Diversity: Indigenous Peoples and Reform of the State in Latin America*, 223–245. Amsterdam: Thela Thesis.

Scott, James. 1985. *Weapons of the Weak: Everyday Forms of Peasant Resistance*. New Haven: Yale University Press.

———. 1990. *Domination and the Arts of Resistance: Hidden Transcripts*. New Haven: Yale University Press.

Sieder, Rachel. 1997. *Customary Law and Democratic Transition in Guatemala*. Research Papers 48. London: University of London Institute of Latin American Studies.

Slater, Candace. 1996. Amazonia as Edenic Narrative. In W. Cronon, ed., *Uncommon Ground: Rethinking the Human Place in Nature*. New York and London: W. W. Norton.

Slater, David, ed. 1984. *New Social Movements and the State in Latin America*. Dordrecht, the Netherlands: Foris Publications/CEDLA.

Smith, Carol A., ed. 1990. *Guatemalan Indians and the State: 1540 to 1988*. Austin: University of Texas Press.

Starn, Orin, 1991. Missing the Revolution: Anthropologists and the War in Peru. *Cultural Anthropology* 6 (1): 63–91.

Stavenhagen, Rodolfo. 1990. Derecho consuetudinario indígena en América Latina. In Rodolfo Stavenhagen and Diego Iturralde, comps., *Entre la ley y la costumbre: El derecho consuetudinario indígena en América Latina*. Mexico City: Instituto Indigenista Interamericano and Instituto Interamericano de Derechos Humanos.

Stephen, Lynn. 1997. Redefined Nationalism in Building a Movement for Indigenous Autonomy in Southern Mexico. *Journal of Latin American Anthropology* 3 (1): 72–101.

———. 2001. *Zapata Lives! Histories and Political Culture in Southern Mexico*. Berkeley: University of California Press.

Stern, Steve, ed. 1987. *Resistance, Rebellion, and Consciousness in the Andean Peasant World: 18th to 20th Centuries*. Madison: University of Wisconsin Press.

Stevens, Stanley, ed. 1997. *Conservation through Cultural Survival: Indigenous Peoples and Protected Areas*. Washington, D.C.: Island Press.

Taussig, Michael. 1987. *Shamanism, Colonialism and the Wild Man: A Study in Terror and Healing*. Chicago: University of Chicago Press.

Trouillot, Michel-Rolph. 1991. Anthropology and the Savage Slot: The Poetics and Politics of Otherness. In Richard Fox, ed., *Recapturing Anthropology: Working in the Present*, 17–44. Santa Fe: School of American Research Press.

Turner, Terence. 1992. Defiant Images: The Kayapó Appropriation of Video. *Anthropology Today* 8 (6): 5–16.

————. 1993. The Role of Indigenous Peoples in the Environmental Crisis: The Example of the Kayapo of the Brazilian Amazon. *Perspectives in Biology and Medicine* 36 (3): 526–545.

————. 1995. An Indigenous People's Struggle for Socially Equitable and Ecologically Sustainable Production. *Journal of Latin American Anthropology* 1 (1): 98–121.

————. 1996. Brazil: Indigenous rights vs. Neoliberalism. *Dissent* 43 (3): 67–69.

Tzian, Leopoldo. 1994. *Kajlab'aliil Maya'iib' Xuq Mu'siib': Ri Ub'antajiik Iximuleew—Mayas y Ladinos en cifras: El caso de Guatemala.* Guatemala City: Editorial Cholsamaj.

Urban, Greg, and Joel Sherzer, eds. 1991. *Nation-States and Indians in Latin America.* Austin: University of Texas Press.

Van Cott, Donna Lee. 1994a. Indigenous Peoples and Democracy: Issues for Policymakers. In Donna Lee Van Cott, ed., *Indigenous Peoples and Democracy in Latin America*, 1–28. New York: St. Martin's.

————, ed. 1994b. *Indigenous Peoples and Democracy in Latin America.* New York: St. Martin's.

————. 2000. *The Friendly Liquidation of the Past: The Politics of Diversity in Latin America.* Pittsburgh: University of Pittsburgh Press.

————. n.d. Andean Indigenous Movements and Constitutional Transformation: Venezuela in Comparative Perspective. *Latin American Perspectives* (forthcoming).

Vasco, Luis Guillermo. 1997. Política, autonomía y cultura a finales del siglo XX. In Ministerio de Justicia y del Derecho, ed., *"Del olvido surgimos para traer nuevas esperanzas": La jurisdicción especial indígena*, 321–326. Bogotá: Ministerio de Justicia y del Derecho/Ministerio del Interior, Dirección General de Asuntos Indígenas.

Wade, Peter. 1993. *Blackness and Race Mixture: The Dynamics of Racial Identity in Colombia.* Baltimore: Johns Hopkins University Press.

————. 1997. *Race and Ethnicity in Latin America.* London: Pluto.

Walker, Christopher. 1996. *Trinkets and Beads* (film). New York: First Run/Icarus Films.

Warren, Kay B. 1978. *The Symbolism of Subordination: Indian Identity in a Guatemalan Town.* Austin: University of Texas Press.

————. 1992. Transforming Memories and Histories: The Meanings of Ethnic Resurgence for Mayan Indians. In Alfred Stepan, ed., *Americas: New Interpretive Essays*, 189–219. New York: Oxford University Press.

————. 1998. *Indigenous Movements and Their Critics: Pan-Maya Activism in Guatemala.* Princeton: Princeton University Press.

————. 2002a. Epilogue: Toward an Anthropology of Fragments, Instabilities, and Incomplete Transitions. In Carol Greenhouse, Beth Mertz, and Kay B. Warren, eds., *Transforming States: Ethnographies of Subjectivity and Agency in Changing Political Contexts*, 379–392. Durham: Duke University Press.

————. 2002b. Introduction: Rethinking Bi-polar Constructions of Ethnicity. *Journal of Latin American Anthropology* 6 (2): 90–105.

Wolf, Eric. 1982. *Europe and the People without History.* Berkeley: University of California Press.

Wright, Robin. 1988. Anthropological Presuppositions of Indigenous Advocacy. *Annual Review of Anthropology* 17: 365–390.

Yashar, Deborah. 1996. Indigenous Protest and Democracy in Latin America. In Jorge I. Domínguez and Abraham F. Lowenthal, eds., *Constructing Democratic Governance: Latin America and the Caribbean in the 1990s*, 87–105. Baltimore: Johns Hopkins University Press:

———. 1998. Indigenous Movements and Democracy in Latin America. *Comparative Politics* 31 (1) (October): 23–42.

———. N.d. *Contesting Citizenship: Indigenous Movements and the Postliberal Challenge in Latin America*. New York: Cambridge University Press.

Young, Crawford. 1976. *The Politics of Cultural Pluralism*. Madison: University of Wisconsin Press.

———. 1993. *The Rising Tide of Cultural Pluralism: The Nation-State at Bay?* Madison: University of Wisconsin Press.

Zapeta, Estuardo. 1999. *Las huellas de B'alam, 1994–1996*. Guatemala City: Editorial Cholsamaj.

2. THE INDIGENOUS PUBLIC VOICE

The Multiple Idioms of Modernity in Native Cauca

David D. Gow
Joanne Rappaport

The past two decades have witnessed an efflorescence of indigenous activism and identity construction in Colombia, culminating in the 1991 Constitution, which recognized the multiethnic character of the Colombian nation and codified the administrative forms by which native peoples would henceforth participate in civil society as ethnic citizens (Triana 1992; Gros 1993; Rappaport 1996).[1] As the indigenous movement accommodated to its new circumstances as an effective player on the national stage, it cultivated new discourses and strategies to penetrate and transform the fields of jurisprudence, development, and education. In the process, a multiplicity of new indigenous actors emerged, most of them young, educated women and men, adept at bridging the discursive gap between their communities and the national society.

This new indigenous leadership is distinct from its predecessors, who were largely men socialized in the land struggle and in preconstitution oppositional ethnic politics (Jimeno 1996). The new indigenous leadership, moreover, articulates a cultural discourse very different from the class discourse of earlier leaders.[2] A good example of the new leadership is Jesús Enrique Piñacué, former president of the Consejo Regional Indígena del Cauca (CRIC: Regional Indigenous Council of Cauca) and national senator. Piñacué, from the Nasa community of Calderas, Tierradentro, is seminary-educated and highly articulate in both Nasa Yuwe—the Nasa language—and Spanish, a masterful orator who magnetically articulates a radical but conciliatory cultural discourse that is appealing to political independents in the dominant society and to indigenous communities alike.[3] In public activities like protest marches, he has tended to serve as one of several indigenous spokespersons, conveying the image of a united and homogeneous native rights movement.

But what appears from the outside to be a monolithic indigenous movement staffed by charismatic and telegenic spokespersons is, from the vantage point of the movement itself, a factionalized assembly of propo-

Colombia

MAP 2.1 Colombia

nents of a broad array of forms of ethnic identity, organizing strategies, and tactics for struggle (cf. Rogers 1996). In the department of Cauca, multiple groups come together at moments of national protest, while at other junctures they contest the demands, methods, and rhetoric of the strongest organizations. The best-known of these is CRIC, the oldest indigenous organization in Colombia, founded in 1971 (Gros 1991; Avi-rama and Márquez 1994). CRIC's platform recently moved from a class discourse to a cultural discourse introduced by its Nasa majority. In the 1980s the Autoridades Indígenas de Colombia (AICO: Indigenous Authorities of Colombia) was founded, its major proponents being the Guambiano (Findji 1992).[4] AICO's noncentralized organization revolves around traditional community authorities — or, at least, its leadership is constituted by elected *resguardo* (reservation) officials; for the most part these authorities are young, educated, and discursively trilingual in the languages of the state, of the movement, and of the communities.[5]

Legal political struggle, however, has historically been only one of several options in Colombia. Indigenous people have also participated in guerrilla organizations, including the Movimiento Armado Quintín Lame (MAQL: Quintín Lame Armed Movement), a majority-Nasa guer-rilla movement named after a turn-of-the-century Nasa leader (Peña-randa 1993). The MAQL was until recently an armed group character-ized by a pluralist vision, incorporating members of multiple indigenous groups as well as mestizos and Afro-Colombians; in 1991 the MAQL ne-gotiated with the Colombian state, becoming a legal organization and a central force in the creation of an indigenous political party, the Alianza Social Indígena (ASI: Social Indigenous Alliance) (Peñaranda 1999).[6]

Within this panoply of political programs and positions, a growing layer of subregional organizations exerts pressure on the larger indige-nous organizations, bringing local communities and "nonaligned" sec-tors — communities not affiliated with any of the regional organizations and Protestant groups, among others — into play at the regional and na-tional levels and creating a complex and constant dialogue. It is at the in-terstices of the movement that the new definition of indigenous identity, forged within the modern constitutional context, emerges. In this new definition, identity arises out of a combination of the civic discourse that developed from the ruins of the leftist parties of the 1970s, the academic discourse of anthropologists who have studied the indigenous communi-ties of Cauca, and the development discourse that claimed the attention of newly empowered indigenous communities and organizations. Partic-ularly in the public sphere, identity must be perceived as both a political and a cultural construct, as Alain Touraine has suggested with reference to social movements:

> A social movement is at once a social conflict and a cultural project . . .
> The goal of a social movement is always the realization of cultural val-ues as well as victory over a social adversary. (1995: 240)

In Cauca, cultural planning is integral to the tasks of indigenous organizations and communities, because cultural demands are central to the political platforms of these movements. Particular cultural projects become areas of contention within the movement, as its multiple players contest the broader ethnic project within the contexts of particular cultural struggles. Conflicting discourses, appropriated from outside the indigenous community and refashioned within the multiple situations in which native people organize themselves, are employed in these encounters: the modernization discourse of development planners, the modernist discourse of ethnographers, and the political ethnic discourse of Latin American indigenous movements contradict and recreate one another in a dialectical relationship out of which political transformations emerge (cf. Holston 1986).

Thus, in order to understand the dynamics of indigenous self-representation in Colombia, we need to go beyond the ethnic boundary or the interstitial zone between ethnic organization and state. While contemporary theorists such as Homi Bhabha (1994) urge us to look at the fuzzy borders where hybrid social discourses emerge at the intersection of minority groups and the dominant society, it is equally important to recognize the existence of an *inside*, a coherent sphere of operation which is tangibly experienced by the actors themselves (Gilroy 1993), furnishing the scenarios in which ideologies are created, transformed, and disputed. In other words, while we certainly recognize that indigenous identity is variable, arising in particular historical contexts and assuming a broad range of forms within a highly heterogeneous and mobile population, there is also a conspicuous, palpable, and passionately defended rubric under which diverse people have united to define themselves as native Colombians. This is what we mean by the inside: a network that defines itself both by political objectives and by what its members perceive as manifest cultural difference, in and out of which actors move in the process of pressing their demands. Whether or not the inside can be defined by anthropologists through discernible cultural characteristics is immaterial in the face of the common experience that this group perceives itself as sharing and the legal reality of the 1991 Constitution (as well as previous legislation going back to the colonial era) (cf. Friedman 1994). This inside is not, however, a bounded entity; at its limits are a variety of players, including indigenous leaders whose lives unfold among the urban intelligentsia (Jackson 1995), non-native advisors (*colaboradores*) who have dedicated their lives to the indigenous movement, and government functionaries who were once *colaboradores* within one of the movements. These actors work full-time in the movement, creating the press releases, organizational newspapers and flyers, public statements, and proposals for funding by which indigenous Cauca represents itself to the world.

So we cannot speak simply of a bipolar struggle between the dominant society and the indigenous movement; nor can we focus exclusively on how a monolithic movement represents itself to the dominant society. We must examine the complex internal dialogue within organizations, between organizations, and between organizations and communities which is framed by the struggle of the movement with the state. For this reason, although at key moments the indigenous movement exhibits a united voice, the cultural and conceptual categories it employs more clearly emerge from its internal multiplicity. Most recently, such moments have included the resettlement of the Nasa in the wake of a 1994 earthquake that destroyed Tierradentro (Rappaport and Gow 1997), the codification of customary law (cf. Ocampo 1997), and the battle for development funds by *cabildos* (*resguardo* councils), subregional organizations, and regional groups (Gow 1997). These three axes of contestation can be comprehended as a series of struggles to redefine the platform of the indigenous movement, which, in the case of CRIC, is known by its slogan "Tierra, Autonomía y Cultura" (land, autonomy, and culture). *Tierra* is a useful gloss for the creation of new post-earthquake Nasa communities; *autonomía*, a reference to the creation of indigenous special jurisdiction in the legal realm; and *cultura*, a constructive metaphor for understanding the objectives of community-inspired development. The remainder of this chapter explores these contexts in which *tierra, autonomía*, and *cultura* are contested and redefined within the indigenous movement in Cauca.

TIERRA: THE CREATION OF NEW COMMUNITIES

Land—access to and control over territory—is one of the defining characteristics of what it means to be indigenous in contemporary Cauca as well as one of the prime arenas within which indigenous politics is contested internally. As the regional indigenous movement and subregional organizations have claimed authority over the past two decades, they have come into conflict over territory with each other as well as with local communities. A case in point is the resettlement of Nasa communities after the June 4, 1994, earthquake and landslide that devastated Tierradentro, killing more than a thousand people, displacing 20 percent of the population, and ruining some 40,000 hectares of land (Desastres & Sociedad 1997; Rappaport and Gow 1997). Those displaced, predominantly

Nasa, were resettled on new lands located in Cauca and the adjacent department of Huila purchased by the Corporación Nasa Kiwe (CNK), the
agency created by the Colombian government to assist with the rehabilitation of the area and to supervise the relocation of its people. At the time
of its creation, the CNK staff included politically progressive environmentalists and nonindigenous professionals whose long-standing collaboration with CRIC belies any facile characterization of the agency as
standing in a polarized relationship to the indigenous movement; CRIC,
which at the time was a weak organization beset by a leadership crisis and
dissent in its ranks, gained a new lease on life through its pivotal role on
the CNK governing board.[7] As a result of CNK's land-purchasing program, new Nasa communities were created as dependent "extensions"
(*ampliaciones*) of existing, legally recognized *resguardos*, subject to the jurisdiction of the *cabildo* (local council) of each community of origin, an
uncomfortable relationship that has bred widespread conflict.

While the major parties involved in the resettlement process agreed on
the importance of purchasing land to settle those displaced, they did not
concur on either the type or the location of this land. The displaced
wanted productive land to complement the traditional agricultural products of Tierradentro and aspired to live near the larger urban centers in
order to benefit from better transportation networks and educational opportunities. In contrast, CNK and CRIC wished to purchase land that
was ecologically complementary to the land available in the communities
of origin, to establish the new settlements in areas where there was little
conflict, and to isolate the displaced from the national society with an eye
toward preserving Nasa culture (CNK 1995: 5–10; Wilches 1995a and
1995b). If successful, this policy of creating new settlements in far-flung
isolated areas would have ensured that many Nasa would have continued
to subsist at near-poverty levels, given the precarious economies and poor
soils in these marginal regions.[8]

Nuevo Tóez, located in the municipality of Caloto, an hour by road
from the industrial center of Cali, is a new settlement which successfully
resisted the CNK mandate and persuaded the agency to buy four productive farms located in an area of sugar cultivation, agroindustry, and intensive livestock production. CNK and CRIC initially opposed the relocation to Caloto on the grounds of cost, the lack of technical expertise for
successful cane cultivation among the people of Tóez, and the potential
for violence in the region, advising the community members to move to
a resettlement site already inhabited by members of another *resguardo*,
where there was land similar to that in Tierradentro and where they could

live surrounded by other Nasa. CNK and CRIC explained their position by arguing that relocation so close to an urban center would inevitably lead to a process of culture loss and that the Tierradentro Nasa were incapable of negotiating violence-prone northern Cauca. In effect, both CRIC and the state agency saw members of the local community as lacking the wherewithal to manage their own future properly, owing to what was perceived as their traditional culture.

This presented somewhat of a contradiction, given that Tóez was one of the most modernizing *resguardos* of Tierradentro and over the previous years had exhibited considerable resistance to CRIC's politics, suggesting that what was at stake was not so much the maintenance of Nasa culture as a concerted effort to bring Tóez into the CRIC fold by resettling the community alongside other communities whose politics was more in accord with the regional organization. The members of the *cabildo* of Tóez persisted in their demands, resisting CNK's stereotyping of them as unsophisticated peasants through recourse to a modernizing project centered in the production of sugarcane, the raising of livestock, the cultivation of food staples, the pursuit of wage labor, and the construction of their own school, whose primary focus would be cultural revitalization. The school was, indeed, a crucial component of the Tóez program, given that the majority of the community is composed of monolingual Spanish-speakers and includes a large proportion of evangelical Protestants who eschew Nasa traditional medicine.

The image of local community that the state constructed, moreover, stood in contrast to the reputation enjoyed by the leadership of CRIC, replete with sophisticated and worldly political negotiators with an aura of Indianness but none of its shortcomings. CRIC supplied ethnic actors whom CNK functionaries more easily understood as political agents with whom they could engage in productive dialogue. In other words, CNK would have CRIC cast as "hyperreal Indians" (Ramos 1994) forged in the state's image, while they painted the displaced communities as unruly and backward, a commonly held and centuries-old stereotype of the Nasa. Thus, the lines of struggle were drawn, both between the state and the indigenous population and within the movement itself, revolving around how each of the players perceived Nasa culture.

CRIC, however, was not as hyperreal as CNK supposed. Instead, defiance of the CNK mandate burst from within the organization itself. Tóez's success in acquiring lands in Caloto was due partly to the strong leadership demonstrated by community members and partly to the support received from the Asociación de Cabildos del Norte del Cauca

(ACIN: Association of Cabildos of Northern Cauca), a regional grouping composed of Nasa *cabildos* that have inhabited northern Cauca since the colonial period.

ACIN, which was instrumental in redirecting CRIC's platform away from an emphasis on regional ethnic politics to a fundamentally Nasa agenda, represents a militant and independent wing of the movement, strongly influenced by Italian priests espousing liberation theology. The northern *cabildo* federation welcomed Tóez into its fold with the hope that the inclusion of this community would dynamize its own cultural project; it perceived the origins of Tóez in the Nasa heartland as project-ing a more "traditional" aura in contrast to the Spanish-speaking north-ern communities, highly integrated into the regional market economy. In short, ACIN's stereotyping of Tóez, while less negative than the helpless image projected by CNK and CRIC, shared the same roots insofar as it posited a metonymic relationship between Tierradentro and traditional Nasa culture. ACIN also hoped that the acquisition of lands for Tóez in northern Cauca, a region known for militant land struggles, would serve as a precedent for acquiring other farms for land-hungry *resguardos* in the area. Thus, the arrival of the people of Tóez in Caloto led to their be-coming enmeshed in a web of conflicting political objectives espoused by different wings of the indigenous movement and fought out in the arena of contestation against the state, as personified by CNK.

In effect, three struggles ensued: between the new settlements and CNK, between CRIC and its constituent *cabildos* organized in federations, and within the *resguardo* itself, between the *cabildo* in the community of origin and the new settlement. The people of Tóez found support within nongovernmental organizations and international funders willing to in-vest in their project and were able to negotiate a good price for the land, thanks to the invervention of ACIN; they also received assistance in their struggle with CNK from the national Office of Indigenous Affairs of the Colombian government: a lawyer who had worked with CRIC since its inception in the early 1970s convincingly argued their position on the na-tional bureaucratic stage. Ultimately, they moved to the northern Caucan site and built a village, complete with an ambitious high school.

Over the years, however, the conflict between resettlement and community of origin has become more pronounced, unfolding through clashes over the allocation of *transferencias*, cash transfers from the central government (CNK 1995: 7) used to finance a variety of development ac-tivities, mainly small public works (Colombia 1993, 1994), an issue that we take up again below in our analysis of a second resettlement, that of

Juan Tama.[9] Five years after the move to northern Cauca, some of these contradictions have been partially resolved, as the differences aired within the movement nourished the creation of a new policy toward indigenous expansion into new lands. CRIC has reconciled itself to the existence of errant settlements such as Tóez and has even conceded that they may have made the appropriate choice in rejecting CNK/CRIC proposals. By 2000 Nuevo Tóez had become an important site for regional meetings of ACIN and CRIC, demonstrating that the move has, in fact, resulted in a rapprochement between this modernizing *resguardo* and the indigenous movement. Indeed, Nuevo Tóez was an active participant in CRIC-inspired blockages of the Panamerican Highway near Popayán in 1999 in response to the lack of government assistance to indigenous communities. Here the movement spoke to the national society with a single voice, masking the conflicts that had preceded the mobilization.

Juan Tama, the resettlement for the displaced of the *resguardo* of Vitoncó, was the new community in which the CNK hoped to relocate Tóez. Juan Tama was established as an extension of the existing *resguardo* in Vitoncó, known as the heartland of Nasa culture and society because the historical and mythical culture hero Juan Tama, for whom the resettlement is named, established his capital here. The settlement is located on the site of an earlier colonization effort by mestizo peasants on the eroded and deforested hillsides of Santa Leticia, now used for small-scale livestock production and virtually useless for agriculture, in an area characterized by a long history of guerrilla activity. The move to Santa Leticia occurred after a fruitless search by the *cabildo* for more productive lands closer to urban centers, a search opposed once again by both CNK and CRIC.

The struggle over the future of Juan Tama was embittered by internal conflicts between sectors of the resettled community allied with larger political actors in Cauca. From the start, there were major differences between the various geographic sections of Vitoncó resettled in Juan Tama, each with its own ideology and relationship with specific movements and institutions, which severely affected their long-term commitment to resettlement and the building of a new community. The sections of La Troja and Vitoncó, for example, were allied with the traditional Catholic church of Tierradentro, which has maintained a stranglehold on education in Tierradentro and is fiercely opposed to CRIC. This constituency clashed continually with El Cabuyo, a group that had enjoyed a long-standing association with CRIC, having established an experimental bilingual school before the disaster which was reconstructed in the resettlement location. Among other issues, the school proved to be a major bone of contention, given that its Nasa-centered curriculum left little room for the Catholic religious instruction championed by families from La Troja and Vitoncó (Cabuyo/CRIC 1996; Camayo and Niqinás 1997). Also crucial was the fact that teachers from the church-sponsored schools of Tierradentro could not work with the CRIC teachers.

The struggle over community education was compounded by a fight over *transferencias* that unfolded between the home community and the resettlement, given that the vast majority of the *resguardo* remained in Tierradentro and thus had the clout to deny Juan Tama its fair share of funds. Those who did not opt for resettlement were from precisely those sections of Vitoncó allied with the church, thus projecting the ideological struggle taking place in Juan Tama over a vaster terrain. In 1997, with differences still unresolved, more than 100 families allied with the church finally moved to another resettlement in Itaibe, within the boundaries of Tierradentro.

While Tóez was more successful in managing to obtain productive lands and relocate near an urban center, its future and the future of its children are closely tied to the regional economy of Cauca and the modernizing discourse of the Colombian state, factors which will influence the type of indigenous identity that its members espouse. While Juan Tama was much less successful in terms of establishing a viable new community, its residents have been obliged to fight against their enforced marginality by attaching increasing importance to the education of their children. Among three pilot schools within CRIC's bilingual education program, not only has the Juan Tama school attracted international funding, but its novel curriculum has had an impact upon the development of bilingual curricula throughout Cauca. The school has played a crucial role in deepening an appreciation of Nasa identity in the resettlement through attention to oral history, the revival of shamanic rituals, and increased value placed on the Nasa language. In the process, the image that CRIC projects about what Nasa culture *should* be is culled from the Juan Tama experience.

Ironically, the families who abandoned Juan Tama for a new community in Itaibe have embarked upon a similar path. While their move was prompted by ideological struggle with those who remained in Santa Leticia, that very confrontation—coupled with their recognition that only as an organized movement can they cull support from state agencies and from the NGO community—has led them to play an instrumental role in the creation of the Consejo Regional Indígena del Huila (CRIH: Regional

Indigenous Council of Huila). The way this organization operates parallels that of CRIC in the neighboring department of Huila, whose boundary Itaibe straddles and where Nasa have lived since the colonial era. Thus, the ideological discord that splintered Juan Tama has led to a new, movement-wide strategy for expanding Nasa territorial control.

AUTONOMÍA: INDIGENOUS SPECIAL JURISDICTION

The 1991 Colombian Constitution makes special provisions for the incorporation of indigenous customary law into the new system of juridical decentralization through the creation of indigenous special jurisdiction:

> The authorities of indigenous communities will be able to exercise jurisdictional functions within their territory, according to their own norms and procedures, so long as these are not contrary to the Constitution and to the laws of the Republic. The forms of coordination of this special jurisdiction with the national judicial system will be established by law. (Colombia 1991: Art. 246)

The form that indigenous special jurisdiction will assume is only now being debated and formulated in public gatherings (Colombia 1997) and constitutional lawsuits (*tutelas*) brought by community members against indigenous authorities in cases in which they feel that the application of customary law violates their constitutional rights as Colombian citizens (Ocampo 1997; Sánchez Botero 1998). The process of articulating customary law with national legislation has begun with the translation of the constitution and consequently of key legal concepts into seven native languages (Muelas et al. 1994; Ramos et al. 1994; cf. Rojas 1997)—including Guambiano and Nasa Yuwe in Cauca—and intensive ethnographic research into the legal systems of a variety of native communities (Gómez 1995, 1999; Perafán 1995).

The complexities inherent in the acceptance of customary law within a national administrative structure have been signaled by indigenous spokespersons (Morales 1997; cf. Ocampo 1997; Perdomo Dizú n.d.), who vehemently reject any steps to codify native legal systems on the grounds that these are inherently consensual, oral, and considerably more flexible than national legal codes; as indigenous leaders have pointed out (Piñacué 1997), the resolution of disputes is the province not only of native political authorities but also of shamans, whose methods are intrinsically antithetical to those employed by judges. In fact, contemporary Nasa discussions of indigenous jurisprudence note that shamanic forms of investigation sidestep the notion of causality, which is central to the Western legal process (ibid.). The very significant move made here by Nasa leaders is to emphasize the fact that native legal procedures are framed by a distinct worldview (*cosmovisión*). It is precisely this appeal to *cosmovisión* that constitutes the basis of indigenous cultural politics, whether in the legal sphere, in education, or in territorial administration.

The nature of *cosmovisión* and its relevance in our understanding of the unique nature of customary law can best be comprehended by consulting the Nasa translation of the Western concept of "culture," *wët üskiwe'n'i*, which is translated as "the form of behavior resulting from a permanent harmonic relationship with Nature" (Ramos et al. 1994: 116). This harmony is seen as the product of the interpenetration of past, present, and future, a notion which is best expressed by Jesús Enrique Piñacué in his intervention regarding the nature of indigenous special jurisdiction, which warrants lengthy quotation here:

> Our *yakni* (thought)[10] corresponds best to the point at which the past and present merge as the foundation of the future. The *Us yakni* (memory) is the unity of our identity. Our ancestors, the elders, are in front, guiding our actions in the present, the foundation of the future of our people. Our actions correspond to the teachings of the elders and determine the future of our existence (*Yatska te' c'indate tengc'a mecue*). Our people walk, observing the footprints of the elders in front of us. Events are unique: this cannot be confused with the law of causation, where an event-effect corresponds to an event-cause. This does not mean that we cannot tell history, but that there are many histories to tell. Events do not cause one another, but an event can influence another in a way that can only be seen by the *Te'wala* (traditional medical specialists). Points are distributed in space, as events are in life, and we can isolate them and give them order. This order obeys the need to achieve harmony with nature and with living beings (*nasa*). To order events is to engage in a political exercise in which two concepts play an important role: cultural reality and cultural vitality, which are present in our conception of life and of justice. (Piñacué 1997: 32–33)

Piñacué's description, which derives in part from the work of Nasa linguists (Yule 1995), exemplifies the efforts of indigenous intellectuals to define their cultural specificity by recourse to a concept—*cosmovisión*—that philosophically reconfigures the relationship between past and present, between time and space, in ways quite familiar to Andeanists.

While contemporary indigenous legal projects employ the notion of customary law—*usos y costumbres* (uses and customs) in the language of the constitution—in their descriptions of native legal systems, a great deal of their attention is drawn to the creation in indigenous territorial and discursive space of legal concepts that parallel those of the constitution. Such analogs in indigenous languages to the Spanish terms in the text of the constitution were created by teams of native linguists, trained in Colombian universities, who coined new political lexicons in their languages. But these new vocabularies do not project concepts and institutional structures that completely mirror those of the Colombian state; instead, they build upon *cosmovisión*, creating uniquely native interpretations of the constitution.

Thus, for example, the Guambiano translation of "participation" is *kan ketøtø linchip purukuyap* (Muelas et al. 1994: 175). Although the Spanish gloss is "accompaniment, help, integration, and solidarity," *linchip* (accompaniment) must be understood within a context of traditional forms of reciprocity within gender relations or political processes: men and women must always accompany each other, and the community must accompany its authorities; such relationships are translated into the visual idiom of movement flags (Rappaport 1992) as well as the legal idiom of the constitution. The translation of "state authority" into Nasa Yuwe is *c'hab wala kiwete npicthë* (Ramos et al. 1994: 115), glossed in Spanish as "leadership of the land of the large town." *Kiwe*, however, holds particular connotations in Nasa Yuwe, including the notion of ritualized political practices performed across a landscape replete with mythic significance (Rappaport 1998b); *c'hab wala* is the name of Vitoncó, the *resguardo* founded by the Nasa culture hero and historical hereditary chief Juan Tama, thus suggesting that the "town" in question is not simply a demographic subdivision of the Colombian population but a discrete cultural and political entity. In the Nasa and Guambiano translations, the terms for archaeological patrimony employ notions of the distant past and of those who peopled such times, which reflect very different models of history from the model employed by Colombians belonging to the dominant, European culture (Muelas et al. 1994: 171; Ramos et al. 1994: 115).

The translation of the constitution into indigenous languages occurred at a moment of intense scholarly activity by native public intellectuals, whose cultural analyses frequently take the form of hierarchically organized word lists in an attempt to redefine the conceptual categories that should be used to study indigenous groups (Rappaport 1998a). The coining of a new legal terminology that transcends the differences between customary and constitutional law must be contextualized within the broader framework of native attempts to decolonize knowledge through the creation of new categories of thought, a project which does not intersect comfortably with that of non-native scholars.

Within the legal arena, this tension is apparent in the difference between the indigenous reconceptualization of ethnographic knowledge and the positivist analyses conducted by mestizo anthropologists, who have attempted to codify customary law by abstracting general rules out of the diverse cases of dispute resolution they have observed in communities (Perafán 1995). Ironically, most of these scholars are themselves employed by the movement, *colaboradores* whose allegiances obscure any neat boundary between an indigenous voice and that of the dominant Colombian society (Rappaport n.d.). The resolution of ideological and intellectual differences between anthropologists and the indigenous movement takes place, then, not at the indigenous/state interface but within the organizations themselves.

The tensions inherent in the project of articulating such diverse and antithetical legal systems as we find in Colombia are underlined by the broader political project within which indigenous special jurisdiction is situated: the relegitimization of the Colombian state (Peñaranda and Montaña 1997), whose legitimacy has been contested by guerrilla movements seeking to introduce new political systems, paramilitary organizations operating as unofficial extensions of the official armed forces, and popular organizations mobilized to fight government corruption and bureaucratic inefficiency. The 1991 Constitution, with all of its neoliberal emphasis on decentralization and its move toward political and ethnic pluralism, is a prime example of governmental efforts to reassert the continued relevance of the nation-state in a period of economic globalization and political fragmentation. The legitimacy sought by the state is partially circumscribed by the primacy of national law. In the final instance, indigenous legal projections cannot contradict the law of the state; the autonomy that native organizations hoped to achieve through the constitutional project thus remains elusive.

This is precisely the problem that comes up repeatedly as members of indigenous communities bring lawsuits against their communal authorities, arguing that their rights as Colombian citizens have been violated by customary law. The clearest example of this is the struggle that has ensued in Jambaló, Cauca, and in the courts after the *cabildo* found a community member guilty of complicity in the guerrilla-inspired murder of a Nasa municipal mayor during the summer of 1996 and decided to condemn him to a public whipping and exile from Jambaló. Among the Nasa, whipping is a highly symbolic activity, conceived as representing the purifying agency of the thunderbolt, harnessed to restore harmony and reincorporate the offenders back into the community (Perafán 1995).

Francisco Gembuel,[11] one of the community members slated to be punished for the murder of Mayor Marden Betancur, is a former president of CRIC aligned with a minority faction that opposes the discourse of its current leadership. Gembuel appealed the *cabildo* decision in the Colombian court system. A 1997 decision by a lower court recognized that Gembuel's constitutional rights—his human rights as a citizen of Colombia—had been violated by the sixty lashes to which he was sentenced by the *cabildo*, but decided that the indigenous authorities were fully within their rights to conduct an investigation into the murder and Gembuel's culpability (Muñoz 1997). The definitive decision of the Constitutional Court reversed the earlier one, arguing that whipping, which is a highly symbolic punishment among the Nasa, does not constitute torture and is an integral component of justice wielded by a competent authority, the *cabildo* (Gaviria 1997).

Francisco Gembuel's appeal (Muñoz 1997), the response of the *cabildo* (Passú and Fiscué 1997), and Gembuel's trial illustrate numerous obstacles to the incorporation of customary law into the national legal system, suggesting the impossibility of such an enterprise and the quandary within which the indigenous movement finds itself, given that its only political option is to support moves toward the institutionalization of indigenous special jurisdiction. Furthermore, these documents powerfully illustrate that the nature of the indigenous/state interface issues from questions internal to the subaltern community.

First, there is the sticky issue of defining Nasa customary law. Gembuel asserted that there was no "tradition, nor use or custom, related to the investigation of homicides, [a procedure] which has always been conducted by the ordinary [Colombian] justice [system]" (Muñoz 1997: 2). He thus put indigenous special jurisdiction to the test, forcing the court to pronounce on the existence of conditions for the official recognition of customary law: the role played by *cabildos*, former *cabildo* members, and shamans in the settlement of disputes (ibid.: 4); their authority to establish norms and procedures; the legal context in which indigenous jurisdiction was established; and the legislative authority by which the two divergent legal systems are to be coordinated (ibid.: 5). In the response of the *cabildo*, written with the assistance of ACIN, a similar set of issues was considered, with the Nasa investigative procedure described in considerably more detail and set within the broader historical context of indigenous jurisprudence and community organization across the Americas (Passú and Fiscué 1997). Interestingly, an anthropological expert was consulted in both documents: Carlos César Perafán, the author of the most extensive positivist ethnographic study of Nasa jurisprudence (Perafán 1995). Perafán's expert testimony legitimized the claims of the *cabildo*, officially recognizing community procedure as "customary law."

Another fascinating facet of the Jambaló decision was the series of arguments made concerning Gembuel's ethnic identity, with the objective of establishing whether or not the *cabildo* of Jambaló could appropriately exercise jurisdiction over him. Francisco Gembuel is a Guambiano from Ambaló who migrated to Jambaló, along with numerous other Guambiano sharecroppers who settled in the Nasa communities of northern Cauca in the mid-twentieth century (Ulcué 1997: 45). Yet, as a Guambiano, he would not necessarily be subject to the rule of the Nasa *cabildo* of Jambaló but to his own ethnic *cabildo* of Ambaló. Thus, the identification of Gembuel as native (*indígena*) was not enough to prove the right of the *cabildo* to conduct its investigation into his culpability; it also had to be proven that he was Nasa. This was achieved in the court brief by conflating residence with ethnicity:

> We can thus affirm without any doubt that both the deceased MARDEN ARNULFO BETANCUR CONDA and FRANCISCO GEMBUEL PECHENE *were once united by that ethnic consciousness* of which the Honorable Constitutional Court makes mention, the former as an inhabitant and member of the *Resguardo* of Jambaló, Vereda Voladero; and the latter equally a member of the same Indigenous *Resguardo* by virtue of having held adjudicated property or improvements for the past year, as he also accepts, and also for having been a recognized indigenous leader who struggled for more than 25 years. Thus it is understood that Mr. FRANCISCO GEMBUEL PECHENE *is a person with all the status and qualities of a. . . . [Nasa] Indian* and in consequence, with respect to his having been accused of having committed an offense against the . . . [Nasa] Community of Northern Cauca, [which] is disposed and equipped to judge him according to its *usos y costumbres*, the former should accept and obey such a decision. (Muñoz 1997: 4; emphasis added)

The three-pronged struggle of petitioner, indigenous authority, and judge thus established that Gembuel was, in fact, Nasa, providing an argument that would become crucial for the definition of the limits of customary law within Colombia's diverse and heterogeneous native communities.

Finally, the Gembuel case was decided internally in a February 1997 trial open to the entire Nasa community: the defendants, the *cabildo* of Jambaló, other ACIN-affiliated *cabildos*, the *cabildos* of Tierradentro, and representatives of CRIC, not to mention a host of outside observers. The *cabildo* of nearby Pitayó presided over the trial as a nonpartisan mediator. This public performance, which was meant to project a broad and united Nasa front in the face of accusations of barbarism by various members of the broader Colombian society (including Amnesty International, which condemned the public whippings), constituted an example of modern Nasa forms of justice of the sort that they hope to institute in the wake of constitutional reform. The social dynamics at the hearing illustrate the complexities of internal struggles within the indigenous movement among a multiplicity of indigenous actors with very different political agendas and methodologies: CRIC, the international voice of the indigenous movement; ACIN, one of its subregional organizations, already locked in a struggle over CRIC's political philosophy; Pitayó, a large *cabildo* that rejects CRIC's program and is trying to found a "nonaligned movement" consisting in great part of Nasa Protestants; and the *cabildos* of Tierradentro, the symbolic Nasa heartland, who are affiliated with CRIC but are also unyielding adherents of the establishment Liberal Party. In the midst of the proceedings, the *cabildos* of Tierradentro left Jambaló in disgust, unhappy because the proceedings did not take into account other crimes committed in Tierradentro of which they accused Gembuel.

Disputes about corporal punishment and its place in a newly codified customary law have indeed widened the breach across the indigenous movement. But at the same time these conflicts have unified the discourse of Cauca's multiple indigenous organizations. However divided CRIC was in the wake of the Gembuel case, all of its constituent organizations and *cabildos* ultimately agreed on a number of key issues. First, while they may have disagreed with the procedures used to convict Gembuel, they have all come to agree on the necessity for corporal punishment in Cauca's indigenous communities. In the resettled community of Juan Tama, home to refugees from Vitoncó, shamans installed stocks some six feet high, which stood silhouetted against the horizon, commanding a view of the whole settlement; they have since been moved to a more unobtrusive location. Those judged guilty of some infraction by the community are hanged upside down by their ankles for a designated time and then whipped; other communities are considering installing their own stocks, and numerous other cases of corporal punishment can be documented over the past few years in Nasa communities.

The Nasa have essentially agreed that such punishments are integral to their policies of cultural revitalization, emphasizing that they are infinitely preferable to long-term imprisonment in Colombian jails, which isolates wrongdoers from their communities and does not allow for their rehabilitation; in fact, they cite instances of public punishments which have led not only to community reintegration but to the election to *cabildos* of those who had been punished and rehabilitated. This consensus, moreover, has created bridges between the CRIC-affiliated Nasa and the nonaligned movement of Protestant-led *cabildos*, who united with Jambaló in judging Gembuel and who have also reintroduced stocks into their communities. Finally, even ethnic groups affiliated with AICO, such as the Guambiano, have defended Jambaló's decision, creating a unified front in the promotion of customary law as well as in issuing a powerful statement to guerrilla organizations, cautioning them to respect indigenous autonomy.

The injection of political discourses from the dominant society continually intrudes upon this consensus, however. The chasm between Tierradentro and the other *cabildos* which opened in the Gembuel trial, exemplified by a breach between adherents of the Liberal Party and supporters of independent indigenous political action, was further accentuated in the summer of 1998, when the validity of Nasa *usos y costumbres* was again put to a test. At the height of the Colombian presidential campaign that pitted Horacio Serpa—the hand-picked successor to Ernesto Samper—against Andrés Pastrana—the politician who had publicly accused Samper of accepting drug-tainted contributions to his campaign, thus opening the floodgates of international public opinion against the embattled president—Jesús Enrique Piñacué, former president of CRIC and recently elected member of the Colombian Senate, appeared on national television in support of Serpa's candidacy. His speech provoked a torrent of criticism in indigenous Cauca, where Nasa communities, particularly those affiliated with ACIN, had advocated abstention from the presidential election.

The most militant of the ACIN *resguardos*, Toribío, proposed that Piñacué be lashed in public, much as Jambaló's *cabildo* (also an ACIN member) had ruled for Francisco Gembuel. The *cabildos* of Tierradentro, who had themselves supported Serpa, opposed such drastic punishment of a native son who had put Tierradentro on the political map during his term of office as president of CRIC and with his election to the Senate.

Tierradentro, moreover, is renowned for its shamans (*thë' wala*), who play a key role in the Nasa process of discipline and punishment. The *thë' wala* of Vitoncó, the heartland of Tierradentro, established by the Nasa hereditary chief and culture hero Juan Tama, advocated a ritual bath in the Laguna de Juan Tama (the lake where Juan Tama disappeared at the end of his life) instead of a whipping; the *cabildos* of Tierradentro assumed control of the negotiations, with the shamans as their vanguard, and succeeded in imposing a more humane mode of punishment. Nevertheless, in the process they widened the breach between the more and less militant branches of CRIC and opened up the process of indigenous special jurisdiction to romanticization and Orientalization by the journalists of the dominant society, who enthusiastically documented the charismatic and photogenic Piñacué's calvary in the national press (Sierra Sierra 1998; Vengoechea 1998a, 1998b).

CULTURA: ETHNIC IDENTITY AND
THE CULTURAL POLITICS OF DEVELOPMENT

In postconstitution Colombia, the indigenous movement has by necessity deviated from its original mission of land claims. Increasing state recognition of indigenous peoples as interlocutors, the administrative decentralization process cemented by the constitution, and the consolidation by violent drug lords of lands slated for indigenous repossession have caused the movement to turn toward development as a means for carving out its economic autonomy in a pluralist world. Increasingly, this has entailed intensive reflection on what it means to be indigenous in the context of contemporary Colombia and the role of indigenous culture in the inevitable process of "development." This cultural politics of development accepts that different cultural meanings and practices come into conflict with each other and that these meanings are part of a process that seeks to redefine development and the relations of social power in which this process is embedded (Alvarez et al. 1998).

At the time of the disaster in Tierradentro, CNK believed that Nasa culture was in a state of crisis, as shown by the loss of traditional values accompanied by the decreasing authority of the *cabildos* and shamans brought on by the economic boom resulting from the cultivation of opium poppies (Wilches 1995a: 130). One of CNK's objectives, then, in trying to create new settlements in isolated areas was the defense and preservation of what was viewed as a culture under threat. Among Nasa communities, both *resguardos* and extensions, Tóez is famous for the quality of the land it received, while Juan Tama is famous for the number of shamans who reputedly live there. To a certain extent, this is a reflection of the two communities' immediate historical past in Tierradentro—the "modernizing" experience of Tóez contrasted with the "traditional" experience of Vitoncó. Yet Tóez, less ethnic and more de-Indianized than Juan Tama, has joined the latter community in making a deliberate and conscious effort to recover—perhaps "rescue" might be a better word— its culture, to preserve it, and to practice it.

The most obvious example of this is the curriculum pursued in the primary school, with its emphasis on Nasa culture and language and its appeal to parents in neighboring Nasa communities, keen that their children should know and understand their own culture; in particular, the curriculum emphasizes culturally appropriate learning techniques, based on the curriculum designer's experience in learning to weave and spin (ADRIT 1995; Mulcué and Yasnó n.d.). Equally important, however, may have been the parents' desire to send their children to a Nasa-controlled school rather than one controlled by the local municipal authorities.

It is tempting to view this effort as more political than cultural. According to the Nasa teacher responsible for teaching Nasa Yuwe in the primary school, this effort is a waste of time, since the process of language acquisition must start at home, yet parents refuse to speak to their children in Nasa Yuwe and have made it perfectly clear that they view this as a responsibility of the school in which they wish to play no part. As a result, little Nasa Yuwe is spoken by young people. For the people of Tóez, the attempts to *preserve* culture may be more important than its *practice* since these attempts can favorably distinguish them from their more de-Indianized, "proletarianized" Nasa neighbors (Gewertz and Errington 1996), thereby functioning as a pivot of identity and making Tóez more attractive and more appealing to outside agencies.

In Juan Tama, in contrast, Nasa Yuwe is spoken widely, and primary education is bilingual and coordinated by CRIC. A relatively large number of *thë' wala* practice in the area. Vitoncó had and still has a large population of religious specialists. Many of them moved at the time of the disaster and were involved in the selection of the settlement, the creation of a nursery for medicinal plants cared for by the schoolchildren, and the collective painting of a series of vivid murals depicting the life of Juan Tama on the walls of the *cabildo* office, where the shamans installed stocks (a practical example of the *autonomía* discussed in the previous section). The school actively promotes and disseminates a Nasa *cosmovisión*, which effectively links the past and the present as a way of dealing with the future (Camayo and Niquinás 1997). For the people of Juan Tama, the culture hero Juan Tama is still an integral part of their everyday reality. At a children's program held there in July 1999, organized by the local school-teachers with assistance from CRIC, the pivotal event was the performance of a distinguished local shaman who recounted a well-known myth about Juan Tama; this particular shaman had played an important mediating role the previous year in arguing that Jesús Piñacué should not be whipped. The details of the myth served as the basis for a whole series of activities undertaken by the children throughout the day, culminating that night in a cultural program attended by a majority of the local population. One of the highlights, which aroused a great deal of interest on the part of both children and adults, was a series of paintings produced by a hand-picked group of children depicting the Juan Tama myth, accompanied by poetry recounting his exploits and their relevance for today's Nasa.

In these two cases, the relationship between culture and development is ambiguous. In Tóez, preservation of culture has been more important than its practice until recently. But that is changing, as practice is assuming more importance. This is evident in ongoing discussions about priorities to be included in their local development plan in response to the increasing influence of the discourse of the indigenous movement on such topics as *autonomía* (autonomy) and *autoridad* (authority), perhaps a politically expedient move by a settlement determined to establish and maintain its indigenous credentials in the face of initial opposition from CNK and CRIC. In Juan Tama, culture continues to provide meaning and structure to the people's everyday lives, while also implicitly helping them to adapt to, to accept, and to begin to live in harmony with a rather inhospitable environment. But only to a certain extent. One of the local schoolteachers wondered aloud about the sort of life for which they are preparing students and what will happen to those who continue their studies in the local mestizo high school, particularly with regard to history, culture, and, of course, *cosmovisión*. It does not necessarily follow, as some have suggested, that development is a means of cultural and ethnic survival for indigenous minorities (Bebbington 1994).

Our second example—from the very different ethnic community of Guambía, affiliated with the rival indigenous organization, AICO—underlines the problematic relationship between culture and development as well as illustrating the extent to which interindigenous relations color the development planning process. Here the notion of culture used by subaltern planners reflects their ambivalent feelings about development and, by implication, about modernity. The major planning document drawn up by the *cabildo*, which stands at the head of some 13,000 Guambiano, is called a *Plan de Vida* or "life plan" (Cabildo, Taitas y Comisión de Trabajo del Pueblo Guambiano 1994). The plan encompasses all aspects of community life and is expected to take some twenty years to implement. As the first document of its kind in the department, it has served as a model for other communities, a kind of metanarrative of indigenous planning (Roe 1994).[12]

The Guambiano strategy revolves around a program of cultural research and alternative development in productive activities that involves the retrieval of local agricultural knowledge and its combination with Western techniques, an objective central to many indigenous development plans (cf. Fundación Sol y Tierra 1995b). There is little evidence, however, presented in the Life Plan to substantiate the potential contribution of local knowledge to increased production (Cabildo, Taitas y Comisión de Trabajo del Pueblo Guambiano 1994: 151): Western technology in the form of chemical fertilizers and pesticides has been a fact of life in Guambía for some four decades, and the Life Plan provides little guidance for incorporating local knowledge into the productive process.[13]

Paradoxically, the section of the plan dealing with the "modernization" of agriculture, specifically the commercial production of potatoes, which began in the 1950s, comes across as both antidevelopment and antimodernist. With the advent of improved varieties of potatoes, the Guambiano farmers needed credit to purchase the seed and the accompanying chemical inputs. Since credit was only approved on an individual basis, the farmer had to provide collateral in the form of a title. Land was owned communally, so the only way to obtain title was through privatization. While the government is blamed for introducing the technology in the first place, the Guambiano are criticized for their lack of understanding of the processes underway and their passivity in the face of internal manipulation by fellow community members:

> If the community does not understand this, everything will continue the same. The individual loans will continue and the settlements/judgments will continue until [we come to] the last piece of Guambiano land. And the sales will continue and a few from the community will fatten themselves with the lands they have purchased and the daily labor of others.
>
> We Guambiano are like crabs: you touch a crab with a straw on one side and it walks to the other; you touch it on the other side and it goes in yet another direction; you touch it in front and it walks backward; you touch it from behind and it walks forward. That is how we Guambiano are. (ibid.: 22)

The Guambiano Life Plan contains an extensive description of Guambiano history, developed by a committee comprised of elder community historians, young schooled investigators, and an anthropologist from Bogotá. The research of the Guambiano history committee (Vasco et al. 1993) attempts to reconfigure historical narrative in such a way that events are organized in a temporal spiral whose contents continuously return to a number of key central themes, thus repeating themselves and replicating a conceptual model developed by Guambiano linguists (Muelas 1995; cf. Rappaport 1998a). One of the significant events in Guambiano history is the birth of Mama Manuela Caramaya and other culture heroes in the major rivers of Guambía, waterways that are emphasized in the historical narrative as masculine and feminine elements that define Guambiano geography, history, and even political action:[14]

> They called the landslide Pikuk, which means water-giving-birth. They named the humans who were born there Pishau. The Pishau came from the landslides. They arrived on the rising floods of the rivers. Below the water came the large stones—dragging and pounding. Above them came mud, the land, then the dirty water. On the surface came the embankment: branches, leaves, uprooted trees and, on top of everything, came the children, drunk.
>
> The ancestors were born from the water, they came on the remains of the vegetation (*shau*) which the flood dragged along. They are native to here, from centuries back. In the place where the landslide started, in the large wound in the earth, there remained the smell of blood. It is the blood watered by nature, just as a woman sprinkles her blood when she gives birth to a child.
>
> The Pishau were not another people, they were the same Guambiano, very wise giants, who ate salt from here, from our very own salt licks, and they were not baptized. (ibid.: 14–15)

Although historical narrative represents an important component of the Life Plan, it is never used in this development document as a framework for conceptualizing new productive activities, administrative reorganization, or land claims strategies.

We frequently think of documents such as the Guambiano Life Plan as tools for communication with the state, as well as models for keeping internal authorities on track, both of which are served by the plan: the document is a tool for self-representation, aimed at both external and internal audiences. Within the line of the argument of our essay, however, we would like to close by recontextualizing the Life Plan, analyzing its role as part of an ongoing dialogue within the indigenous movement itself. It is precisely the history section, so key to Guambiano philosophy but so distant from their development proposals, which reflects interindigenous conflict in Cauca.

During the summer of 1998, Rappaport participated in a new indigenous university established by CRIC, in which forty-one students, mostly Nasa bilingual teachers, were pursuing a degree in community pedagogy. In a course on historical methodology, the students were invited to comment on the work of the Guambiano history committee, opening the floodgates to bitter criticism of the Guambiano by the Nasa. In brief, the students disputed the provenance of Guambiano narratives of chiefly births in rivers, suggesting that this is a strictly Nasa account appropriated by the Guambiano historians or added to Guambiano history by the elder historian Abelino Dagua, who, they argued on the basis of his surname, must be of Nasa descent; they demanded that the Nasa character of this origin story be recognized by the Guambiano.

Historically, the Nasa and Guambiano have been enemies, struggling over the centuries for territory and taking opposing sides in the Spanish invasion (Rappaport 1998b). Today the two groups are crucial players in the two rival indigenous organizations of Cauca: the Nasa in CRIC and the Guambiano in AICO, although most recently they have become uncomfortable electoral allies. Clearly, from a Nasa point of view, the cultural analysis inserted into the Guambiano Life Plan responds to historical and contemporary interethnic rivalries in such a way that the plan represents a positioning by the Guambiano vis-à-vis their Nasa political opponents. Guambiano self-representations meant for internal use and for dialogue with the state are distinctly mediated by myriad relationships among ethnic groups at the heart of indigenous Cauca.

CONCLUSION: INDIGENOUS MODERNITY

The multiple idioms in which the indigenous public voice speaks in Cauca point to some of the fundamental difficulties in using existing theoretical approaches to modernity to analyze contemporary native Latin American struggles. García Canclini's (1989) evocative model of multitemporal heterogeneity suggests that Latin American modernity is constituted by the juxtaposition and simultaneity of multiple symbolic and practical systems belonging to different periods. While this vision permits us to grasp the complexities of modernity from the indigenous point of view, it relegates indigenous people to a prior temporality, denying them a place in a modernity that, we argue, is clearly demonstrated by our cases—a modernity which frames the multiple dialogues that go on within the indigenous movement. García Canclini assumes that (indigenous) culture is a static thing and not a changing process. As we hope to have illustrated in this chapter, culture is, instead, a complex and ever-changing construct that assumes different forms and fills different functions depending upon the context in which it is deployed. Thus, for instance, at the organizational level, culture is exemplified by *cosmovisión*, the philosophical underpinnings of indigenous forms of social and territorial control, a constellation of concepts which are currently under study by indigenous intellectuals and which are explained in nonacademic form in the contributions that native politicians and planners have made in the discussion of indigenous special jurisdiction and in the historical interpretations that accompany *resguardo* life plans. In the locality, culture is better understood in terms of concrete forms of material and narrative culture, particularly language, mythology, handicrafts, and the tools of social control embodied in the stocks and in whips. In both cases, culture must be understood as an eminently modern construct, as a vehicle for intercultural dialogue and planning—processes which are themselves informed by modernist ethnography (cf. Jackson 1995; Rappaport 1998a).

In the hands of indigenous activists, then, the notion of culture is neither essentialist romanticism nor nostalgia (Hanson 1989; Keesing 1989; Gewertz and Errington 1996), nor, as Jackson, in her earlier work, suggests, is it a generic European form. Instead, it constitutes an effective subaltern political tool (Trask 1991; Friedman 1994; Tobin 1994) framed in ethnographic terms, through which the movement hopes to achieve autonomy in a pluralist—but also hegemonic—political and intellectual environment. For it is only by laying the conceptual groundwork for the cultural difference that is lived on the inside that the movement can begin to wrest power from the state by erecting institutions that the movement controls. Nevertheless, this groundwork is in dispute on the inside, as the Francisco Gembuel affair and the differences between Nasa/CRIC and Guambiano/AICO so clearly attest.

Homi Bhabha's (1994) concept of hybridity, which focuses on the boundary between the minority and dominant cultures and which inordinately emphasizes artistic production, disregarding the production of other cultural forms, ignores the ideological struggles that occur at the center of a cultural group—the place where, we have argued, the public face of the indigenous movement is negotiated. While at a mass mobilization the Nasa speak as a unified whole, their tactics and strategy are subject to constant contestation from within—by individual *cabildos* and their members, by subregional organizations, by the various political lines within the regional organization. This is clear in the struggle of multiple indigenous actors with the Colombian state in the reconstitution of earth-quake-damaged Nasa communities. Only through close ethnography of these movements, such as anthropologists are achieving in Guatemala (Warren 1998; Nelson 1999) and in Brazil (Ramos 1998) and as exemplified in the other contributions to this volume, can we begin to understand how internal conflict and boundary negotiation interact. We cannot simply interpret the texts that emanate from the boundary—as de Certeau (1986) did with CRIC documents—as though they represented monolithic institutions, but must instead comprehend the political, social, and discursive contexts in which they were constructed, including the key events (disaster relief, alternative forms of punishment) that we analyze here.

Indigenous modernity in Cauca can best be understood as a process that occurs simultaneously within native groups and organizations and between them and the institutions of the dominant society, in a trajectory in which the notion of "multitemporal heterogeneity" is used to represent the indigenous *political* relationship with the dominant society, as opposed to a *temporal* relationship. This process is mediated by numerous historically constituted relationships, differences, and struggles, which we must demonstrate ethnographically. If Latin American modernity is multiple, indeed, indigenous modernity is too.

Acknowledgments

The research upon which this chapter is based was conducted during the summers of 1995–1998, thanks to a 1995–1997 research grant from Colciencias to an international team coordinated through the Instituto Colombiano de Antropología and in 1998 by summer research grants from the Graduate School of Georgetown University and the Elliott School of International Affairs of George Washington University. We would especially like to thank María Victoria Uribe, director of the Instituto Colombiano de Antropología; María Lucía Sotomayor, coordinator of the Cauca–Sierra Nevada project; and ICAN researcher Carlos Vladimir Zambrano for sharing their funding with us and for creating the conditions for a stimulating process of dialogue and exchange. Our analysis of Cauca emerged from continued dialogue with a number of key individuals to whom we owe a tremendous debt of gratitude: Graciela Bolaños,

Ruby Bolívar, Henry Caballero, Luis Alberto Escobar, Myriam Amparo Espinosa, Claudia Inseca, Jorge Eliécer Inseca, Felipe Morales Paja, Alfonso Peña Chepe, Adonías Perdomo, Daniel Piñacué, Susana Piñacué, Jesús Enrique Piñacué, Inocencio Ramos, Manuel Sisco, Pablo Tatay, Segundo Tombé Morales, Lilia Triviño, Luis Carlos Ulcué, Gustavo Wilches Chaux, and Marcos Yule. The exchange of ideas and documents with Donna Lee Van Cott expanded our understanding of indigenous special jurisdiction in Colombia and with Robert Dover and Jessica Mulligan broadened our comprehension of the intricacies of the Colombian indigenous movement.

Notes

1. The research leading to this chapter was conducted during the summers of 1998–2000 in various communities of Cauca, Colombia, with the support of Colciencias/Instituto Colombiano de Antropología, Georgetown University Graduate School, George Washington University's Elliott School for International Affairs, and an international collaborative grant from the Wenner-Gren Foundation for International Research. We could not have conducted ethnographic research in Cauca without the support of the Consejo Regional Indígena del Cauca and the *cabildos indígenas* of Juan Tama, San José, and Tóez. We are thankful to the following individuals for their stimulating conversation and ideas: Lucho Escobar, Myriam Amparo Espinosa, Jorge Eliécer Inseca, Felipe Morales, Adonías Perdomo, Susana Piñacué, and Inocencio Ramos. The 1991 Constitution also recognized Afro-Colombians of the Pacific Coast and of the Caribbean islands of San Andrés and Providencia as ethnic minorities. Their participation in the decentralized administrative structures and the new face of legislative bodies that emerged with the 1991 charter has not been specified to the degree that it has for indigenous people (Triana 1992; Arocha and Friedemann 1993; Wade 1995).

2. This move, which positioned indigenous demands within ethnic discourses as opposed to class politics, is true of other Andean countries in addition to Colombia (Albó 1987; Ramón 1993; Ticona et al. 1995). In Colombia, this shift is explained in terms of a move from an emphasis on indigenous peoples (*indígenas*) as a category (*gremio*) to a focus on the specific means by which particular indigenous groups (*pueblos*) organize themselves internally and have an impact upon a multiethnic external political field.

3. The approximately 200,000 Nasa (formerly called Páez) live in the northern and eastern regions of the department of Cauca, in the western part of the neighboring department of Huila, and also have moved as colonists to western Cauca, Caquetá, and Putumayo. In the sixteenth and seventeenth centuries,

the Nasa fanned out from an isolated region called Tierradentro, which is located in eastern Cauca, to settle on the more accessible slopes of the Central Cordillera, nearer to the administrative center of Popayán.

4. The approximately 13,000 Guambiano live in various communities in the municipality of Silvia, Cauca, and are establishing new settlements in the coffee-growing municipalities of Morales and Piendamó, to the north of Silvia, as well as in the neighboring department of Huila.

5. The *resguardo* is an institution specific to Colombia, through which indigenous communities that hold colonial title to their land or that have been approved as *resguardos* in the past two decades are granted a limited autonomy as communal landholding corporations. The *resguardo* is governed by an elected council, the *cabildo*, which, since the 1991 Constitution, is responsible for managing funds for public works emanating from the national government (*transferencias*) and for administering justice in the community. Given the centrality of the *resguardo* in indigenous life, it is not surprising that it has emerged in the past thirty years as a pivot around which the indigenous movement has organized, distinguishing Colombian native politics from its counterparts in other Latin American nations.

6. In the October 1997 municipal elections, ASI won several mayoral races in Cauca. In coalition with AICO, peasant organizations, and labor unions, it successfully launched a gubernatorial campaign, resulting in the election in 2000 of Colombia's first indigenous governor, Floro Alberto Tunubalá, a Guambiano.

7. Nasa Kiwe is the Nasa-language term for the territory of that ethnic group. The CNK has served since 1994 as an umbrella organization for disbursing government funds, international grants and loans, and private bequests to the affected populations, streamlining bureaucratic procedures and providing a means for circumventing the administrative rules of other government agencies. Thus, for example, CNK has been able to purchase lands for affected communities beyond the limitations of the agrarian reform agency, whose policy for land acquisition is unfavorable to sellers—taking the form of bonds, as opposed to cash payments—and whose procedures are extremely lengthy and complicated.

8. Surveys conducted in Tierradentro by CNK and CRIC immediately after the disaster indicated just how precarious the domestic economies of many of the families were, and still are, in terms of access to productive land (Carvajal 1995; López Garcés 1995). Another study conducted at the same time concluded that only 13.7 percent of the area directly affected, some 172,000 hectares, is safe for permanent human settlement (INGEOMINAS 1995: 52). The historical process of impoverishment is discussed briefly by Pachón (1996). Most of the large farms purchased by CNK were formerly the property of large landowners who, because of depleted soils and threats from guer-

rilla organizations, were keen to divest themselves of these white elephants. Sales of these properties to CNK were negotiated through a lawyer in Popayán, who served as an effective intermediary, creating a united front that the state agency could not afford to resist.

9. There has also been a growing symbiosis between the new settlement and the *resguardo* of origin, stimulated by the latter's comparative advantage for the cultivation of opium poppies, an unintended ecological complementarity encountered in other new settlements. Reports indicate that Tóez, like other *cabildos* in northern Tierradentro, was engaged in intensive opium poppy production before the disaster (Gómez and Ruiz 1997).

10. Note that the orthography used for Nasa Yuwe in this quotation does not correspond to the normalized orthography recently adopted by Cauca's Nasa communities, which is used for writing Nasa Yuwe in the text of this chapter but not necessarily in all of the quotations or references.

11. Although Francisco Gembuel was also subject to exile, a punishment that precludes the restoration of his own harmonic relations with the community of Jambaló, the others who were tried along with him remained in the community—and thus, presumably, whipping would have a harmonic effect upon their relationship with the community. In practice, however, the conflicts that gave rise to the trial have persisted in Jambaló, because the punishments were never completely carried out in the wake of the protracted constitutional issues they brought to the fore.

12. Now that a Guambiano, Floro Alberto Tunubalá, has been elected governor of the department of Cauca, the plan will serve more broadly as a template throughout the region's native communities.

13. See Gow (1997) for a detailed analysis and description of this and other life plans from indigenous Cauca.

14. The Guambiano land claims strategy focused upon an *hacienda* located at the point of union of two rivers, where their cultural heroine was born.

References

Albó, Xavier. 1987. From MNRistas to Kataristas to Katari. In Steve Stern, ed., *Resistance, Rebellion, and Consciousness in the Andean Peasant World, 18th to 20th Centuries*, 379–419. Madison: University of Wisconsin Press.

Alvarez, Sonia, Evelina Dagnino, and Arturo Escobar. 1998. Introduction: The Cultural and the Political in Latin American Social Movements. In Sonia Alvarez, Evelina Dagnino, and Arturo Escobar, eds., *Cultures of Politics/Politics of Cultures: Re-visioning Latin American Social Movements*, 1–29. Boulder: Westview Press.

Arocha Rodríguez, Jaime, and Nina S. de Friedemann. 1993. Marco referencial histórico-cultural para la ley sobre los derechos étnicos de las comunidades negras en Colombia. *América Negra* (Bogotá) 5: 155–172.

Asociación de Damnificados del Resguardo Indígena de Tóez (ADRIT). 1995. *Estudio de factibilidad: Construcción de un colegio de enseñanza media diversificada*. MS.

Avirama, Jesús, and Rayda Márquez. 1994. The Indigenous Movement in Colombia. In Donna Lee Van Cott, ed., *Indigenous Peoples and Democracy in Latin America*, 83–105. New York: St. Martin's Press.

Bebbington, Anthony. 1994. Theory and Relevance in Indigenous Agriculture: Knowledge, Agency and Organization. In David Booth, ed., *Rethinking Social Development: Theory, Research and Practice*, 202–225. Harlow, U.K.: Longman Scientific and Technical.

Bhabha, Homi K. 1994. *The Location of Culture*. London and New York: Routledge.

Cabildo, Taitas y Comisión de Trabajo del Pueblo Guambiano. 1994. *Diagnóstico y plan de vida del Pueblo Guambiano*. Territorio Guambiano-Silvia: Cabildo de Guambía/CENCOA/Corporación Autónoma Regional del Cauca/Visión Mundial Internacional.

Cabuyo/CRIC. 1996. *Proyecto educativo comunitario: Construcción de una escuela intercultural*. Popayán: PEB-CRIC.

Camayo B., Mélida, and Luz Mary Niquinás. 1997. KWE'S' TUL como estrategia pedagógica y cultural. *C'ayu'ce* (Popayán) 2: 4–8.

Campbell, Howard, Leigh Binford, Miguel Bartolomé, and Alicia Barabas, eds. 1993. *Zapotec Struggles: Histories, Politics, and Representations from Juchitán, Oaxaca*. Washington, D.C.: Smithsonian Institution Press.

Carvajal, Edmundo. 1995. *Censo de población CRIC–Nasa Kiwe en el área del desastre de Tierradentro, Cauca, CRIC–Nasa Kiwe: Análisis descriptivo de la producción y usos del suelo e impacto del desastre del 6 de junio de 1994 en la región de Tierradentro*. Popayán: Consejo Regional Indígena del Cauca/Corporación Nasa Kiwe.

Colombia, República de. 1991. *Nueva constitución política de Colombia*. Pasto: Minilibrería Jurídica Moral.

———. 1993. *Ley 60 de 1993*. Bogotá.

———. 1994. *Ley orgánica del plan de desarrollo (Ley 152)*. Bogotá.

Colombia, República de, Dirección General de Asuntos Indígenas, ed. 1997. *"Del olvido surgimos para traer nuevas esperanzas": La jurisdicción especial indígena*. Bogotá: Ministerio de Justicia y del Derecho/Ministerio del Interior, Dirección General de Asuntos Indígenas.

Corporación Nasa Kiwe (CNK). 1995. *Primer semestre: Informe resúmen de actividades realizadas entre julio y diciembre de 1994*. Popayán: Corporación Nasa Kiwe.

Crush, Jonathan. 1995. Introduction: Imagining Development. In Jonathan Crush, ed., *Power of Development*, 1–23. New York: Routledge.

de Certeau, Michel. 1986. *Heterologies: Discourse on the Other*. Minneapolis: University of Minnesota Press.

Desastres & Sociedad. 1997. *Especial: Cauca y Huila, Colombia, junio 1994–junio 1995: El desastre y la reconstrucción del Páez*. Special Issue of *Desastres & Sociedad* 4 (3).

Espinosa, Myriam Amparo. 1996. *Surgimiento y andar territorial del Quintín Lame*. Quito: Abya-Yala.

Findji, María Teresa. 1992. From Resistance to Social Movement: The Indigenous Authorities Movement in Colombia. In Arturo Escobar and Sonia Alvarez, eds., *The Making of Social Movements in Latin America: Identity, Strategy, and Democracy*, 112–133. Boulder: Westview Press.

Fischer, Edward F., and R. McKenna Brown, eds. 1996. *Maya Cultural Activism in Guatemala*. Austin: University of Texas Press.

Fiszbein, Ariel. 1997. The Emergence of Local Capacity: Lessons from Colombia. *World Development* 25 (7): 1029–1043.

Friedman, Jonathan. 1994. *Cultural Identity and Global Process*. London: Sage.

Fundación Sol y Tierra (FST). 1995a. Formación integral e investigación, Pueblo Nuevo, Centro de Capacitación "Luis Angel Monroy." Popayán. MS.

———. 1995b. Plan de desarrollo Resguardo Indígena de Vitoncó municipio de Páez-Cauca, años 1996–1997–1998: Elaborado por la Comunidad Indígena y el Cabildo de Vitoncó. Popayán. MS.

García Canclini, Néstor. 1989. *Culturas híbridas: Estrategias para entrar y salir de la modernidad*. Mexico City: Grijalbo.

Gaviria Díaz, Carlos. 1997. *Diversidad étnica y cultural: Reconocimiento constitucional*. Sentencia no. T-523/97. Bogotá: Sala Cuarta de Revisión de Tutelar de la Corte Constitucional.

Gewertz, Deborah, and Frederick Errington. 1996. On PepsiCo and Piety in a Papua New Guinea "Modernity." *American Ethnologist* 23 (3): 476–493.

Gilroy, Paul. 1993. *The Black Atlantic: Modernity and Double Consciousness*. Cambridge: Harvard University Press.

Goff, Brent. 1994. Reviving Crafts and Affirming Culture: From Grassroots Development to National Policy. In Charles David Kleymeyer, ed., *Cultural Expression and Grassroots Development*, 185–206. Boulder: Lynne Rienner Publishers.

Gómez, Herinaldy. 1995. El derecho étnico ante el derecho estatal. *Convergencia* (Mexico City) 3 (8–9): 295–316.

———. 1999. Crisis de la justicia y la jurisdicción indígena en Colombia. *Convergencia* (Mexico City) 6 (18): 285–308.

Gómez, Herinaldy, and Carlos Ariel Ruiz. 1997. *Los paeces: Gente territorio: Metáfora que perdura*. Popayán: Fundación para las Comunidades Colombianos/ Universidad del Cauca.

Gow, David D. 1997. Can the Subaltern Plan? Ethnicity and Development in Cauca, Colombia. *Urban Anthropology* 26 (3–4): 243–292.

Gros, Christian. 1991. *Colombia indígena: Identidad cultural y cambio social*. Bogotá: CEREC.

———. 1993. Derechos indígenas y nueva constitución en Colombia. *Análisis Político* (Bogotá) 19: 8–24.

Hanson, Allan. 1989. The Making of the Maori: Culture Invention and Its Logic. *American Anthropologist* 91 (4): 890–902.

Holston, James. 1986. *The Modernist City: An Anthropological Critique of Brasilia*. Chicago: University of Chicago Press.

INGEOMINAS (Instituto de Investigaciones e Información Geocientífica, Minero-Ambiental y Nuclear). 1995. *Zonificación para usos del suelo en la cuenca del río Páez*. Bogotá: INGEOMINAS.

Jackson, Jean. 1995. Culture, Genuine and Spurious: The Politics of Indianness in the Vaupés, Colombia. *American Ethnologist* 22 (1): 3–27.

Jimeno, Myriam. 1996. Juan Gregorio Palechor: Tierra, identidad y recreación étnica. *Journal of Latin American Anthropology* 1 (2): 46–77.

Keesing, Roger. 1989. Creating the Past: Custom and Identity in the Contemporary Pacific. *Contemporary Pacific* 1 (1–2): 19–42.

Kleymeyer, Charles David, ed. 1994a. *Cultural Expression and Grassroots Development*. Boulder: Lynne Rienner Publishers.

———. 1994b. Cultural Expression and Grassroots Development. In Charles David Kleymeyer, ed., *Cultural Expression and Grassroots Development*, 39–67. Boulder: Lynne Rienner Publishers.

López Garcés, Carlos Alfredo. 1995. *Censo de población CRIC–Nasa Kiwe en la zona de desastre del 6 de junio de 1994: Análisis descriptivo del medio ambiente en Tierradentro*. Popayán: Consejo Regional Indígena del Cauca/Corporación Nasa Kiwe.

Morales Tunubalá, Alvaro. 1997. Sistema tradicional de juzgamiento en el pueblo guambiano. In República de Colombia, Dirección General de Asuntos Indígenas, ed., *"Del olvido surgimos para traer nuevas esperanzas": La jurisdicción especial indígena*, 75–85. Bogotá: Ministerio de Justicia y del Derecho/Ministerio del Interior, Dirección General de Asuntos Indígenas.

Muelas Hurtado, Bárbara. 1995. Relación espacio-tiempo en el pensamiento guambiano. *Proyecciones Lingüísticas* (Popayán) 1 (1): 31–40.

Muelas Hurtado, Bárbara, et al. 1994. *Nupirau nu wamwan trek køntrai isua pørik: Apartes de la constitución política de Colombia—1991 en guambiano*. Bogotá: CCELA-UniAndes.

Mulcué Mulcué, Adela, and Nydia María Yasnó González. n.d. Participación de la familia y la comunidad en la propuesta pedagógica del grado cero del CET. Nuevo Tóez. MS.

Muñoz Alvear, Leoxmar Benjamín. 1997. Acción de tutela impetrada por el señor Francisco Gembuel Pechené, en contra de los señores Luis Alberto Passú, gobernador del Cabildo Indígena de Jambaló y Luis Alberto Fiscué, presidente de la Asociación de Cabildos de la Zona Norte del Departamento del Cauca. Sentencia del Juzgado Primero Penal Municipal, Santander de Quilichao (Cauca), 8 January.

Nelson, Diane M. 1999. *A Finger in the Wound: Body Politics in Quincentennial Guatemala*. Berkeley and Los Angeles: University of California Press.

Ocampo, Gloria Isabel. 1997. Diversidad étnica y jurisdicción indígena en Colombia. *Boletín de Antropología* (Medellín) 11 (27): 9–33.

Pachón, Ximena. 1996. Los nasa o la gente páez. In Ximena Pachón, Diana Oliveros, and Luis Eduardo Wiesner, eds., *Geografía humana de Colombia: Región andina central*. Bogotá: Instituto Colombiano de Cultura Hispánica.

Passú, Luis Alberto, and Luis Alberto Fiscué. 1997. Letter to Dr. Leodxmar [*sic*] Benjamín Muñóz Alvear, Juez Primero Municipal de Santander de Quilichao. 13 January.

Peñaranda, Claudia Helena, and Juan Montaña. 1997. Elementos de un diálogo. In República de Colombia, Dirección General de Asuntos Indígenas, ed., *"Del olvido surgimos para traer nuevas esperanzas": La jurisdicción especial indígena*. Bogotá: Ministerio de Justicia y del Derecho/Ministerio del Interior, Dirección General de Asuntos Indígenas.

Peñaranda, Ricardo. 1993. Los orígenes del Movimiento Armado Quintín Lame. In Amado Guerrero, ed., *Cultura política, movimientos sociales y violencia en la historia de Colombia.* Bucaramanga: n.p.

———. 1999. De rebeldes a ciudadanos: El caso del movimiento armado Quintín Lame. In Ricardo Peñaranda and Javier Guerrero, eds., *De las armas a la política,* 75–131. Bogotá: Tercer Mundo.

Perafán Simmonds, Carlos César. 1995. *Sistemas jurídicos páez, kogi, wayúu y tule.* Bogotá: Colcultura/Instituto Colombiano de Antropología.

Perdomo Dizú, Adonías. n.d. Autonomía, autoridad y justicia interna en los resguardos de Pitayó Silvia, Pioyá Caldono y Pat Yu' Cajibío. Pitayó. MS.

Piñacué, Jesús Enrique. 1997. Amplicación autonómica de la justicia en comunidades paeces (una aproximación). In República de Colombia, Dirección General de Asuntos Indígenas, ed., *"Del olvido surgimos para traer nuevas esperanzas": La jurisdicción especial indígena,* 31–52. Bogotá: Ministerio de Justicia y del Derecho/Ministerio del Interior, Dirección General de Asuntos Indígenas.

Ramón Valarezo, Galo. 1993. *El regreso de los runas: La potencialidad del proyecto indio en el Ecuador contemporáneo.* Quito: Comunidec/Fundación Interamericana.

Ramos, Abelardo, et al. 1994. *Ec ne'hwe's': Constitución política de Colombia en nasa yuwe.* Bogotá: CCELA-UniAndes.

Ramos, Alcida. 1994. The Hyperreal Indian. *Critique of Anthropology* 14 (2): 153–171.

———. 1998. *Indigenism: Ethnic Politics in Brazil.* Madison: University of Wisconsin Press.

Rappaport, Joanne. 1992. Reinvented Traditions: The Heraldry of Ethnic Militancy in the Colombian Andes. In Robert Dover, Katharine Seibold, and John McDowell, eds., *Andean Cosmologies through Time: Persistence and Emergence,* 202–228. Bloomington: Indiana University Press.

———, ed. 1996. *Ethnicity Reconfigured: Indigenous Legislators and the Colombian Constitution of 1991.* Special issue of *Journal of Latin American Anthropology* 1, no. 2.

———. 1998a. Hacia la descolonización de la producción intelectual indígena en Colombia. In María Lucía Sotomayor, ed., *Modernidad, identidad y desarrollo: Construcción de sociedad y re-creación cultural en contextos de modernización,* 17–45. Bogotá: Instituto Colombiano de Antropología.

———. 1998b. *The Politics of Memory: Native Historical Interpretation in the Colombian Andes.* Durham: Duke University Press.

———. n.d. Los nasa de frontera y la política de la identidad en el Cauca indígena. In Joanne Rappaport, ed., *Retornando la mirada: Una investigación colaborativa interétnica sobre el Cauca a la entrada del milenio.* Popayán: Editorial Universidad del Cauca (in press).

Rappaport, Joanne, and David D. Gow. 1997. Cambio dirigido, movimiento indígena y estereotipos del indio: El estado colombiano y la reubicación de los nasa. In María Victoria Uribe and Eduardo Restrepo, eds., *Antropología en la modernidad,* 361–399. Bogotá: Instituto Colombiano de Antropología.

Roe, Emory. 1994. *Narrative Policy Analysis: Theory and Practice.* Durham: Duke University Press.

Rogers, Mark. 1996. Beyond Authenticity: Conservation, Tourism, and the Politics of Representation in the Ecuadorian Amazon. *Identities* 3 (1–2): 73–125.

Rojas Curieux, Tulio. 1997. La traducción de la Constitución de la República de Colombia a lenguas indígenas. In República de Colombia, Dirección General de Asuntos Indígenas, ed., *"Del olvido surgimos para traer nuevas esperanzas": La jurisdicción especial indígena,* 229–244. Bogotá: Ministerio de Justicia y del Derecho/Ministerio del Interior, Dirección General de Asuntos Indígenas.

Sánchez Botero, Esther. 1998. *Justicia y pueblos indígenas de Colombia.* Bogotá: Universidad Nacional de Colombia, Facultad de Derecho, Ciencias Políticas y Sociales.

Sierra Sierra, Silvio. 1998. Piñacué, al borde del fuete. *El País,* 8 July, E1.

Stephen, Lynn. 1996. The Creation and Re-creation of Ethnicity: Lessons from the Zapotec and Mixtec of Oaxaca. *Latin American Perspectives* 23 (2): 17–37.

Ticona A., Estéban, Gonzalo Rojas O., and Xavier Albó C. 1995. *Votos y wiphalas: Campesinos y pueblos originarios en democracia.* La Paz: Fundación Milenio/CIPCA.

Tobin, Jeffrey. 1994. Cultural Construction and Native Nationalism: Report from the Hawaiian Front. *boundary 2* 21 (1): 111–133.

Touraine, Alain. 1995. *Critique of Modernity.* Oxford: Blackwell.

Trask, Haunani-Kay. 1991. Natives and Anthropologists: The Colonial Struggle. *Contemporary Pacific* 2: 159–167.

Triana Antorveza, Adolfo. 1992. Grupos étnicos: Nueva Constitución en Colombia. In Esther Sánchez B., ed., *Antropología jurídica: Normas formales, costumbres legales en Colombia,* 103–114. Bogotá: Sociedad Antropológica de Colombia/Comité International para el Desarrollo de los Pueblos.

Ulcué, Luis Carlos. 1997. El yu'kh "monte" y la política de conservación en los nasa de Pueblo Nuevo, municipio de Caldono—Cauca. M.A. thesis, Problemas Políticos Latinoamericanos, Universidad del Cauca, Popayán.

Vasco Uribe, Guillermo, Abelino Dagua Hurtado, and Misael Aranda. 1993. En el segundo día, la Gente Grande (Numisak) sembró la autoridad y las plantas y, con su jugo, bebió el sentido. In François Correa, ed., *Encrucijadas de Colombia amerindia,* 9–48. Bogotá: Instituto Colombiano de Antropología.

Vengoechea, Alejandra de. 1998a. Entre dos aguas. *Cambio16 Colombia* 266: 44–46.

———. 1998b. Veinte fuetazos por Serpa. *Cambio16 Colombia* 265: 28.

Wade, Peter. 1995. The Cultural Politics of Blackness in Colombia. *American Ethnologist* 22 (2): 341–357.

Warren, Kay B. 1998. *Indigenous Movements and Their Critics: Pan-Maya Activism in Guatemala.* Princeton: Princeton University Press.

Wilches Chaux, Gustavo. 1995a. Particularidades de un desastre. *Desastres & Sociedad* 4 (3): 119–139.

———. 1995b. Tierra de la gente: Principios orientadores de la Corporación NASA KIWE: Tierra de la gente. *Desastres & Sociedad* 4 (3): 91–104.

Yule, Marcos. 1995. Avances en la investigación del Nasa Yuwe (lengua páez). *Proyecciones Lingüísticas* (Popayán) 1 (1): 23–30.

3. CONTESTED DISCOURSES OF AUTHORITY IN COLOMBIAN NATIONAL INDIGENOUS POLITICS

The 1996 Summer Takeovers

Jean E. Jackson

INTRODUCTION

This chapter is about the form that assertions about Colombian indigenousness, in particular about indigenous authority, took during the summer of 1996, when a series of takeovers of buildings to protest the situation of Colombia's indigenous people erupted throughout the country. The protests highlighted a debate currently taking place in Colombia concerning who best represents the country's indigenous people: traditional leaders in local communities or leaders from the national indigenous movement. The chapter explores the nature of this debate, its roots, and the stakes for the debaters.

I first provide an overview of the history of indigenous organizing in Colombia and a brief description of national indigenous organizations, followed by a description of the summer's events. I then analyze why the dispute that began the takeovers evolved into a much bigger confrontation between national indigenous organizations and the director of the National Office of Indigenous Affairs, an agency of the Ministry of the Interior (Dirección de Asuntos Indígenas: DAI), over who should represent the nation's indigenous peoples in their relations with the state. The director claimed that the "traditional authorities" in the local communities possessed an authority superior to that of the national indigenous organizations and that it was DAI's job to strengthen the local authorities. This position was opposed by leaders from the National Indigenous Organization of Colombia (Organización Nacional de Indígenas de Colombia: ONIC) and their allies. Information on these events was obtained during a trip to Colombia from August 13 to 28, 1996, in the form of interviews, unpublished documents, audiotapes of meetings, and press reports.[1]

BACKGROUND: HISTORY OF THE
INDIGENOUS MOVEMENT IN COLOMBIA

Colombian indigenous mobilization on a national level began early in the twentieth century in Andean sectors of the country and was originally tied to Colombian Marxists who spoke of "indigenousness" and championed an "indigenous proletariat," partially breaking with the assimilationist positions held by both the left and the right. The most famous leader, Manuel Quintín Lame, a Páez,[2] participated in protests organized by the Marxists during the 1920s but came to espouse indigenous separatism during the 1930s. During the 1930s and 1940s peasant struggles for land were taken up by the Movimiento Agrarista in the southern part of the department of Tolima; in the 1950s Marxist and Liberal guerrillas continued the struggle against the Conservatives in power, forming "independent republics," which gave rise in 1947 to the largest guerrilla organization now operating, Fuerzas Armadas Revolucionarias de Colombia (FARC: Colombian Armed Revolutionary Forces).[3] Indigenous mobilizing at the time focused on repossessing illegally expropriated lands titled to Andean indigenous communities during the colonial era. In 1970 the Asociación Nacional de Usuarios Campesinos (ANUC: National Association of Peasant Users) was formed to ensure enactment of the land reform laws passed in the early 1960s. ANUC soon divided, and Indians[4] from Cauca, Nariño, Putumayo, San Andrés de Sotavento and Kuna from Antioquia formed a Secretaría Indígena Nacional within one faction.

Upon realizing that ANUC's only interest was to "peasantize" (*campesinar*) its indigenous members, the Consejo Regional Indígena del Cauca (CRIC: Regional Indigenous Council of Cauca) was formed in 1971 to fight for land rights and as a defense against severe repression from guerrilla armies and the national armed forces. Despite being specifically indigenous, CRIC has never identified itself with a particular pueblo, although most of its members are Nasa.[5] María Teresa Findji states that CRIC lacked an "ethnic" vision (she also calls it anti-indigenist),[6] its organizing principle being social class (1992: 118). While CRIC certainly maintained links with other sectors of the rural society, helping to amplify its potential for mass mobilization, and CRIC's own version of its history does acknowledge that "we ourselves believed that being *indio* wasn't good, and that in order to progress we had to copy what came from outside" (Consejo Regional Indígena del Cauca 1981: 11), in the fall of 1971 CRIC's charter was modified to include the defense of "indigenous history, language, and customs" (ibid.: 12). *Unidad Indígena*, a newspaper currently published several times a year, began in 1974.

The indigenous movement definitively split from ANUC in 1976. The First Indigenous Congress, held in Bogotá in 1982 and attended by more than 2,000 indigenous delegates, created ONIC, with a mandate to defend indigenous autonomy, history, culture, and traditions and to continue the campaign to recuperate the lands of *resguardos* (reservations established during colonial times).[7] ONIC was recognized by the government in 1983 and became an official participant in several governmental programs concerned with indigenous affairs.

NATIONAL INDIGENOUS ORGANIZATIONS

Four indigenous organizations currently claim to have a national presence and more than one noncontiguous indigenous pueblo as their constituency. ONIC's structure, with its national office and thirty-five regional affiliates, has been likened to that of a labor union. Most of its regional affiliates represent more than one pueblo, and many are formed along departmental, rather than ethnic, lines (e.g., Regional Indigenous Council of Cauca), an arrangement that sometimes results in a pueblo's communities belonging to more than one regional affiliate. ONIC and its affiliates see themselves as transcending a territorial-based ethnicity, achieving a superior, supracommunity administrative level.[8]

Over the years ONIC has had both internal problems (organizational and economic—it was restructured in 1987) and external ones. An example of the latter is the decision, reached after much debate, not to participate officially in international organizations.

Another national organization, Autoridades Indígenas de Colombia (AICO: Indigenous Authorities of Colombia), was born in the 1980s out of Guambianos' desire not to be seen as peasants or even as indigenous in the generic sense: "We don't want to be 'humiliated' *indígenas*—we want to defend, for our children's sake, our right to be Guambianos" (as cited in Findji 1992: 122). It adopted the slogan "We are not a race, we are a pueblo." AICO was formed out of alliances forged with the Aruaco (Ika), and the Emberá, two pueblos located in other parts of the country. But AICO has never had ONIC'S federated structure, in part because it was formed as a reaction against the kind of organization model represented by CRIC and others. The image AICO projects more or less prevents it from being a national movement representing all of the country's pueblos. Its cultural ties and its claims to legitimacy are with Andean peoples, in particular Guambiano (although not all Guambiano *cabildos*—the governing bodies—belong to the organization). AICO has criticized ONIC for being authoritarian, too vertical, and too dismissive of traditional authorities (Muyuy 1992: 52). Lorenzo Muelas, earlier elected to the senate by majority vote (i.e., not occupying one of the two seats reserved for Indians), is associated with AICO.

Both of the other two indigenous organizations are political parties. Alianza Social Indígena (ASI: Indigenous Social Alliance) was created by CRIC and Movimiento Armado Quintín Lame (Quintín Lame Armed Movement), an indigenous guerrilla group that demobilized to participate in the National Constituent Assembly (ANC). ASI's members include non-Indians; hence, strictly speaking, it is not an "indigenous organization." At times ASI supports ONIC and other times opposes it. It has been strongly criticized by ONIC, which said that such alliance strategies fed into capitalist visions (see Muyuy 1992: 52). More recently ASI has managed the campaign of Jesús Piñacué, a co-founder and former president of CRIC, elected to the senate in 1997 and still serving. ASI's candidates won more offices in 1997 overall than either AICO or Movimiento Indígena de Colombia (MIC: Movement of Indigenous People of Colombia), the other organization. MIC, the party of Senator Gabriel Muyuy, was founded in 1994 to campaign for Muyuy's reelection when ONIC got out of electoral politics (until then Muyuy had been its candidate). MIC is primarily allied with the Inga people of the Putumayo (Jimeno 1996: 73; MIC n.d.).

A great deal more could be said about the division between ONIC and AICO (see M. Jimeno 1996; Padilla 1996; Rappaport and Dover 1996). ONIC sees its lack of association with a given region of the country or group of pueblos as an advantage; but, as shown below, the shifts in indigenous politics discourses in the 1990s are increasing the visibility of the disadvantages inhering in the way ONIC is organized. Although both organizations must employ European-derived categories in their construction of ethnic difference and are concerned with making their cultural characteristics "more palatable for outside observers" (Dover and Rappaport 1996: 5), there are differences in the way they represent indigenousness. ONIC employs a "trait list" of indigenousness that essentializes identity "in much the same way that national legislation and social science have done for the past century by associating native culture with discrete cultural traits such as language, social organization, and traditions, or with expanses of land" (Rappaport and Dover 1996: 28). AICO, in contrast, eschews such "outmoded anthropological criteria" in favor of the "romanticizing of indigenous resistance in an appeal to history as the prime definer of native identity" (Rappaport and Dover 1996: 25).

In its discursive political strategies, ONIC for the most part has used a rather straightforward Western political language which only recently has begun to perform indigenous cultural difference. Cultural difference is certainly asserted, but, as we shall see, it is *performed* far less than when "traditional authority" leaders address a metropolitan audience. The following quote about the mobilization of nearly all Colombian pueblos during the summer from Abadio Green, president of ONIC at the time of the takeovers,[9] provides an example of a fairly minimal performance of cultural difference. The language used is entirely Spanish, and the statement contains relatively few symbols of indigenousness like the ones discussed by Graham (this volume): "We spoke with a single voice. The advantage we have is that we speak of our culture, our language, and our Mother Earth." Although he was speaking to me, the comment is very representative of Green's public statements. A generic indigenous cultural difference is being asserted, but of necessity a very generalized one.

In fact, some nonindigenous activists have complained that ONIC and its affiliates have pursued an over-appropriation of European-derived discursive forms—in particular a fetishization of legal discourse, a "rituality concerning legal institutions and law," as Guillermo Padilla, a Colombian anthropologist, puts it.[10] Padilla complains that now that the parameters of the struggle for indigenous rights and autonomy have changed, the national indigenous movement places too much emphasis on "parliamentary machinery" and on the "game" of forming political alliances (see Ramos, this volume).

THE TAKEOVERS

On June 24, 1996, forty-five Wayúu (formerly known as Guajiro) Indians occupied DAI's Bogotá offices.[11] This was followed by a Wayúu occupation of the branch office of DAI in Uribia, in the Wayúu region of Guajira. Discussions began, but no settlement was reached.[12] Insofar as I understand it, the dispute started when a Wayúu woman submitted a proposal for a project involving the not inconsiderable sum of 3,000,000 pesos via her local NGO to a mayor. The mayor wrote DAI, asking what criteria to apply, and letters of protest arrived from surrounding communities complaining that "we don't know anything about this project!" DAI wrote back to the NGO, saying the community had to be involved. Following this, the group of Wayúu traveled to Bogotá and began the occupation.

Then, on July 5, a group of sixty Indians from many areas of Colombia[13] occupied the Episcopal Palace in Bogotá in the name of Colombia's eighty-five indigenous pueblos. Because the takeover occurred during the bishops' annual meeting, the event received a great deal of publicity. Horacio Serpa Uribe, the minister of the interior, agreed to meet with Msgr. Alberto Giraldo, the president of the Episcopal Conference, and various indigenous leaders. The indigenous activists presented a list of demands concerning the situation of all the indigenous pueblos of the country; the government agreed to seek a solution, and a negotiating commission was set up.

By July 21, sixteen days later, several things had become clear. First, the indigenous movement was, at least publicly, united. Lorenzo Muelas and Gabriel Muyuy, the two indigenous senators,[14] joined with the occupiers—who were for the most part connected to ONIC and its regional affiliates—and issued a document distributed from the Episcopal Palace. Other leaders, among them Jesús Piñacué, the Nasa leader from Cauca and at the time head of CRIC, and Francisco Rojas Birry, an Emberá who was a former member of the Constitutional Assembly and at the time a member of the Bogotá city council, also visited the Episcopal Palace and helped in negotiations with the government. Such a sign of unity was significant, for the national indigenous movement has been characterized by internal disputes from the beginning. As Víctor Jacanamejoy, vice-director of MIC, put it in an interview with a reporter, the activists in the Episcopal Palace agreed that they would not refer to the distinct indigenous organizations, as this would be divisive, and the truth was that "they [guerrillas, military, and paramilitaries] are killing all of us!"[15] For the moment at least, a unifying discourse had emerged; as Green said: "We are united around the issue of life, because we are being killed; we are also united around the issue of our territories: it is Mother Earth who calls us together, who convenes her children" (as cited in Navia 1996).

The negotiations with the government advanced to the point of agreeing to create a bipartite commission (earlier, indigenous representatives had turned down the official proposal to create another commission that would "study the theme of indigenous territories"). The activists insisted that the occupation would end only when a concrete method was found for creating indigenous territories, a feature of the Territorial Ordination Process mandated by the 1991 Constitution but stalled in its implementation.[16]

In the succeeding days, other takeovers in support of the actions in the capital (and also to protest local problems) were carried out in Montería, Cali, Ipiales, Quibdó, Puerto Carreño, Riohacha, Mocoa, Ibagué, and Vichada.

Support from many sectors began to come in. Between July 5 and 25 many national nongovernmental organizations (NGOs) and human rights groups paid for ads in the national press.[17] Peasant organizations came on board, saying that "hundreds of us are being killed too!"; they helped occupy various regional INCORA (Instituto Colombiano de Reforma Agraria, the government agency in charge of land reform) offices. Many church officials and international organizations sent letters to then-president Ernesto Samper.

On August 1 more than 3,000 members of various *cabildos* in the Cauca valley blocked the Panamerican Highway, applying pressure—successfully, it turned out—on the government to negotiate locally and with the occupiers of the Episcopal Palace. Local demands concerning autonomy, health, education, and environment were included in the agreement that was signed. This action was carefully planned; in fact, two sites were blocked to prevent traffic from taking a detour and rejoining the highway past the first blockade. Over 3,000 Indians and campesinos participated in the mobilization. Several people I spoke with believed that the Panamerican blockade was what really brought the government to its knees, so that in a sense what was happening in Bogotá was in support of the Cauca action and not vice versa—although this was not Green's position, of course: "One week CRIC blockaded the Panamerican Highway, and it had an impact. I had to go there to support them." The agreement, titled "La María Piendamó," sets up policies relating to human rights, a committee concerned with indigenous territories and *mesas de concertación* (roundtables for dialogue).[18]

Finally, on August 8 in Bogotá, chicha (manioc beer), music, and shouts of "viva!" accompanied the signing of two decrees (1396, 1397) that "defend the fundamental rights of Colombian indigenous people" (*El Espectador* 1996b). The Episcopal Palace had been occupied for thirty-six days. The agreement, similar to the one signed in Cauca, established a committee on human rights, a national commission of lands, and a permanent interinstitutional *mesa de concertación*, where government and indigenous leaders would periodically meet. The Interamerican Organization of Human Rights, the International Labor Organization, and the Episcopal Conference would supervise to see that the promises were kept. August 9 was declared "The Day of a New Dawn."[19]

INDIGENOUS GRIEVANCES LEADING TO THE OCCUPATIONS

In July Gabriel Muyuy summed up the indigenous movement's progress so far:

> In some respects we have advanced a little bit, but not in the fundamental issues. For example, progress on the theme of territory is zero. Human rights abuses grow more serious each day. In some places ground has been gained in social investment, but most indigenous communities continue to be poor, marginalized, and victimized by land invasions. (cited in Navia 1996)

Specific grievances raised during the takeovers included the following:

1. Land (both with respect to the ongoing process of "territorial ordination"[20] established by the 1991 Constitution and with respect to the older types of struggles for land involving legal denunciations and repossessions).

2. Control over development in indigenous territories.[21]

3. Transfer of resources to indigenous communities.

4. Continued repression of indigenous leaders and human rights violations.

5. Failure to legislate the 1991 Constitution in domains other than territorial ordination.

Other issues emerged as well—for example, complaints about tokenism and inappropriate government-sponsored social services in several indigenous communities.

The most serious complaint concerned the state's failure to promote legislation implementing the fundamental ("organic") law regarding territorial ordination, a law which applies to the entire country, not just indigenous communities.[22] Once the Constitution's mandates are legislated and put in place, indigenous pueblos, constituted into indigenous territorial entities (*entidades territoriales indígenas:* ETIs), will receive funds directly from the state; in the meantime, however, the funds are administered by local mayoral offices, an unsatisfactory arrangement in indigenous eyes. The funding problem became particularly acute following implementation of Law 60 in 1994, which instituted direct transfer of funds. This was the main issue fueling the debates about traditional authorities and autonomy—exacerbated, according to one lawyer,[23] by the state's having "changed the game two years ago," when powerful officials in then-president César Gaviria's administration began to strongly resist implementing the Constitution. Van Cott (personal communication, 2001) notes that Gaviria himself (and DAI) strongly supported implementing the sections of the Constitution pertaining to indigenous matters. And the decline continued; according to Gabriel Muyuy, attention paid to indigenous politics diminished 90 percent during the Samper administration (*El Espectador* 1996a).

The clear momentum building against the 1991 Constitution in other quarters was also worrisome. Critics, some Colombian anthropologists among them, had begun to say that the Constitution went too far, resulting in a fragmented country ("like the former Yugoslavia") and producing ethnic conflict in areas where coexistence had been possible earlier (in particular in places where Afro-Colombians and Indians or Indians and *colonos* [settlers] lived near one another).[24]

That many of the takeovers occurring outside of Bogotá involved offices of INCORA (the land reform agency) was no surprise. Colombian agrarian reform, instituted in order to dampen conflict and make more territory available to modern agriculture, has been characterized as "minimalist," clearly never intended to make the fundamental structural land tenure changes that would truly benefit small-scale farmers (see Gros 1996: 254; Rappaport and Gow 1997: 379). During the 1960s and 1970s INCORA had wanted to dismantle the *resguardos*, seeing them as a retrograde form of land tenure. But every attempt was met with opposition from activists, and confrontations often ensued. The extensive repression that resulted in areas where landlessness was most acute was met with indifference or at times hostility from both DAI and INCORA (M. Jimeno and Triana 1985: 118). INCORA's mandate involved titling lands to the small-scale peasants working them and creating reserves in the country's *baldíos* (lands legally designated as "empty territories" in Amazon and Orinoco regions) to facilitate migration, reducing the population pressure in the heartland of the country. In fact lowland indigenous communities were found throughout these territories, however, and indigenous organizations successfully pressured INCORA to convert most of the reserves into *resguardos*, giving the pueblos inalienable collective ownership. Between 1961 and 1986 INCORA constituted 158 new *resguardos*, totaling over 12 million hectares; and between 1986 and 1989 it created 63 new *resguardos* totaling over 13 million hectares (Pineda 1995: 31). Despite such impressive achievements, INCORA's antagonism to the organizations, its very spotty success in places where the problems were gravest, and its utter failures in some of the highest-conflict areas (involving the Zenú, Nukak-Makú, U'wa, Pasto, and Kofán: Echeverry 1998) virtually guaranteed the extensive criticism heard during the summer.

Specific complaints about INCORA focused on overly close ties between local INCORA functionaries and landlords. Gaps between its policies and local indigenous communities' vision of autonomy frequently produced tensions as well. Protesters complained that INCORA officials often did not identify with the community, resulting in their actually preferring that money designated for indigenous projects be lost. Indigenous leaders also complained about the small amount of funds assigned to INCORA for land acquisitions, the lack of institutional infrastructure, the legal hurdles impeding the acquisition and titling process, and the unattractive amounts the agency offered to pay to landowners, resulting in purchases of land of the worst quality.[25] Others criticized INCORA agents for seeming to treat the land tenure crisis as if it were a problem between indigenous, peasant, and Afro-Colombian communities themselves. In fact, said some critics, INCORA's politics was clearly oriented toward impeding the titling process, the lack of political will being due to government links to multinational companies and their Colombian affiliates (ONIC 1998: 335–336).

ONIC also complained that Decree 2164, a regulation of Law 160 of 1994 concerned with land reform, was legislated without consulting Colombia's indigenous organizations; in particular several unfavorable key changes had been made at the last minute that limited autonomy and impeded the enlargement and restructuring of indigenous *resguardos* and the relocation of nonindigenous individuals.

Finally, to understand the series of occupations, it is crucial to keep in mind the enormous crisis the country is facing. Colombia is undergoing its worst recession in seventy years; at the beginning of the 1990s approximately 50 percent of the population was living in absolute poverty (Van Cott 2000: 49), and neoliberal policies have produced a deterioration of the standard of living for the vast majority of citizens. A significant amount of the civil war is being fought in indigenous territory. The military and civil authorities' failure to prosecute vast numbers of crimes successfully and an outrageously high degree of repression have resulted in more than 35,000 lives being lost and 1.2 million citizens displaced—an appallingly large number for a country of less than 40 million that is not formally at war (Schemo 1999). A United Nations International Children's Emergency Fund (UNICEF) report states that this total exceeds the internally displaced refugees of Rwanda, Burundi, and Congo combined (as cited in Van Cott 2000: 251–252). Colombia has the highest homicide rate in the world; according to Amnesty International, fourteen homicides per day are considered politically motivated (website posting, December 21, 2000). *Plan Colombia*, an aid package legislated by the U.S. Congress in 2000, ostensibly to help the government fight the drug war, is already worsening the situation in regions like the Putumayo and Caquetá because so much of the aid comes in the form of military support. In such a context, it was a tall order to have a *mesa de concertación* that addressed violations of indigenous rights not only by the formal political system (the police, the army) but also by "everything underneath—kidnappers, assassins, paramilitaries, guerrillas," as Víctor Jacanamejoy put it in an interview with me.

In sum, Colombia's indigenous peoples face extremely grave threats: in regions like Córdoba, Sucre, Urabá, Tierradentro, the Chocó, and the plains and Amazonian regions of Guaviare, Vaupés, Putumayo, and Caquetá, their very lives are endangered by narcotraffickers, landlords willing to commit heinous acts to avoid handing over land, paramilitary forces, guerrillas, and, unfortunately, the military. All indigenous communities are subject to human rights abuses, and the vast majority live in the most miserable of conditions. As a sector of the population, Colombia's indigenous people always come out the lowest with respect to poverty, health, education, and other standard of living indices.

WHAT THE DISPUTE REVEALS: DAI'S SIDE

According to Gladys Jimeno, director of DAI, the Wayúu in the original group that came to Bogotá were corrupt and lacked a real political agenda—evident from the "ridiculous" agreement they presented for DAI to sign. At this stage, their demands centered exclusively around money.[26] One of the lawyers I spoke with told me that the argument presented by this delegation of Wayúu to Horacio Serpa (the minister of the interior when he visited DAI offices) was: "Do what we ask, because we voted for you [i.e., for Samper]." This lawyer concurred with Jimeno that these Wayúu had not planned such a drawn-out confrontation but simply wanted to get Jimeno to reverse her decision denying them funds. He criticized these individuals for behaving in a "very ugly" manner during their stay; for example, although he was accustomed to a very politicized discourse, he said that this was the first time he had heard Indians personally insult their opponents in so offensive a manner. He said ONIC also had disapproved of the trashed offices and ripped-out telephones.

Although many grievances were aired, even after ONIC joined the protest a major focus continued to be Jimeno herself. Relations between national indigenous leaders and DAI have always been fraught with difficulty: they both need each other but often hold strikingly different opinions about a given project.

DAI began as an agency in the Ministry of Government, in part as a response to the International Agreement Colombia had signed with the Instituto Indigenista Interamericano in Mexico.[27] Its story illustrates the pitfalls that loom when a centralized modern state attempts to control its ethnic minorities. As in earlier periods, the state continued to consider its "indigenous problem" solvable by eliminating the country's Indians qua Indians, but DAI was to accomplish this goal by implementing a new, progressive policy. No longer would the government allow "forced acculturation" or religious domination[28] or legitimize territorial expropriation; rather, the agency would promote penetration through various programs that would turn Indians into "citizens useful for society," mainly by introducing a money economy.

DAI documents of the period, as in other Latin American countries, describe Indians in terms of marginalization and isolation, descendants of preconquest peoples and hence "relics of the past." Rather than being due to political powerlessness and shocking poverty, the "indigenous problem" resulted from a mentality that stubbornly maintained precolonial customs despite, in some cases, a long period of contact (as in many Andean areas).

DAI's specific approaches included discrediting the power and legitimacy of native authorities by promoting the development of communal leaders (envisioned as directors of cooperatives), primary school teachers, health care promoters, and so forth. According to Myriam Jimeno and Adolfo Triana (1985: 92), at that time (1962–1966) the agency shared with INCORA the goal of eliminating the *resguardo* system; all property was to belong to individual families, and nomadic peoples were to be sedentarized. In certain locations the agency worked to classify Indians as ordinary peasants; not surprisingly this effort always occurred in areas with land conflicts (M. Jimeno and Triana speak of DAI's anxiety over maintaining exclusive authority to decide who was and was not indigenous as "obsessive" [1985: 91]).

From the beginning DAI functionaries were appointed along clientalist lines, trained poorly (if at all), and paid very little. M. Jimeno and Triana note that *politiquero* (entirely self-interested) politics and clientalism have always characterized the organization, particularly at the regional level—for example, where local authorities opposed DAI programs (favoring, for instance, lumber concessions in indigenous territory), the agency would leave. Funding for the agency's programs was always scarce, greatly restricting its ability to maneuver. DAI's initiatives also often failed because, as happens throughout the Colombian state, new administrations appointed bureaucrats who put new plans into place and discarded the old ones. For a while DAI basically competed with INCORA, promoting virtually identical programs. More technically efficient and better funded, INCORA always won.

The 1970s brought a proliferation of totally uncoordinated state programs targeted at indigenous communities. In 1980 the Department of National Planning assumed the role of coordinator of all indigenous policy and restructured DAI. Its agents were limited to serving as technical assessors of other agencies' programs in the field, and the functionaries in Bogotá found themselves with virtually nothing to do. M. Jimeno and Triana note that, paradoxically, the growth of indigenous organizations during the 1970s and 1980s revivified DAI. Indigenous communities had resisted the new policies all along, and DAI, threatened, had often been on a collision course with the activists.[29] But the state's ultimate conclusion that it would have to pay attention to the organizations' claims resulted in DAI gaining a modicum of legitimacy and authority, especially following ONIC's insertion into state structures.

What emerged in the 1996 dispute between DAI and the organizations—which often took the form of a feud—was the inadvisability of Jimeno's public statement that the indigenous organizations did not and could not adequately represent Colombian indigenous pueblos and that the traditional authorities deserved much more support from agencies like DAI. Jimeno's position was that—while there was a role for the national and regional indigenous organizations—traditional authorities should have greater authority.

The consensus was that Jimeno had committed a grave political error with her remarks, because they were "for the record"; while everyone knew of indigenous leaders' problems—losing touch with their roots, becoming overly bureaucratized, and overly identifying with mainstream Colombian society—nonetheless a government official should not publicly suggest that the indigenous organizations' leadership ignored and looked down on the traditional authorities. Jimeno became DAI director as a political appointee with the Samper administration; this was her first administrative office in the area of indigenous affairs.[30] Although her sister, Myriam Jimeno, is viewed as one of the country's best authorities on indigenous matters, Gladys Jimeno was seen to be somewhat ill-informed on DAI history and policy-making, especially with regard to crucial tacit knowledge about how to do business. (The DAI consultant Hernán Correa was seen by all as very knowledgeable.)

When I asked Jimeno about the nature of DAI's policies, she spoke of "political projects" and "ethnic projects." One part of DAI's mission, she said, was to support indigenous social systems, which meant reinforcing the traditional authorities. Of course, DAI also needed policies for dealing with intermediaries, both regional and national. Contrary to accusations, she said DAI did not want to ignore the intermediaries—that it was indeed necessary to deal with indigenous representatives throughout the state system (i.e., senators, councilors, department-level deputies, and mayors) as well as the regional and national indigenous organizations. Jimeno criticized the government of the previous president, Gaviria, for thinking it could exclude many sectors and deal only with the offices of the two indigenous senators. She added, however, that for a "micro project" DAI should deal only with the traditional authorities of a given community or pueblo. "We simply want to support the traditional authorities and reduce corruption."

If ONIC were chosen by a pueblo's traditional authorities as their representative, she said, things would be fine; but as this did not happen in most areas of the country, of course, ONIC's political project conflicted with DAI's. She also asserted that ONIC did not, in fact, support indigenous rights insofar as they concerned community autonomy; for example, the idea that traditional authorities were to make decisions only in internal matters had been invented by the organization. "Secrets" had come out in discussions with ONIC during the takeovers that demonstrated that it did not want discussions about autonomy to take place (for instance, what does autonomy consist of?), because it wanted to be the intermediary in all dealings between local communities and organizations at the national and international level. As ONIC was like a guild organization, she said, it could not really respect the ethnic diversity in the country's indigenous pueblos. Furthermore, although ONIC had regained its *personería jurídica* (the mechanism by which the state recognizes an individual or organization as a legal entity), by no means did this support its claim to be the sole representative of Colombia's indigenous people. Finally, ONIC's argument that the traditional authorities could easily be tricked was not true. "Give them time to reflect and consult with the communities, and no matter how traditional they might be, they can do it." Indigenous communities in some parts of the country knew these facts very well, she said, in particular those of the Sierra Nevada de Santa Marta in the north.

It is clear that since the early 1990s government agencies like DAI that deal with indigenous pueblos have increasingly opined that the traditional authorities have the real authority and that communities in the hinterland represent the real indigenous culture. The authority of other parties, whether local indigenous NGOs claiming to represent the will of the communities or national indigenous organization leaders, is increasingly challenged.[31] Several causes, some of them structural, lie behind the increasing emphasis on the traditional authorities. One of them is the neoliberal move to decentralize power, extensively reorder Colombia's political landscape, institute participatory democracy, and reduce government presence as much as possible, in an attempt to reorient power away from the traditional clientalist two-party political system.

That Colombia's mineral exports now earn more revenue than agricultural exports also plays a role in the moves to strengthen local traditional authorities. Industrial exploitation of most bioenergetic resources, mining, and oil involves large corporations, often multinational, and primarily takes place in indigenous territories. Substantial evidence exists that corporations and the government agencies in charge of their proposals prefer trying to convince local indigenous authorities to allow mining or oil exploration rather than negotiating with the national organizations. These attempts do not always succeed; as in the U'wa case discussed below, which group of individuals constitutes a pueblo's "traditional authorities" and just what "consultation" means are by no means always clear.

In the 1980s ONIC's efforts to represent all the nation's pueblos employed discourses and practices for the most part based on such Western notions as compliance with the law (in the case of illegal appropriations of land), social justice, minority rights, and human rights. During the 1990s "indigenous culture" (and, more ambivalently, Afro-Colombian culture) gained a privileged place in the Colombian imaginary as an emerging discourse championing pluralistic national identity. As a result, culturalist language has increased in ONIC's statements; but, as noted above, generic language about the country's indigenous people is vague and generalized, for in fact very little can be said about what the totality of Colombian indigenous pueblos exclusively shares in the way of culture. Most of the time "Colombian indigenous culture" appears as a motif, with actual content coming from specific pueblos. While the phrase "Colombian Indians" does precisely designate the collectivity of indigenous people who reside within the country's borders, and while this population has shared a great deal of postcontact history, at present the phrase lacks any but the most generalized references to cultural content.

The situation resembles that of other countries with both lowland and Andean indigenous communities but differs strikingly from the case of countries like Guatemala and to some extent Brazil, which are fashioning a nationwide indigenousness that more or less coincides with the country's boundaries (see, for example, Albert 1997: 183). Thus, when challenged by arguments in support of the traditional authorities, ONIC finds that the inapplicability of the "distinct culture" discourse at the national level limits its usefulness for buttressing ONIC's claim to be the appropriate institution to represent the nation's indigenous peoples. Yet it increasingly finds itself having to make a gesture toward cultural distinctiveness, for the culturalist rhetoric that emerged during the 1990s has been remarkably well received not only by non-Indians who support the indigenous cause but by much of the metropolitan public as well. For example, the following excerpt—weighty with non-Western authority—from a 1991 letter written by the Ika *mama* (spiritual leader) Kancha Navinquma from Nabusímake, the central sacred site in the Sierra Nevada de Santa Marta, to Constitutional Assembly constituent Lorenzo Muelas appeared in several publications at the time:

> For us it is strange that a law could change, as happens with the *bunachis* or civilized people. It is strange but we respect it . . . Yes, it is strange, not because we do not understand it but because for us the law is permanent, to [help us] remain indigenous in conformity with our law, in conformity with our origin and tradition. The new Constitution of Colombia is not our fundamental law [*ley de origen*], but if it helps us achieve the mandate of our forefathers, and recognizes our territory, then we can well create an equilibrium that incorporates elements of this Constitution, subject to our traditions.[32]

The popularity of this letter and others like it appearing in the press clearly derives from the way it signals an alternate way to see the world.

The consistently and defiantly non-Western self-representation of the U'wa,[33] who number about 6,000 and live in the departments of Boyacá, Arauca, and Norte de Santander, in their protests against government licensing of Occidental Petroleum ("Oxy") to conduct seismic testing is another example of the appeal of the "distinct culture" discourse. Their plight received a great deal of sympathetic attention during and following the occupations. Given their small size and anonymity prior to the 1990s, the national and international attention their campaign received following their statement that they were at the point of collective suicide[34] illustrates the power of a claim based on the necessity of preserving a pueblo's culture. For example, one journalist commented that, as oil exploration and exploitation would ruin the U'wa's land and identity, of course they would prefer to die right away rather than slowly.

The vast majority of U'wa complained that the "consultation" required by law prior to issuing a license simply did not take place and that the Ministry of Environment's claims to the contrary were spurious, for the pueblo's traditional authorities had not been present, and only they were authorized to represent the community (Diago García 1996). (One lawyer sympathetic to the U'wa case commented to me that "at times the state so essentializes indigenous people that if a functionary in the Ministry of Environment or DAI is indigenous, his participation in a consultation is felt to suffice.")

All nonindigenous supporters of the U'wa agreed that the pro-Oxy parties had indeed failed to understand and comply with local traditional authority structures. A journalist, criticizing the government's handling of the case, argues that the U'wa have practiced "human sustainable development" for years and that they "walk down a single road, and speak with a single voice, that of their traditional authorities who say":

> Our law is not new. It is not to take more than what one needs, like the land which gives food to every living being, but not to eat too much, because then everything will be finished; we ought to take care of our environment and not maltreat it. For us it is forbidden to kill with a knife, machete, or bullet; our arms are thought and words; our power is wisdom; we prefer death before seeing our sacred elders profaned. Oil (Ruiría) is a sacred living being, a living resource, just as is the blood (of Mother Earth) . . . Eternal Father (Sira) left it below in order to take care of us. Its exploitation would provoke the destruction of our culture and bring our death. (Diago García 1996: 18A)

The text is accompanied by a rather contrived-looking photograph of a young U'wa man in a ceremonial feather crown in a field aiming a bow and arrow; its message, while not as successfully communicated as the text, is the same. The language is compelling; like the letter written by the Ika *mama*, it powerfully critiques Western practices and shows a superior way of thinking about humans' place in the world. Although the text and the photograph illustrate the way the Colombian media sometimes essentialize and romanticize the country's indigenous communities (see Gow and Rappaport, this volume), the overall argument rings true. Most remarkable, however, is the simple fact that it appeared in a national media publication; prior to the 1990s, when beleaguered indigenous communities were sympathetically portrayed in the media, arguments focusing on human rights abuses and economic exploitation were employed. Here sympathy is elicited by drawing attention to the U'wa's distinct culture, in particular their values. Imagining how ONIC could elicit support through similar means, by referring to the distinct culture of the totality of Colombian Indians, shows the discourse's limited usefulness for furthering ONIC's agenda in the dispute pitting it against the traditional authorities.

Note that Green and other national leaders successfully employ generic discourse in other contexts. Indigenous pueblos depicted as guardians of Mother Earth, as protectors of biodiversity, as champions of ethnodevelopment and sustainable development—such language figures prominently in the evolving discourse greatly favored by many ecologically focused international NGOs (see Albert 1997) as well as by the Colombian state at times (see Gros 1996: 270–271). While such arguments convince many people inside and outside of Colombia that ONIC's leadership is crucial to safeguarding the nation's natural resources, however, the arguments are less successful in ONIC's struggles with government agencies over the issue of traditional authorities.

According to Jimeno, the case of the Wayúu dramatically revealed the many interests that were constantly trying to avail themselves of funds going directly to the Wayúu as a result of Law 60. Among the competitors were NGOs (local and extralocal, indigenous and nonindigenous); local non-Indians; other intermediaries; ethnic fence-straddlers (among the Wayúu the example is often given of a non-Indian who has married a Wayúu woman; the Wayúu are matrilineal); *politiqueros*, indigenous and not; and mayors, whom she cast as outright thieves (see Uscátegui Martínez 1996). Jimeno spoke of a case in the High Guajira where several mayors stole a great deal of money. They were denounced and tried, and some of them went to jail. Following this, "other mayors with similar ideas realized that it was unwise to steal outright, better to rob with the help of indigenous partners . . . Finding corruptible Wayúu is not difficult; local NGOs are set up, and the money disappears."

It is not hard to see why the Wayúu case provoked such concern and resulted in denial of funds. Jimeno argued that

> the requirement that "you have to be an Indian" to be allowed to represent indigenous people is no longer sufficient; rather, any claims to authority should be accompanied by evidence of a collective, local agreement regarding who is entitled to represent that community. And

especially in the Wayúu case, the traditional authorities should be *traditional*, and their right to represent clearly validated.

ONIC'S SIDE

Leaders in the national indigenous organizations were delighted with the takeovers, saying that—contrary to their enemies' assertions—the protests demonstrated that the movement was indeed united and that it included many traditional authorities. The takeovers provided ample spaces for airing grievances, a major one being the claim that it was government officials who were producing divisions in the movement. Also seen as very beneficial was the opportunity to demonstrate how hard ONIC and the other indigenous organizations were working to change relations between the movement and local traditional authorities.

For example, Jacanamejoy rejoiced in the unity that was achieved: "The occupation of the Episcopal Palace was an example of acting together . . . MIC, ONIC—rather than thinking that each one only works for their own benefit. Such a thing would be very easy for the senators [Muelas and Muyuy] to do, but to work unilaterally is not the idea. Everyone felt the unity. There are specific problems, but we have a lot in common."

Green also felt that the occupations taught that coming together and speaking from a unified position was indeed possible—and much more effective:

> . . . although now everyone wants to be a senator or a mayor [i.e., there are many divisions], the *compañeros* Muelas, Muyuy were with us, as well as [Francisco] Rojas. No one thought it, but *tac!* We were all of one voice. The solidarity was a very good thing, more important than obtaining the decree.[35] No one spoke about individuals; it was "the indigenous pueblos of Colombia."

Especially important was the evidence of support from far-flung communities, particularly those traditional authorities who participated in local protests. Green said:

> An old U'wa shaman was with us . . . those from the Sierra [Nevada de Santa Marta, where four pueblos that have never linked up with ONIC are found] said they could not occupy a site in Valledupar, but said they were praying for us—and we do not have a tight relationship with them. So we *had* support. So the government found out that we were not just a group seated in Bogotá with no representation . . . found out

that these indigenous activists are not just ordinary people . . . we can have our advisors—anthropologists, lawyers—and participate.

Green spoke darkly of "attempts to separate us [coming] from these vested interests." ONIC has publicly claimed that the division between traditional authorities and the younger men and women who belong to indigenous organizations has been the result of insidious efforts on the part of various government officials to divide the indigenous community:

[The government] imposes divisions that do not exist in our communities. This happens when it treats our elders and our wise men and women as "elderly indigenes" and favors some of them in order to foster oppositions between them and others, and between them and the entire community, bringing them goods, taking advantage of the food crisis in almost all indigenous communities. This promotes paternalism and dependence. (*Utopías* 1996: 24)

Green was of the opinion that the Wayúu situation escalated because Jimeno and Hernán Correa, the DAI consultant (who works with Wayúu communities, see, e.g., Correa 1995), could "do what they wanted" with the Wayúu, in large part because ONIC "has not formed a big movement there . . . this was an example of these efforts to divide the pueblos." The argument DAI made—that its mission should focus on strengthening cultural institutions in indigenous communities—was spurious, he said; the current DAI administration took such a position because it was unaware of the three decades of struggle that members of indigenous organizations had undertaken to secure their rights: "The traditional authorities are the point of conflict. Gladys doesn't like the indigenous organizations and doesn't want the pueblos to organize themselves. She is ignorant about all of the struggle we have had. She puts a lot of emphasis on the traditional authorities and ignores us. We are authorities, but not traditional ones."

Green further criticized DAI, maintaining that it continued to be based on the assimilationist politics of indigenism as forged in Mexico in the 1940s. He added that in far-flung places like the Vaupés, DAI plays no role: its agents have neither money nor, being political appointees, credibility. One lawyer I spoke with agreed that DAI did indeed lack a coherent politics appropriate to the 1990s and did continue to use the indigenist language of its founding charter—still speaking, for example, of "the indigenous problem."

However, other Colombian Indians, while doubtless quite critical of the state, continue to level criticisms at ONIC. For example, a member of the Aruaco (Ika) pueblo, studying for a law degree, said: "One has to criticize ONIC. [When mobilizing the takeovers] they just called the organizations, not the traditional authorities, who are more valuable." She said ONIC was not, in fact, representative and that its leaders did not travel to the communities and consult with them. In contrast, "because AICO works out of the communities, it is more representative, something lacking in ONIC's way of operating."

Note that the criticism that nonindigenous activists leveled at Jimeno concerned what she had said publicly. When speaking off the record, those who have worked long and hard for indigenous rights in Colombia will seriously criticize indigenous organizations and their leadership. The legal and political advances of the past three decades notwithstanding, everyone agrees that the situation of Colombia's indigenous people is very grave and that some of the blame clearly rests with the organizations. Knowledgeable nonindigenous individuals I spoke with were highly critical of some of the actions taken by ONIC during the occupations.

Despite the upbeat tone of many of my conversations regarding the takeovers, a sense of the indigenous movement's being fundamentally divided permeated talk about the current situation. For example, Green commented: "We have advanced but we also have regressed. Indians now can be governors, deputies, senators, but a chaos has come that divides us. Instead of building solidarity, there are more divisions."

The problems that can arise due to divisiveness were illustrated early in the occupations. After the initial group of Wayúu came to Bogotá, many other Wayúu wrote in protest, supporting DAI. A second Wayúu delegation subsequently came to Bogotá (paid for by DAI, which is apparently illegal) to denounce the first group. The divisiveness among the Wayúu has occurred in several other cases where a faction of a given pueblo denounces the local branch of DAI, but another faction supports it.

When Green spoke of the divisiveness—"the *politiqueros* are able to divide the pueblos . . . we continue to fight, but the government is trying to divide our movement"—he noted somewhat defensively that splits were happening elsewhere as well: "the labor movement has two parties, the teachers fight as well, the *campesinos* [peasants] are divided." He said it was ironic that the single most important factor in accomplishing the unity during the takeovers was Jimeno herself. "Even if the various organizations could agree on nothing else, everyone agreed that she had to be opposed."

ANALYSIS

A new indigenous discourse is emerging in the national arena, one that increasingly refers to traditional local authorities and their communities as the appropriate locus for making decisions affecting Colombia's indigenous people. Of course, much decision-making has always occurred at this level; what is changing is the idea that traditional authorities should have state-sanctioned authority because they represent and manifest the authentic cultural difference inhering in a pueblo and because authority is assigned in keeping with traditional custom. Opinions are also changing about the role indigenous organizations should play. The state-conferred mandate empowering ONIC and the regional organizations to represent the pueblos is increasingly scrutinized and questioned along culturalist lines. Criticisms made during the 1980s did not focus nearly so much on the question of whether these organizations' leaders could claim an authority rooted in the traditions of individual pueblos.

Both DAI and ONIC are struggling, within a highly politicized arena, to adjust to these changes and use them to their political advantage if possible. But many people feel that both institutions are outmoded. Both have been criticized for being out of touch with current issues, locked into their own history and their own authority structures. One lawyer speculated about possible solutions to this problem—perhaps a federation of pueblos, or perhaps an entirely new entity, a group of professional indigenous leaders. But who would push for such reforms, given the current circumstances?

We have seen that Green himself considered the problems facing indigenous people to be in part internally generated:

> The situation of Colombia's Indians is more uncertain than before. If we speak about the year 1600, it was the Spaniards and the Indians. Our forefathers knew who they were, what was their culture. But the years have passed and more actors opposed to the pueblos appeared. Not Spaniards but even mestizos opposed to indigenous pueblos . . . there are Protestant sectors wiping out cultures. Some NGOs don't have close relationships with the pueblos, and the money that comes serves to divide them.

In short, Indians now can be the enemy. Those who have converted to Protestantism can be enemies. Mestizos, despite self-identifying as Indians, can be the enemy (an interesting thing to say, given how many ONIC officials have been mestizos). Those aspiring to *politiquero* status can be the enemy. Those who establish NGOs unresponsive to the needs of indigenous communities can be the enemy. But the enemy of what? Indigenous interests, of course. But who gets to decide which interests need to be defended and which defeated? Clearly some Indians are corrupt, and some are *politiqueros*, but not the majority. The enemy's identity is not always evident by any means.

One lawyer strongly criticized ONIC, saying the organization had lost a great deal of legitimacy because of internal contradictions, to the extent that "ONIC calls a meeting, but the regional organizations don't attend."[36] We have seen that some of ONIC's problems in 1996 had originated during the Gaviria administration, which thought the indigenous senators and other elected officials could handle everything between the state and indigenous pueblos, and excluded the organizations. This exacerbated the already difficult relationship between ONIC and Muyuy and Muelas and their respective organizations, MIC and AICO. ONIC has had financial problems as well (which Green acknowledged in his interview).[37] One nonindigenous activist I spoke with, although quite critical of ONIC, felt that such an organization was necessary and was in favor of 1 percent of the funds designated for indigenous communities being earmarked to support ONIC—an idea that had been proposed but not accepted.

It is generally agreed that the internal divisions within ONIC and its problems with the other organizations and the country's pueblos play a major role in the difficulties it faces. Many of its problems ultimately stem from the fact that, being an institution, it behaves like one—protecting itself, attempting to decrease competition, and in general trying to make itself look good and its enemies look bad. Unfortunately, such strategies often only work in the short term. An example of such self-protectiveness is that AICO is not mentioned in the decrees coming out of the takeovers, and this was not accidental. AICO therefore lacks representation in the permanent *mesas de concertación*. Sadly, many examples can be found of attempts by ONIC to discredit its rivals during the summer's events. Another example of self-protectiveness comes from the negotiations to end the occupations, in which ONIC continually argued in favor of language giving power to the indigenous organizations and the government representatives continually insisted on language giving power to the traditional authorities. One of the lawyers who had written some of the documents stated that sometimes DAI simply would not budge on this matter and so in the end prevailed.

ONIC's guarded responses to the increased visibility and legitimacy of local traditional authorities were clearly motivated by self-protection. On the one hand, leaders obviously have to speak with respect and deference about the elders and others who hold positions of authority via traditional means. On the other hand, leaders of indigenous organizations also need to claim and perform a distinct authority, difficult when traditional authorities operate independently of the national indigenous organizations. Green's argument that ONIC is entitled to represent Colombia's Indians because it has fought for so long can be turned on its head by an official like Jimeno. Speaking of how the indigenous movement was born in a time of great racism and powerful capitalist interests that opposed land repossessions, what the movement conquered in the way of lands and what it acquired in the way of political experience (especially CRIC and CRIT, the Regional Indigenous Council of Tolima) provided leaders with a specific political perspective. Furthermore, the nonindigenous intermediaries in these two organizations had been extremely politicized (a point often made by people knowledgeable about the indigenous movement) and had favored alternatives to the state, including socialist, revolutionary solutions. Jimeno asked, "Given that ONIC comes out of this experience and this perspective, what *is* the relationship between it and these sixty-four or sixty-five languages and eighty-five pueblos? ONIC emerges from all of this history and cannot reflect all of the diversities represented by the pueblos."

Jimeno provided many examples of indigenous pueblos organizing themselves along other lines: the Kogui of the Sierra Nevada de Santa María, the Awá (Kwaiquer), the Pasto, the Kankuamo, some Wayúu, the Aruaco (Ika), and some Emberá;[38] all these pueblos oppose such a militant politics, she said. She added that while AICO's political proposal was indeed to support and strengthen the traditional authorities, because it is an actor in the national arena, in fact it had come to have a "joint position" and hence was vulnerable to some of ONIC's institutional problems.

We see that ONIC, and the kind of activism it represents, is in a precarious position—one reason why it took such a risky action, according to a knowledgeable lawyer. It must be a political movement and be effective, but some of the measures it must take to be maximally effective (such as relying on nonindigenous advisors) invite criticism. Maintaining a tight, efficient bureaucratic structure is criticized as following a "white model." If its officers and activists are young men (and a few women), some of them university-educated, accusations about not including "the old ones" appear. Celebrating the movement's history of thirty years of struggle encourages an unfavorable image of a militant, anticapitalist movement that cannot adapt to current reality—cannot, despite its rhetoric, deal with the fact that it represents an extremely diverse constituency, some of whom reject such representation. ONIC's and its regional affiliates' legitimacy to a large extent derives from nonindigenous institutions: the Colombian state and international governments and NGOs. Its labor-union structure and organizational principles mitigate against restructuring itself, for such a process would weaken it further. Faced with criticism from other indigenous leaders in Bogotá, the communities, and a growing number of "individualist" indigenous state officials, some of them would-be *politiqueros*, with decreasing financial support, and with challenges from bad-faith government agencies, it hunkers down and at times engages in behavior that only fuels the criticism.[39]

Green did affirm that part of ONIC's project was indeed "to strengthen the culture and to strengthen the traditional authorities" (he added, "because we'll *have* to"). He acknowledged that ONIC did have to work harder at having a tighter relationship with "the old ones." Jacanamejoy also spoke of devising ways to include the traditional authorities—"the *cabildos*, the *mamas*"—in decision-making at the national level. But despite the risk, ONIC also must periodically demonstrate that in certain contexts its abilities to represent the indigenous pueblos surpass those of the traditional authorities. Describing the way the U'wa had been "tricked" into approving a license for seismic exploration, Green noted that "the government said, 'We'll do it directly [with the communities], not with the organizations.' But this harms them much more, because those leaders don't know the dangers. The government only says, 'We're going to give you money,' and the community is content." Such statements can be interpreted as generalized assertions about the incompetence and ignorance of traditional authorities. Finding a way to promote an image of indispensability and maintain ONIC's legitimacy and political strength, while managing to avoid being seen as casting aspersions on the pueblos' elders and their traditions, requires great political skill and spaces to employ it in.

The Wayúu case dramatically reveals the contradictions that inevitably emerge in arrangements involving a switch to more direct interaction between the state and its indigenous pueblos. Among the highly decentralized Wayúu, where leadership is confined to local settlement and local matrilineage, traditional mechanisms for determining what the Wayúu collectively think simply do not exist. Neither *cabildos* nor other kinds of federation models are a Wayúu tradition; ironically, when the new forms of "traditional authority" structures Jimeno is asking for are constituted, her assertion that "the Wayúu are not obeying Wayúu norms" will continue to be correct. While the Wayúu case exploded for many reasons, a major one was because (unlike the U'wa, who are said by the press to speak with a single voice) the Wayúu speak with thousands of voices—their leaders are thousands of maternal uncles. Finding a way to represent themselves collectively at any level higher than the local matrilineage in a manner respecting the traditional authority structures would seem to be a difficult task.[40]

CONCLUSIONS

Colombia's indigenous rights movement has focused on a struggle for recognition, greater autonomy and self-determination, rights to land, and basic human rights. The events of the summer of 1996 brought to national attention the slow pace of implementation of legislated changes and in some respects a retreat from earlier gains. The events validated some changes and provided ample evidence that other changes had not occurred. Everyone agrees that Colombia's indigenous people have progressed in their fight in several important respects. As Jacanamejoy put it, "It's not the same as during the 1960s and 1970s when the policy was 'hit them on the head.' Now the government listens to the indigenous officials [such as the two senators]." Comments are sometimes heard to the effect that poor peasants are now worse off than Indians—for example, Jacanamejoy stated: "There are others as well—Afro-Colombians, campesinos, workers. At times we are better off than these other sectors, so we have to make claims for them as well."

The summer's events brought to the surface a building tension that formed during the 1980s, and increased during the discussions leading to the 1991 Constitution, between the organized indigenous movement and various government agencies, in particular DAI. To what degree should these organizations be constituted by the state as the legitimate representatives of Colombia's indigenous peoples, and to what degree should the traditional authorities play this role? The original group of Wayúu traveled to Bogotá precisely over this issue: they claimed a right to funds intended for Wayúu communities, but DAI claimed that they were not, in fact, traditional authorities. Of course, many other indigenous grievances were aired during the series of takeovers and strikes sparked by this dispute, but this problem remains one of the most intractable ones, for it is not only a dispute between the indigenous movement and various government agencies but an issue that all of Colombia's indigenous people are debating as well.[41]

The conflict between traditional authorities in many communities and ONIC and its regional affiliates is growing in importance because of the structural changes following the 1991 Constitution, which by awarding significant power to "indigenous authorities" considerably raised the stakes for the winner of this struggle. Given that some of the indigenous movement's legitimacy rests on indigenous people being seen as culturally distinct, the more a person becomes equipped to deal with nonindigenous society (i.e., speaking Spanish fluently, receiving a university education, living in Bogotá or other urban site), the less "authentic" (and hence the less legitimate a representative) that person will be considered by some sectors, and this of course applies to organizations as well. We have an interesting situation in which certain skills can be both an advantage and a handicap. The ways in which traditional local authorities increasingly successfully perform their identity in the metropolitan arena, as illustrated by the U'wa case, significantly contrast with the ways in which indigenous activists and leaders have represented themselves until now. Both indigenous identity and political and administrative skills were required to ensure that the leaders would be taken seriously by the non-Indians they dealt with (some of whom, of course, did everything they could to undercut this authority). But during the 1990s, for certain activists, the very fact of being a leader in a national indigenous organization began subtly but significantly to increase the probability that their right to represent Colombian Indians would be challenged. A new set of criteria had appeared (new in the sense of being taken seriously for the first time); in a way, winning some of the battles for recognition and institutionalization permitted an imaginary of indigenousness to emerge that privileges, in a favorable manner, alterity, "authenticity," tradition, and hinterland far more than previously.[42]

In a study of Inga Indians in the Sibundoy valley, Robert Dover distinguishes between *traditional authorities* and *leaders:*

> . . . whereby the former achieve a measure of structural and *de jure* legitimacy because community members select them in a traditional manner to be their authorities; and the state, through its legislation, sanctions these selections; whereas the latter have neither a place in the traditional structure of community authority, nor were they recognized until recently by the state. Indigenous *líderes* do have a *de facto* au-

thority that they have both appropriated and to a certain extent been granted by their traditionalist communities. (1995: 2–3)

Dover is talking about local leaders; if we examine the national level we find a significant amount of *de jure* (state-sanctioned) and *de facto* authority in national leaders' hands as well and an extremely dynamic situation with respect to the perceived legitimacy, or lack thereof, of both kinds. What is interesting about the summer's events is how, during the negotiations, these claims to legitimacy and the affirmations or challenges that came in response (by the government, by the media, by other institutions such as the church) revealed some of the underlying problematic concerning indigenous authority in its dealings with the state. Some of this, Dover argues, derives from the multiple meanings of the terminology:

> ... there appears to be a measure of ambiguity to the term *authority*, not only as regards who is able to exercise it, but also to whom is *authority* responsible, how is *authority* expressed both in traditional as well as non-traditional terms, and from what or from whom does *authority* draw its cultural and social legitimacy. (1995: 3)

ONIC and to some degree other organizations that aspire to represent all of the nation's indigenous pueblos are in a quandary. The way ONIC leaders represent themselves and the organization when justifying their claims to speak for all of Colombia's indigenous people is to refer to the past struggle. But the claim that Green was able to make—"we are authorities, but not traditional ones"—is less and less persuasive and even sounds a bit defensive in today's discussions, which look to traditions seen to have sedimented over a long time in rural settings to confirm the validity of a claim to represent an indigenous community, pueblo, or collectivity of pueblos. Clearly the paradigm for indigenous self-representation characterizing the 1990s differs in certain important respects from the one that put the indigenous movement on the map during previous decades.

Because language that champions the local, the traditional, and the culturally different has gained in popularity, both sides of the dispute between ONIC and DAI had to jump on this discursive bandwagon, and the two sides accused each other of not really supporting the local traditional authorities. Clearly, both sides were correct: neither in fact totally supported the new decentralization discourse, Jimeno's and Green's assertions to the contrary, because the implications do not favor their institutional interests.

The indigenous population of Colombia is conceived of in two, at times contradictory, ways: collectively as a sector of the nation's citizenry and as members of pueblos. Of course all citizens of a country are both members of the nation and of smaller units; but the state's increasing tendency to construct its indigenous authorities as "leaders of a pueblo," as opposed to "representatives of indigenous Colombian citizens," poses problems for leaders like ONIC officers. Unlike Guatemalan activists' ongoing successful (albeit partial) work to establish a Pan-Mayanism, Pan-Colombian indigenousness lacks Colombia-specific symbols other than those deriving from shared colonial and neocolonial history. Generic cultural alterity discourse at the national level is in the process of being invented; and ONIC leaders are probably trying to figure out how to borrow a page or two from U'wa leader Roberto Cobaría's book on how to reach an international audience while performing traditional indigenousness, for the U'wa have achieved a remarkable visibility.[43] However, activists in the indigenous movement often cannot avail themselves of local authority-conveying symbols because they signal knowledge gained over many years in a rural site and explicit recognition by a community. Ironically—because organizations like ONIC played a major role in securing the constitutional guarantees—the way indigenous people in Colombia are coming to be perceived, in part due to the effects of the 1991 Constitution and subsequent legislation, is calling into question the adequacy of the kind of representation provided by the leaders of such organizations.[44]

In the last twenty years, indigenous mobilizing has characterized virtually all Latin American countries containing indigenous populations. This mobilizing has never intended to establish a sovereign, exclusively indigenous state or even a "state within a state." In general, indigenous activists seek to ensure land rights, human and civil rights, rights to political and cultural autonomy (Yashar 1996: 93, 96), and an increase in participation in the national arena (see Assies et al. 2000: 301).

Expectably, the shape these movements take in their respective countries varies. For example, Guatemala's indigenous majority has mobilized as Mayas, an example of ethnogenesis, since thirty years ago "Maya" was a term used largely by anthropologists and archeologists. The contrasts between Colombia's indigenous mobilizing and the Guatemalan case are telling. While a lot of diversity is found within Guatemala's movement, to one who is familiar with the Colombian case Guatemala's movement appears to be far more politically and ideologically united, despite the far greater numbers of activists, and cultural recovery has played a far more prominent role (see Warren 1998). Although one finds many statements in Colombia about its indigenous people in the aggregate, culturalist discourse referring to a distinctively Colombian panindigenism is a work in progress. While Colombia's activists speak of a shared history of oppression and exploitation, when speaking of shared culture they use symbols from the international indigenous movement—in fact, they often speak of the incredibly rich cultural *diversity* found within the nation's borders.

The summer's events revealed the familiar scenario of two organizations frequently at odds once again squaring off, each accusing the other of acting out of "petty interests" or of being corrupt. But when the director of DAI states publicly that its policies must work to strengthen the nation's traditional authorities rather than indigenous organizations, more is going on than simple ill-advised bureaucratic mischievousness (although the accusation that DAI is promoting a policy aimed at introducing divisions and inequities into indigenous communities is not without validity). Clearly, the issues are more important than the at times silly spats between indigenous leaders and government bureaucrats, for the dispute reveals one of the more important issues the entire country is trying to work out: who has the right to represent Colombia's indigenous peoples? If leaders in the regional and national organizations are to continue to achieve respect and legitimacy in the eyes of Colombia's citizenry and interested international parties, the degree to which gaining such respect and authority requires performing and embodying a culturally distinct indigenousness needs to be established. There are potential solutions; one of them, mentioned above, would be local pueblos' selection of their national representatives, eliminating the regional organizations and ONIC. The current situation in which local authorities are pitted against the ONIC leadership is lamentable, for the perceived incompatibility of their state-conferred authority with the authority held by local traditional leaders provides abundant ammunition to indigenous Colombia's many enemies.

Notes

1. In Colombia, thanks to all who have helped my research on indigenous organizing, in particular Raúl Arango, Jaime Arocha, Ana Cecelia Betancourt, Guillermo Carmona, François Correa, Segisfredo Franco, Abadio Green, Leonor Herrera, Victor Jacanamejoy, Myriam Jimeno, Hernando Muñoz, Guillermo Padilla, Roberto Pineda, María Clemencia Ramírez, Elizabeth Reichel, Roque Roldán, Enrique Sánchez, Esther Sánchez, María Lucía Sotomayor, Adolfo Triana, Carlos Uribe, Simón Valencia, Miguel Vázquez, Mar-

tín von Hildebrand, the Instituto Colombiano de Antropología, the Department of Anthropology at the Universidad de los Andes, members of the Consejo Regional Indígena del Vaupés (CRIVA), and officials of the Organización Nacional de Indígenas de Colombia (ONIC). Martín Franco greatly facilitated interviewing and collecting documents. Thanks is particularly due to Gladys Jimeno, director of the Dirección General de Asuntos Indígenas, who gave so much of her time and provided access to DAI's archives. Trips to Colombia (1985, 1987, 1989, 1991, 1992, 1993, 1996, 2000) have been funded in part by the Dean's Office, School of Humanities and Social Sciences, MIT. The materials examined in this chapter were discussed earlier at a conference on "Language Communities, States, and Global Culture: The Discourse of Identity in the Americas," held at the University of Iowa in October 1996. I would like to thank the conference's organizers, Laura Graham, Nora England, and Mercedes Niño-Murcio, for inviting me to participate. For help thinking through the ideas presented here, thanks to David Gow, Joanne Rappaport, Terence Turner, Donna Lee Van Cott, and Kay Warren. Not all of those acknowledged above agree with this chapter's analysis, and the responsibility for the ideas set forth here is entirely my own.

2. The Páez are called Nasa now; see Gow and Rappaport (this volume).
3. On Quintín Lame, see Pineda (1984), Rappaport (1990), Gros (1991: 179), and Molano (1994). On land struggles and armed insurgency, see Triana (1993) and the articles in NACLA (1998).
4. Where stylistically possible I use "indigenous" rather than "Indian," but I retain the latter term when a noun must be used, despite its controversial status. "Indigene" is not really English, and I find "native" (see Gow and Rappaport, this volume) equally problematic.
5. Van Cott (personal communication, 2001) has suggested that CRIC is not identified more tightly with the Nasa because many of the organization's leaders have been from the Coconuco pueblo. The Coconuco are less able to perform indigenousness successfully because they lost their language years ago; nor do they wear pueblo-specific costume. Drawing on the political purchase of pueblo identity, therefore, might empower the Nasa section of CRIC.
6. Note that "indigenist" has two well-established, often confusing meanings. The first, negatively valenced and most often used in reference to state policy toward indigenous peoples, indicates an integrationist position; this is particularly the case with the word's Spanish and Portuguese cognates. The second meaning refers to any individuals (Indian or non-Indian) or institutions in favor of indigenous rights.
7. Beginning in 1549, the Crown granted *resguardos* to New Spain's indigenous populations, which collectively managed and worked them and paid tribute (Triana 1993: 101–106). From then on the numerous efforts to expropriate *resguardos* led to many of them falling into decline. In 1890 Law 89 reversed the previous "progressivist" legislative trend during the nineteenth century that

attempted to eliminate tribute-paying and privatize collective lands. The new legislation strengthened indigenous claims to *resguardo* lands and became the foundation for repossessions during the 1970s and 1980s. In addition to territory granted during the colonial era, new lands have been given to indigenous communities during the past thirty years: most in the form of *resguardos*, some as *reservas* (reserves; see Roldán 2000: 49–53).

8. Dover and Rappaport (1996: 13). Gros (1991) provides a history and analysis of the Colombian indigenous movement up to the 1980s and discusses the broader implications of Latin America's indigenous movements in his most recent book (2000).

9. Born in 1959 in the Comarca of Kuna Yala in Panama, Green (whose Kuna name is Manipiniktikinya) studied in Catholic schools in Panama City. He then studied philosophy and theology at the Universidad Bolivariana de Medellín in Colombia and earned a postgraduate degree in linguistics at the Universidad de los Andes in Bogotá. He became a Colombian citizen in 1994 (Navia 1994). He has traveled widely and published a significant amount (e.g., 1996, 1997, 1998). During his tenure as president of ONIC several important volumes co-written by ONIC appeared (e.g., ONIC et al. 1995; ONIC and Ministerio de Agricultura 1998).

10. He notes that some scholars feel that this tendency, a legacy from Spain, characterizes Colombians as a whole. All quotes are from Padilla (1993: 14).

11. The context of this protest is, expectably, quite complicated. First, as leadership among the Wayúu is very horizontal, any Wayúu who seek to represent large units are almost automatically suspect. Second, Wayúu regions differ significantly in their interactions with government officials, in particular those in DAI.

   The main grievance had to do with impediments to fulfilling the mandate of Law 60, established in 1993, which provides for direct transfer of state funds to local indigenous communities, administered by local mayoral offices. Given that there are 150,000 Wayúu in Colombia, the sums of money are considerable—Jimeno said that the treasury of the mayoral offices contained 12,000,000 pesos belonging to them.

12. Abadio Green told me that negotiations stalled because the Wayúu delegation kept insisting that Jimeno not be present during the negotiations, and the government said it could not negotiate without her. "Days, days, seventeen days dealing with this issue of one person."

13. Caquetá, Amazonas, Putumayo, Guainía, Guaviare, Vaupés, Cauca, Chocó, Córdoba, Valle, and Caldas.

14. People I spoke with were divided with respect to whether Muelas and Muyuy were there as representatives of their organizations or simply as high-profile and respected Indians. Neither AICO nor MIC was formally represented during the negotiations at the Episcopal Palace.

15. Quotation from Navia (1996). The degree of nationwide communication and coordination was a notable achievement. ONIC members inside the Episco-

pal Palace communicated via cellular telephones and a radio transmitter that allowed them to maintain contact with thirty-five organizations throughout the country.

16. See Betancourt and Rodríguez (1994: 22) and Rappaport (1996).

17. For instance, an ad placed by various leftist and liberal organizations on July 25 in the newspaper *El Espectador* supports the Indians' demands. It highlights the dearth of progress five years since the 1991 Constitution, saying that although successive administrations had signed multiple agreements, these had not been kept. The ad also criticizes the government's refusal to implement the decree establishing the mechanism through which the ETIs, the constitutionally mandated new indigenous territorial units, are to be established.

18. *Concertación* means a coming together to achieve a goal. The state also agreed to give 12,000 hectares of land over a period of three years and to make every effort to assure that the perpetrators of a massacre in El Nilo (in which twenty Nasa were killed) would be punished and the victims' families would be taken care of. Special groups to study the indigenous problematic in Cauca and Nariño were also created (García 1996). Note that the agreement was signed at the beginning of a series of violent mass demonstrations against government-sponsored fumigation of coca crops in the Caquetá, Putumayo, and Guaviare departments. During the takeovers national indigenous leaders, while occasionally speaking of the plight of other marginalized people in Colombia, did not ever link their protest with the predicament of the coca-growing campesinos; some analysts saw a link between the two actions, however, saying that the government did not want to fight battles on two fronts at the same time. Green voiced the frequently heard complaint that the campaigns to fumigate coca fields resulted in *colonos* invading indigenous territories, clearing the forest, and bringing the violence with them. See Ramírez (n.d.).

19. However, some of the demands the Indians had originally made were not part of the agreement. A solution to the plight of the Zenú living in the highly conflictual zone of Córdoba, whose leaders have been systematically wiped out by guerrillas and paramilitaries, was not found. Nor were several demands relating to the government's failure to live up to the mandates of the 1991 Constitution resolved (*El Espectador* 1996b). The most polemical part of the negotiation was the creation of indigenous territories. Despite the fact that the Constitution had mandated an even more comprehensive territorial order, indigenous territorial entities (ETIs), no resolution had been found even on how to establish indigenous *territories* (Navia 1996).

20. Territorial ordination can be glossed as territorial legislation or legislation promoting a new territorial regime in which the political map of Colombia would be redrawn.

21. "If the Constitution is not applied as it ought to be, they are going to finish us off not only with bullets but with highways, with oil exploration, hydro-

electric dams, interoceanic canals. The indigenous person is not consulted as to whether the project should be undertaken, but to negotiate reimbursements after the decision has been made" (Green, as cited in Navia 1996). This complaint is intimately tied to the land issue but should be analyzed separately, because some of the issues are fundamentally different from the long history of land disputes concerning indigenous subsistence efforts—agriculture or foraging and hunting. Green's comment refers to the new forms of commercial development, said to harm indigenous communities by the extraction of a given resource itself and by the infrastructural development projects (e.g., new roads, canals, military bases) needed for successful exploitation. An additional complaint concerned prospecting for pharmaceuticals and the testing, patenting, and ultimate marketing of human genetic resources (*Utopías* 1996: 25).

22. See *Utopías* (1996: 23). While Colombia's indigenous people appear to control an abundant quantity of land (approximately 28 million hectares), according to some estimates, non-Indians are found in as much as 80 percent of these territories, and the majority of Indians continue to live in the most isolated and least fertile zones.

23. I identify Abadio Green, Víctor Jacanamejoy, and Gladys Jimeno because they were speaking for the record. Others, both indigenous and nonindigenous, did not want to be identified. I interviewed several lawyers, all of whom had been involved in indigenous issues; some, but not all, are acknowledged in note 1.

24. See Ramírez (1995) on Afro-Colombian/indigenous confrontations; see Ramírez (n.d.) on indigenous/*colono* conflicts.

25. The occupiers of the Episcopal Palace stated: "Paradoxically, once the Constitution recognized that Indians owned their lands, even greater institutional obstacles arose to guaranteeing this. During the fiscal period of 1995 INCORA failed to execute 50% of the $11 thousand million (pesos) available for buying lands and improving and cleaning *resguardos* [i.e., clearing them of non-Indians]. The Executive Junta stated that it did not buy lands because of lack of anything to buy" (*Utopías* 1996: 25; see also Navia 1996).

26. One lawyer described various factors which contributed to the dispute between the Wayúu delegation and DAI. The extensive decentralization characteristic of the Wayúu is one; another major one is struggle over the future of the port of Maicao, a center for a lot of smuggling (including coca, arms, and other kinds of contraband), prostitution, and with it AIDS. The port is in a single *resguardo;* how to help its members is a problem because there are so many interests behind these activities. There is also a dispute with the state over the Salinas de Manaure salt flats. State exploitation had resulted in the virtual disappearance of the birds, fish, and other species found in the mangrove swamps, the community's source of food. The state responded by saying that 20 percent of the owners would be Wayúu; although some Wayúu

politicians liked this arrangement, much remained unresolved, so the dispute continued (see Correa 1995).

27. All of the information on the history of DAI is from M. Jimeno and Triana (1985).

28. According to M. Jimeno and Triana, the church lost power because its mission—ideological penetration and political subjection—had been almost completed (1985: 81). The main indication of this decline in church power was the 1962 agreement between the Ministry of Government and the Summer Institute of Linguistics/Wycliffe Bible Translators (SIL/WBT), justified in terms of "scientific and practical investigation" to aid acculturation. Hence, although the church lost ground, in a sense religious colonialism continued, albeit sub rosa: public documents concerning the agreement lacked any mention whatsoever of SIL/WBT's proselytizing aims (M. Jimeno and Triana 1985: 102).

29. DAI's strongest effort to control indigenous communities occurred during the several attempts between 1977 and 1981 to pass legislation (Proyecto de Ley) that would have given extensive power to the state, clearly along clientalist lines. Again, DAI reserved for itself the power to recognize the existence of an indigenous community as such. Communities could not become legal entities under this law and were not able to make contracts; rather, permission from DAI to do virtually anything would be required. But strong opposition led to the bill's defeat every time (Triana 1978; M. Jimeno and Triana 1985: 105–106).

30. Jimeno, a psychologist, had previously worked on human rights issues, including indigenous rights (see Jimeno 1994), and had been a negotiator in the Wayúu dispute with the government over the Manaure salt flats (see Correa 1995).

31. Jimeno illustrated this point with the Guambiano case, stating that the pueblo is in crisis because some of its advisors and even some of the *cabildo* governors are allied with narcotraffickers. "But, being the state, *we* can't accuse them of corruption. Because they are minorities, they deserve their lands, they deserve to have their human rights respected; their cultures are fragile." She repeated that whereas *she* could not say that the organizations were corrupt, someone like me could, giving me a clue as to why she agreed to talk to me.

32. Cited in Gros (1993: 8; my translation). Padilla (1993: 27) also cites this letter; its entire text can be found in Carta Abierta (1996).

33. Also known as Tunebo; see Osborne (1995).

34. See Camargo (1996) and Morales Manchego (1996). The main complaint had to do with whether U'wa permission was granted or not. Following a meeting in January 1996, the Ministry of the Environment issued a license in February. ONIC accused Jimeno of arranging a farcical "consultation" in the city of Arauca in which the U'wa were "consulted" by being told what was going to happen. ONIC quotes Jimeno as saying: "The consultation is not to say yes

or no to a project, but to inform the community how they might be affected by the works that are going to happen" (citing the *acta* of the meeting, quoted in *Utopías* 1996: 23). Green commented to me that to inform the members of a community about how they are going to die is not a consultation.

Who among the U'wa actually indicated that seismic exploration would be acceptable is not clear; some U'wa claimed that those who agreed were not in fact recognized as U'wa by the community, and others said that an *acta* was signed; but, rather than constituting a legal agreement, it was only an acknowledgment of having "attended a simple meeting" (Diago García 1996: 18A).

35. Several knowledgeable people commented that, in signing the decree, the national indigenous movement once again revealed that it had been coopted by the government, settling for too little when it agreed to end the occupations: the leaders should have been able to see that, after all is said and done, they had won merely promises written on two pieces of paper. One lawyer remarked that a lot of the language negotiated was on the order of "that the government carry out such-and-such decree." But, as he pointed out, once a decree is signed, legally it *has* to be carried out. Writing decrees that mandate carrying out previous decrees is a pointless exercise because the problem is one of political will.

36. ONIC by no means always supports the regional affiliates. For example, in 1998 it issued a stinging rebuke to the Vaupés regional affiliate, CRIVA (Regional Indigenous Council of the Vaupés), accusing it of restricting candidates for elected positions to members of the highest Cubeo clan and attributing the "little credibility" it commands to the "unethical" transfer and mismanagement of funds by a string of indigenous mayors of the capital, Mitú (ONIC and Ministerio de Agricultura 1998: 251).

37. Not only Green but Jacanamejoy too lamented the end of the period during the 1970s and 1980s when there was international support for building indigenous organizations: "at present, the European countries are abandoning us." My interview with Green revealed other worries about ONIC weakness. Discussing how the takeover began, he said it had indeed been spontaneous in the sense that ONIC had not planned that the Wayúu would take over DAI offices; however, ONIC had been waiting and hoping for something like this to happen. During their executive meetings everyone would agree that a mobilization needed to occur, but nothing ever happened. (Every six months indigenous representatives from the twenty-seven departments come to Bogotá for a meeting in ONIC's headquarters.)

38. For example, in 1998 the Emberá-Katío members of one *resguardo* expelled ONIC, complaining about an "indigenous elite" who did nothing but personally profit from their position. In particular, nonindigenous ONIC consultants "ignored our highest authorities, made decisions without consulting with the communities," and only paid attention to the contracts ONIC had

signed (Guzmán 1998). ONIC responded, defending itself (*El Espectador* 1998a).

39. ONIC is by no means unique in this respect. Michael Brown (personal communication, 1996) notes that indigenous federations throughout lowland South America grapple with this problem: unlike tribal governments in the United States and Canada, these federations' assertions are at times backed up neither by law nor by the sentiments of their constituencies. See Brown (1995).

40. Note that smuggling along the Colombia/Venezuela border is an extremely important, decades-old, and widespread Wayúu practice, often managed by the traditional authorities. Which authority should prevail, the state or the local elders? Although my example is tongue in cheek, similar issues come up again and again in the courts, with verdicts concerning illegal activities often favoring the pueblos. See Sánchez on constitutional court decisions concerning required abandonment of disabled children among the nomadic Nukak, abandonment of newborn twins among the U'wa (also see Saravena 1999), and the use of whipping and stocks (*cepo*) among the Nasa (Sánchez 2000).

41. The question of creating supracommunity indigenous organizations is fraught with difficulties in many Latin American countries. Stephen, for example, analyzes the negotiations among indigenous representatives from different regions of Mexico following the San Andrés Peace Accords over this issue, which depends in part on how autonomy is defined. Single-ethnicity organizations were preferred by some, multiethnic (including local mestizos) by others (Stephen 1997). Also see Ramos (1998) and Albert (1997) on Brazil.

42. An article by Green (1998: 4) illustrates creative use of local symbols to make arguments about Colombian pueblos as a collectivity. For example, he mentions the Yuruparí ritual of the Vaupés Tukanoans to make a point about the need to unify: "The Yuruparí ritual can only be carried out if there is community; without community it's an empty ritual. Without indigenous organization, one cannot be a part of all indigenous pueblos; without universal community it isn't possible to sustain the world."

43. The U'wa won Spain's Bartolomé de las Casas prize for pro-indigenous activism and the U.S. Goldman award for ecology (*El Tiempo* 1998; *El Espectador* 1998b). Sadly, FARC's murder of three North American pro-indigenous environmentalists put the pueblo on the front page of thousands of newspapers (see *El Espectador* 1997). Fortunately, the pueblo has so far won the campaign against Oxy. See Albert (1997: 194–198) for an insightful discussion of the "dialectic" between generic ethnicity and specific tradition during the successful Kayapó-organized Altamira protests in 1989 and later "eco-indigenist" projects.

44. National leaders wear their pueblo dress all the time, don it under certain circumstances, or signal indigenousness in some fashion. Green has shoulder-length hair and wears a Kuna *mola* (a colorful reverse-appliqué panel of cloth)

sewn on the back of his denim jacket, utilizing the best-known symbol of the Kuna pueblo. As *molas* are traditionally worn by women, the message being sent by Green's jacket is a fine example of Graham's (this volume) second-order indexicality.

References

Albert, Bruce. 1997. Territorialité, ethnopolitique et développement: A propos du mouvement indien en Amazonie Brésilienne. *Cahiers des Amériques Latines* 23: 177–210.

Alvarado, Raimundo. 1994. Al debate, la ley territorial. *El Tiempo*, August 15, 7A.

Arocha, Jaime Rodríguez. 1992. Los negros y la Nueva Constitución Colombiana de 1991. *América Negra* 3: 39–56.

———. 1993. El sentipensamiento de los pueblos negros en la construcción de Colombia. In Carlos Uribe T., ed., *La construcción de las Américas*, 159–174. Bogotá: Universidad de los Andes.

Assies, Willem, Gemma van der Haar, and André Hoekema. 2000. Diversity as a Challenge: A Note on the Dilemmas of Diversity. In Willem Assies, Gemma van der Haar, and André Hoekema, eds., *The Challenge of Diversity: Indigenous Peoples and Reform of the State in Latin America*, 295–313. Amsterdam: Thela Thesis.

Avirama, Jesús, and Rayda Márquez. 1994. The Indigenous Movement in Colombia. In Donna Van Cott, ed., *Indigenous Peoples and Democracy in Latin America*, 83–105. New York: St. Martin's.

Betancourt, Ana Cecilia, and Hernán Rodríguez. 1994. After the Constitution: Indigenous Proposals for Territorial Demarcation in Colombia. *Abya Yala News: Journal of the South and Meso American Indian Information Center* 8 (1–2): 22–23.

Brown, Michael F. 1995. Facing the State, Facing the World: Amazonia's Native Leaders and the New Politics of Identity. *L'Homme* 33 (2–4): 307–326.

Buenahora Febres-Cordero, Jaime. 1991. *El proceso constituyente: De la propuesta estudiantil a la quiebra del bipartidismo.* Bogotá: Tercer Mundo Editores.

Camargo, Gabriela. 1996. Comunidad Uwá a punto del suicidio. *El Espectador*, July 5.

Campos Zornosa, Yesid. 1984. Colombian Indian Organizations. *Cultural Survival Quarterly* 8: 26–28.

Carta Abierta. 1996. *Journal of Latin American Anthropology* 1 (2): 18–21.

Centro de Investigación y Educación Popular (CINEP), et al. 1996. Demandamos pronta y satisfactoria respuesta a las exigencias indígenas. *El Espectador*, July 25.

Colombia Update. 1995. International Aid Needed to Solve Colombia's Crisis: Call for a Special UN Rapporteur. (Spring) 7 (1–2): 1–2.

Consejo Regional Indígena del Cauca (CRIC). 1981. *Diez años de lucha: Historia y documentos.* Serie Controversia Nos. 91–92. Bogotá: CINEP (Centro de Investigación y Educación Popular).

Correa, François. 1993. A manera de epílogo—Derechos étnicos: Derechos humanos. In F. Correa, ed., *Encrucijadas de Colombia Amerindia*, 319–334. Bogotá: Instituto Colombiano de Antropología.

Correa, Hernán Darío. 1995. Las Salinas industriales de Manaure, el territorio de los Wayúu y las dificultades de una concertación intercultural. In ONIC, CECOIN, and GhK, *Tierra profanada: Grandes proyectos en territorios indígenas de Colombia*, 235–258. Santafé de Bogotá: Disloque Editores.

Diago García, Vanessa. 1996. U'wa: No a exploración de petróleo: Aunque fuentes de la petrolera Occidental señalan que detrás de su posición está la guerrilla, los U'wa no hablaron de lucha de clases, sino de religión. *El Tiempo*, September 1, 18A.

Dirección General de Asuntos Indígenas. 1998. *Los pueblos indígenas en el país y en América: Elementos de política colombiana e internacional.* Bogotá: Ministerio de Gobierno.

Dover, Robert. 1995. Nucanchi Gente Pura: The Ideology of *Recuperación* in the Inga Communities of Colombia's Sibundoy Valley. Ph.D. thesis, Indiana University.

Dover, Robert V. H., and Joanne Rappaport. 1996. Introduction. In Joanne Rappaport, ed., *Ethnicity Reconfigured: Indigenous Legislators and the Colombian Constitution of 1991.* Special issue of *Journal of Latin American Anthropology* 1 (2) (1996): 2–17.

Dover, Robert, and María Eugenia Vargas. 1999. Reindianization and Language Politics in the Sierra Nevada de Santa Marta. Paper given at the American Anthropological Association Chicago meeting, November.

Echeverry, Blanca. 1998. Editorial. *El Tiempo*, February 12.

El Espectador. 1996a. Indígenas desprotegidos. July 6, 5-A.

———. 1996b. Nuevo amanecer indígena: Desalojada la conferencia episcopal, cuya mediación fué decisiva. August 10.

———. 1997. "Ella tenía permiso de Farc": El esposo de Ingrid Washinawatok dijo ayer que su mujer estaba autorizada por las Farc para estar con los U'was. March 28.

———. 1998a. Organización indígena aclara las acusaciones de los embera. March 27.

———. 1998b. Otro premio para los u'wa. April 21, 13-A.

El Tiempo. 1998. U'was recibieron el Bartolomé de las Casas. July 22, 7-B.

Findji, María Teresa. 1992. From Resistance to Social Movement: The Indigenous Authorities Movement in Colombia. In Arturo Escobar and Sonia E. Alvarez, eds., *The Making of Social Movements in Latin America: Identity, Strategy, and Democracy*, 112–133. Boulder: Westview Press.

Friedemann, Nina S. de. 1993. Africa y los negros en la construcción de América. In Carlos Uribe T., ed., *La construcción de las Américas*, 131–140. Bogotá: Universidad de los Andes.

García, Fernando. 1996. Almuerzo y rumba sellaron las protestas en el Cauca: El ministro de gobierno se comprometió a indemnizar a los familiares de las víctimas de la masacre de Nilo y devolver parte de sus tierras. *El Espectador*, August 6.

Green, Abadio. 1996. Life Belongs to Us: We Don't Want to Be Immortalized in Laboratories! *Colombia Update* 8 (2–3): 1, 12.

———. 1997. Aplicación autonómica de la justicia en las comunidades indígenas. In Ministerio de Justicia y del Derecho, ed., *"Del olvido surgimos para traer nuevas esperanzas": La jurisdicción especial indígena.* Bogotá: Ministerio de Justicia y del Derecho/Ministerio del Interior, Dirección General de Asuntos Indígenas.

———. 1998. ¿El otro, soy yo? *Su Defensor* 5 (49): 4–7.

Gros, Christian. 1991. *Colombia indígena: Identidad cultural y cambio social.* Bogotá: Fondo Editorial CEREC.

———. 1993. Derechos indígenas y nueva constitución en Colombia. *Análisis Político* 19 (May–August): 8–24.

———. 1996. Un ajustement à visage indien. In Jean-Michel Blanquer and Christian Gros, eds., *La Colombie: A l'aube du troisième millénaire*, 249–279. Paris: Editions de L'Iheal.

———. 2000. *Políticas de la etnicidad: Identidad, estado y modernidad.* Bogotá: Instituto Colombiano de Antropología e Historia.

Grueso, Libia, Carlos Rosero, and Arturo Escobar. 1998. The Process of Black Community Organizing in the Southern Pacific Coast Region of Colombia. In Sonia E. Alvarez, Evelina Dagnino, and Arturo Escobar, eds., *Cultures of Politics, Politics of Cultures: Re-visioning Latin American Social Movements*, 196–219. Boulder: Westview Press.

Guzmán Arteaga, Ramiro. 1998. Emberá expulsan a organización indígena. *El Espectador*, March 23, 7-A.

Hoffman, Odile. 2000. Titling Collective Lands of the Black Communities in Colombia: Between Innovation and Tradition. In Willem Assies, Gemma van der Haar, and André Hoekema, eds., *The Challenge of Diversity: Indigenous Peoples and Reform of the State in Latin America*, 123–136. Amsterdam: Thela Thesis.

Jimeno, Gladys. 1994. Pueblos indígenas, derechos humanos y participación política. *Derechos Humanos* (May–August): 4–9.

Jimeno, Myriam. 1996. Juan Gregorio Palechor: Tierra, identidad y recreación étnica. *Journal of Latin American Anthropology* 1 (2): 46–77.

Jimeno, Myriam, and Adolfo Triana. 1985. *Estado y minorías étnicas en Colombia.* Bogotá: Ediciones Cuadernos del Jaguar.

Molano, Alfredo. 1994. Los Paeces. *El Espectador*, September 8, 4-A.

Morales Manchego, Marta. 1996. Los uwa no dejan de cantar. *El Espectador*, August 25, 11-A.

Movimiento Indígena Colombiano (MIC). n.d. *Movimiento Indígena Colombiano: Origen, antecedentes y situación actual.* Bogotá: n.p.

Muyuy Jacanamejoy, Gabriel. 1992. Taking Responsibility: Interview with Gabriel Muyuy Jacanamejoy. *Cultural Survival Quarterly* 16 (3): 49–52.

———. 1996. Del senador Muyuy Jacanamejoy. *El Espectador*, July 11.

Navia, José. 1994. Abadio para los blancos. *El Tiempo*, September 25.

———. 1996. Protesta sin señales de humo. *El Tiempo*, July 21.

North American Congress on Latin America (NACLA). 1998. The Wars Within: Counterinsurgency in Chiapas and Colombia. *NACLA Report on the Americas* 31 (5) (March/April).

Organización Nacional de Indígenas de Colombia (ONIC), Centro de Cooperación al Indígena (CECOIN), and University of Kassel, Germany (GhK). 1995. *Tierra profanada: Grandes proyectos en territorios indígenas de Colombia.* Santafé de Bogotá: Disloque Editores.

Organización Nacional de Indígenas de Colombia (ONIC) and Ministerio de

Agricultura. 1998. *Memorias: Los pueblos indígenas de Colombia: Un reto hacia el nuevo milenio.* Santafé de Bogotá.

Osborne, Ann. 1995. *Las cuatro estaciones: Mitología y estructura social entre los U'wa.* Bogotá: Banco de la República.

Pachón, Ximena. 1980–1981. Los pueblos y los cabildos indígenas: La hispanización de las culturas americanas. *Revista Colombiana de Antropología* 23: 297–326.

Padilla, Guillermo. 1993. Derecho mayor indígena y derecho constitucional: Comentarios en torno a su confluencia y conflicto. Paper given at Thirteenth International Congress of Anthropological and Ethnological Sciences, Mexico City.

———. 1994. Los indígenas en la nueva constitución. *Coama* 1: 2–4.

———. 1996. La ley y los pueblos indígenas en Colombia. *Journal of Latin American Anthropology* 1 (2): 78–97.

Pineda, Roberto. 1984. La reivindicación del indio en el pensamiento social colombiano (1850–1950). In J. Arocha and N. S. de Friedemann, eds., *Un siglo de investigación social: Antropología en Colombia,* 197–252. Bogotá: ETNO.

———. 1995. Colombia étnica. In ONIC, CECOIN, and GhK, *Tierra profanada: Grandes proyectos en territorios indígenas de Colombia,* 1–37. Santafé de Bogotá: Disloque Editores.

Plan Colombia. www.ciponline.org/colombia/aid/aidprop4.htm.

Ramírez, María Clemencia. n.d. The Politics of Identity and Cultural Difference in the Colombian Amazon: Claiming Indigenous Rights in the Putumayo Region. In David Maybury-Lewis, ed., *Identities in Conflict: Indigenous Peoples and Latin American States.* Cambridge, Mass.: DRCLAS.

Ramírez, Yaned. 1995. Suspenden creación de resguardos: Las tierras dividen a los indios y a los negros del Chocó. *El Tiempo,* May 4.

Ramos, Alcida Rita. 1998. *Indigenism: Ethnic Politics in Brazil.* Madison: University of Wisconsin Press.

Rappaport, Joanne. 1990. *The Politics of Memory: Native Historical Interpretation in the Colombian Andes.* Cambridge: Cambridge University Press.

———, ed. 1996. Ethnicity Reconfigured: Indigenous Legislators and the Colombian Constitution of 1991. *Journal of Latin American Anthropology* 1 (2).

Rappaport, Joanne, and Robert Dover. 1996. The Construction of Difference by Native Legislators: Assessing the Impact of the Colombian Constitution of 1991. *Journal of Latin American Anthropology* 1 (2): 22–45.

Rappaport, Joanne, and David D. Gow. 1997. Cambio dirigido, movimiento indígena y estereotipos del indio: El estado Colombiano y la reubicación de los Nasa. In María Victoria Uribe and Eduardo Restrepo, eds., *Antropología en la modernidad: Identidades, etnicidades y movimientos sociales en Colombia,* 361–399. Bogotá: Instituto Colombiano de Antropología.

Roldán, Roque. 1992. Notas sobre la legalidad en la tenencia de la tierra y el manejo de los recursos naturales de territorios indígenas en regiones de selva tropical de varios paises suramericanos. In *Derechos territoriales indígenas y ecología en las selvas tropicales de América,* 37–74. Bogotá: CEREC and Fundación GAIA.

———. 2000. *Pueblos indígenas y leyes en Colombia: Aproximación crítica al estudio de su pasado y su presente.* Bogotá: Fundación GAIA.

Sánchez Botero, Esther. 2000. The Tutela-System as a Means of Transforming the Relations between the State and the Indigenous Peoples of Colombia. In Willem Assies, Gemma van der Haar, and André Hoekema, eds., *The Challenge of Diversity: Indigenous Peoples and Reform of the State in Latin America*, 223–245. Amsterdam: Thela Thesis.

Saravena. 1999. U'was condenarían a muerte a gemelos. *El Espectador*, February 19, 11-A.

Schemo, Diana Jean. 1999. Colombian Rebel Chief Is Absent as Peace Talks Start. *New York Times*, January 8.

Serpa Uribe, Horacio. 1997. Introducción: Justicia, diversidad y jurisdicción especial indígena. In Ministerio de Justicia y del Derecho, Ministerio del Interior Dirección General de Asuntos Indígenas, ed., *"Del olvido surgimos para traer nuevas esperanzas": La jurisdicción especial indígena*. Bogotá: Ministerio de Justicia y del Derecho/Ministerio del Interior, Dirección General de Asuntos Indígenas.

Stavenhagen, Rodolfo, and Diego Iturralde, eds. 1990. *Entre la ley y la costumbre: El derecho consuetudinario indígena en América Latina*. Mexico City: Instituto Indigenista Interamericano/Instituto Interamericano de Derechos Humanos.

Stephen, Lynn. 1996. The Zapatista Opening: The Movement for Indigenous Autonomy and State Discourses on Indigenous Rights in Mexico, 1970–1996. *Journal of Latin American Anthropology* 2 (2): 2–41.

———. 1997. Redefined Nationalism in Building a Movement for Indigenous Autonomy in Southern Mexico. *Journal of Latin American Anthropology* 3 (1): 72–101.

Triana, Adolfo. 1978. El estatuto indígena o la nueva encomienda Bonapartista. *Controversia* 79: 29–41.

———. 1993. Los resguardos indígenas del sur del Tolima. In F. Correa, ed., *Encrucijadas de Colombia Amerindia*, 99–140. Bogotá: Instituto Colombiano de Antropología.

Uscátegui Martínez. 1996. $4.282 millones no llegaron a indígenas. *El Espectador*, July 25.

Utopías: Presencia Cristiana por la Vida. 1996. Los 82 pueblos indígenas de Colombia: Por la autonomía, la cultura y el territorio. 4 (37): 22–27.

Van Cott, Donna Lee. 2000. *The Friendly Liquidation of the Past: The Politics of Diversity in Latin America*. Pittsburgh: University of Pittsburgh Press.

Wade, Peter. 1993. *Blackness and Race Mixture: The Dynamics of Racial Identity in Colombia*. Baltimore: Johns Hopkins University Press.

———. 1997. *Race and Ethnicity in Latin America*. London: Pluto.

Warren, Kay. 1998. *Indigenous Movements and Their Critics: Pan-Maya Activism in Guatemala*. Princeton, N.J.: Princeton University Press.

Yashar, Deborah J. 1996. Indigenous Protest and Democracy in Latin America. In Jorge I. Domínguez and Abraham F. Lowenthal, eds., *Constructing Democratic Governance: Latin America and the Caribbean in the 1990s—Themes and Issues*, 87–105. Baltimore: Johns Hopkins University Press.

4. THE MULTIPLICITY OF MAYAN VOICES

Mayan Leadership and the Politics of Self-Representation

Víctor Montejo

Mach xhjiloj stzoti' heb'ya' komam komi' yinh janma. Hatik'a sb'elen heb'ya ha' b'ay xhkawxi ko k'ul. Don't forget the teachings of the ancestors. In their paths we will find hope for the future.—A Mayan elder

INTRODUCTION

The promise of anthropologists to understand themselves more critically while portraying and representing non-Western cultures (Marcus and Fisher 1986) has not been fulfilled. In most parts of the Americas, anthropologists have continued to represent indigenous people as "primitives" and as objects of study (Tierney 2000),[1] although their rhetoric and terminology have shifted to more relativistic modes (e.g., from informants to collaborators). Many talk about the postcolonial and postmodern eras, but from a local or regional perspective we can see that most indigenous people are still living in a colonized world. Others with more resources live in a neocolonized world (economically and intellectually), while most of them cannot call their world postmodern. The rhetoric used in anthropology is a powerful device for maintaining the indigenous worlds intellectually colonized (Said 1979).

I am not saying that all anthropologists have created works that are designed to colonize the minds of indigenous people, since ethnographies are unlikely to be read by the people themselves, except by a few intellectuals from those cultures. Some anthropologists are writing ethnographic descriptions and analyses that value the current contributions of indigenous people to their communities in the search for ways to promote the process of self-representation (Warren 1998). In the case of Guatemala, the role of anthropologists should not be focused only on working with indigenous people but on starting a process of dismantling the stereotypes and images created by early anthropologists, which have fossilized the image of the Classic Maya, covering over the contemporary Maya. To represent themselves, the Maya must now focus their attention on the construction of texts (autohistory) that could destroy the negative images that are embedded in the minds of the Ladino (non-Mayan) population of Guatemala. Contemporary Maya are living in the present, and the Mayan writers of today are telling the world that they too carry the creative power of their ancestors (Montejo 1991, 1999).

As a Mayan anthropologist and writer, I am contributing to the present Mayan renewal. I believe that anthropologists must contribute to the self-determination of the indigenous people that they study. This may be a more difficult task for foreign anthropologists; but in my case, being a Maya, I can see the multiple ways in which I can contribute to the autorepresentation of my people. I have been writing testimonial literature to denounce the injustices to the Maya. I have also engaged in creative writing, including the writing of children's books, because the negative stereotypes about the Maya must be destroyed at an early age. The multiple voices of the contemporary Maya should be heard, because they are no longer silent or sunken in centuries-old amnesia. We remember who we are and where we come from as we fashion our hopes for the future. We are active subjects of our histories and Guatemalan history too, which was written during the past two k'atuns (twenty years each) with Mayan blood. We are alive, and we are now (at least the Mayan intellectuals) using print capitalism (Anderson 1990) to manifest the persistence of Mayan roots into this new century. This time, I insist, we have to listen to the multiplicity of Mayan voices, because in the past the international solidarity community, mostly leftist, has created pictures that purported to represent Mayan or Indian America as a homogeneous whole: for example, the portrayal created for Rigoberta Menchú as the only "voice" of Indian America.

Maya must be critical in the construction of their images and Mayanness through a process of ethnocriticism. This ethnocriticism should be placed at the juncture of epistemic roads, Mayan truths and Western truths. In other words, a Mayan ethnocriticism should position itself in between discourses, at the contested frontier, in order to be an interactionist discourse.

As proposed by Arnold Krupat, ethnocriticism "is concerned with differences rather than oppositions, and so seeks to replace oppositional with dialogical models" (Krupat 1992: 15). This dialogical model must be used by Maya to carry out autocriticism of their own Mayan culture in relation to foreign, discursive and ideological control. It is sometimes said that

Maya should not criticize some major Mayan figure because the "solidarity internationalists" would say that it is anti-Mayan. I am willing to criticize my own culture because like any other civilization it has its own problems and little hidden monsters and demons.

I would like to open this dialogue by referring to the multiplicity of Mayan voices in Guatemala within the current process of self-representation. As a part of the implementation of the peace accords, there is an urgent need for Maya to revise and reorient their current politics and projects for self-representation. In this context, the two prevailing forms of Mayan leadership, the popular (leftist) movement and the Pan-Mayan movement described below, need to be reoriented. Their previous roles have already been bypassed and taken over by non-Mayan politicians, who are now negotiating the future of the Mayan population with the formation of new political parties. Also, the problems of leadership among the Maya *are* visible; there is a need for an organized effort to step beyond sectarian-reductionist ideas in order to reconstruct a new Mayan political front that would make Mayan voices and knowledge relevant to the current process of national reconstruction. There is a sense of voicelessness, which is unfortunate at this historical moment when the implementation of the peace accords requires strong and effective Mayan leadership. In order to achieve stronger expression and reaffirmation of Mayan identity, Maya need to redefine their goals and use their ancestral heritage, both material and spiritual, as major symbols for their self-representation. This recharging of Mayan identity will dispel the political amnesia of the majority of Maya and ignite a stronger desire to empower ourselves and promote our identities for the future.

This chapter focuses on the current problem of leadership among the Maya and suggests the political avenues possible for articulating this intercommunity effort to reaffirm their Mayanness. [goal] One of these avenues is the Pan-Mayan movement (Warren 1998), which is developing a bridge between Mayan traditionalists and Mayan activists, who then would coalesce into a more viable political entity or regenerationist movement of self-representation. The data that inform this essay are based on regional politics and cultural identity in Guatemala. They focus on national efforts to revitalize Mayan culture and the search for ways to achieve political power at the national and international level. But the major issue is to eliminate the stereotypes created about the Maya and other indigenous people of the Americas. Scott Vickers has noted that "[t]he Indians of the Western hemisphere have suffered not only the denigration of their own tribal religions, but also the brutalization of being stereotyped as less-than-human entities, unworthy of basic human decency" (Vickers 1998: 27).

MAYA AND THE SELF-REPRESENTATION PROJECTS

I believe that the Mayan revitalization movement going on in Guatemala has not yet seriously focused its attention on strategies for self-representation. Until now political struggles have tried to take power away from the dominant elite through the popular movement's protests and uprisings or by emphasizing the division between two major ethnic communities making up the Guatemalan nation, Maya and Ladinos. That is why the proposals for the construction of a unified Guatemalan nation-state have always been antagonistic. The most radical representatives of Pan-Mayanism argue that Maya and non-Maya cannot develop a united nation-state and that Maya must have a nation separate from the Ladino nation-state. The rhetoric focuses heavily on the issue of internal and external colonialism (Cojtí Cuxil 1996) but offers no clear proposal for achieving such autonomy. In reality, some Mayan ideologists are busy thinking about ways of creating a multicultural and multiethnic nation state, while the majority of the Mayan population, which is rural, is living in a state of political amnesia. The reason is that there is still a high rate of illiteracy among the Maya, and their participation in national politics is minimal. It is hoped that, as Guatemalan citizens, they will fully exercise their rights to vote. One factor is that literate Maya, like most Guatemalans, do not have the habit of reading, and the few who want to write in national newspapers are not given the space by those who control the media. In other words, print capitalism is not yet fully available to the Maya. The production of knowledge is important; for as we can see in the case of Guatemala, those who write and voice their concerns are more likely to be recognized as leaders of the Mayan movement (Warren 1998).

Unfortunately, most of these intellectual leaders are not very effective in convincing other intellectuals and the majority of the Mayan population to follow their leadership. Their projects are mostly individual and do not respond to the necessity of bringing changes and prosperity to the Maya. Also, those Mayan leaders who talk about decolonization and autonomy are mainly immersed in the political and international patronage of institutions like UNESCO (United Nations Educational, Scientific, and Cultural Organization), AID, and the World Bank that maintain the neocolonialist system in Guatemala.

So-called Mayan leaders are now competing individually against the rich Ladinos, and their attention is focused mostly on economic advantages. Mayan leaders in Guatemala are always asking or inquiring if such and such an individual is already *nivelado*, that is, enjoying the status and perks of the affluent dominant class. In other words, to be *nivelado* is to own and drive an expensive car; have a house in Guatemala City; and have a good-paying job with the government or with an international organization such as UNICEF, AID, or a powerful international NGO. However, those leaders who claim to be progressive are not free to act unless the Guatemalan National Revolutionary Unity (URNG), the former guerrilla leadership, allows them to. When Mayan leaders respond to the dictates of political groups directed by non-Maya, the movement is impaired and channeled to sectarian interests. This is where the popular Mayan movement and, to a lesser degree, the cultural movement stand now. Obviously, this situation has its own reasons for being and presents a difficult historical background to understand and interpret.

For the past thirty-six years, Guatemala was immersed in an internal war that claimed the lives of tens of thousands of Maya and drove thousands of others into exile (Montejo 1987; Carmack 1988; Manz 1988). Finally, on December 29, 1996, the government/army and the URNG signed the peace accords which put an end to the armed conflict. Maya are now hopeful that the agreements will be implemented, especially those concerning Mayan identity, education, land, and spirituality. Even if the legacy of terror persists, such as the thousands of war widows, orphans, and displaced persons, the Maya have clearly survived, and so has their culture. This survival is expressed through the current Pan-Mayan movement, which is presently restructuring its projects and visions for the future.

The prophetic words of those elders who were concerned about survival are now obviously relevant. In 1982, during the height of the military violence, the elders reminded Jakaltek youth: *Mach xhqiloq stzoti' heb' ya' komam komi' yinh qanma. Hatik'a sb'elen heb'ya' ha' b'ay xhkawxi ko k'ul:* "Don't forget the teachings of the ancestors. In their paths we will find hope for the future." These prophetic and hopeful words are now being listened to. Maya believe that when their culture is under attack the younger generation will pass on the torch and reconstruct Mayan culture for following generations. The revitalization of Mayan culture responds to this faith and hope for a better future. The Mayan movement has developed little by little, and it needs the support of all Guatemalans and the international community in order to be effective in its contribution to the economic development projects and positive historical changes that must stem from community bases.

The Maya have struggled for centuries against marginalization and the lack of educational and economic opportunities. In addition to the long internal warfare, Maya had to cope with forced indoctrination, fear, and death as a result of guerrilla warfare, army scorched earth policies, and paramilitary organizations such as the civil patrols.[2] It is important to be aware of the current struggles of Mayan people and their efforts to make their presence visible in this historical moment of national reconciliation. There are several ways in which the revitalization of Mayan culture is taking shape. Most importantly, it is an effective and nonviolent form of historical reconstruction and a peaceful alternative to conflict. For example, the revitalization of Mayan culture is the main goal of the Pan-Mayan movement, which has taken enormous pride in the Mayan cultural heritage. The revitalization of Mayan languages, religion and spirituality, native knowledge, Mayan schools, and political consciousness is one of the most expressive forms of this Pan-Mayan movement of self-representation and cultural resurgence (Montejo 1997; Warren 1998).

THE RISE OF MAYAN ACTIVISM

As mentioned above, contemporary Mayan activism resulted from the chronic violence that enveloped Mayan life and history. Little by little, contemporary Maya began voicing their concerns and increased their activism. At the same time, they were also being studied by anthropologists. Foreign scholars have followed the rise of Mayan activism very closely and have either collaborated with or ignored it. Anthropologists working in Guatemala since the 1950s have written extensively about Mayan politicization and tried to explain this phenomenon according to their own outsiders' perspectives. The early investigators considered themselves pure scientists who went to the field and wrote about Mayan culture. In their works, the modern Maya were seen as objects of study and the Mayan region as a place to collect artifacts for museums and private collections (Castañeda 1996).

Some Ladino scholars and literary critics who work on the periphery of the Mayan movement have been examining this process from a vaguer and less accurate, if not cynical, position. For example, Mario Roberto Morales has characterized the Mayan revitalization movement as a regressive or fundamentalist movement (Morales 1996). Others believe that this is a movement devoted only to reviving ancient patterns of Mayan culture as essential relics to be worshiped (Fischer and Brown 1996).

I personally believe that the agenda of Mayan scholars and activists is not to embellish ourselves with a romantic past or to wrap ourselves in ancient Mayan garb but to revitalize our Mayan identity and weave back in the sections worn away by centuries of neglect. Contemporary Maya are constantly creating and recreating their Mayan culture and redefining themselves. I have argued elsewhere that the Mayan culture of the future will be conceptually different from the Classic and Postclassic Maya. Many minds are engaged in building our future, thinking about it, and recreating it. The idea is to use the powerful symbols of the past to reconstruct the present and build the future, as we retrace the footprints of our ancestors on the ancient bridge that links the past to the present. From those building blocks we want to create the Mayan culture of the future. It is not, then, a bad thing to have the essential parts of our culture, such as language and respect for land and the elders, as the foundation of this dynamic process of self-representation we are promoting for ourselves. This will only be possible if we understand the prophetic time in which we are living and contribute to the writing of our own histories within the cyclical patterns of our worldviews.

Another issue raised to explain the process of revitalization of Mayan culture is the concept of invented traditions, "the use of ancient materials to construct invented traditions of a novel type for quite novel purpose" (Hobsbawm 1988: 6). The concept of invented traditions applies to Mayan culture, of course, but not to the same degree as in Western cultures. And as stated by Eric Hobsbawm: "The element of invention is particularly clear here, since the history which became part of the fund of knowledge or the ideology of nation, state or movement is not what has actually been preserved in popular memory, but what has been selected, written, pictured, popularized and institutionalized by those whose function it is to do so" (Hobsbawm 1988: 13).

For colonizers and nonindigenous ideologues, what has been preserved in popular memory may not be important, as they interpret and invent traditions to accommodate themselves among established and deep, historically rooted indigenous cultures and communities. For us, the Mayan cultural heritage is clearly visible, and its roots are still strong and firmly embedded in Mayan soil. The fund of knowledge that Hobsbawm mentions is what has been preserved in the Mayan memory, such as the ceremonies performed at sacred sites by Mayan priests and the use of the Mayan calendar. For example, when I reaffirm my Mayanness, I don't need to go into a time machine and travel back in time visiting imaginary worlds to see my ancestors as Westerners do through films and science fiction. Instead, I just have to visit the sanctuary of the Jakaltek hero

Xhuwan Q'anil and recharge my identity by participating in the Mayan ceremonies and prayers carried out in my native Mayan language, Pop-b'alti'. This is to belong to a tradition with roots still strong and deeply embedded in the land, its sacred places and geography (Montejo 2001). Also, we Maya can go to Tikal, to Palenque, or to other sacred sites in our own communities and see, touch, and feel all around us the presence and power of the ancestors. Mayan spirituality helps us in this way, and that is why the role of the Mayan spiritual leader is also essential in this project of Mayan reconstruction and representation. The land is essential for Mayan survival, and perhaps during this new century we will be playing a role that will definitely go beyond survival. I am not saying that Mayan culture is static; it changes, but not like Western culture, which invents and creates nationalism in new postcolonial settings. Maya have been struggling to express their Mayanness through the centuries and even millennia, but their culture is substantially and essentially based on Mayan languages and worldviews.

There are several reasons why Mayan leaders and scholars use an essentialist approach in the revitalization of Mayan culture. First, they are descendants of the magnificent ancient Maya. The persistence of Mayan languages and the visibility of Mayan monumental architecture make them proud of their heritage. Unfortunately, those who are in positions of power in Guatemala may continue to deny this ancient heritage and invalidate the Mayan land claims and struggles for self-determination. The reaffirmation of their Mayanness is important at this time of implementation of the peace accords, which were negotiated and signed by the bilateral commissions in December 1996. We could say that we are living in much the same kind of political environment as when the *Popol Wuj*, the *Anales de los Kaqchikeles*, and the *Título de Totonicapán* were written in the early colonial period.[3] After the Spanish invasion, the Maya had to rely on the power of their own traditions, especially the origin myths. They insisted on their roots and origins, while they claimed communal ownership of the land which was taken from them after the Spanish conquest.

Another reason for Maya to insist on their links to the ancient Mayan culture is because they are interested in writing their own histories and representing themselves from their own indigenous perspectives. They want to be called Maya, and their link to the ancient Maya legitimates this desire. In other words, not all of them are interested in theorizing about what they are doing or how they are doing this or that. I believe this is where the role and contributions of anthropologists will be important. Nevertheless, I would caution anthropologists to be careful with their analyses and interpretations of the process as well as the methods they use for gathering their data. Foreign anthropologists are very visible, and their role is definitely very important. Now, in the postwar period in Guatemala, more young anthropologists from around the world are arriving "to study the Maya." Another reason why Maya are drawing strength from their heritage is that some Ladinos continue to insist that what we have or what we are is not Mayan. This is an issue where Mayanists can help people to understand why Maya are using this name to create and recreate their culture. Maya know that what we have now is not Classic Mayan, because identity changes in time and space, but we call ourselves Maya because we have clear links to the prehispanic Mayan culture. In other words, we are aware that the Classic Maya were not the same as the Preclassic or the Postclassic and were of course different from the contemporary Maya. But because of these links we consciously call ourselves Maya, and this makes our identity historically powerful.

THE MAYAN MOVEMENT OF SELF-REPRESENTATION

The tremendous hiatus in Mayan writing and self-representation during the colonial and postcolonial periods (1600–1900) is truly painful for us to remember. The Maya during this time were unable to express pride in their heritage. Instead, they were placed under colonial domination, including forced labor, and obliged to pay tribute. They were labeled "Indians" and therefore were considered inferior. Under such extreme exploitation, the Maya had to find ways to send letters to the king of Spain asking him to stop the abuses against them. Those who exploited the indigenous population were military leaders, *encomenderos*,[4] and clergy, including some bishops who were known to be protectors of the Indians, such as Bishop Francisco Marroquín. The Indians from the central valley of Guatemala complained to the king of Spain, denouncing the abuses of their rights as human beings. From a recent publication, *Nuestro pesar, nuestra aflicción* (Dakin and Lutz 1996), we have become aware of the extent of Mayan suffering under colonial rule. The oppressed Mayan leaders wrote letters asking for the intervention of the king of Spain to ease their pain. "Help us, you, who are our King, Philip the II, King of Castile. We the *macehuales* [common people] are suffering excessively. The *macehuales* go about naked, without clothing. The people suffer too much, having to keep paying the tribute ordered by Pedro de Alvarado and Bishop Francisco Marroquín" (Dakin and Lutz 1996: 79).

Despite the continuous resistance by indigenous people in Guatemala,

Maya produced no texts in Mayan languages during this period; the letters just mentioned were written in Náhuatl. The lack of written histories of this Mayan suffering means that non-Maya have forgotten how their forebears perpetuated this suffering for the Maya. This atrocious enslavement was of course responsible for weakening the roots of Mayan culture during the colonial period. As a Mayan writer, I believe that the greatest loss of all was the loss of the knowledge of reading and writing the Mayan hieroglyphs. Modern Maya greatly lament that knowledge of the glyphs was not passed down through the generations. The colonial Maya did realize this great loss of knowledge and protested: "We complain in great sorrow, in loud voices and death. Our grief is torment. We are pierced with a great longing to read the books of wood and the writings on stone, now in ruins. They contain the seven wellsprings of life! They were burned before our eyes at the well. At noonday we lament our perpetual burdens" (Makemson 1951: 5).

Until the beginning of the twentieth century, the voices of Maya were heard again, but only in the writings of ethnographers. That much of the culture had survived was documented systematically by early ethnographers such as Robert Redfield (1950), Ruth Bunzel (1981 [1952]), Oliver La Farge and Douglas Byers (1931), and many others. After the Jacobo Arbenz reforms of the 1950s, Guatemala's indigenous people began to talk and express themselves in writing. Contrary to the belief that the Maya would disappear or be totally assimilated, they began to organize themselves, and some began to pursue higher education. Guatemalans and people of other nationalities realized that the days of submission and silence imposed on the Maya were over. The pioneering works of the K'iche' educator Adrián Inés Chávez promoted self-expression and representation of the Maya. Chávez (1979) utilized the *Popol Wuj* to represent the Maya and their literary contribution to the world. In the words of Carlos Guzmán Böckler, "The originality of his work and his erudition have challenged the impositions of Western linguistics. By presenting and using his own alphabet, he challenged intellectual colonialism" (Guzmán Böckler 1979).

While this was happening among the K'iche' Maya with Chávez, a younger generation throughout Guatemala gained the opportunity to be educated in urban schools with scholarships offered by missionaries. Some of those who graduated from schools run by these missionaries became involved in party politics, making Maya more visible as subjects of history. Since then, the indigenous people of Guatemala have carried out a campaign of autorepresentation, as they demanded their rights while becoming involved in national politics. One of the first major efforts to push forward the process of self-representation was the formation of a political party, Frente Indígena Nacional (National Indigenous Front: FIN), by Mayan intellectuals. Their strategy was to show pride in their heritage, and they presented themselves to the national community as "indios." This was the common term used by Mayan leaders during the 1970s, since the term "Maya" was used by Mayanists to refer solely to the builders of ancient Mayan civilization or to refer to Yukatek Maya.

Unfortunately, these Mayan leaders fell into the traps of party politics, and the FIN ended up supporting the brutal and repressive government of Fernando Romeo Lucas García (1978–1982). With this coalition supporting a repressive government, the leaders of this political party were seen as opportunists, no different from Ladino politicians. They wanted to obtain positions in government, so they allied themselves with the Partido Revolucionario (Revolutionary Party: PR) then headed by General Lucas García.

The proximity of Guatemala City to the territory of these K'iche' and Kaqchikel leaders playing these political roles provided them with more opportunities and access to political power. At the same time, in the most remote areas of western Guatemala, a different kind of cultural revival was underway but on a more regional scale. In the Jakaltek region, two local and regional newspapers were founded, *El Jakalteko* and *Despertar Maya* (Mayan Awakening), which I edited in 1978. We had to cease publication of *Despertar Maya* because of death threats. The use of Mayan languages in these newspapers was not the immediate goal. At that time, it was more necessary to let people know that Mayan culture was alive and that the people of the region were related to each other culturally. It was necessary to recover our Mayan identity and be proud of it despite Ladino discrimination. This Mayan awakening after centuries of voicelessness and inaction was headed by Mayan intellectuals, mostly schoolteachers. The idea was to develop the habit of reading among the Maya, while making them aware of the local, regional, and national situation.

At the end of the 1970s the existing indigenous organizations were forced to redefine their goals and strategies because of governmental repression against their leaders. Most of these organizations had Ladinos as leaders, so it was easy for them to opt for a militant strategy with strong links to the guerrillas (Carmack 1988; Smith 1990; Perera 1993; Carlsen 1997). The divergent interests of the traditional Maya as opposed to the militant Maya became apparent, as some agreed with and supported the guerrilla movement, while others continued with their nationalist and cultural agendas (Smith 1990). The so-called popular movement became nationally well known, and international solidarity organizations began to support it. Unfortunately, their agenda was mostly prepared by nonindigenous leaders who continued to manipulate the popular movement until the signing of the peace accords. The involvement of leftist non-Mayan leaders in the decision-making of these organizations was evident. For example, representation of the Maya by the umbrella organization COPMAGUA (Coordinator of Organizations of the Mayan People of Guatemala) was weak and stumbled because of the lack of solid Mayan leadership. The desire for personal gain and political position by some of these leaders rendered the negotiational ability of COPMAGUA less than powerful as an umbrella organization.

At the same time, the leadership of the culturalist Mayan movement was radicalized to the point that nothing could be accepted if it was not aimed at the creation of an autonomous Mayan nationalism (Cojtí Cuxil 1996). The strategy for negotiation by these leaders was not appropriate, since they undiplomatically proposed bold, radical changes in their relations with the non-Maya. At this political juncture, and after a bloody undeclared civil war between the army and the guerrillas that killed tens of thousands of Maya, it was not a convenient time for radicalized action, because the Mayan majority was not fully represented by the political and cultural leaders of the popular and the Pan-Mayan movements.

I think it is important at this time to have a middle-ground leadership, which could be called "regenerationist." The regenerationist group should be flexible and careful about preaching an extreme nationalist ideology along Western lines. We must think about the multicultural and multiethnic reality of Guatemala. Maya must realize that not all Ladinos belong to the elite and that they cannot be treated as outsiders either, since they share Mayan blood. On the contrary, Maya may help them to recognize their mixed heritage so that both may collaborate in the construction of a multicultural nation-state in Guatemala. The Ladinos have long attached themselves to the ruling class and rejected their other side, the Mayan component. They must search for their own identity and cherish the sources of their mixed blood equally in order to find the Mayan way not to be backward or dangerous to the Ladinos.

Similarly, the Maya must try to explain what it is to be Mayan to these Ladinos, to prevent mistrust of the Mayan projects of revitalization. For this reason, the radical nationalism proposed by some Mayan leaders as a solution to the Mayan neocolonial situation cannot help in the implementation of the peace accords but would only deepen the century-old division. The construction of a multicultural nation-state means the contribution of all the ethnic groups in Guatemala to the consolidation of those nationalist-pluralist goals. We must think about the future in realistic terms. To use Eric Wolf's metaphor (Wolf 1982), we should not promote the creation of small independent nation-states that may clash continuously like billiard balls within the Guatemalan territory. To create the Guatemalan imagined community (Anderson 1990) as a multicultural nation-state, is to share and create the future from the contributions and particularities stemming from Maya and Ladinos alike.

When talking to a high-ranking Guatemalan diplomat in the Alvaro Arzú government, I asked why President Arzú had not appointed any Mayas to positions of power in his cabinet, as he had promised before the elections. The diplomat answered that the Maya did not want the Secretaría Indígena that the president had proposed for them. The Maya argued that it was a form of separatism which they did not want, so the government stopped considering it and gave them nothing instead. The issue is not whether or not the Maya want the proposed *secretaría*, which should be called Secretaría de Asuntos Mayas. The government has the responsibility to fulfill its promises to the Mayan people, a majority of the population, and create institutions that benefit them. I believe that Mayan leaders should have accepted the Secretaría Indígena and the political power that would have come with it, if run by Mayas. It is better to achieve something than nothing at all. I strongly believe that it is necessary to create institutions run by Mayas to deal with Mayan issues. Maya are now considered Guatemalan citizens but continue to lack the opportunities and rights enjoyed by citizens belonging to the dominant group. Maya should be equal partners in any joint projects for the future. It is time for Maya to be fully part of the nation and not just part of the labor force (Peeler 1998). The efforts to achieve self-representation are advancing slowly, although some critics say that the paternalistic attitude of the scholars behind some Mayan leaders suggests that they cannot do things for themselves. This may be the case with a few Mayan leaders, but the majority are really engaged in creating and producing knowledge. To do this, modern Maya are making use of the tools provided by print capitalism as they write books and make contributions to the Guatemalan media, projecting their ideas and enriching the Mayan movement. Among such scholars are Estuardo Zapeta, an anthropologist whose polemical work is aimed at shaking the bushes of both camps, Mayan and mestizo. Luis Enrique Sam Colop writes in the newspaper *Prensa Libre*; his articles are critical and reach the Mayan population, as he uses the K'iche' Mayan language in his editorials. Then we have the Mayan writers who have published works which have been translated into other languages. Among the best known are Humberto Ak'abal (K'iche'), Gaspar Pedro González (Q'anjob'al), and Víctor Montejo (Jakaltek).

In Chiapas, the Mayan presence in the media is becoming more noticeable, and women are among those who are at the forefront of writing and producing theater pieces for public performance. As Warren (1998: 27) notes, "The production of cultural representation in a variety of media is used quite self-consciously by public intellectuals to support struggles for social change." The multiplicity of Mayan voices and the lack of formal representation of Maya and their ideas for a unified Mayan movement are due to the fact that the most visible leaders play opposite roles, siding with radicalized groups. For this reason, it is necessary for Maya to be represented by the voices of peasants, intellectuals, and students from rural and urban areas. We need to refine our rhetoric and create a middle position which is viable, nonviolent, and feasible for all Maya and non-Maya. Mayan leaders must develop a new approach to their own linguistic communities, such as more direct consultation with the communities by using the traditional political forms of consensus-making in order to reflect the concerns and needs of the community. This is one of the goals of the Pan-Mayan movement. Mutual respect within each Mayan linguistic community must be emphasized as well as a commitment to their collective survival and resurgence (Wilson 1995; Montejo 1999).

The early forms of Pan-Mayan associations can be traced to the special teachers' institutes that train Mayan women and men. Among these institutions have been the Instituto Indígena "Santiago" and the Instituto Indígena "Nuestra Señora del Socorro" (the latter for women). These institutes for secondary and vocational education were run as boarding schools by religious orders. The establishment of these Indian institutes was a result of the struggle against communism in Guatemala by Bishop Mariano Rossell y Arellano after the downfall of the Arbenz government. This was a measure to stop Maya from falling into the traps of Communist manipulation. It is interesting to note that some of the most prominent Mayan leaders of the present were trained in these institutes.

The functioning of these institutes, which brought young men and women from most Mayan linguistic communities, opened up possibilities for becoming acquainted with other linguistic communities. Also, interethnic marriages took place, weakening the endogamous tradition that Mayan communities have maintained for centuries. In other words, the migration of Maya to the cities for economic and educational purposes put them in contact with people from other Mayan linguistic communities, thus broadening their views of themselves, their people, and the country.

Attendance at universities also helped Mayan academics to construct an ethnic identity which encouraged pride in the Mayan heritage. Better educated than previous generations, Maya after about 1950 began to rethink their position as mediators and interlocutors between the two worlds. They recognized and experienced the problems of the past, but now there was a possibility of influencing or at least envisioning a better future.

On the local and regional level, Mayan revitalization is also occurring. One of the major symbols now used for self-representation is the Mayan New Year Ceremony, demonstrating that the revitalization of Mayan religion and spirituality has become a powerful moving force for all the Mayan groups. The hope is to develop a Mayan unity and consensus within the multiple ways of being Mayan and to guarantee a better future for all Guatemalans. In this way Maya are reviving those values that emphasize respect for the land. The land is the source of their being and the place of their roots and identities. At the same time, they are developing a strong and respectful relationship with other ethnic groups beyond the borders of modern Guatemala.

MAYAN POLITICAL AND CULTURAL AWAKENING

The major changes in Mayan political views were generated during the brutal repression the people have endured since the 1970s. The massacre of one hundred Q'eqchi' Maya in Panzós in northern Guatemala in 1979 marked the beginning of a strong politicization of the Mayan population. When news that the army had killed these Mayan peasants spread throughout the country, so did condemnation of this criminal act. As a form of response from the communities, poems and songs were written honoring the victims of the massacre, denouncing this violation of human rights by the army. This was a wake-up call for the Maya, who began more fully to recognize the terrible restrictions and lack of opportunities to which they were subjected. Another event that had a national impact was the killing of radio announcer Timoteo Curruchiche. He had a Kaqchikel-language program listened to by Maya which addressed the problems of violence in the nation. The death of a voice with which people identified symbolized the death of their own voices, as Maya had become silent and fearful of death-squads during the Lucas García regime. The cultural revitalization which was beginning to take place in most Mayan communities during the 1970s stagnated, and its leaders were silenced. There was persecution of university students and professors, missionaries, labor leaders, and politicians who had denounced the aggression against peasants and indigenous people. The killing of congressman Alberto Fuentes Mohr and the former mayor of Guatemala City, Manuel Colom Argueta, was a turning point in the political violence instigated by the government against those who opposed its repressive methods of control. Leftist Mayan organizations such as the Committee for Peasant Unity (CUC) were under attack; most of its leaders went underground and became guerrillas to continue their struggle.

Ironically, an important development during this period of violence was an increase in the numbers of young Mayan men and women pursuing careers in vocational schools in the cities. The Catholic church provided scholarships to Mayan students to attend vocational institutes, seminaries, and universities. This was a major change in the educational structure for Mayan communities, where schoolteachers had been Ladinos who came from the cities and did not speak the local language or share the indigenous culture. Mayan schoolteachers who graduated began to take jobs in their own linguistic communities, and there was an increase in the awareness of Mayan values and pride in their cultural heritage.[5]

With the awareness of their cultural heritage, Mayan intellectuals began to organize their efforts for cultural revival and revitalization. The work of Mayan writers was important; they concentrated on the use of the language as a means of ensuring that Mayan culture and worldviews would be passed on effectively from one generation to the next. At the beginning of the 1980s this organized effort led to the creation of the Academy of Mayan Languages of Guatemala (ALMG). The recognition of ALMG in 1985 as an autonomous institution funded by the government was one of the major achievements of the Maya working for self-representation. ALMG is a Pan-Mayan institution in which the twenty-one Mayan linguistic communities of Guatemala are represented (Warren 1998). Another major achievement of the Mayan movement was the organization of projects of cultural and religious revival by Mayan religious leaders, such as the National Association of Mayan Priests, the *ah q'ijab'* or experts on the Mayan calendar. The so-called popular organizations also have a Pan-Mayan view but operate mostly in the political arena. Mayan umbrella organizations such as COMG (Mayan Council of Guatemala) and COPMAGUA (Coordinator of Organizations of the Mayan People of Guatemala) significantly influenced the negotiations for the peace accords. Although there has been a division of leadership within and among these organizations, their tenacity in mobilizing mass demonstrations has had its effect. The major achievement of these umbrella organizations is their recognition as institutions that voice the demands of indigenous people concerning the implementation of the peace accords.

In spite of its contribution to the Mayan popular movement, COP-MAGUA has lost its power of convocation and leadership by being seen as too attached to the left. On the issue of Mayan identity, COPMAGUA organized multidisciplinary commissions to study and present proposals and projects for the implementation of the accords relating to Mayan rights and identity. Unfortunately, the referendum or national consultation on May 8, 1999, failed when the voters said no to the proposed constitutional reforms. The rejection of the constitutional reforms made it clear that the majority of the people who had the ability to vote, mostly Ladinos, did not want to give "more rights" to the Maya. According to them, all of the Guatemalans are equal under the constitution, so changing it to accommodate indigenous rights meant dividing the nation. For this reason, those who opposed the changes argued that an ethnic war or indigenous uprising against the Ladino population might result. This was a manipulation to infuse fear in the population, so those who could vote voted against the reforms. The referendum was also proof of the discontent in the rural populations. There was an 80 percent abstention rate in the voting, which was a message to the government and to the leftist opposition that the people were unhappy with the system and did not believe the politicians' promises.

Another important factor in the signing of the peace accords was the Assembly of Civil Society (ASC), which managed to push the agenda of indigenous issues in the discussions between the army and the URNG. Unfortunately, the ASC has disintegrated and cannot help monitor the implementation of the peace accords. But the formation of Guatemala's truth commission (formally the Commission for Historical Clarification—Comisión para el Esclarecimiento Histórico de Guatemala: CEH) brought some hope to the Guatemalan population. It was necessary to let the people know about the history of violence and its sources and to name the perpetrators of the crimes. Two Mayan intellectuals were members of the truth commission, which documented the horrors of the violence experienced in rural Guatemala. But, as is usually the case with these investigatory commissions, those who organized and planned the investigation were mostly foreigners assigned by the United Nations; few Maya participated, except as informants. For this reason, the recommendations of the truth commission to follow up with a process of "reparation" to the affected communities has not been taken seriously by the present government of President Alfonso Portillo (2000–2004).

Similarly, the Catholic church organized its own investigatory commission and publicized a document called *Guatemala: Nunca más* (Guatemala: Never Again) (REMHI 1998). This commission documented the atrocities by the army and guerrillas and named the perpetrators of these crimes. Both commissions carried out the tremendous task of calling for the Maya to write down their own stories, so that the martyrs will not be forgotten. Unfortunately, the killing of Bishop Juan Gerardi a few days after he made public *Guatemala: Nunca más* shattered the hopes of the Guatemalan people for a lasting peace. The document was a compilation of the testimonies of thousands of people who had been victims of the armed conflict. With the violent death of Bishop Gerardi, Guatemala is now concerned about the impunity of those who have not only avoided justice but are committing new crimes.

THE MAYA: A NEW FORCE IN GUATEMALAN POLITICS

At the present time, it is obvious that a new indigenous political front is developing. During the past elections, most indigenous communities decided to support candidates for mayors who had been nominated by local civic committees. Some of these committees had links to the newly formed, left-leaning Frente Democrático Nueva Guatemala (FDNG).[6] An increasing number of Mayas are now interested in politics, although some favor the ideologies of the old right-wing political parties. In reality these parties had not been interested in having Mayas in positions of power. This pattern was changed when the FDNG won some seats in Congress. The FDNG was seen as a democratic force with possibilities for promoting unity among Guatemalans for national reconciliation. Nevertheless, little has been achieved by the opposition parties, for the ruling party Frente Republicano Guatemalteco (FRG) has the majority of representatives in Congress. The signing of the peace accords, however, provided Mayas with the possibility to speak up freely and without fear. Now they can tell their stories of how both sides, army and guerrillas, committed crimes against indigenous people. This is a positive result of the peace agreements, and now Mayas are voicing their concerns and breaking the silence imposed on them as a result of the armed conflict.

The past election in Guatemala (1999) resulted in many changes in the political arena. Many old political parties died out (e.g., Partido Institucional Democrático: PID) since they no longer provided alternatives for change and democracy in Guatemala. Mayan communities in western Guatemala have benefited from this because the old local caciques who had strong links to the leaders of the national parties lost their power and no longer could manipulate the Mayan peasants. The caciques that I am referring to here are strongmen who have served political parties for decades and are friends with the Ladino mayors and secretaries of the towns. They were the only people knowledgeable about national politics, because they were the parties' representatives in the towns. These old Mayan political leaders were loyal to their parties and were feared by the communities. One of the strategies commonly used by the leaders of national political parties was to distribute communal lands among their followers. At present some young leaders, mostly intellectuals, are taking their places; but they owe no loyalty to these new parties. These leaders can shift allegiance from one political party to another. They are interested in becoming mayors of their towns and frequently become corrupt as they use the office for personal gain. Most other Mayan leaders in western Guatemala are reluctant to join political parties, preferring to organize civic committees and participate in elections. They are the ones who are likely to be involved in the revitalization of Mayan culture, and they reject party politics.

The opposition parties have been widely divided ideologically and politically. The FDNG leadership, for example, reached out only to those members who were already identified with the left. Because of its limited political strategies and vision, the FDNG lost all that it had gained as a political party, as it also became extinct after the November 1999 elections. I would say that the URNG, which became a political party after the signing of the peace accords (1996), has been stillborn as a political party. A major problem has to do with its name, which symbolizes combat and clandestine activities, carrying with it the stigmatizing associations of war, violence, and failure. Similarly, General Efraín Ríos Montt's political party, Frente Republicano Guatemalteco, which reminded people of military repression and massacres, against all odds won the presidential elections of 1999, with Alfonso Portillo as its presidential candidate. Some Mayas won seats in Congress by supporting the FRG; the most intriguing event after the election was the appointment of Mayan critics to the governmental cabinet, as a form of silencing Mayan leaders. Despite this, I believe that Mayan intellectuals should get more involved in politics and seek positions in government. Maya should be able to represent themselves and be in charge of the decision-making that will affect their own future.

PAN-MAYANISM: MAYAN SELF-REPRESENTATION

As I have mentioned, there are several Mayan projects concerned with cultural revival. These achievements are astonishing because of the restricted spaces and limited resources out of which they have been developing. The new Mayan movement is emerging from the ashes of the 36-year-old armed conflict which finally came to an end in December 1996. In this context, the Maya have shown a powerful will to survive in the midst of extreme political violence. Once again the resurgence of Mayan culture is underway, responding to the extreme pressures imposed upon indigenous cultures during the past decades—for instance, the massacres that disrupted Mayan worldviews and traditions. The present revitalization of Mayan culture is also a reflection of the continental mobilization of indigenous people to achieve self-determination. On the cultural, linguistic, political, and religious levels Maya are engaged in the process of unifying the diverse Mayan ethnic groups or Native Nations into a Pan-Mayan movement of cultural revitalization and resurgence (Warren 1998; Montejo 1999).

The current process of building a coordinated effort for subsistence and cultural reaffirmation among these Mayan linguistic communities (Pan-Mayanism) results from the violent history of the past decades through which they have lived. Mayan culture was affected dramatically during the military confrontation between the army and the guerrillas, so now Maya are in the process of organizing themselves into a cultural movement concerned with self-representation. This cultural resurgence emphasizes the necessity of Maya being allowed to express themselves freely and to contribute from their own knowledge system, ideology, and communal politics to the construction of a multicultural Guatemalan nation-state.

Pan-Mayanism is a cultural movement focused on self-understanding and validation of Mayan heritage (Montejo 1997). Maya prefer to call their own efforts a process of self-determination which will help to create a pluralistic Guatemalan nation-state. Pan-Mayanism is the basic first step for achieving further goals. This is because, first, Maya must take pride in their Mayan culture in order to promote it as a source of powerful identities. And second, the stereotypes and images embedded in the minds of the different non-Mayan groups in the nation-state must be radically changed to positive ones, with an appreciation of Mayan history and culture, past and present. The construction of a Guatemalan nationalism must come from a compromise between both Maya and non-Maya. If Guatemala wants to continue proclaiming its uniqueness as a nation by using Mayan elements and symbols, it must recognize the active role of Mayan culture as an integral part of the process of nation-state building (Smith 1991).

It is evident that Mayan culture is very complex. It is the expression of various levels of understanding or worldviews being reworked by each Mayan linguistic community. It is also the expression of different sectors of the Mayan population, such as intellectuals, advocates, peasants, and traditional religious leaders. All voices must be heard so that action is not radicalized. Otherwise, only one highly politicized sector will prevail, limiting the ability of other sectors of the Mayan population to express themselves. Maya must understand and be aware of the political environment, nationally and internationally. The world is changing dramatically, and each sector must strengthen its national feelings through the recognition of other ways of thinking and being Mayan. The distinctiveness and cultural expression of each Mayan linguistic community is being recognized and valued within the developing Pan-Mayan movement. Pan-Mayanism recognizes the way different Mayan linguistic groups have contributed to the continuous transformation and maintenance of Mayan culture as a whole.

The diversity of Mayan culture should be seen as an advantage and not as an obstacle. This is a healthy sign, which affirms the continuity of Mayan culture despite centuries of violence and forced assimilation. Similarly, we must insist that Mayan identity be historically based and that contemporary Maya continue to sustain and recreate it. But as Joane Nagel has argued for Native Americans in the United States:

> The knowledge that Native American ethnicity is historically based, however, must not obscure the fact that Indian ethnic boundaries and identities are continually socially constructed and negotiated. It is important to note that for both traditional and emergent Indian communities, the work of social and cultural survival represents an ongoing challenge. There is nothing "automatic" or "natural" about Native American tribal or supra-tribal ethnicity. No matter how deeply rooted in tradition, Indian ethnicity, like all cultures and identities, must be sustained and strengthened. (Nagel 1996: 9)

The Maya definitely need to sustain and strengthen their Mayanness. Maya must write and rewrite their own histories in order to eliminate the negative images imposed on them. This is possible, since Maya now are more prepared and sophisticated, as they make use of modern technology and media information to promote their own views of themselves.

CONCLUSIONS

The recognition and value of the cultural distinctiveness of each Mayan linguistic community make Pan-Mayan identity very strong and complex. Pan-Mayanism argues for a common Mayan global identity, that is, sharing the base Mayan culture. Pan-Mayanism also values and recognizes that the diversity greatly increases the probability that Mayan culture will continue in the future. Pan-Mayanism is not about a political imposition that dictates the role that each Mayan linguistic community must play but rather about mutual recognition that each community values its own share of Mayan civilization.

The position of the movement for Pan-Mayan identity can be summarized as follows:

1. Today's Maya should be recognized as such, because there are elements that strongly link them to the millennial history and tradition of their Mayan ancestors.

2. Pan-Mayanism is an effort to make the diversity of Mayan cultures strongly visible, reaffirming their presence as Maya in the present century.

3. Pan-Mayanism is an interethnic movement valuing and recognizing the importance of diversity in the unity of Mayan culture, including those in Mexico, Belize, and Honduras.

4. Any and all ruthless violence affecting a particular Mayan linguistic group must be considered as an attack against Mayan culture as a whole; this will bring broader international awareness of Mayan culture.

5. Stereotypes found in different Mayan linguistic communities are the result of their forced isolation from other groups. All Maya should understand and recognize that there are different ways of being Mayan.

6. Defense of the cultural heritage of the Maya must be seen as a global concern of all Mayan linguistic communities. In some areas, like Chia-

pas, Mexico, the recognition of the uniqueness and diversity of Mayan culture and the respect for those differences and autonomies are being created.

Thus Maya must seek this Pan-Mayan identity in order to legitimize their cultural projects of revitalization within and outside the nation-state. The Pan-Mayan cultural and political movement is being extended to other Mayan communities in Mexico, Belize, and Honduras as they develop projects of cultural revival like that of the Guatemalan Maya. The recognition of belonging to a common root or base culture as Maya and developing a Pan-Mayan solidarity must be encouraged (Montejo 1999). This cooperation will provide the basis for a more permanent peace and security instead of a continuation of the unequal relationship imposed by elite Ladino nationalism. Maya do not want to isolate themselves into little nation-states. We do not need to create a new Yugoslavia or replicate the ethnic warfare and tribal conflicts raging on the African continent. All Guatemalans, Mayan and non-Mayan, must work toward the construction of a pluralistic Guatemalan nation-state.

In the construction of a global Pan-Mayan ethnic identity, the role of Mayan organizations and the media is essential, as they help to promote the revitalization of Mayan culture. Among the organizations dedicated to the diffusion of Mayan ideas and information are at least two publishers, Cholsamaj and the Yax Te' Foundation, as well as the multilingual weekly newspaper *El Regional.* Similarly, the work of Mayan leaders at the national and international levels is also important. One of these Mayan figures is the Nobel Peace Prize winner Rigoberta Menchú, whose efforts have helped to bring indigenous issues to the forefront of discussion in Guatemala and elsewhere. Similarly, the role of the spiritual leaders has become a symbol for the revival and unification of Mayan culture nationally. It is my hope that the current demands of indigenous people for their self-determination and the support of the United Nations will help Maya to coordinate efforts to know and value their own uniqueness, a great asset for the multicultural nation-state building in Guatemala. There is still much to be done for the resurgence of Mayan culture in the whole Mayan area. At this point, Maya are becoming aware of their cultural heritage and focusing on the revival of institutions and ceremonies. Unfortunately, the Mayan movement is divided and has a weak leadership. There are at least some 200 Mayan organizations in Guatemala, each with its own agenda. Some are offshoots of political parties, members of NGOs, and religious Mayan and non-Mayan organizations. The Mayan organizations with strong links with the left, like the URNG, still use confrontational rhetoric in their demands and promote the invasion of lands and ecological reserves. It is unfortunate that members of Congress have not come out with legislative initiatives that attend to the demands of the Mayan population. Even worse, the current government of the FRG is not interested at all in the implementation of the peace accords.

Nevertheless, the Maya continue their struggles to make their presence visible. Among the projects being contemplated is the creation of a Mayan university. It is imperative that the leadership of the Mayan movement achieve higher education in order to develop a critical vision of the educational system. They must have the freedom and power of decision-making in the elaboration of educational curricula that are more global and inclusive. Similarly, the organization of a Mayan political party (one not exclusive of Ladinos) seems appropriate at this time when Maya have come to realize that they have been used by political parties, by institutions, and even by the contenders in the armed conflict. Maya must bring their creativity to the forefront and make their presence stronger and more visible. Also, a regenerationist Mayan leadership should organize a Mayan commission to monitor the implementation of the peace accords. The Maya must be in charge of developing and implementing projects for reparation to the communities affected by the recent armed conflict.

In order to achieve any level of political and cultural autonomy and self-determination, the Guatemalan Mayan movement must put an end to the centuries of silence. Maya must speak and write about everything, because we have been affected on every political or institutional front. Yes, the Maya need lawyers, anthropologists, Mayan priests, educators, politicians, poets, and writers. We are a civilization that must flourish in all of its creative expressions. All Guatemalans must recognize that Mayan culture is a vital part in the current efforts to lead the country to sustainable development and positive historical change. This is the challenge Mayan leaders and organizations confront now at the beginning of this new millennium.

Notes

1. The Chagnon-Tierney controversy over the Yanomami Indians of Venezuela portrayed in *Darkness in El Dorado: How Scientists and Journalists Devastated the Amazon* (Tierney 2000) is a good example of this continued misrepresentation of indigenous people in anthropology.
2. The civil patrols were paramilitary organizations for self-defense organized among the civilian population by the army, serving as the "eyes" and "ears" of the Guatemalan army (Schirmer 1998).

3. The *Popol Wuj, Anales de los Kaqchikeles,* and *Título de Totonicapán* are ethnohistorical documents written in Mayan language by indigenous writers after the Spanish conquest of Guatemala in 1524.

4. *Encomenderos* were captains of war and lords who were rewarded with *encomiendas:* royal grants which gave them a full title to the Indian serfs living on the land, which became Spanish estates.

5. This was the case at the Instituto Indígena para Varones "Santiago," where the author received his teaching degree in 1972.

6. Frente Democrático Nueva Guatemala was a political party organized by Rosalina Tuyuc, who was the head of the widows' organization CONAVIGUA. Tuyuc became one of the first Mayan women appointed to the Guatemalan Congress and nominated by the FDNG.

References

Anderson, Benedict. 1990. *Imagined Communities: Reflections on the Origin and Spread of Nationalism.* London and New York: Verso.

Bunzel, Ruth. 1981 [1952]. *Chichicastenango.* Guatemala City: Editorial José de Pineda Ibarra.

Carlsen, Robert S. 1997. *The War for the Heart and Soul of a Highland Maya Town.* Austin: University of Texas Press.

Carmack, Robert M., ed. 1988. *Harvest of Violence: The Maya Indians and the Guatemalan Crisis.* Norman: University of Oklahoma Press.

Castañeda, Quetzil E. 1996. *In the Museum of Maya Culture: Touring Chichén Itzá.* Minneapolis: University of Minnesota.

Chávez, Adrián Inés. 1979. *Pop Wuj.* Mexico City: Ediciones de la Casa Chata, Centro de Investigaciones del INAH.

Cojtí Cuxil, Demetrio. 1996. The Politics of Maya Revindication. In Edward F. Fischer and R. McKenna Brown, eds., *Maya Cultural Activism in Guatemala,* 19–50. Austin: University of Texas Press.

Dakin, Karen, and Christopher H. Lutz. 1996. *Nuestro pesar, nuestra aflicción: Memorias en lengua náhuatl enviadas a Felipe II por indígenas del Valle de Guatemala hacia 1572.* Mexico City: UNAM and CIRMA.

Fischer, Edward F., and R. McKenna Brown, eds. 1996. *Maya Cultural Activism in Guatemala.* Austin: University of Texas Press.

Guzmán Böckler, Carlos. 1979. Prólogo to Adrián I. Chávez, *Pop Wuj,* 7–27. Mexico City: Ediciones de la Casa Chata, Centro de Investigaciones del INAH.

Hobsbawm, Eric. 1988. "Introduction: Inventing Traditions." In Eric Hobsbawm and Terence Ranger, eds., *The Invention of Tradition,* 1–15. Cambridge: Cambridge University Press.

Krupat, Arnold. 1992. *Ethnocriticism, Ethnography, History, Literature.* Berkeley: University of California Press.

La Farge, Oliver, and Douglas Byers. 1931. *The Year Bearer's People.* Middle American Research Series, Publication No. 3. New Orleans: Tulane University.

Makemson, Maud. 1951. *Book of the Jaguar Priest*. New York: Henry Schuman.

Manz, Beatriz. 1988. *Refugees of a Hidden War: The Aftermath of Counterinsurgency in Guatemala*. Albany: State University of New York Press.

Marcus, George E., and Michael M. J. Fischer. 1986. *Anthropology as Cultural Critique: An Experimental Moment in the Human Sciences*. Chicago: University of Chicago Press.

Montejo, Victor D. 1987. *Testimony: Death of a Guatemalan Village*. Willimantic, Conn.: Curbstone Press.

———. 1991. *The Bird Who Cleans the World and Other Maya Fables*. Willimantic, Conn.: Curbstone Press.

———. 1997. Pan-Mayanismo: La pluriformidad de la cultura maya y el proceso de autorrepresentación. *Mesoamérica* 18 (33): 93–123.

———. 1999. *Voices from Exile: Violence and Survival in Modern Maya History*. Norman: University of Oklahoma Press.

———. 2001. *El Q'anil: Man of Lightning*. Tucson: University of Arizona Press.

Morales, Mario Roberto. 1996. *Fundamentalismo maya*. Guatemala City: Periódico Siglo Veintiuno.

Nagel, Joane. 1996. *American Indian Ethnic Renewal: Red Power and the Resurgence of Identity and Culture*. New York: Oxford University Press.

Peeler, John A. 1998. Social Justice and the New Indigenous Politics: An Analysis of Guatemala and the Central Andes. Paper presented at the 1998 International Congress of Latin American Studies Association, Chicago, September 24–26.

Perera, Victor. 1993. *Unfinished Conquest: The Guatemalan Tragedy*. Berkeley: University of California Press.

Redfield, Robert. 1950. *A Village That Chose Progress*. Chicago: University of Chicago Press.

REMHI (Proyecto Interdiocesano de Recuperación de la Memoria Histórica). 1998. *Guatemala: Nunca más*. Guatemala City: Oficina de Derechos Humanos del Arzobispado de Guatemala (ODHA).

Said, Edward W. 1979. *Orientalism*. New York: Vintage Books.

Schirmer, Jennifer. 1998. *The Guatemalan Military Project: A Violence Called Democracy*. Philadelphia: University of Pennsylvania Press.

Smith, Carol A., ed. 1990. *Guatemalan Indians and the State, 1540–1988*. Austin: University of Texas Press.

———. 1991. Maya Nationalism. *NACLA Report on the Americas* 25 (3): 29–33.

Tierney, Patrick. 2000. *Darkness in El Dorado: How Scientists and Journalists Devastated the Amazon*. New York: W. W. Norton.

Vickers, Scott B. 1998. *Native American Identities: From Stereotype to Archetype in Art and Literature*. Albuquerque: University of New Mexico Press.

Warren, Kay B. 1998. *Indigenous Movements and Their Critics: Pan-Maya Activism in Guatemala*. Princeton: Princeton University Press.

Wilson, Richard. 1995. *Maya Resurgence in Guatemala: Q'eqchi' Experiences*. Norman: University of Oklahoma Press.

Wolf, Eric R. 1982. *Europe and the People without History*. Berkeley: University of California Press.

5. VOTING AGAINST INDIGENOUS RIGHTS IN GUATEMALA

Lessons from the 1999 Referendum

Kay B. Warren

This essay views Guatemala's transition from counterinsurgency warfare to electoral democracy through the controversies unleashed by the national referendum on indigenous rights in May 1999 and the subsequent congressional and presidential elections. The analysis pays special attention to the marketing of alternative interpretations of indigenous rights by political groups that clashed during the YES and NO referendum campaigns.

The 53 percent to 47 percent defeat of the *consulta popular*, as the referendum was known in Spanish, came as a great shock, though not as a surprise, to many who have worked in Mayan organizations and communities over the last decade. The emerging character of indigenous and national politics, given the persistent disputes over the implementation of the 1996 peace accords, was at issue in this vote. Observers and Mayan leaders alike now wonder if leftist *popular* groups, which mobilized class-based movements against repression in the 1980s and early 1990s, and Mayan culturalist groups, which have had some success making the national political imaginary a more multicultural one in the 1990s, will be able to maneuver successfully within the established system of political parties and electoral politics. In the midst of a transition to democracy when the Maya could finally participate openly in national politics, many wondered why they appeared not to vote in their own interests. Were indigenous Guatemalans failing to embrace the carefully crafted political subjectivity that twenty years of Pan-Mayan social movements had crafted for them?

Even more striking was the fact that the vast majority of the electorate chose not to vote at all. In a country that bore witness to three decades of conservative authoritarian military rule and continues to suffer from endemic corruption in national politics, it is not surprising that abstention rates for the nation as a whole averaged 53 percent across both the presidential primaries and the runoff election, held after the referendum. Yet, given the sustained public controversy over indigenous rights, the striking 81 percent abstention rate for the referendum calls for further scrutiny.

Electoral politics is often seen as the most important marker of democracy, a crucial way in which citizens can seek to influence their government.[1] Yet, once one probes the meanings of voting in general or the particulars of a given vote, it becomes clear that the fact of casting ballots is overshadowed by the contested meanings of the process and its results. For the United States, the disputed Florida vote count in the 2000 presidential election between Albert Gore and George W. Bush focused attention on how local the nationwide practice of casting ballots and counting them is. From recent U.S. referendums—anti-immigrant propositions, English-only initiatives, and votes to disestablish affirmative action and bilingual education—it is clear that electoral politics influences wider understandings of what is socially and politically desirable, and whose interests are at odds in moments of social and economic reconfiguration, especially with current shifts in perception of the nation's ethnic composition. As Clifford Geertz argues in *The Social History of an Indonesian Town* (1965), the issues at stake behind the formal politics—the cultural as well as the political interests in play—can be just as important as the final outcome. Voting tallies, as this essay suggests, leave a great deal of unfinished business for their societies.

Guatemala has undergone two dramatic political transformations in the last thirty years: the guerrilla rebellion and horrific counterinsurgency war of the late 1970s and 1980s, and the more recent move to incorporate indigenous issues and protagonists within electoral politics after the return to civilian rule in 1985 and the peace accords of 1996. Across this period, Mayas have emerged from their fragmented status at the margins of the nation to be recognized as constituting the *majority* of the national population. However emblematic the 63 percent majority figure may be (see note 33 in the introduction), this new social fact constitutes a revolutionary change in the way that Guatemalans think about their social world.

As Julia Paley (2001) argues in her study of the 1988 Agusto Pinochet referendum in Chile, political marketing involves using the media to target particular sectors of the electorate with powerful images designed to manipulate consumer desire and create the illusion of choice. In addition to flyers, Chilean activists on both sides used sophisticated national TV campaigns and designed short advertising spots to reach wide audiences with catchy jingles and images.

In Guatemala, the YES and NO campaigns on indigenous rights targeted urban voters through talk show radio programming; carefully crafted, seemingly objective presentations of the pros and cons of each of the proposed reforms in brochures that were circulated by a variety of groups; and propagandistic flyers tactically deployed for selected markets. As will become evident, the referendum was a complex, even cynical vehicle for citizen participation in a country where illiteracy rates range from 11.2 percent in the department of Guatemala, the site of the nation's capital, to 58 percent in Alta Verapaz, a predominately rural and indigenous department.

Of course, one can halt all analysis at the onset by focusing on the alarming abstention rate, dismiss voting as not meaningful when so few actually vote,[2] and conclude that the language of rights is an abstract and alien imposition far from people's daily concerns in the countryside.

Or one can declare that this is not really an anthropological project because it involves abstract charts of vote counts and political issues that belong to another field of inquiry.[3] Why, however, should anthropology not engage in the study of democracy, employing our meaning-centered approaches that examine the complex interrelation of discourses and practices in their wider political and social contexts? The stakes are particularly high in this case because analysts outside Guatemala are citing the referendum's defeat as the end of effective indigenous organizing, in contrast to what they see as more successful models of activism in other Latin American countries. Wider evaluations by social scientists of the significance of this defeat and the viability of the Pan-Mayan movement—which has sought culturally and politically to unify people from historically related indigenous communities across local loyalties and language diversity—have the potential to affect international support and funding for reforms in Guatemala.[4] This essay argues that any such assessment needs to be developed in a less reductive way, focusing on the state and its failures as much as on the Pan-Mayan movement.

I would suggest that a closer examination of the referendum—including the meaning of the vote for partisans of both sides, the political process involved, a finer-grained consideration of the voting patterns, and the surprising turn of events in its aftermath—yields many political lessons for the Pan-Mayan movement and its allies, who together seek to create a viable multicultural nation-state. All would agree that voting is a necessary but insufficient indicator of democracy for a country that has been haunted by periods of immobilizing instability during its troubled transition to civilian rule.

Along with this case study, I hope to generate a comparative discussion of the ironies and significance of democratic participation in a world in which state sovereignty has been eroded on many fronts. Several streams of recent theorizing relate to this project: Deborah Yashar's (1996, 1998) view of indigenous activism as a response to neoliberal economic and political pressures, Michel-Rolph Trouillot's (2001) reconsideration of globalization, and Richard Falk's (1997) view on the politics of utopian thought in indigenous movements that threaten to fragment existing states.

THE EMERGENCE OF INDIGENOUS RIGHTS AND ACTIVISM

Few observers anticipated that indigenous rights would become a central element in Guatemala's peace process, which took seven years of on-and-off-again negotiations to get underway during the country's low-intensity warfare, which followed three decades of brutal counterinsurgency war. This fortuitous change was a result of the tactical convergence of indigenous groups, particularly of activists in the popular left and others in the Pan-Mayan cultural revitalization movement, who together successfully pressured for inclusion in the civilian wing of the negotiations through what came to be recognized as the Assembly of Civil Society (Asamblea de Sociedad Civil: ASC) during the drafting of the accords. Both groups came to see the language of rights as a way to push for indigenous recognition and representation in the powerful social and political institutions from which they had been largely excluded in the past. Both groups were radicalized as they were forced to come to a consensus over a common agenda of indigenous issues through the newly created Coordination of the Mayan Pueblo of Guatemala or Saqb'ichil/COPMAGUA, as their wing of the ASC was called (Bastos and Camus 1995, 1996; ASIES 1996; Cojtí Cuxil 1997; Warren 1998).

This surge in indigenous activism is consistent with Deborah Yashar's (1996, 1998) regime-focused findings that attribute politicized resurgence in the Americas to the democratic opening in many Latin American states in the 1980s and 1990s. The opening brought many tensions, including neoliberal economic reforms mandated by the international foreign aid community that called for reductions in government services and subsidies and the expansion of free markets, which endangered rural communities' subsistence. As dictatorships were pressured by international organizations to liberalize their regimes, hold elections, and honor basic civil and political rights, indigenous groups emerged publicly to press for concerns that had no legal channel in the repressive years before.

Throughout this period, indigenous organizing was a transnational affair with frequent regional and international meetings that focused on articulating a common language of rights-based demands addressed to national governments. The state's and civil society's continual marginalization of Mayas by excluding them from regular channels for citizen participation—including the congress, political parties, and major social institutions—forced Mayas to organize themselves politically outside the grammar of conventional community groups.

Trouillot (2001) suggests another analytic language for comprehending these events. The heart of the matter for him is the growing intensity of globalization. Despite the vibrant rhetorics of sovereignty and nationalism, it is now impossible to sustain the bounded or container view of states as autonomous entities. Rather than viewing the state as a composite of formal political institutions that monopolize coercive powers and contrast with civil society, Trouillot stresses the importance of conceptualizing the state as a collection of social fields, boundaries, and institutions. States are knowable through the ethnographic study of ongoing events and processes that capture transnational power relations, the circulation of capital and growing concentration of economic power, and the restructuring of labor markets. Trouillot suggests a conceptual innovation, the study of the interplay of transnational and state powers through their effects. Among these "state effects" are the production of atomized individualized subjects, collective identities, languages of governance, and boundaries and jurisdictions (2001: 4). With neoliberal globalization, which calls for privatization in order to cut state expenditures for public services, states are yielding functions to other groups, and international institutions and NGOs are appropriating state spheres of activity which produce state effects in their own right. Thus, one needs to look at state effects as just as much a product of globalized interventions as a result of domestic politics. The trick, I would add, is coming to a fuller understanding of the interplay.

Finally, Richard Falk (1997) argues that a characteristic of indigenous movements in the Americas is the combination of utopian radicalism— the dream of total autonomy from dominant states, which by implication would lead to the breakup of existing states—with the capacity to forge compromises that involve novel power-sharing arrangements within states. For him, a deeper history of activism needs to be revealed. Such dual political imaginaries are reflected in the history of Mayan activism in Guatemala. In an early wave of activism dating from the late 1970s and early 1980s, leftist Mayas from the student and labor movements, as well as rural activists from what became the Comité de Unidad Campesino

(CUC), joined or directly supported the armed insurgency in the western highlands. The radical utopianism of those times was revolutionary socialism. Interestingly, a number of activists from culturalist groups also joined their ranks in places like Huehuetenango in the sometimes chaotic early highland guerrilla mobilization. When culturalist activists were killed in what were then understood as internal disputes within the rebel forces, many of their peers were discouraged from supporting armed opposition as a route to social change. The wider history of Ladino-Maya relations within the guerrilla movement has often been idealized, although revisionist accounts from Mayan former guerrillas who have begun to discuss the racism within the guerrilla fronts are now emerging.

A second wave of radical utopianism, this one distinctively separatist in tone, flowered in the speeches and writings of Demetrio Cojtí Cuxil (1991, 1994, 1995, 1996b, 1997) in the 1980s and 1990s. Cojtí Cuxil was instrumental in passionate behind-the-scenes discussions that spurred the formation of many of the culturalist groups in the 1980s. Through endless meetings and workshops, the dream emerged of a separate Mayan state built on the regionalism of Mayan language groups reconfigured as ethnic variations of Mayan cultural nationalism. The Pan-Mayan embrace of cultural rights is clear from the initial manifesto of the Council of Mayan Organizations (COMG 1995), read at the 1991 Second Continental Meetings for Indigenous and Popular Resistance in Quetzaltenango. Furthermore, one can see their emphasis on publishing regionalized language maps as an attempt to make this vision spatially legible, even as state organizations have been reluctant to promote spatial representations that would rewrite basic administrative units (see Maps 5.1 and 5.2). Those who read this separatism literally can choose to overreact to indigenous activism, just as Falk would predict. Officials of the Guatemalan government, MINUGUA (United Nations Verification Mission in Guatemala), and U.S.-AID often referred to Cojtí Cuxil during the 1990s as a dangerous radical rather than a nation builder.

In fact, as early as 1994 Cojtí Cuxil's writings turned to self-consciously articulating a federalist solution to Ladino-Maya coexistence as a compromise solution and counterpoint to a wished-for Mayan nation-state. This is clear from his writings in the national newspaper *Siglo Veintiuno:*

Isn't it possible to conceive of Guatemala as a free association of Mayan and mestizo communities which undertake common objectives but preserve their respective integrity and identity? Pan-Mayanists consider this federal form of political organization an ideal that is still not feasible, and therefore accept the location of their project for national

MAP 5.1 Mayan language map of Guatemala. Pan-Mayanists use this language map to argue that language diversity and indigenous identity are regional issues. By contrast, the Guatemalan state insists on the primacy of the administrative division of the country (see Map 5.2) into departments (*departamentos*), which ignore language divides, and counties (*municipios*), which reflect the existing patterns of community loyalty. The government has long resisted representations of the nation that could be used as a framework for regional self-administration. Source: Warren (1998).

liberation within the framework of the pyramidal State . . . In this model, the ethnic diversity and autonomy of each ethnic group would not be complete, but would function at the intermediate level of government. Autonomous regions or microregions would be formed from *municipios* (counties) composed of the speakers of the same language. (*Siglo Veintiuno*, February 16, 1995)

MAP 5.2 Political-administrative divisions of the country. Source: Warren (1998).

There can be no other choice than that the central state apparatus car-ries out the supraethnic functions that concern all individual and col-lective members of society (such as national defense, diplomatic re-lations, common standards) while the particular ethnic region could and should exercise administrative and legislative powers in areas that directly affect its existence and well-being (education, culture, social work, police, heath, etc.). (*Siglo Veintiuno*, August 28, 1994)

One sees in Cojtí Cuxil's writings a vigorous critique of Ladino racism and the tactical possibility of working within or outside the system, as conditions permit.

In my view, regime-focused, globalization-focused, and dual political imaginary-focused approaches offer different languages for understanding the tensions and conflicts of democratic transition in Guatemala. Each is useful in its own way for making sense of these complex currents of change in Guatemala, if we are to avoid seeing this instance of ethnic resurgence as an isolated phenomenon.

THE INDIGENOUS ACCORDS

The first surprise was that the peace process involved indigenous rights at all. What is distinctive about the peace process in Guatemala is that it has occurred after decades of chronic internal warfare that culminated in a horrifying crescendo of violence in the early 1980s during which 20 percent of the nation's people were displaced from their homes, hundreds of communities were attacked by counterinsurgency troops, some 200,000 refugees fled to other countries, and at least 80,000 people were killed, the vast majority being from indigenous communities in the western highlands. While some analysts have denied that this was an ethnic war (Stoll 1993), the Guatemalan truth commission used the word "genocide" in its final report (CEH 1999) and made it clear that the vast majority of the victims of this phase of counterinsurgency warfare, including the bloodiest offensives in 1982–1983, were Mayas killed by the Guatemalan army (CEH 1999). Ethnicity became politicized and militarized in a number of ways during the counterinsurgency war. First, military indoctrination of its troops built on the imagery of subduing the rebellious Indian (Schirmer 1998; Montejo 1999). Second, President Ríos Montt's imposition of civil patrols in 1981 to divide insurgents from sources of civilian support meant that Mayan towns and villages were forced to monitor their own communities. Third, death squads organized by the government with army collaboration targeted indigenous leaders in rural communities who were active in Catholic Action (a lay Catholic group), the agrarian cooperative movement, and grassroots leftist groups (Warren 1978, 1999).

To the surprise of many Guatemalans, the main peace negotiators, including representatives of the military, the government, and the rebels, signed a separate accord on indigenous rights in 1995. The United Nations–brokered negotiations had been influenced by lessons from the El Salvador peace process so that they included a range of social and political issues beyond the immediate demobilization of the rebels and wartime army (ASIES 1996). In 1996 the separate indigenous rights accord became part of the final peace agreement, which dealt with demilitarization, postwar reconstruction, and democratization. While the country was jubilant about the formal end to civil war after years of stalled peace talks, it was clear that the disarming of the guerrilla forces, which occurred rapidly and successfully, was only one step in a much longer process (ASIES 1996). The accords were not, in fact, binding agreements but rather calls for further discussion, congressional legislation, and constitutional reform. To implement the peace accords, there would have to be consensus on how to operationalize them and then referendums or constitutional assemblies to ratify reforms. A list of the issues from the indigenous accords (Saqb'ichil/COPMAGUA 1995) illustrates how complicated implementation would be if it were successfully to transform abstract commitments to concrete programs that might attract funding:

- Recognition of Guatemala's indigenous people as descendants of an ancient people who speak diverse, historically related languages and share a distinctive culture and cosmology.

- Officialization of indigenous languages and recognition of the legitimacy of using them in schools, social services, official communications, and court proceedings.

- Recognition and protection of Mayan spirituality and spiritual guides and the conservation of ceremonial centers and archaeological sites as indigenous heritage, which should involve Mayas in its administration.

- Commitment to educational reform, specifically the integration of Mayan materials and educational methods, the involvement of families in all areas of education, and the promotion of intercultural programs for all children.

- Indigenous representation in administrative bodies on all levels, the regionalization of government functions, and the recognition of localized customary law and community decision-making powers in education, health, and economic development.

- Recognition of communal lands and the reform of the legal system so Mayan interests are adequately represented in the adjudication of land disputes. The distribution of state lands to communities with insufficient land.

As U.N.-sponsored MINUGUA has monitored the process of implementation (MINUGUA 1998), ambivalence about cultural rights and the political mobilization of the national population that is of Mayan descent continues.

On the right of the political party spectrum, Ríos Montt's Guatemalan Republican Front (FRG) sought to derail the reforms procedurally in the congress to make sure they were never implemented. The left created its own political party, the New Guatemala Democratic Front (FDNG), which included many *popular* leaders such as Rosalina Tuyuc from CUC, former guerrilla sympathizers, and ex-guerrilla leaders who supported accord implementation. Direct support also flowed from COPMAGUA, the still active Mayan umbrella group from the peace process. The Pan-Mayan leadership participated in official commissions to make the case for particular strategies for accord implementation. On the independent left, public intellectuals like Mario Roberto Morales argued that the leadership of the Pan-Mayan movement was full of urban opportunists who did not authentically represent their people (Morales 1998; Warren 1998). Heated debates continued from the mid-1990s in the mass media on a range of fronts, and Mayan leaders such as Demetrio Cojtí Cuxil and Estuardo Zapeta, who had not had wide public exposure before this time, emerged as regular commentators in the mass media. Enrique Sam Colop joined this lineup, and in 1999 Víctor Montejo became another Mayan voice in the national press.

THE REFERENDUM: VOTE TALLIES AND QUALITATIVE CONCERNS

In the summer of 1999 the vote was seen as a pivotal moment in indigenous organizing because it revealed that the political interests and benefits of the reforms which appeared to be of obvious importance to those in the Pan-Mayan movement were not transparently significant for indigenous people nationally. The success of the NO vote generated Mayan debates over alternative political strategies—some ethnic nationalist and others intercultural—appropriate to this phase of the troubled transition to democracy. I had the opportunity to discuss the referendum with members of both camps while the constitutional reforms were being publicly debated earlier in the year, and at a variety of Mayan forums after the vote, where shell-shocked leaders engaged in postmortems in the months immediately after the vote.

The 1999 referendum was designed to measure the civilian support for a wide range of reforms, many of which dealt with indigenous issues and the redefinition of Guatemala as a "multicultural, ethnically plural, and multilingual state." By any measure the referendum failed to attract substantial support for a more inclusive definition of national culture. As this was a nonpresidential election, only 18 percent of the registered voters bothered to vote at the polling places located in their county seats, often at a great distance from people's homes. In some departments such as the predominantly Ladino Jutiapa in the eastern part of the country, the abstention rate was over 91 percent; in others such as the predominately Mayan department of Sololá, the rate was a lower 70 percent. Table 5.1 summarizes the results by department, with predominately Mayan departments in boldface. It is interesting that the referendum's high abstention rates contrast strikingly with the respective abstention rates of 46.7 percent and 37.1 percent in these same departments for the presidential primaries and general elections held later that year.

Telling details about the structuring of the referendum are presented below. At this juncture, it is important to note that the YES vote for the referendum *as a whole* took the majority in only four of eight predominately Mayan departments. Yet the referendum was actually composed of four questions, covering different sets of issues. The number increases to six of eight predominately Mayan departments when the different questions of the referendum are disaggregated so that Question 1, which contained the lion's share of constitutional reforms on indigenous issues, is the measure. What is clear in general is that Mayas, in fact, did carry their own regions. For the western highlands, then, those voters who were engaged in the process supported the YES vote with Question 1 totals as high as 58–69 percent for the departments of Huehuetenango, Quiché, Alta Verapaz, and Sololá (see Table 5.2). At 49.8 percent, the referendum barely lost in the department of San Marcos. At 42.5 percent, Quetzaltenango, home to Guatemala's second largest city, appears to be anomalous in its lower support (discussed at greater length below).

On the national level, none of the proposed reforms was approved by voters. For the indigenous issues which were concentrated in packet 1, the national YES vote was 47 percent and the NO vote 53 percent. Another highly controversial question, dealing with major reforms of the armed services, received a 43 percent YES vote and a 57 percent NO vote. Dinorah Azpuru's (1999) data show that greater Guatemala City had 26.5 percent of the nation's voters and produced an aggregate YES vote of 26 percent on the referendum as a whole. Many observers argue that winning the capital was crucial. But as she points out, the Mayan highlands also contain a substantial proportion of the electorate. By my calculations, it turns out that departments with over 40 percent indigenous population represent 38.1 percent of the nation's voters. These departments produced an aggregate YES vote that ranged from 54 to 75 percent of their electorates, with the exception of Quetzaltenango, the location of the country's second city, where the YES vote was 42 percent (Azpuru

Presidential Election

Region	Illiteracy	Consulta		Presidential Primary				Presidential Election		
	Illiteracy Rate (%)	Mean "Yes" (%)	Abstention Rate (%)	PAN (%)	FRG (%)	DIA-URNG (%)	Abstention Rate (%)	FRG (%)	PAN (%)	Abstention Rate (%)
Guatemala	11.20	24.51	80.09	34.82	47.84	8.03	45.30	65.80	34.20	54.61
El Progreso	26.37	27.44	84.57	35.08	52.60	3.02	42.16	69.70	30.30	54.28
Sacatepéquez	18.62	28.40	79.21	26.31	54.80	8.88	40.47	73.40	26.60	53.81
Zacapa	29.24	28.76	80.93	30.97	63.96	2.35	39.37	78.30	21.70	49.88
Santa Rosa	28.92	30.95	87.16	31.84	48.27	8.54	46.21	71.00	29.00	62.63
Escuintla	25.88	35.41	84.28	25.38	53.58	13.08	49.50	78.00	22.00	59.32
Suchitepéquez	35.25	36.08	81.66	21.36	56.34	12.34	41.65	78.60	21.40	55.52
Jutiapa	32.12	36.76	91.68	32.09	55.30	3.32	46.71	74.50	25.50	60.94
Retalhuleu	29.12	37.66	82.98	24.29	50.67	19.57	48.11	75.10	24.90	60.48
Quetzaltenango	**26.48**	**37.89**	**79.41**	**26.02**	**45.18**	**17.54**	**47.65**	**66.80**	**33.20**	**62.32**
Chiquimula	41.65	40.11	85.01	40.50	49.96	3.74	39.86	65.00	35.00	54.15
Izabal	31.72	43.07	83.35	22.39	53.60	16.26	50.81	79.30	20.70	61.03
Jalapa	38.86	44.80	89.39	38.31	49.74	3.52	42.63	66.30	33.70	55.90
San Marcos	**34.00**	**47.14**	**82.99**	**24.34**	**47.98**	**14.30**	**50.29**	**70.00**	**30.00**	**66.44**
Baja Verapaz	**44.10**	**47.77**	**81.88**	**31.69**	**50.87**	**9.49**	**43.93**	**77.90**	**22.10**	**60.07**
Totonicapán	**43.97**	**48.68**	**78.80**	**23.92**	**47.74**	**15.98**	**44.40**	**67.70**	**32.30**	**64.38**
Chimaltenango	31.71	48.85	74.87	25.39	42.81	20.68	44.70	68.70	31.30	60.18
Huehuetenango	**45.88**	**55.64**	**80.16**	**22.01**	**44.41**	**13.09**	**48.02**	**78.30**	**21.70**	**70.71**
El Quiché	**56.63**	**60.86**	**80.77**	**25.85**	**44.46**	**18.88**	**46.66**	**71.10**	**28.90**	**67.65**
Alta Verapaz	**58.24**	**62.75**	**73.76**	**21.37**	**50.14**	**20.58**	**45.50**	**74.80**	**25.20**	**58.26**
Sololá	**49.84**	**67.03**	**70.01**	**25.15**	**36.00**	**28.60**	**37.13**	**66.80**	**33.20**	**60.39**
Petén	35.83	71.16	86.66	27.83	39.97	25.53	51.62	63.90	36.10	63.81
COUNTRY	31.90	40.40	81.45	30.32	47.72	12.36	46.24	68.30	31.70	59.61
Guatemala City	11.20	22.36	78.78	42.56	41.93	8.52	47.42	54.30	45.70	54.37

Source: Data from Tribunal Supremo Electoral de Guatemala, World Development Indicators Database 2001, Resultados Finales de las Coberturas de Atención Etapa Inicial.

Note: Sorted by *consulta* YES votes; boldfaced departments have Mayan majorities.

TABLE 5.2. Guatemalan Referendum Results by Ballot Question and Department

Region	Question 1 National Social Rights (%)	Question 2 Legislative Branch (%)	Question 3 Executive Branch (%)	Question 4 Judicial Branch (%)	Mean "Yes" (%)	Abstention Rate (%)
Guatemala	27.00	20.89	23.57	26.58	25.51	80.09
El Progreso	31.41	24.39	25.94	28.03	27.44	84.57
Sacatapéquez	32.88	24.51	26.01	30.20	28.40	79.21
Zacapa	30.19	27.63	27.80	29.42	28.76	80.96
Santa Rosa	33.85	28.49	29.38	32.08	30.95	87.16
Escuintla	37.80	33.12	34.21	36.50	35.41	84.28
Suchitepéquez	38.65	33.74	34.74	37.19	36.08	81.66
Jutiapa	39.70	34.01	35.32	37.99	36.76	91.68
Retalhuleu	40.26	35.34	36.18	38.87	37.66	82.98
Quetzaltenango	**42.46**	**33.90**	**35.28**	**39.90**	**37.89**	**79.41**
Chiquimula	41.84	37.97	39.33	41.28	40.11	85.01
Izabal	45.33	41.51	41.80	43.62	43.07	83.35
Jalapa	47.93	41.79	43.39	46.07	44.80	89.39
San Marcos	**49.78**	**45.09**	**45.86**	**47.83**	**47.14**	**82.99**
Baja Verapaz	**50.80**	**45.63**	**45.99**	**48.67**	**47.77**	**81.88**
Totonicapán	**59.53**	**41.00**	**41.30**	**52.87**	**48.68**	**78.80**
Chimaltenango	53.05	45.17	46.97	50.19	48.85	74.87
Huehuetenango	**58.16**	**53.62**	**54.17**	**56.61**	**55.64**	**80.16**
El Quiché	**62.22**	**59.87**	**59.94**	**61.42**	**60.86**	**80.77**
Alta Verapaz	**65.11**	**60.93**	**61.59**	**63.37**	**62.75**	**73.76**
Sololá	**69.21**	**65.21**	**66.01**	**67.68**	**67.03**	**70.01**
Petén	72.08	70.37	70.25	71.94	71.16	86.66

Source: Data from Tribunal Supremo Electoral de Guatemala, World Development Indicators Database 2001, Resultados Finales de las Coberturas de Atención Etapa Inicial.

Note: Sorted by *consulta* YES votes; boldfaced departments have Mayan majorities.

1999). It is important to note once again that departments with substantial indigenous populations continued to have abstention rates in the 70–80 percent range. That voters must travel great distances from their dispersed homes to the municipal center in order to vote contributes to chronically low voter turnouts for referendums when they are not combined with presidential elections.

The Mayan vote count is consistent with Richard Adams's (1996) argument that over time the twentieth-century departments with higher Mayan populations have became increasingly Mayan, while swing departments have lost Maya-identified populations to assimilation into the

Ladino "mainstream." The referendum results highlight precisely these departments.

As one national Mayan leader commented after the vote tallies were clear, "Now we have our Maya map" (see Map 5.3, which includes Quetzaltenango, famed for its Mayan mayor, Rigoberto Quemé Chay). While the state could inhibit the recognition and distribution of the Mayan language map because it does not follow the contours of the official departmental divisions, and thus to some seemed dangerously seditious, the state-mandated process of the referendum in effect produced an alternative Mayan map. If one compares these attempts to render a Mayan state legible (Scott 1998), the dual consciousness of utopian separatism versus everyday living within state discipline is made visible.

Few were surprised by the Ladino support of the NO vote, since any change in the ethnic status quo was deeply problematic to many Ladinos who see themselves as the westernized mainstream of the country and the rightful representatives of its hispanic national culture. Nevertheless, many Mayan leaders were disappointed by the low turnout of Mayan voters in rural areas where they constitute the majority of the population. Why would the Mayan highlands fail to deliver more votes and cut into the high rate of abstention?

Mayan responses—from public discussions at the Maya-run conferences I attended and from interviews of local teachers, heads of regional organizations, and national leaders—varied as to what many saw as a serious setback to the Mayan cause. Some leaders argued that the moment was right to focus on activism in party politics; others argued that the only solution was to create an explicitly Mayan party. Many were skeptical of the electoral process and felt that the lesson of the referendum was that organizing efforts needed to return to the grassroots to promote a social movement that would find alternative avenues of political influence through a strategy of cultural revitalization and social institution building, including schools and community centers. This would be, in effect, building on the dominant model in the Mayan movement since the late 1980s. Others felt that the movement needed to work on a wider scale, to transcend the localism of Mayan self-identification with home community, which is the deepest cultural affinity for many people in the countryside.

Everyone agrees that a major reason for the referendum's failure as a vehicle for electoral participation was its complexity. Many interests shaped its final form during congressional deliberations. Until two months before the vote, it was not clear if voters would be given only one item to vote on, if they would vote on fifty separate articles for constitutional

MAP 5.3 The indigenous rights section of the 1999 referendum. Although the referendum as a whole was defeated 54 percent to 47 percent, activists point out that Question 1, which focused on the "nation and social rights," passed by a majority (or near majority) of votes in the western highlands where Mayas make up the majority of the population. With these official results, Mayan leaders were able to assert: "Now we have our Maya map." The shaded areas on this map represent departments where the YES vote gained a plurality, ranging from 50.8 percent in Baja Verapaz to 69.2 percent in Sololá. The striped areas of Quetzaltenango and San Marcos came in very close to pluralities, with 42.4 percent and 49.8 percent YES votes. (It is unclear why El Petén in light gray gained a 72 percent plurality, as it is located outside the Mayan highlands.)

5.1 Mayan leaders Martín Chacach, Narciso Cojtí, and Víctor Montejo speaking at the First Mayan Education Congress in Quetzaltenango, Guatemala, in 1994. Photo by Kay B. Warren.

reform, or if there would be successful Supreme Court challenges of the referendum. Mayan leader Cojtí Cuxil (1999) described how some Mayan indigenous congressional representatives wanted to separate different aspects of the indigenous reforms so that a racist vote on one question would not negate all the proposed reforms. In the end, Mayan congressional representatives created a consensus, with support from COPMAGUA and leftist coalitions in the party system, for a set of reforms dealing with the "nation and social rights." Among them were:

- Recognition of Guatemala as a multiethnic, multilingual, and pluricultural nation.
- Access to sacred sites for Mayan descendants.
- Consultation with indigenous people concerning laws that would affect them.
- State recognition of twenty-five indigenous languages.
- Congressional formation of a language officialization committee.

If passed, these reforms would have involved substantial revisions of the country's constitution. Yet it is interesting to note that land issues from the original accords were omitted from the referendum.

5.2 Mayas voting at an agrarian cooperative meeting in San Andrés Semetabaj in 1971. Photo by Kay B. Warren.

5.3 Schoolchildren from a Pan-Mayan elementary school on a field trip to the mayor's office in San Andrés Semetabaj in 1996. Photo by Kay B. Warren.

5.4 Mayan linguists in training in 1997 at OKMA in Antigua, Guatemala. Photo by Kay B. Warren.

5.5 The revitalization of Mayan ritual performances in San Andrés Semetabaj in 1989. Photo by Kay B. Warren.

5.6 Mayan journalist Estuardo Zapeta, who came to play a central role in the 1999 NO campaign, shares a light moment three years earlier at the Mayan Studies Conference with truth commission member Otilia Lux de Cotí (center) and social scientist Margarita López, who supported the YES campaign. Photo by Kay B. Warren. Courtesy of Princeton University Press.

Voters were confronted with three additional packets of reforms pertaining to the "legislative branch," "executive branch," and "judicial branch." Reforms continued to be added and others challenged during the congressional deliberations; thus the referendum did not jell until the last moment. Each of the final packets of reforms, identified by color, contained ten to nineteen separate articles which were markedly diverse in content. For instance, free health care, compensation reform for government employees, and compulsory military or social service were added to what some had envisioned as the "indigenous" section, that is, as Question 1.

In some cases, specific reforms pertaining to indigenous communities were included in the other packets. For instance, the formation of community-level development councils was incorporated into the executive branch packet, and the recognition of customary law into the judicial branch packet. To add to the confusion, while in the case of the nation and social rights packet all the articles represented substantial reforms, 69 percent of the judicial branch reforms were refinements rather than changes in substance.

No powerful political group seemed satisfied with the final product.

5.7 Marta Elena Casaus Arzú, a historian and elite ally of the Mayan movement, with Demetrio Cojtí Cuxil, a driving intellectual force in the movement who has played a central role in international education for UNICEF and, after the defeat of the referendum, became the vice minister of education in the Portillo government. Photo by Loy Carrington.

The party in power, President Arzú's Partido de Avanzada Nacional (National Advancement Party: PAN), condemned the referendum with faint praise and prohibited government agencies from campaigning on the issue. Ríos Montt's FRG strongly opposed the referendum. The Coordinating Committee of Agricultural, Commercial, Industrial, and Financial Institutions (CACIF), the powerful rightist business group, dragged its feet even as it moved just days before the vote to support the NO position (Ríos de Rodríguez 1999).

PAN-MAYANIST VIEWS OF THE REFERENDUM

Many indigenous leaders I spoke with complained that it was impossible to condense their complex opinions about the issues into a single vote on each packet of constitutional reforms.[5] This was also the problem for savvy voters presented with such seriously flawed referendum choices. Activists I interviewed found themselves "in favor of seven [of the articles] and opposed to three, or vice versa," and many simply decided not to vote. Furthermore, while strongly in favor of the indigenous reforms in general, some activists could not support the creation of community development councils because they would erode the autonomy of municipal governments, a crucial issue for cities like Quetzaltenango, whose Mayan mayor, Rigoberto Quemé Chay, was backed by the powerful Xelaju' Civic Committee, which functioned as an alternative to party politics. This was the double bind for those in a position to do a sophisticated analysis of the substance of the referendum. Hence, the crosscurrents of indigenous interests evoked by the referendum explain some of the low YES vote in Guatemala's second city, located in a majoritarian Mayan area.

The net effect was that the national leadership of many important culturalist organizations in the highlands did not work with local leaders from their communities to mount a systematic campaign in support of the YES vote. The congress produced such a flawed vehicle for their participation that many Mayan professionals found themselves unable to endorse the indigenous rights that they supported in their everyday work lives when it came to having to decide on either a YES or a NO vote on the referendum's passage. As a result, some of the most successful groups dedicated to indigenous rights did not work actively for the passage of the referendum.

Also puzzling is the YES coalition's spotty organization on the grassroots level despite its years of *popular* organization and more recent Pan-Mayanist language committees in many Mayan communities. On the whole, local and regional organizations were not able to get out the vote on any massive scale or to stand up to the opposition's rhetoric. Some of the leaders I interviewed in the far west said that the campaign did not reach their rural communities at all. Local leaders described activists' last-minute attempts to get out the vote with truck caravans and banners, but this appeared to be too little, too late in motivating people so that they could find out about the packets and travel to municipal centers on election day. Some departmental capitals such as Sololá were able to get out the vote because they had strong grassroots organizations and activist mayors (see Smith 2001). Their rates of abstention were among the lowest and their participation in the subsequent congressional and presidential elections among the highest. Many leaders noted that where the indigenous population represented the great majority there was a higher Mayan vote and the YES vote took the referendum.

Perhaps most telling was the account of a human rights activist who has been involved in exhumations of clandestine cemeteries from the counterinsurgency war in order to document the violence and bring closure to the families of the disappeared. He reported that when Mayanist organizations visited rural communities to explain the referendum, local populations sometimes saw them as strangers rather than fellow Mayas. Evincing a long-standing distrust, these people wondered, "If I vote for this referendum, am I voting for the guerrillas or for the military?" One sees in this activist's narrative the wounds from the counterinsurgency war that can run especially deep in rural areas, far from the cosmopolitanism of urban Guatemala. For outlying areas, Cold War dichotomies resonate with new freedoms in discordant ways.

THE OPPOSITION

Just as important as the problems inherent in mobilizing the YES vote was the NO campaign's clever media strategy, which was orchestrated by the Mayan journalist Estuardo Zapeta, known for his free-spirited independence and commitment to Mayan causes, if not always to Pan-Mayanism. Zapeta and the NGO he worked for ran a very effective opposition campaign, financed by conservatives, which sought to influence the urban vote. As he quipped in our interview shortly after the referendum, "This was the *consulta* where no one was consulted." In reconstructing the politics that surrounded the drafting of the referendum's inchoate list of reforms, Zapeta suggests that the representatives of each political party in the multiparty planning committee pressured relentlessly for their immediate interests as they negotiated behind closed doors. Zapeta wrote commentaries for the national press and served as the host of a radio show, aired daily, during which he put a series of ambivalent, clearly uncomfortable political figures in the hot seat. Zapeta championed the following lines of argument in the media:

- Since the 1996 peace accords are political and not constitutional documents, a referendum is the wrong vehicle for such reforms. Identity is not a constitutional question but rather a social and political one, which, therefore, lies beyond the realm of constitutional reform.

- By means of their funding of the peace process, international donors have called the shots and pressured Mayan activists and the government with enormous quantities of money in the name of rights, reforms, and democratization. This money has corrupted those who are involved in indigenous issues because they end up "selling themselves as representatives of their communities" and "believing their own lies" when it comes to issues such as language policies.

How can Mayan languages be officialized when "Mayan linguists and their foreign mentors are inventing new languages as we speak"? [This charge referred to the fact that descriptive linguists trained at Oxlajuuj Keej Maya' Ajtz'iib' (OKMA, which as the major Mayan research center on indigenous languages maintains a fruitful association with the North American linguist Nora England) had concluded, in some cases, that what had been conventionally thought of as dialects of a single Mayan language are in reality distinct languages. In other cases, what have been considered distinctive Mayan languages by their speakers have been found through linguistic research to be dialects of the same language.]

It does not make sense to recognize customary law because there is no constitutional basis for several systems of laws in the country. Moreover, how will such laws apply to local Ladinos?

Mayan spirituality should not have been included in the reform package, given that the separation of church and state is central to governance. Furthermore, some Mayan elders have protested the recognition of Mayan spirituality in the reforms by arguing that Mayan religion is not negotiable. Given this stance by religious leaders, how can indigenous religion be part of a political campaign?

With respect to reforms that call for consulting local communities whenever they might be affected by new laws, the real question is what national issues—education, health, justice, and social security—*do not* affect indigenous communities. Reforms that single out one ethnic community and not others are deeply paternalistic.

The ethnic focus for constitutional reforms has become a dogma of victimization that divides people into sectors and generates separatism and ethnic ghettos rather than a unified nation. Those who promulgate this position, whether they are leftists or Pan-Mayan intellectuals, do not represent their constituencies. In effect activists are arguing for unacceptable "special rights" based on cultural uniqueness.

Zapeta's urban campaign was seen by Pan-Mayan activists as complementing the "dirty campaign" mounted by the opposition in hotly contested cities like Quetzaltenango, where leaflets distributed to the public argued that constitutional reforms would fragment the country. Scare tactics were indeed used to stir up voters, who were told by local leaders that their children would be forced to learn indigenous languages, that indigenous people would receive special rights under the reforms, and that indigenous people would be pressured to dress in traditional dress and to speak their own language even if they were monolingual in Spanish. The underlying threat, an old one, was that ethnic conflict, even civil war, would result from constitutional changes. Evangelical groups were encouraged to challenge the Mayan spirituality clause because it would promote paganism; property owners were told that under the referendum they would have to open their lands to traditionalist religious groups.

There is little doubt in Guatemala that the combination of these two campaigns helped delegitimize the reform process in the eyes of many voters. The YES campaign was caught between its own ambivalence about specific reforms and its underlying assumption that indigenous rights were transparently worthy to the wider population. Tactically, they could not stand up to the media-savvy NO campaign that targeted specific audiences—such as political liberals, evangelicals, Ladinos, and urban Mayas who are fluent in Spanish rather than in regional Mayan languages.

On a deeper level, it is important to identify what Zapeta was marketing during the referendum campaign. I would suggest that if one sees the counterinsurgency war and peace process as re-ethnicizing the Guatemalan nation in a particular way after a decade of genocidal violence disproportionately targeted at rural Mayas, then Zapeta's arguments can be seen as a counterproject to factor ethnicity out of the nation and create an alternative political subjectivity for indigenous citizens through an interesting combination of discourses. His anti-internationalist stance was designed to provoke Guatemalan nationalism in the face of the country's dependence on foreigners to fund peace and monitor demilitarization and human rights through the United Nations' MINUGUA after the peace accords. His liberal agenda from the human rights movement stressed the constitutional basis of law, the separation of church and state, and the individual rather than the community as the locus of rights. Moreover, Zapeta advocates a singular transcendent system for the nation, one which he portrays as nonethnic in contrast to the arguments advanced by the indigenous rights camp that stress the incommensurability of Mayan and Ladino cultures as exemplified by Mayan spirituality and customary law.

In short, Zapeta's arguments for unification are designed to undercut multiculturalism as a political agenda formulated by its own Mayan experts, to take cultural issues out of the arena of public debate,[6] and to relocate culture and ethnicity to the realm of private celebration. In effect, Zapeta would strip the Pan-Mayan movement of its dual vision and its capacity to make claims on the state. For its part, a dirty campaign functioned on the local level to argue that cultural difference promotes dangerous and intolerant cultural fundamentalism, a charge reminiscent of Samuel Huntington's (1996) "civilizations" argument. The imagery used in Quetzaltenango—intended to serve as a catalyst for the Ladino vote and to fragment the Mayan community—echoes the recent wartime imagery of the rebellious, culturally different Indian who will, if given a chance, retaliate against the Ladino populace for past wrongs.

THE AFTERMATH

Many ironies have surfaced in the aftermath of the referendum. In the subsequent presidential election, the *popular* left Día-URNG coalition, which continued to promote indigenous rights, did surprisingly well with Alvaro Colom Caballeros as their candidate. Many were satisfied with the 12.4 percent of the vote that the left gained, hoping this would be a base that *populares* and the Pan-Mayan culturalists, who crossed old political cleavages to join them, could build on in the future. As the field narrowed to two major parties in the final round of the presidential elections, these voters and many others were caught in the double bind of having to choose between the FRG, a rightist party long controlled by former dictator Efraín Ríos Montt, which mounted Alfonso Portillo as its candidate, and the PAN, the party in power, which nominated Oscar Berger. The resentment of PAN's pervasive corruption, especially its involvement in the privatization of public services at the cost of the public welfare, seriously eroded support for the status quo. Many voted against the PAN rather than in favor of the FRG. While abstention rates dipped during the first round of the presidential election in predominately Mayan departments, they increased in the final round. These statistics clearly reflect the narrowing of the options for voters.

While many observers worried that the triumph of the conservative FRG meant the end of the indigenous question, others argued that Portillo's energy and populist concern for the poor allowed for some optimism that the new government might be more responsive to rural concerns. In a surprising move, Portillo appointed major Mayan leaders to key governmental posts. Demetrio Cojtí Cuxil, who as vice-minister of education is reviewing textbooks, reformulating the national curriculum, and promoting Mayan-language education, has become an activist in the administration, along with Raxche' Demetrio Rodríguez, who was appointed as head of the newly revitalized national bilingual education institute, Dirección General de Educación Bilingüe (National Board for Bilingual Education: DIGEBI). Otilia Lux de Cotí, the Mayan representative to the high-profile truth commission that denounced the army's atrocities during the war (CEH 1999), has become the minister of culture. Time will tell whether these leaders are able to have as much impact working within the system as they did before they chose to join the government. None of them share the FRG's rightist politics. They felt they could not reject the opportunity to influence government policies at this historical juncture, when the implementation of the multicultural reforms hangs in the balance. Of course they face being tainted by their association with Ríos Montt and his violent past as one of the architects of the counterinsurgency policies in the early 1980s. Some argue that these Mayan functionaries have lost all credibility in the process of working within the bureaucratic system as it stands (see Ramos, this volume).

In contrast, Estuardo Zapeta, who might have been rewarded for his work to undermine the referendum, was not asked to join the FRG government. He continues to be proud of his independence, noting that Mayan leaders are settling for soft "indigenous" positions in the administration. He is waiting for the day when a Maya can be appointed to a major position dealing with the economy or international affairs.

One can examine this turn of events—the survival of indigenous issues in national politics despite the failure of the referendum—in several lights. First, in keeping with Yashar's focus on regime changes that occur with the transition to democracy, the openness of the FRG to indigenous issues can be seen as an instance of a government strategically realizing that it must incorporate a new constituency which is making demands that must, from its point of view, be channeled institutionally.

Second, in keeping with Trouillot, the incorporation of Mayan critics into the government can be seen as a state effect of the international community, which has become a major funder of development initiatives and peace accord implementation in the country. As the international community—particularly the European Union—has been a sponsor of indigenous rights, a supporter of Mayan projects in cultural revitalization, and the source of billions of dollars of reconstruction funding, this move is instrumental in another sense. In fact, European countries, including Norway and Germany, have threatened to withdraw development aid during the current economic crisis as the government continues to fail to make headway in efforts to promote peace accord reforms. Trouillot would stress that European intervention is part of larger patterns of globalization which have redefined political subjectivity and important social categories in national society, leading to a formal recognition of Guatemala as a "multicultural, ethnically plural, and multilingual" polity. Nevertheless, as this analysis has shown, this redefinition is hardly hegemonic; the tensions over multiethnic definitions of the country can only continue.

For his part, Falk would make more space for Pan-Mayanists, and the various permutations of the movement's dual consciousness, as they flexibly set an agenda that continues to have utopian commitments in the field of education, even as it is constrained by working within the system.

There is no dearth of critics of the Mayan culturalist leadership that has accepted positions in a rightist administration. For everyone, such a high-risk experiment on the part of Mayan leaders is worthwhile only until their dream of more progressive parties might gain its own momentum. In the meantime, the failure of the referendum has taught activists of all Mayan groups important lessons in democracy.

Appendix 1. A Timeline of Indigenous Rights and Guatemalan Politics

Last wave of the counterinsurgency war	1978–1988
Democratic opening with the Vinicio Cerezo election	1986
Consolidation of the Mayan movement and organizations	1988–1991
On-and-off peace process	1988–1996
Indigenous accord signed	1995
Guatemalan ratification of ILO 169	1995
Peace Accords signed	1996
Implementation commissions (*comisiones paritarias*) established	1997
Truth commission report released	February 11, 1999
Referendum (*consulta popular*) defeat	May 16, 1999
National election, first round	November 7, 1999
Presidential election runoff: Berger (PAN) vs. Portillo (FRG)	December 26, 1999
Inauguration of Alfonso Portillo (FRG)	January 14, 2000

Notes

1. This essay is, in effect, an epilogue to my book *Indigenous Movements and Their Critics* (1998), in which I argued that Mayas involved in cultural revitalization were not pursuing their politics through the formal government and party system because of the cynical manipulation of Mayan communities in the past. My thanks go to participants who shared their views with me at the May 30–June 5, 1999, Pop Vuj conference in Quetzaltenango and the August 4–6, 1999, Segundo Congreso de Estudios Mayas in Guatemala City, where Mayan

leaders met to discuss the future after the referendum. I have shared this analysis in presentations at Harvard, the School of American Research, the Ecole des Hautes Ètudes en Sciences Sociales, and the American Political Science Association (APSA). I am grateful for the useful feedback I have received at each of these venues, though the final analysis remains my own. Bret Gustafson provided invaluable research assistance for the tables in this essay. Special thanks go to Jean Jackson for discussions of the issues that knit this collection together, for feedback on this analysis, and for the opportunity to collaborate on this project.

2. In fact, the rate of abstention was *not* unusual for a national referendum in a nonpresidential election.

3. It has been fascinating to see anthropologists designate this analysis as nonanthropology the minute they see the tables. In fact, one of the reasons I took on the topic was because of its transgressiveness and the nonconventional kinds of data it forces anthropologists to deal with. The way in which this phobia serves as a boundary marker for cultural anthropology deserves more attention.

4. On the ethical dilemmas of doing social science in highly political situations, see Warren (1998).

5. For North Americans to understand the feeling of Guatemalan voters, one has only to reflect on the bewildering complexity of propositions that routinely face one in the voting booths and the common reaction of not bothering to vote or intensely puzzling over the real political implications of one's vote before pulling the lever.

6. See Ferguson (1994) on the issue of depoliticizing processes of change with development.

References

Acción Ciudadana, CEPADE, CIDECA, et al. 1999. *Quién es quién: Catálogo electoral 1999.* Guatemala City: Magna Terra Editores.

Adams, Richard N. 1996. Un siglo de geografía étnica guatemalteca, 1893–1994: Evolución y dinámica de los sectores étnicos durante los últimos cien años. *Revista USAC* (Guatemala City) 2: 7–58.

Arnson, Cynthia, and Mario Quiñones Amézquita, eds. 1997. *Memoria de la conferencia: Procesos de paz comparados.* Guatemala City: Asociación de Investigación y Estudios Sociales (ASIES) and the Latin American Program of the Woodrow Wilson Center.

Asociación de Investigación y Estudios Sociales (ASIES). 1996. *Acuerdo de paz firme y duradera: Acuerdo sobre cronograma para la implementación, cumplimiento y verificación de los acuerdos de paz.* Guatemala City: ASIES.

Azpuru, Dinorah. 1999. The Consulta Popular: A Vote Divided by Geography. In Dinorah Azpuru, Demetrio Cojtí Cuxil, Carroll Ríos de Rodríguez, et al., *The Popular Referendum (Consulta Popular) and the Future of the Peace Process in Guatemala,* 1–20. Latin American Program Working Papers Series. Washington, D.C.: Woodrow Wilson Center for Scholars.

Bastos, Santiago, and Manuela Camus. 1995. *Abriendo caminos: Las organizaciones mayas desde el Nobel hasta el Acuerdo de Derechos Indígenas*. Guatemala City: FLACSO.

———. 1996. *Quebrando el silencio: Organizaciones del pueblo maya y sus demandas*. Guatemala City: FLACSO.

Carmack, Robert. 1995. *Rebels of Highland Guatemala: The Quiché-Mayas of Momostenango*. Norman: University of Oklahoma.

CEDIM (Centro de Documentación e Investigación Maya). 1992. *Foro del pueblo maya y los candidatos a la presidencia de Guatemala*. Guatemala City: Editorial Cholsamaj.

Cojtí Cuxil, Demetrio. 1991. *Configuración del pensamiento político del pueblo maya*. Quetzaltenango, Guatemala: Asociación de Escritores Mayances de Guatemala.

———. 1994. *Políticas para la reivindicación de los mayas de hoy*. Guatemala City: Editorial Cholsamaj.

———. 1995. *Ub'aniik Ri Una'ooj Uchomab'aal Ri Maya' Tinamit: Configuración del pensamiento político del pueblo maya, 2da. parte*. Guatemala City: Seminario Permanente de Estudios Mayas and Editorial Cholsamaj.

———. 1996a. Estudio evaluativo del cumplimiento del Acuerdo sobre Identidad y Derechos de los Pueblos Indígenas. In Carlos Aldana et al., *Acuerdos de paz: Efectos, lecciones y perspectivas*. Debate 34. Guatemala City: FLACSO.

———. 1996b. The Politics of Mayan Revindication. In Edward Fischer and R. McKenna Brown, eds., *Maya Cultural Activism in Guatemala*, 19–50. Austin: University of Texas Press.

———. 1997. *Ri Maya' Moloj pa Iximulew: El movimiento maya (en Guatemala)*. Guatemala City: Editorial Cholsamaj.

———. 1999. The Impact of the Popular Referendum on Compliance with the Indigenous Accord and on Democratization in Guatemala. In Dinorah Azpuru, Demetrio Cojtí Cuxil, Carroll Ríos de Rodríguez, et al., *The Popular Referendum (Consulta Popular) and the Future of the Peace Process in Guatemala*, 21–26. Latin American Program Working Papers Series. Washington, D.C.: Woodrow Wilson Center for Scholars.

Comisión para el Esclarecimiento Histórico (CEH). 1999. *Guatemala: Memoria de silencio*. Washington, D.C.: American Association for the Advancement of Science. http://hrdata.aaas.org/ceh/.

Consejo de Organizaciones Mayas de Guatemala (COMG). 1995. *Construyendo un futuro para nuestro pasado: Derechos del pueblo maya y el proceso de paz*. Guatemala City: Editorial Cholsamaj.

de Paz, Marco Antonio. 1993a. *Maya' Amaaq' xuq Junamilaal: Pueblo maya y democracia*. Guatemala City: Seminario Permanente de Estudios Mayas and Editorial Cholsamaj.

Editorial Saqb'e. 1996. *Recopilación de los Acuerdos de Paz*. Guatemala City: Editorial Saqb'e.

Esquit Choy, Alberto, and Víctor Gálvez Borrell. 1997. *The Mayan Movement Today: Issues of Indigenous Culture and Development in Guatemala*. Guatemala City: FLACSO.

Falk, Richard. 1997. The Right of Self-Determination under International Law: The Coherence of Doctrine versus the Incoherence of Experience. In Wolfgang Danspeckgruber with Arthur Watts, eds., *Self-Determination and Self-Administration: A Sourcebook,* 47–63. Boulder: Lynne Rienner Publishers.

Ferguson, James. 1994. *The Anti-Politics Machine: "Development," Depoliticization, and Bureaucratic Power in Lesotho.* Minneapolis: University of Minnesota Press.

Fischer, Edward, and R. McKenna Brown, eds. 1996. *Maya Cultural Activism in Guatemala.* Austin: University of Texas Press.

Geertz, Clifford. 1965. *The Social History of an Indonesian Town.* Cambridge: MIT Press.

Huntington, Samuel. 1996. *The Clash of Civilizations.* New York: Simon and Schuster.

Jonas, Susanne. 2000. *Of Centaurs and Doves: Guatemala's Peace Process.* Boulder: Westview Press.

MAYA (Programa de Desarrollo de los Pueblos Mayas). 1995. *Acuerdo sobre Identidad y Derechos de los Pueblos Indígenas y documentos de apoyo para su comprensión.* Guatemala City: Cholsamaj.

MINUGUA (United Nations Verification Mission in Guatemala). 1998. *The Situation in Central America: Procedures for the Establishment of a Firm and Lasting Peace and Progress in Fashioning a Region of Peace, Freedom, Democracy, and Development.* A/52/57. New York: United Nations.

Montejo, Victor. 1999. *Voices from Exile: Violence and Survival in Modern Maya History.* Norman: University of Oklahoma Press.

Morales, Mario Roberto. 1998. *La articulación de las diferencias o el síndrome de Maximón.* Guatemala City: FLACSO.

Nash, June C. 2001. *Mayan Visions: The Quest for Autonomy in an Age of Globalization.* New York: Routledge.

Paley, Julia. 2001. *Marketing Democracy: Power and Social Movements in Post-Dictatorship Chile.* Berkeley: University of California Press.

Rappaport, Joanne, ed. 1996. *Ethnicity Reconfigured: Indigenous Legislators and the Columbian Constitution of 1991.* Special issue of *Journal of Latin American Anthropology* 1 (2) (Spring).

Raxché, Demetrio Rodríguez Guaján. 1989. *Cultura maya y políticas de desarrollo.* Guatemala City: COCADI.

Ríos de Rodríguez, Carroll. 1999. The Organized Productive Sector and the Consulta Popular. In Dinorah Azpuru, Demetrio Cojtí Cuxil, Carroll Ríos de Rodríguez, et al., *The Popular Referendum (Consulta Popular) and the Future of the Peace Process in Guatemala,* 27–42. Latin American Program Working Papers Series. Washington, D.C.: Woodrow Wilson Center for Scholars.

Saqb'ichil/COPMAGUA (Coordinación de Organizaciones del Pueblo Maya de Guatemala). 1995. *Acuerdo sobre Identidad y Derechos de los Pueblos Indígenas.* Punto 3 del Acuerdo de Paz Firme y Duradera. Suscrito en la Ciudad de México por el Gobierno de la República de Guatemala y la Unidad Revolucionaria Nacional Guatemalteca. Guatemala City: COPMAGUA.

———. 1996. *Acuerdo sobre Identidad y Derechos de los Pueblos Indígenas, versión maya ilustrada.* Guatemala City: Editorial Saqb'e.

Schirmer, Jennifer. 1998. *A Violence Called Democracy: The Guatemalan Military Project.* Philadelphia: University of Pennsylvania Press.

———. n.d.a. Prospects for Compliance: The Guatemalan Military and the Peace Accords. Paper presented at the Guatemala after the Peace Accords Conference, Institute of Latin American Studies, University of London, November 1997.

Scott, James C. 1998. *Seeing Like a State: How Certain Schemes to Improve the Human Condition Have Failed.* New Haven: Yale University Press.

Sichar Moreno, Gonzalo. 1999. *Historia de los partidos políticos guatemaltecos: Distintas siglas de (casi) una misma ideología.* Quetzaltenango: Editorial Los Altos.

Sieder, Rachel. 1997. *Customary Law and Democratic Transition in Guatemala.* London: University of London, Institute of Latin American Studies Research Papers.

Smith, Carol, ed. 1990. *Guatemalan Indians and the State: 1540–1988.* Austin: University of Texas Press.

Smith, Timothy J. 2001. Maya Nationalism in the Resurgence of Kaqchikel-Maya Government in Sololá, Guatemala. AAA Meetings, Washington, D.C., November.

Stoll, David. 1993. *Between Two Armies in the Ixil Towns of Guatemala.* New York: Columbia University Press.

Trouillot, Michel-Rolph. 2001. The Anthropology of the State in the Age of Globalization: Close Encounters of the Deceptive Kind. *Current Anthropology.*

Van Cott, Donna Lee, ed. 1994. *Indigenous Peoples and Democracy in Latin America.* New York: St. Martin's Press.

Velasco Bitzol, Miguel Angel, and Carols Ochoa García, eds. 1997. *Los pueblos indígenas y el primer año de gobierno.* Guatemala City: CECMA.

Warren, Kay B. 1978. *The Symbolism of Subordination: Indian Identity in a Guatemalan Town.* Austin: University of Texas Press.

———. 1998. *Indigenous Movements and Their Critics: Pan-Maya Activism in Guatemala.* Princeton: Princeton University Press.

———. 1999. Conclusion. Dilemmas for the Anthropology of Violence: Death Squads and Wider Complicities. In Jeff Sluka, ed., *Death Squad: The Anthropology of State Terror,* 226–247. Philadelphia: University of Pennsylvania Press, 1999.

Yashar, Deborah. 1996. Indigenous Protest and Democracy in Latin America. In Jorge Domínguez and Abraham Lowenthal, eds., *Constructing Democratic Governance: Latin America and the Caribbean in the 1990s,* 87–105. Baltimore: Johns Hopkins University Press.

———. 1997. *Demanding Democracy: Reform and Reaction in Costa Rica and Guatemala, 1870s–1950s.* Stanford: Stanford University Press.

———. 1998. Contesting Citizenship: Indigenous Movements and Democracy in Latin America. *Comparative Politics* 31 (1) (October): 23–42.

Zapeta, Estuardo. 1999. *Las huellas de B'alam, 1994–1996.* Guatemala City: Editorial Cholsamaj.

6. HOW SHOULD AN INDIAN SPEAK?

Amazonian Indians and the Symbolic Politics of Language in the Global Public Sphere

Laura R. Graham

The rivers, fish, and forest call out for help, but the government does not know how to listen. It says that we will die of hunger if it shuts down the mining. Surely we will die of hunger if the mining doesn't stop. But if it does stop, we will plant macaxeira [sweet manioc], bananas, roots, taioba [taro], papaya, sugarcane, pupunha [peach palm], and no one will die of hunger from lack of things to eat.

These words are excerpted from a letter dated August 31, 1989, addressed "to all peoples of the earth" signed by the Yanomami leader Davi Kopenawa (Ação pela Cidania 1990). In this open letter, and in various other speeches addressed to national and international audiences, Davi Yanomami—as he is known to outsiders—broadcast his plea for aid to his people's cause. The background to this plea began in the late 1980s, when disaster struck the Yanomami: thousands of independent gold prospectors invaded their lands, bringing disease, ecological destruction, and violence. As a result of their appeal, the Yanomami, who number some 22,000 (Ramos 1995) and are the largest indigenous group in the Amazon basin, captured international attention as a "primitive" tribe threatened with extinction by global forces. Media reports seized upon the drama of a violent clash of cultures and accusations of genocide.

In the flurry of attention to the Yanomami, Davi Kopenawa emerged as the chief Yanomami spokesperson to the outside world. Davi also earned distinction as an environmental advocate. In 1988, at a time when Westerners were beginning to express appreciation for Indians as "natural guardians of the forest," the United Nations conferred upon him a Global 500 Award, its highest environmental honor. Davi Yanomami came to be sought after as a representative not only of the Yanomami but of all native Amazonian peoples. For Western[1] audiences, he achieved the position of a metonymic voice, one that articulated the concerns of endangered indigenous peoples who—"by their very nature"—practice en-

MAP 6.1 Brazil: Locations of indigenous groups discussed

vironmental conservationism. Davi made speaking appearances in prominent national and international forums. In 1992, at the opening ceremonies commemorating the United Nations International Year of Indigenous
Peoples, he addressed the U.N. General Assembly (Yanomami 1993).

In addressing outside audiences in national and international arenas,
indigenous spokespersons make strategic decisions about language use. In
addition to deciding what to say, they make politically weighted choices
about the linguistic forms they use—speaking in native languages, using
translators, or adopting a dominant Western language, for instance. Western linguistic ideologies, in which language is perceived to be a principal

sign of identity based on the assumption that monolingualism is the norm, are filters through which their messages are heard and understood and thus have profound implications for their choices. For instance, choices about language may emphasize "Indianness" or may have the opposite effect, raising questions about legitimacy and authorship. What interests me in this chapter is the importance of language use in indigenous self-representation, specifically ways in which Western ideologies of language and identity influence outsiders' interpretations of Indians' speech and ways in which Indians deploy language as a vehicle for expressing identity.

Using examples from the Brazilian Amazon, I identify four types of linguistic interaction that represent ways in which indigenous spokespersons negotiate the linguistic barriers of transcultural encounters. I argue that indigenous leaders must creatively balance symbolic gains earned by using native linguistic forms against their ability to communicate content. In the process some create new hybrid forms. Creative use of language in indigenous culture may be interpreted through the lens of Western linguistic ideology as evidence of "inauthenticity" or cultural "contamination." Creative mixing in language and other cultural domains is typical of native Amazonians' practice and has been a factor in their historic adaptivity (see Turner, this volume, for instance).

THE DAVI CONTROVERSY

After he achieved high-profile status in national and international arenas, Davi Yanomami's legitimacy as a leader and representative became the subject of considerable debate. His language was the lightning rod of controversy. His principal critic, anthropologist Napoleon Chagnon, who has worked with the Venezuelan Yanomami, questioned Davi's status as a legitimate Yanomami spokesman. Chagnon (1992: 276, 1997: 108) and others (for example, Sanford 1997) pointed out that the widely dispersed Yanomami communities are autonomous, and there is at present no political structure that would permit any one individual to speak for all Yanomami.[2] The Yanomami are linguistically heterogeneous, consisting of speakers of four related languages: Sanumá, Yanomam, Yanomamɨ, and Yanam (Ramos 1995: 19).

Beyond pointing out that no individual can represent all Yanomami, Chagnon specifically critiques Davi's integrity as an indigenous spokesman in language-centered ways. Chagnon charges that Davi's discourse does not appear to represent Yanomami at all. He accuses Davi of being a parrot, of imitating the words and positions of his First World activist mentors, and of giving voice to opinions or positions that he does not fully understand.[3] He objects to portrayals of Davi as a "Yanomami leader" "who represents anything other than himself or what his NGO creators tell him to say" (Chagnon and Brewer-Carías 1994; also Chagnon 1992a: 234–235, 1992b: 276). Chagnon publicly charges Davi with speaking in "scripted" ways and questions whether he really speaks his own thoughts in his own words. "When I read his [Davi's] proclamations, I am moved— but I am also sure that someone from our culture wrote them" (Chagnon 1992b: 276; also Chagnon 1996: 36).

By accusing Davi of being a ventriloquist's pawn, Chagnon publicly calls Davi's credibility into question. As a "created" spokesman, as Chagnon labels him, Davi cannot be the author of his speech. Chagnon asserts that Yanomami who speak Spanish (and presumably other European national languages) are not really authentic Yanomami (see Salamone 1997: 22). "To the extent that natives become fluent in a dominant language, they become less fluent in their own" (Chagnon, personal communication, 1996). These criticisms raise important issues about indigenous language use. They point to Western assumptions about language and its relation to identity and bring the polemics and political implications of language choice in contemporary indigenous representational politics directly into the political spotlight.

Before addressing these issues, I turn to a brief discussion of the events surrounding Chagnon's accusations so that readers may understand something about the context in which they were situated. The episode centered around issues of access to the Yanomami and the question of who has the right to represent and "speak for" them to the outside world (see Salamone 1996, 1997). It involved questions of representation as well as issues of credentials, political advantages, and academic trends and their detractors. The situation raised interesting questions about the roles of missionaries, anthropologists, and NGOs in indigenous movements.[4] As in the representational politics of "who speaks for whom" in the development of the Pan-Mayan movement, the question "who speaks *with* whom" is perhaps more productive and telling (Warren 1998: 19–20). Because Chagnon states that the positions Davi advocates are, in his view, generally "consistent with the Yanomamö's future" (Chagnon 1992b: 276), his accusations against Davi must be interpreted in light of his problems with Davi's outsider allies.

Background to the Controversy: Chagnon vs.
Salesians, Anthropologists, and NGOs

Chagnon publicly denounced Davi Yanomami in the mainstream press (see, for example, 1993b, 1996) and in the fourth edition of his well-known and widely read textbook on the Yanomami (1992a: 233–234; also 1992b: 275–277). These denunciations have less to do with Davi than with Chagnon's relationship to outsiders with interests in helping and researching the Yanomami with whom he does not align. His critique of Davi became highly visible through the international media in the context of a bitter clash involving himself, Salesian missionaries, and other pro-Yanomami advocates in the immediate aftermath of a grisly massacre of Yanomami by illegal mineral prospectors in August 1993. While his criticisms predate the massacre (see Chagnon 1992b: 275–276), they became especially prominent in this context. Following the massacre, Chagnon felt insulted and slighted in his efforts to participate in an investigation (see Salamone 1997) and lashed out publicly in the press.

Chagnon and a close Venezuelan associate, Charles Brewer-Carías, who had been appointed to a special presidential commission to investigate the massacre, were expelled the day after they arrived in the Yanomami area, when a second government-appointed team arrived.[5] Chagnon interpreted his expulsion as the work of Salesian missionaries—who, in his view, had in the past obstructed his access to the Yanomami—as well as of "left-wing" politicians and anthropologists (Chagnon 1993b). He drew Davi into the controversy because he feared that the Salesians would put forward their own spokesman who would "parrot" the Salesians' opposition to him in the same way that he believed Davi previously had parroted the words of foreign anthropologists and NGO supporters with whom he had clashed (Salamone, personal communication, 1999). According to anthropologist Frank Salamone (1997: 103), who investigated the Chagnon-Salesian debate at the request of the Salesians, it is doubtful that the Salesians had such plans, since they asserted that in some cases *they* must speak for the Yanomami (see Bortoli 1997).[6]

The circumstances surrounding Chagnon's expulsion and the two investigative commissions are still not entirely clear (see Salamone 1997: 1; also Tierney 2000: 196–198). There was widespread opposition to the involvement of Brewer-Carías and Chagnon in the investigation among many sectors of Venezuelan national society as well as among Yanomami (see Tierney 2000: 196–198). What is clear is that Chagnon's past conflicts and disagreements with missionaries and other Yanomami advocates supplied him with ready targets at which to direct his anger and frustrations. The occasion led to one of the most virulent public clashes between missionaries and an anthropologist as well as among anthropologists themselves. Chagnon publicly accused missionaries and the principal Brazilian-based Yanomami support group, the Committee for the Creation of a Yanomami Park (CCPY), of attempting to "own" the Yanomami and of using them for their own political agendas (see Chagnon 1993b, 1997). Davi was caught in the middle of the outsiders' fracas.

The Salesians believed that Chagnon and Brewer-Carías were involved in illegal mining and were suspicious of their plans to develop a biosphere preserve, which they feared would be a kind of "human zoo."[7] Opposition to Brewer-Carías, according to anthropologist Terence Turner (1994), came from indigenous organizations, anthropologists and other academics, politicians, and missionaries, who pointed out that Brewer-Carías's participation in the investigation entailed a conflict of interests stemming from his great wealth and political influence (he is an ex–cabinet minister) as well as his history of exploiting gold and other minerals in the Amazon, possibly on Indian land. Chagnon and Brewer-Carías deny this charge (Chagnon and Brewer-Carías 1994). Chagnon had also clashed with anthropologists and "Survival groups" (Chagnon's term), specifically French anthropologist Bruce Albert, Brazilian anthropologist Alcida Ramos, and the CCPY, who had criticized him for misrepresenting the nature of Yanomami violence and accused him of neglecting the political implications of his sociobiological interpretations of Yanomami warfare. Chagnon's portrayals of endemic warfare driven by males' biological drives for reproductive success, they asserted, are used as justifications for genocide and for Brazil's neglecting to take action against the invasion by miners.[8] This academic debate was also brought into the fray after the massacre.

When Chagnon lashed out in the press at his perceived opponents, a group of Salesians (presumably) responded with a smear campaign of anonymous mailings to U.S. anthropologists aimed at discrediting Chagnon's research and reputation. Accusations and counteraccusations aired in such publicly visible places as the *Anthropology Newsletter,* the *Chronicle of Higher Education,* the *New York Times,* the *London Times Literary Supplement,* and *Véjà,* a prominent Brazilian weekly analogous to *Time Magazine* in the United States.[9] Terence Turner expressed concern that the high-profile Chagnon-missionary conflict might have had the effect "of transforming the tragedy of the Yanomami massacre into a stage for the drama of Chagnon versus the Salesians, and the persecution of Chagnon's sociobiological theories. Worse, it threatens to have grave political consequences for the Yanomami themselves and those who are working to help them" (Turner 1994).

This clash, which took place in the theater of the international print media, evidences the power of words as weapons.[10] It also illustrates the way that indigenous people can get caught in the crossfire of outsiders' rhetoric in political and ideological conflicts. The debate over "who speaks for the Yanomami" underscores that, when Indians are the subjects of outsiders' debates, the motives of each side must be constantly and critically questioned. After the dust settled, Davi's stature as Yanomami representative remained relatively unscathed, and the overall effect of Chagnon's criticism on Brazilian-based Yanomami supporters has been minimal.

INDIGENOUS MEDIATORS AND LANGUAGE CHOICE

While the circumstances surrounding accusations that Davi did not speak for himself are unique to the Yanomami situation, any indigenous leader could be subject to similar doubts or accusations.[11] Indian mediators are often what Frances Karttunen (1994) calls "uncomfortable bridges" between worlds. Outsiders may become suspicious of leaders who become "too skilled" or familiar with the workings of Western political machineries.[12] Conversely, a leader's legitimacy in local communities may be compromised through recognition from outsiders.[13]

Questions of authorship may arise in any politically laden situation where an individual is taken to represent a group. In modern Western politics it is well known and accepted that members of a paid staff write the speeches of prominent politicians. Authorship in this case is generally not an issue. When Indians—or members of other politically disenfranchised groups—claim to speak on behalf of their people, however, questions of authorship and authenticity are especially politically charged. By attacking authorship, adversaries seek to undermine the spokespersons' credibility as legitimate representatives and, by extension, the legitimacy of their position.

Questioning authorship, accusing spokespersons of being parrots of others' words, can be an especially potent weapon against peoples who are not native speakers of the language of dominant political discourse, such as Indians. This questioning represents a politicization of the dialogic nature of discourse (Bakhtin 1981). Any individual discursive expression, because of discourse's nature as a publicly circulating product, necessarily implicates others' words and expressions. No single individual is ever the sole author of his or her speech. Discourse, as Mikhail Bakhtin pointed out, is constituted by a diversity of voices. "Language lies on the border between oneself and the other. The word in language is half someone else's" (1981: 292; see also Duranti 1988; Vološinov 1979). All speech— that of Indians as well as others—blends voices that circulate in the public sphere.

The relevant linguistic issue for me in this essay is not whether individual leaders are or are not legitimate representatives. Rather it has to do with Western audiences' imputed perceptions of what counts as a legitimate linguistic sign of indigenous "authenticity." Westerners who have experienced what James Clifford (1988) calls "modernity's loss of authenticity" discursively attempt to locate "purity" and "authenticity" in indigenous peoples. These notions, however, must be understood as relational, culturally constructed, and politically charged.[14] The concept of authenticity is a colonial folk category that emerges out of contact imperialism and was circulating in notions of the "folk" in Europe by the late eighteenth and early nineteenth centuries. It becomes an essentialized quality which entails a new moment of colonial subjectivity.[15] Indigenous culture and discourse, like the culture and discourse of any social group, are constantly evolving. They are continuously being reinvented as social actors meet new social and political challenges. Indigenous spokespersons, like individuals and groups everywhere, "improvise local performances from (re)collected pasts, drawing on foreign media, symbols and languages" (Clifford 1988: 14).

Although anthropologists have demonstrated the constructed nature of authenticity, the concept "remains nonetheless entrenched in popular thought and is an emotional, political issue for indigenous peoples" (Linnekin 1991: 446). During the height of the Amazonian environmentalist-Indian alliance of the late 1980s and early 1990s, Westerners focused on Amazonian Indians as icons of naturalness and purity. Essentialized representations of natives proliferated, tapping into and reinvigorating Western notions of Indians as ahistorical, unchanging, "pure," and free from foreign influences. Environmental groups used these images as leverage for their own projects, which were decidedly Western (see Brysk 1994). Language and expressive verbal performances—like exotic body images (Conklin 1997)—carry a strategic weight in Western perceptions, as well as in indigenous assertions, of symbolic claims to legitimacy in contemporary indigenous identity politics.[16] Facing national and international audiences, indigenous spokespersons invoke language, among other expressive forms such as bodily adornments, to "perform"[17] or instantiate identity. Conscious of the "pragmatic salience" (Errington 1985: 294–295) their languages hold for members of dominant society, Indians strategically deploy linguistic practice to legitimate their "otherness."[18]

Western ideologies of identity posit essential ties between language and culture and impose external definitions of what counts as legitimate in Indians' discursive practice. Despite the fact that a "pure" indigenous discourse is a nonexistent, reified notion, popular Western audiences look for signs that to them uphold their idealized images. "Real" Indians should speak Indian languages; for in the Western idealized image, language is a principal defining feature of indigenous identity.[19] Consequently, Indians who speak Western languages may be vulnerable to questions about authorship. Like Davi Kopenawa, they may be easy targets for accusations of ventriloquy.[20]

THE SYMBOLIC POLITICS OF LINGUISTIC MULTIFUNCTIONALITY

Indigenous representatives to national and international publics thus face a linguistic dilemma. If an Indian spokesperson chooses to speak in a dominant language, his[21] credentials can come into question. He loses the Bourdieuan "symbolic value"[22] (1977 [1972], 1984 [1979]) that his language bestows. In those instances when native language is a positively valued resource, speaking in the native language may enable an indigenous spokesperson to capitalize on this linguistic symbolic value. Yet speaking his native language may compromise his ability to communicate the propositional content of his message.

This dilemma casts linguistic multifunctionality into sharp relief. The types of linguistic interaction and the political implications of language choice in transcultural encounters are in fact considerably more complex than this simple dichotomy presents. My aim here is to begin to tease apart the complexities and political ramifications of language use in public arenas that arise because of language's multifunctional nature.

The notion that language is a complex and multifunctional semiotic system became influential in Western Europe and the United States through the work of Czech linguist Roman Jakobson (1960; see Hymes 1975). Building on Jakobson, Michael Silverstein (1976, 1993) and others (for example, Hymes 1962; also Urban 1991, 1996) moved thinking about language beyond the Western focus on message content (known to linguists as "denotational," "propositional," or "semantico-referential" meaning)[23] to describe ways in which linguistic forms acquire meaning through associations with aspects of the social context ("pragmatic" or "indexical" meaning). According to Jakobson (1960), who identified six functions for language, in any given instance of speech or writing one function may predominate. The focus or "set" (*Einstellung*), as Jakobson called it, fixes attention on one functional aspect of an utterance or text above others. In poetry or verbal art, for example, aesthetic practice calls attention to form over message content.

Because of language's double nature, as a semiotic medium that consists of nondenotational pragmatic signs that contextualize it in cultural realities of identity, as well as signs that represent things and states-of-affairs that are talked about, it holds unique status among the signs that Indians can invoke to express Indianness. Using language's denotational function, Indians can convey propositions—representations of the world—that are taken by those who receive the messages to represent uniquely Indian perspectives. Message content—mythological themes, for example—can thus itself come to be indexical of Indianness, even when uttered in a non-Indian language. And those wishing to be considered "Indian" can heighten the density of such themes as a performance of identity.

At the same time, the acoustic form in which a message is delivered can be taken as a sign or emblem of "authentic"—or counterfeit—identity. This is true for language per se as a formal grammatical system: language choice can signify identity. It is also true of discourse practices—forms of oratory and rhetorical strategies—that are unique to individual indigenous groups. Discourse style can also index Indian identity or "Indianness." Processes of what Silverstein (1996, 1998) calls "second-order indexicality"—the processes by which signs take on novel indexical meanings in new contexts that were only latent in earlier ones—are thus intensively operative when languages become emblems of identity, indexing some "essence," in this case "Indianness." In contemporary national and international contexts, when languages are taken as "emblems" (see Anderson 1991 [1983]: 133) of "Indian identity," use of a language which happens to signal membership in a particular indigenous group (first-order indexicality) becomes a deployable "naturalized index" of a general "Indian essence" (second-order indexicality) as a function of emerging performance expectations of audiences for "Indianness."

Turning now to the Brazilian Amazon, I identify four types of linguistic interaction that represent ways indigenous spokespersons negotiate the linguistic barriers of transcultural encounters. Each strategy differentially weighs the balance between language's referential and pragmatic functions, playing the potential gains and losses of referential communication against potential gains and losses in the symbolic (or pragmatic) arena. I then turn to the invention of complex hybrid discursive forms, creative mixings of languages, discourse styles, content, and other expressive forms that some Indians use to meet the representational and political challenges presented by Indians' increasing interactions in the global arena.

LANGUAGE AND VOICELESSNESS

In 1991 a Waiãpi chief and his two associates traveled to Brasília to meet with government officials concerning the legal demarcation of a Waiãpi reserve in the Brazilian state of Roraima. Gold prospectors had invaded their territories, bringing disease, violence, and destruction. In a series of meetings the Waiãpi leaders sought to convince the appropriate officials that the situation required immediate attention (see O'Connor 1991). Accompanied by their translator, anthropologist Dominique Gallois, who had worked in the area for over twenty years and documented the invasion of goldminers, they met with representatives of FUNAI (Fundação Nacional do Índio, the National Indian Foundation) and IBAMA (Brazilian Institute for the Environment and Natural Resources). At the most critical official meeting of their visit with an executive committee that deals with indigenous lands, O Groupão, government officials unexpectedly barred the Indians' translator from participating. The Indians, who spoke no Portuguese, were left voiceless. They had no means of joining the official discussion that was deciding the legal fate of their land. Unable to speak the language used for this discussion, they sat on the sidelines through the meeting—angry and humiliated. Subsequently they took their case to the attorney general, who is charged with defending indigenous interests under the Constitution of 1988. He stated that "[those] who can promise, didn't even allow you to speak" (Gallois 1996; also O'Connor 1991).

This is a case of extreme linguistic powerlessness. Government officials forced a situation that gave them the linguistic advantage; they used language to reinforce their dominance. The Indians' dependence on their native language placed them at maximal linguistic disadvantage. The Waiãpi's inability to speak Portuguese effectively excluded them from the discussion: they could not communicate their proposal themselves, and, without a translator, no one could convey it for them. The government's treatment of the Waiãpi caused an uproar among supporters both in Bra-

6.1 Waiãpi leaders meeting with Brazil's attorney general in Brasília (anthropologist and translator Dominique Gallois seated at the far right). Photo by Geoffrey O'Connor, 1992. Courtesy of Geoffrey O'Connor, Realis Pictures, Inc.

zil and abroad. Eventually, through hard-fought battles with anthropologists and NGO assistance, the Waiãpi secured rights to the territory they demanded (see O'Connor 1991).

In this situation, what was at stake for the Waiãpi was the ability to communicate propositions. To borrow Jakobsonian terminology, the "set" or focus was toward message content. Here the Waiãpi's status as native representatives was not in question. In this case, government bureaucrats attached little, if any, value to the native language. They certainly perceived no symbolic worth in Waiãpi discourse, and there were no symbolic gains to be made from speaking the native tongue. The Waiãpi language had no positive symbolic value in this context.

In situations where the potential for political gain rests solely on a speaker's ability to communicate propositional content—when the focus is on the message—dependence on an indigenous language may be a serious political liability. This is the reason why many indigenous groups place tremendous importance on Western education, and some make considerable sacrifices so that their youth may become conversant in the dominant language. For example, soon after contact, leaders of the central Brazilian Xavante community of Etéñritipa made the decision to send a number of young boys out of the community to learn Brazilian ways and specifically to learn Portuguese, the national language. A group of men from this community committed to the idea of finding non-Indian Brazilian homes for some of their sons traveled hundreds of miles from their community to the city of Riberão Preto in São Paulo state, where they had a contact, to broadcast over the radio their appeal for families to take the boys.

Of six boys sent out during the 1970s, two will likely never return to live in the community, although each endeavors to work for the Xavante from outside. Some community members cast aspersions on one who has fallen out of favor, stating that "now he doesn't even speak the [Xavante] language." The other four who did return have acted as translators for elder leaders and have now assumed leadership positions themselves, often displacing their seniors and interacting in new arenas.[24] For several, acting as translators for their elders played an important role in the development of their leadership skills. The act of translation, however, has its own incumbent problems.[25]

TRANSLATORS: LANGUAGE MEDIATORS OR LANGUAGE MEDDLERS?

Indian leaders often negotiate the "language barrier" by relying on translators to mediate linguistic interactions by converting semantico-referential messages from one language into another. There are advantages and disadvantages to this strategy. One advantage of using a translator is that a speaker can employ the native language to make symbolic gains in situations where the indexical, or pragmatic, properties of an indigenous language are valued. To Western audiences who hunger to hear messages directly from native spokespersons, hearing the spoken Indian language may be a positively valued signal of Indian authenticity. Speaking in a native tongue, an Indian spokesperson may appear to romanticizing outsiders to represent the "true" voice of the rainforest. Moreover, Indians who use their native language to address a foreign audience often speak eloquently, using marked oratorical styles that Westerners—although they cannot understand the propositional content of the message—can appreciate for their acoustic distinctiveness. Westerners perceive an aesthetic value in these performances.

Both the indigenous language as a grammatical system and distinctive forms of delivery can operate to deepen an appreciation for the semantico-referential message when it is eventually translated into the dominant language. The positive value derived from the performance can transfer to the propositional message, thereby increasing the performance's overall symbolic value. Use of translators can thus enable indigenous culture brokers to capitalize on the pragmatic value of their native languages in transcultural encounters.

Native languages and oratorical styles are thus a form of cultural capital that Indians can deploy to advance their political agendas. The disadvantage of using a translator, however, is that speakers necessarily lose control over the semantico-referential content of their message. The presupposition of translation is that the value of a proposition will remain constant across languages. Yet unless speakers are sufficiently proficient in the target language, they have no way of knowing whether or not their message is faithfully converted. The speakers are dependent upon the translator and must assume that the translator will accurately convey their speech.

In most cases, those who do the translating for Indian representatives are allies—sympathetic Westerners (anthropologists or missionaries, for example) or native youths who have become more or less proficient in the dominant language. The speaker must assume that such individuals would not consciously manipulate a message to bring some disadvantage upon him. Nevertheless, the very act of translation opens up this possibility. Translation, as Alcida Ramos points out, "is always an act of treason (as captured in the phrase 'traduttore, traditore')" (1988: 222).[26] Even the most well-intentioned of translators may unwittingly alter a message in the belief that she or he is making the speaker's message more accessible to a Western audience, as the following example shows.

In November 1987 one of the first encounters of indigenous peoples, landless forest occupants, and rubber tappers took place in Goiânia, Goiás. This meeting marked an important step in the formation of the unprecedented "Forest Peoples Alliance," a grassroots movement that became a significant political force during the late 1980s and early 1990s (see Hecht and Cockburn 1990). This event, called Semana da Paz (Peace Week), brought together indigenous leaders from the Xavante, Krahò, Karajá, and Kayapó tribes and well-known rubber tapper organizers, including Chico Mendes, the highly visible leader of the Brazilian Rubber Tappers Union, whose 1988 murder brought international attention to the social struggles and violence of the Brazilian Amazon during the late 1980s. Here, and in other meetings, old enmities began to melt as participants began to perceive their common goals and mutual adversaries.

Despite their long history of conflict, a new solidarity emerged between Indians and rubber tappers, built around defending rights to land, natural resources, and traditional lifeways. Speaking of the newly established alliance, Jaime Araújo, a member of the governing board of the Rubber Tappers' Council, noted that "we have the same way of life, and the same enemies: the rancher and the logger. The isolation we live in as tappers and Indians intensifies the solidarity among men and reinforces the bonds of family, friendship and cordiality between people" (quoted in Hecht and Cockburn 1990: 210). Within the alliance, which evolved over a number of years, rubber tappers and Indians articulated the common goals of earning recognition of Indian and rubber-tapper land rights in agrarian reform, establishment of extractive reserves, and an end to the debt-peonage on traditional rubber estates. They demanded local authority over health and education and called for cooperatives and public investment in the processing of forest products (Hecht and Cockburn 1990: 216). With the objectives of giving indigenous peoples control over production and processing of forest commodities while providing financial credits to producers rather than to intermediaries' several initiatives between Indians and private corporations (including the Body Shop[27] and Aveda) and Indians and NGOs (for example, Cultural Survival) were established during this exciting time.

At the Semana da Paz, meetings that took place apart from sessions open to the public were important forums in which participants became familiar with each other's situations. For example, Xavante participants met with Krahò and Kayapó leaders, including the well-known Ropni (also known to Westerners as Raoni), and discussed problems common to Indians. These indigenous leaders also met with landless peasants and rubber tappers and learned about their shared problems. The public events were important arenas for divulging common concerns and experiences of injustice and maltreatment as well as for symbolic displays, particularly on the part of the event's indigenous participants. Throngs of journalists and photographers mobbed the Indians in anterooms and doorways, seeking photo opportunities and sound bites.

Several Indian leaders gave addresses at the Semana da Paz public forums. Among them was the Xavante elder Warodi. Warodi attended the conference with his bare torso and forehead anointed with babaçu coconut oil and red body-paint made from urucum seeds (*Bixa orellana L.*), in red shorts, wearing a cotton necktie and his distinctive Xavante earplugs. Warodi displayed himself as a Xavante and as a leader, and his bodily adornments indicated the seriousness with which he approached the proceedings. Appearing this way, Xavante men signal their unique indigenous identity and warrior heritage.

Ailton Krenak, one of the conference organizers and then president of Brazil's Union of Indigenous Nations (UNI), introduced Warodi as a "traditional person." Warodi was among the eldest Indians to attend the conference and gave his address in his native language. His participation was valued, as Krenak's comment suggests, because he represented a "traditional" Indian lifestyle and way of thinking. Warodi embodied these attributes in his manner of dress and comportment and in his way of speaking. Warodi adopted an eloquent speech style known as *ĩhi mréme* or elders' speech (see Graham 1993).

The audience of some 100 people, including local intellectuals and activists, college students and professors, and journalists, remained silent as Warodi spoke. Although these people could not understand a word he said, his vocal performance was captivating. The repetition of short phrases and characteristic intonational contours of his elders' speech made the presentation interesting to listen to. For most Western members of the audience, the performance was unusual, even exotic. A palpable hush fell over the auditorium as Warodi spoke. Although the referential content of Warodi's message was opaque, the aesthetic value of the acoustic performance was unmistakable.

When Warodi finished, Paulo—one of the young men who had spent several years away from the community and who speaks good Portuguese—translated. Overall his translation captured the gist of Warodi's speech. What is interesting about the translation is the fact that Paulo omitted precisely the material that might have had the most symbolic value for this sympathetic audience. He left out what are perhaps the most significant referential indicators that Warodi's speech represents a distinctly Xavante perspective on the world and on the current events that were the subject of the conference proceedings.

In his speech, Warodi critiqued FUNAI for its consistent failure to assist indigenous peoples and for its positive stance toward large-scale ranching and agribusiness. Anybody can comment on FUNAI, but no one can do it like a Xavante sage, especially one like Warodi:

And where
And where, when you die
Where are you going to live?

Are you [FUNAI administrators] going to shed your skin and have a
    new life?
Are you going to shed your skin?
No, you will die [cease]
It [FUNAI] will certainly cease

That, the way of life [custom]
All of our ancestors
Our ancestors' way of life
They live again

Unlike the ancestors who live again
because you [FUNAI] dislike us
and always give poor assistance
Unlike the always living ancestors, you will not live again

And the One Who Pierced His Foot
Unlike him, you will not continue living
And well
And the one whose stomach swelled from his mother and made the sea
The One Who Made The Sea
Are you going to continue living like the One Who Made The Sea?
You are going to die, day after day.

In his critique of FUNAI Warodi refers to two Xavante creators—The One Who Pierced His Foot and augmented the population and The One Who Created the Sea (see Graham 1995). In mythological times, these creators gave things to the Xavante; and, like Xavante who pass on, they continue living. For Warodi, the events and actions of the creators' lives give meaning to events in the present. Their memory and the stories of their lives provide a backdrop against which to interpret current events like FUNAI's work and ecological destruction. These creative blendings and blurring of discursive genres—such as myth, history, politics—are typical of native Amazonian discourse (see Gallois 1993; also Ramos 1998: 134–137).

Warodi's references to these creators mark his speech as uniquely Xavante. This passage sets his commentary apart from the critiques of any other person. Only a Xavante elder could interpret FUNAI in the context of "the always living" creators. These mythological references are indexical of Warodi's distinctly Xavante perspective. Here referential material works as a type of referential index (Silverstein 1976). The propositions act indexically, conveying an unmistakably Xavante message. The unique Xavanteness of this passage contributes to the overall symbolic value of Warodi's speech.

Ironically, by failing to translate these mythological references, Paulo diminished the symbolic weight of Warodi's discourse in the context of an audience seeking to hear a distinctly Indian perspective. Part of the performance's symbolic value is literally lost in translation. Paulo translated Warodi's critiques of FUNAI and condemned the damage wrecked by ranching but never mentioned Warodi's invocation of the ancestral mythological figures. For Paulo, without a lengthy explanation that was not germane to the principal topic of Warodi's discourse, these references could have no meaning for outsiders. They were incommensurate with the interpretive background of the primarily Western audience and were therefore unwieldy references that did not merit translation. Failing to recognize the potential symbolic value that Warodi's mythological passages held, Paulo left them out.

With these references deleted in the translation, nothing—apart from the performance—stood out from Warodi's speech as particularly noteworthy. Given the translation, it seemed to me as a member of the audience, the speech did not capture the attention it deserved for its creative blend of mythological and contemporary themes. Without the mythological references, Warodi's speech did not appear to be particularly representative of a "traditional" perspective. The absence of "exotic" and uniquely Indian themes left the speech comparatively unremarkable. Consequently, while Warodi's legitimacy as a representative of indigenous perspectives was never in doubt, the translation compromised the uniquely Xavante content of his speech. After it was translated, Warodi's speech received polite but not particularly enthusiastic applause, and the press courted other participants more than him.

Over time, through repeated encounters with sympathetic outsiders and NGO representatives, Paulo learned more about the power of language and representation and what certain outsiders want to hear from Indians. In February 1989, when a group of some twenty leaders from different Xavante communities traveled to the Amazonian town of Altamira to support the Kayapó protest against a proposed dam complex (discussed further below), Paulo went along to translate for the monolingual elders. There representatives from the GAIA Foundation, a London-based environmental organization, sought out the Xavante to be recipients of GAIA funding. The foundation, which had provided substantial sums to the Kayapó, was seeking other native Amazonian groups that would fit its image of environmental stewards to be beneficiaries of its financial support. In an interaction between GAIA representatives and Xavante leaders, Paulo demonstrated his awareness of outsiders' idealistic agendas and astutely adjusted his speech to dovetail with their expectations. Anthropologist Catherine Howard, who was also at the Altamira event acting as a

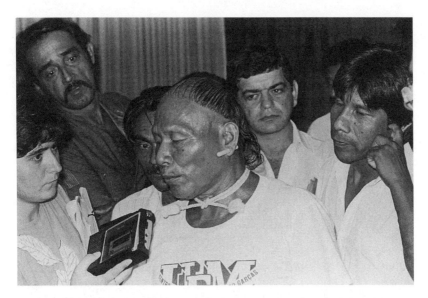

6.2 Warodi Xavante speaking with a journalist following a Semana da Paz meeting. Photo by Laura R. Graham, 1987. Courtesy of Laura R. Graham.

translator for non–Portuguese speaking journalists and NGO representatives, participated in this exchange and later recounted it to me. In this encounter, which was videotaped by GAIA, she was translating for the NGO representatives.

After explaining GAIA's philosophy that the earth is a living thing, the representative stated that the foundation was committed to protecting the environment and the rights of indigenous peoples who have knowledge about environmental preservation that industrialized peoples have lost. She outlined a number of ways that the foundation had supported indigenous peoples and then stated that she wanted to hear what the Xavante needed. "You can trust us. We are not like other whites who have betrayed you," she said. "We want to help you and we are here today to hear what you natives want. We are videotaping so that we have a record of what you want, directly from you."[28]

When the leaders heard this, their eyes widened, and they asked for some time to prepare their proposals. They went off into a huddle, pulled paper and pens from their pockets, and—having experienced the power of the written word and contracts in the Xavante fight for land—went to work writing out their requests. When they returned to the GAIA representatives, the camera, which had been stopped, rolled again. One by one the elders stood in front of the camera, held up their pieces of paper, and stated their requests in Xavante, which Paulo, and then Howard, translated. They requested tractors, trucks, and generators, and each reiterated that he would return to his people trusting that the GAIA Foundation would not betray them as FUNAI had betrayed them in the past. Each ceremoniously handed over his neatly folded paper stating, "Let this be a record of my request."

As the requests came in, one after another, the GAIA representatives exhibited greater and greater discomfort. After the eighth or ninth one, they shut the camera off. Realizing the bind they had gotten into, the head of their team turned to Howard and asked with exasperation, "Don't they understand what we want them to do? The things they are asking for destroy the environment!"

Recognizing that the Xavante elders were not conforming to the environmentalists' idealized image of Indians, Paulo, a keen observer, stepped forward. To Howard he said, "These elders stay in the villages, and they don't understand who folks like these GAIA people are. I can help. Let me say something." He launched into an eloquent speech in Portuguese telling GAIA about an agricultural regeneration and fruit-processing project that was being initiated via the Union of Indigenous Nations (UNI) in his community. He went on to explain an innovative collaborative experiment, the Centro de Pesquisa Indígena (CPI) or Indian Research Center, whose objective was to provide Brazil's indigenous peoples with Western knowledge and skills in applied biological sciences so that they could combine them with traditional knowledge and technologies in their reserves. Paulo explained that they needed scholarships so that young Indians could come and learn from one another about "ethnobotany" and native agriculture at the CPI. This was an opportunity, he said, for Indians to exchange knowledge in order to revitalize traditional wisdom and simultaneously regenerate nature.[29]

Elated that Paulo was giving them what they sought, the GAIA representatives turned the video camera on again, and Paulo stole the show. In this encounter, two years after he translated for Warodi in Goiânia at the Semana da Paz, Paulo clearly understood Western environmentalists' agendas. Going beyond simply translating for his elders, he formulated his own speech, one that closely fit the outsiders' expectations. Paulo also took the opportunity to promote a project that involved his community.

Had Paulo possessed the knowledge that he had gained over the last two years at the time of the Semana da Paz, it is possible that he might have translated Warodi's speech differently, although this is something we cannot know. Here Paulo stepped beyond the bounds of simply translating and upstaged the elders by presenting a proposal that he knew the outsiders would find more palatable. Paulo's move underscores the point that translators wield considerable power—power they may consciously or unconsciously wrest from the principal speaker.

BILINGUAL CULTURE BROKERS: AUTHENTIC OR COUNTERFEIT REPRESENTATIVES?

When culture brokers become sufficiently proficient to make their public addresses in the dominant language of political discourse they have, unlike Warodi, full control over the content that can reach their audience. As the case of Davi Yanomami illustrates, however, questions of legitimacy may arise. Because of the Western ideology that equates Indian identity with language, an Indian's ability to speak the dominant language may potentially set him up for accusations of counterfeit. Questions of "authenticity" also stem from the Western "personalist" ideology of language (Holquist 1983) that conflates individual subjectivity with discursive expressions. What one says, according to this ideology, is the exclusive product of one's self.[30] If an Indian uses "Western" concepts and words such as "biodiversity" or "ecology" in his speech (words which are relatively recent innovations in Western environmentalist rhetoric), he risks accusations of Western corruption. This ideological perspective on language ignores the very public nature of circulating discourse. Others' words and ideas necessarily enter into the speech of those who participate in public spheres.

The problem confronting an Indian culture broker who chooses to speak in the dominant language is how to make himself appear to be a legitimate Indian spokesman in the face of these Western linguistic ideologies. Speaking the dominant language may afford an Indian better control of the propositional content of his message—control he potentially loses when using a translator—but this choice forces him to sacrifice the symbolic value that his native language may bestow. However, because of its multifunctional nature, language offers other resources that an Indian can deploy to signal Indianness, even when he adopts the dominant language in public discourse. Although speaking in the dominant language forces him to forgo the cultural capital that his language and discursive practices may offer, he may draw upon other linguistic resources to convey his legitimacy. An Indian can insert culturally specific content into speeches he delivers in the dominant language. This, for example, is a strategy that

6.3 Davi Yanomami speaking to Westerners via the video camera. Photo by Beto Ricardo/Instituto SocioAmbiental, 1993. Courtesy of Instituto SocioAmbiental.

Davi Yanomami has employed. To understand the sophisticated cultural blending Davi achieves in his speech, it is useful to know something of Davi's background and personal history.

Davi, who was born in the early 1950s, learned to read and write in Yanomami from evangelical New Tribes Missionaries.[31] He became disillusioned with "the Word of God" after his mother died in a 1967 measles epidemic brought by a missionary couple's daughter. In the 1970s he went to work for FUNAI, first as an interpreter and eventually as chief of post (Albert 1995: 7). While Davi was working as a FUNAI interpreter, his father-in-law trained him as a shaman. In the 1980s, during the Yanomami campaign for land, and through his efforts to establish health-care initiatives, Davi interacted intensively with anthropologists and members of CCPY. Through his interactions with missionaries, government representatives, anthropologists, and pro-Indian activists, Davi learned about "becoming Indian" as well as "being Indian" (see Jackson 1991).[32] He became adept at communicating with outsiders. Eventually Davi became known regionally, nationally, and ultimately internationally for his declarations in defense of Yanomami territory and for his proclamations against illegal mining in Yanomami land (see Albert 1995: 8).

Davi's unique knowledge of Yanomami cosmology and his familiarity with outsiders made him a particularly effective cultural mediator (see Albert 1995). This is evident in Davi's speech, especially in the ways that he achieves a discursive blend that weaves Yanomami themes with language and issues familiar to Western audiences. In a 1992 interview he gave to Terence Turner, who was chair of the American Anthropological Association's special commission to investigate the Yanomami situation, Davi includes distinctly Yanomami material. This gives a particular Yanomami flavor to his discourse. The interview, conducted in Portuguese, was transcribed by French anthropologist and Yanomam speaker Bruce Albert, who has worked with the Yanomami for over twenty years. Albert glossed Yanomami expressions in Davi's speech.

Hutucara [the spirit of the sky] can call a powerful wind from under the earth, where the wind stays, call it forth thus [swirling arm gesture] and command it to clean away all that smoke, all that pollution, and carry it back under the earth. Thus the world might be cleansed once again. (Turner and Kopenawa Yanomami 1991: 63)

This is an excellent discursive example of Silverstein's "second-order indexicality," the process by which utterances take on new and sometimes very different meanings—here meanings of speaker identity as opposed to presupposed ideas about Yanomami spirituality—when embedded or recontextualized (Bauman and Briggs 1990) in new discursive contexts. Here the words and gestures index "Yanomaminess" for outsiders, rather than calling forth particular spiritual or mythological referents as they would do for fully traditional Yanomami listeners who understand the way these propositions and imitated supernatural gestures index the traditional beliefs underlying them. Similarly, in his open letter "To All Peoples of the Earth," Davi Yanomami includes referential material that marks his perspective as uniquely Yanomami. He finishes his plea to all peoples by invoking spirits of the Yanomami pantheon.

The mountains are sacred places, places where the first Yanomami were born, where their ashes were buried. Our elders left their spirits in these places. We Yanomami want these mountains to be respected, we don't want them to be destroyed. We want these places to be preserved to conserve our history and our spirits. We call the Hekura to cure our illnesses. We have used them for many years, they don't cease. Omamë [a mythological figure] left these spirits to defend the Yanomami. Omamë is very important for the Yanomami, Makuxi, and Wapixana Indians, and for all the whites and blacks: he is the origin of them all, of the entire world. (Ação pela Cidania 1990: 44–45; my translation from Portuguese)

In his 1992 interview with Turner, Davi indicates that he has coined certain phrases to make Yanomami concepts accessible to outsiders. In answering a question Turner poses about the importance of preserving mountains in the Yanomami area, he says:

I like to explain these things to the whites, so that they may know . . . This sacred place, the high mountains, the beautiful mountains, are places of *spirit* [emphasis added]. Now "spirit" (*espirito*) is not a word in my language. I have learned this word *spirit* and use it in the mixed language I have invented [to talk to whites about these things], but my own indigenous word is *hekurabe;* [also] *saboribe* [literally, "old gardens"]. These are the spirits of shamans (*shabori*) who live in the mountains. (Turner and Kopenawa Yanomami 1991: 63)

In this passage Davi himself speaks of his discourse as a "mixed language." His discourse is a creative, highly constructed semantic hybrid invented to traverse the borders between Yanomami notions of the world and those of his international interlocutors. Davi's hybrid discursive form is characterized by what Albert calls a "double articulation" of cosmological and interethnic competence. Such combinations enable indigenous leaders to convey their "authenticity" while simultaneously entering into the discursive space of a broader transnational public. Albert notes:

Indigenous discourse legitimates itself by making reference to cosmological knowledge, and in the process it reconstructs its own coherence in light of other discourse. If indigenous political discourse limits itself to merely reproducing white categories, it will be reduced to empty rhetoric. If, on the other hand, it remains exclusively in the realm of cosmology, it will not escape cultural solipsism. In either case, failure to articulate these two dimensions results in political failure . . . It is the capacity to articulate these that makes great interethnic leaders. (Albert 1995: 4–5; my translation)

As Albert points out (1995: 7), Davi embodied dual competencies; he was adept in Yanomami cosmology and had unique skills in interethnic relations. "He is an exemplary manifestation of the double articulation of the new indigenous discourse, which . . . does not necessarily entail a division between 'old and modern' leadership" (Albert 1995: 7).

According to Albert, certain semantic features characterize the hybridity of Davi's discourse. Of the "ecological" themes in Davi's discourse, Albert notes that certain Portuguese terms have a wider semantic domain for Davi than they do for Westerners. For example, expressions such as "save the forest" or "demarcate the land" do not simply mean guaranteeing the existence of a physical space exclusively for Yanomami use. The terms imply preserving a whole series of social coordinates and cosmological exchanges that constitute and affirm Yanomami's cultural existence and status as human beings (Albert 1995: 10). The "forest" is not simply a physical space or the source of alimentary staples. It is a deeply cosmological space, the source of spiritual nourishment as well. "Nature" implicates a vast metaphysical world. Words such as "forest" or "earth" are not merely objects. These conceptual spaces are alive and replete with complex shamanistic notions (Albert 1995: 19). Portuguese translations of Yanomami concepts thus entail drastic semantic contractions (Albert 1995: 19).

The power of Davi Yanomami's speech therefore derives in part from his ability to link local Yanomami concerns with the concerns of a broader public. It also stems from the poetic way he weaves Yanomami themes into the content of his speech. These themes are potent indexical resources that imbue his entire speech with symbolic value. They give his speech the exotic cast that environmentally oriented Western audiences crave.[33] His invocation of Yanomami spirits and creators marks him as unique and legitimate. Note that these are the same sorts of invocations that Warodi made but that Paulo left out of his translation. These referential indexes of Indian identity are positively valued by sympathetic Western audiences and can be used by Indian leaders who speak the dominant language to offset criticisms of inauthenticity.

PERFORMING LANGUAGE: MAXIMIZING THE SYMBOLIC

These three cases illustrate that language offers multiple resources that an Indian spokesperson may use to differentially emphasize referential content or symbolic messages in transcultural encounters: one may speak in a native language using a translator so as to underscore Indian identity through grammatical form, choose a distinctive rhetorical style, or include uniquely Indian content while adopting the dominant language. A further type of language-centered interaction is a performance in which Indian leaders deliberately address Western audiences in the native language. In such instances an Indian leader seeks to maximize the symbolic value of his language's indexical functions with little, if any, intention of communicating a propositional message. The "set," or focus, is toward the message form.

With the understanding that authenticity is their biggest asset in national and global arenas, some Amazonian Indians make efforts to display signs of "Indianness" to members of the dominant society, conscientiously deploying aspects of their culture to capture the attention of Western audiences. International attention has, in some cases, helped Amazonian Indians to achieve concrete political gains. In public appearances Indians often draw heavily on visual signs that connote Indianness to Western audiences. Body paint, feather headdresses, and body ornamentation are signs that play to a Western fascination with the exotic and have potent symbolic value as signs of Indianness. They supply the media with the visual images to nourish the Western appetite for the exotic (see Conklin 1997; Ramos 1998). Certain adornments, such as feather headdresses, have come to stand for Amazonian Indianness so much that Indians who no longer have their own ornaments adopt them to authenticate their Indian identity (see Conklin 1997: 727). These visual signs, strategically used to invoke Western essentialized notions, are one way that Indians seek to legitimate their position, adopting what Gayatri Spivak has called "strategic essentialism." [34]

Language use and displays of verbal artistry also figure among the signs that Indian leaders have deliberately employed, for political gain, to play into the stereotyped Amazonian version of what Robert Berkhofer calls the "white man's Indian" (1978, 1988). Alcida Ramos notes that as part of their interethnic strategies Indians "intentionally use their own languages as a political vehicle to impress Brazilian authorities" (1995: 269). A particularly vivid example are the Pataxó of the northeastern Brazilian state of Bahia, who no longer speak their native tongue. The recognition that language can be used as an important strategic tool for dealings with representatives of the dominant society is so powerful that the Pataxó have sought to acquire the language of another indigenous group to mark their "essential" Indianness to outsiders. They have made a special effort to learn the language of the remotely related Maxakali in the distant state of Minas Gerais with the purpose of adopting it as their own (Ramos 1995: 268). "Portuguese, the only language they speak, is not regarded, with good reason, as the most appropriate means to communicate legitimate otherness to the society that engulfs and dominates them" (Ramos 1995: 269–270).

Verbal artistry and other cultural forms are often deployed as projections of pride and cultural strength as well as to win political advantage by appealing to Western idealizations. In the late 1980s and early 1990s the Kayapó became masters in the art of using cultural performance, a magnificent sense of theater, and verbal arts for political gain (see Turner 1991b, 1992). When Brazil's plans to construct a series of hydroelectric dams that would flood portions of Kayapó land became public, the Kayapó leader Payakan conceived of staging a huge protest demonstration in the Amazonian town of Altamira. The event, which took place in February 1989, was designed to be a media spectacle that would appeal to the Western appetite for Indian exotica. In addition to 500 Kayapó, hundreds of other Indians came to Altamira to show their support. Assured of an aesthetically stunning display, as well as a politically fascinating encounter between natives and high-level government officials, journalists from around the globe flocked to the remote Amazonian frontier town where some 1,200 people had gathered.[35]

The Indian participants staged dramatic cultural performances that drew heavily on visual signs of Indianness, verbal arts, and dances. Indians' spectacular oral performances, both song and dance and oratorical displays, attracted the attention of news crews. National and international press often documented these native-language performances on the basis of their aesthetic appeal alone. For example, a Xavante leader held the attention of film crews as he delivered a speech to the camera in the oratorical style of Xavante political discourse with no accompanying translation. By delivering his speech in Xavante, and using a form that is obviously acoustically marked, he captivated the media's attention. The orator deployed his speech to capitalize on its symbolic potential, further objectifying the outstanding acoustic dimension of this distinctive oratorical style. The form of this delivery eclipsed the referential dimension of his discourse for Western viewers. The Kayapó leader Ropni also held journalists and other Westerners spellbound as he orated in Kayapó (Catherine Howard, personal communication, 1999). In effect, these two and many other Indians held a series of press conferences where the contents of their pronouncements were entirely incomprehensible to their addressees.

One of the most stunning displays at the Altamira event was staged by a Kayapó woman, Tuíre, who approached the podium brandishing a machete. Gracefully and deliberately she symbolically swiped it against the cheeks of the director of the regional power company as she orated in

6.4 Tuire Kayapó orating to the director of the regional power company at the Altamira protest. Photo by Paulo Jarez, 1989. Courtesy of Interfoto.

Kayapó. Her gestures and speech were so symbolically powerful that no translation was necessary. None was offered, and the audience roared with applause in support of her performance.

Documentary films of the Altamira event feature these and other oratorical performances because they present fascinating visual and acoustic images (see Beckman 1989 and O'Connor 1997b, for example). These oratorical displays have symbolic value as material forms in much the same way visual images of "exotic Indians" have symbolic value as material forms. Western audiences appreciate verbal arts as aesthetic forms. These forms were particularly interesting at this historical moment because of their association with indigenous peoples.

While discourse captures the attention of Western audiences, content—if translated—may also be valued, for certainly Western audiences are interested in what Indians have to say. The point, however, is that in many cases Indians—aware of the symbolic value they hold for Western audiences—deploy verbal artistry to grab outsiders' attention. Having captivated outsiders' attention with an acoustic performance, an Indian may then be able to communicate his or her referential message using another means, through a translator or perhaps even using the dominant language. Performing in the native language, speakers capitalize on the symbolic value Westerners attach to oral performance as an aesthetic form. In such oratorical displays, where the focus is on the form itself, questions of authenticity are minimized, and the speaker's authority as a legitimate Indian voice is maximized. Indians who are conscious of the social significance that their languages hold for outsiders strategically deploy language practices to benefit from their "pragmatic salience" (Errington 1985: 294–295).

Westerners' fascination with expressive forms of native Amazonia may explain the recent proliferation of CDs featuring native Amazonian musics in First World markets. Native Amazonian musics debuted in the popular First World market as featured cuts on recordings made by well-known celebrities, following the typical World Beat pattern whereby local artists are introduced to international audiences. Musics of remote indigenous peoples reach international audiences by this means (see Meintjes 1990). For example, Milton Nascimento's 1990 album *Txai* features a track of Kayapó singing. In the 1996 CD release *Roots*, the heavy metal rock group Sepultura features cuts of the band singing with Xavante as well as photos of the band in the community and band members painted for Xavante ceremonials.

A number of native Amazonian groups have themselves featured their musics on CDs directed to First World markets, especially European audiences. In 1994 the Xavante of Pimentel Barbosa released *Etenhiritipa*, a CD of exclusively Xavante recordings (Núcleo de Cultura Indígena 1994). It has done well in both Brazil and Europe. Members of the community produced the album, under the name Associação Xavante de Pimentel Barbosa, so that non-Xavante, particularly Westerners, could listen to and appreciate their music and to earn revenue from sales. According to Paulo and other Xavante men, hearing their music will enable outsiders to value this important dimension of their culture. The Xavante Association has exclusive rights to the material on the recording and a portion of the proceeds from sales (see Giron 1994). Other Amazonian groups—such as the Guaraní, Maxakali, Krenak, Pataxó, and Krahò—are now being featured in CD releases which are packaged as cultural representations to outsiders.[36] While the music and liner notes do not have an overtly political message, representation itself can be considered a political act.

These musics are finding sympathetic listeners in large measure because of the Western fascination with expressions of Amazonian Indianness. Untrained Western ears, which are tuned to listen for melody and rhythm, may not appreciate the complexities of Amazonian musics. These often elaborate qualities of timbre and volume in ways that are unfamiliar to, or perhaps not even perceived by, many Westerners. Listening for signs of "otherness," Westerners appreciate Amazonian musics as decontextualized aesthetic forms in much the same way that they appreciate indigenous linguistic forms and bodily adornments available through the global market. All are decontextualized by the process of globalization and then recontextualized as commodities or as symbols of movements that have themselves become globalized—for instance, indigenous rights or environmental movements.

A potential danger that lurks in this otherwise positive orientation to native Amazonian musics is that it fosters the romanticization and essentialization of Indians. This fascination can be seen as a form of "imperialist nostalgia," to use Renato Rosaldo's term (1989). Implicit in this orientation is the reality that those Indians whose forms of cultural expression do not meet outsiders' standards of what is deemed to be "Indian" may be politically disadvantaged (see Thomas 1994: 189; Conklin 1997).

As language and other forms of aesthetic representation, including music, dance, and bodily ornamentation, are assuming prominence in indigenous revitalization movements, they simultaneously engender pride on the part of users and can be used to win outsiders' support. As the example of the Pataxó language illustrates, Indians may go to great lengths to adopt signs to legitimate their Indianness to outsiders. However, as Ramos cautions, insofar as Indians mold their appearance and behaviors to fit outsiders' images and ideals, they risk becoming a type of Baudrillardian simulacrum, a simulation of real Indians (Ramos 1994: 163, 1998: 267–283). This native Amazonian simulacrum or "hyperreal Indian" is a model Indian that becomes increasingly removed from the lived experiences of indigenous people (Ramos 1998: 175). Yet, at the same time, these very interactions—in national and international arenas—are increasingly part of native Amazonians' lived experience.

DISCURSIVE HYBRIDS AND THE LINGUISTIC INVENTIVENESS OF BRAZIL'S NATIVE AMAZONIAN LEADERS

In their interactions with others in national and global arenas, native Amazonians are creatively responding with linguistic and expressive innovations. Turner (1988) reports, for example, an instance in which the Kayapó leader Ropni begins an address to a mixed audience in Kayapó (speech directed primarily to Kayapó youth) and then switches to Portuguese (speech directed primarily to Brazilians). Ropni also juxtaposes commentary on contemporary events with commentary on the culture hero Ipéré. Ropni thus mixes whole languages, oratorical styles, *and* semantic content in a complex discursive hybrid.

If one regards larger performances, such as the Altamira event, as complex expressive wholes, the creative mixing is taken to another level. In such events, Indians mix language (as a grammatical system) and discursive forms such as oratory, song, dance, and keening with discussions of contemporary events that incorporate culturally specific material such as myths.

For a full analysis of the creative and unique ways Indians are blending languages, discourse forms, semantic content, and other performance genres, further documentation of these hybrid performances is needed. Transcriptions of cultural mediators' speeches need to indicate what marked linguistic forms are used as well as provide details on culturally specific information, style, and semantics that will enable analysis of such usages. Detailed documentation would allow researchers to answer a number of questions about the actual mechanics of such hybrid discursive forms. For example, do indigenous spokespersons adopt traditional rhetorical styles when making speeches in Western languages? What is the intended (and actual or imputed) effect of such oratorical transpositions? In what contexts do spokespersons insert distinctive indigenous cultural materials? Similarly, when do they consciously insert decidedly "Western" themes and concepts, such as "biodiversity," "ecology," or "extractive reserves"? Precise documentation of such performances is certain to provide rich material for future analyses.

The innovative hybrid forms that indigenous leaders are creating in the context of their interactions with outsiders make myth, indigenous perspectives, and discourse styles relevant to contemporary events. These hybridizations must not be taken as evidence of "culture loss," as Albert points out. Rather, these adaptations are manifestations of the creativity that is "traditional" among native Amazonians (Albert 1995: 12). A characteristic of Yanomami shamanism, for example, is the ability to make creative analogies and to "constantly update the group's mythology in relation to novel situations and the immediate historical context" (Albert 1995: 12).[37] The notion that the integration of "traditional" or culture-specific themes with new or Western concepts or topics is evidence of "cultural corruption" or inauthenticity is rooted in the Western penchant for compartmentalization. Such compartmentalization is not inherent in indigenous discourses themselves. It is, as Ramos points out regarding the Western tendency to construct neat distinctions between myth, history, and political discourse, for example, the result of "our need to organize ethnographic material into familiar categories in order to make sense of it on our own and our readers' terms" (1998: 136–137).

In their speeches to outsiders, indigenous spokespersons include non-indigenous voices and concepts, drawing on elements from the discursive fields of the national and international arenas they increasingly move in. This incorporation enables Indians to take part in the debates and discussions of these arenas. Daniel Mato (1997: 182), for example, notes that the rhetoric of COICA (Coordinating Body for the Indigenous Peoples of the Amazon Basin, an organization which links indigenous peoples' organizations from Brazil, Bolivia, Colombia, Ecuador, Peru, Venezuela, Surinam, and Guyana) reveals high levels of exchanges with the rhetoric of environmental organizations, in a vocabulary that often talks in terms of "biodiversity" and "global concerns." And journalist Joe Kane, in his book *Savages*, gives an example of such rhetorical engagement for strategic purposes. He recounts an episode in which an Ecuadorian Huaorani spokesperson, Moi, was preparing for a speech in which he would confront representatives of indigenous federations and the state oil company. After hearing an oral draft of the speech, Kane commented, "That is powerful." "Yes it is," Moi said. "But it needs more cannibal [outsider] words—words they will understand. Like . . ." He paused. "*Environment*—that is a word that pleases them, no?" (Kane 1995: 199).

Failure to incorporate new words, ideas, and formulations would condemn Indians to discursive isolation, sealing them off from the global context and its dialogues. Inclusion of new concepts—incorporation of words like "biodiversity," "environment," "copyright," and "intellectual or cultural property"—expresses creative engagement with the global world in which Indians now find themselves. Such inclusions are predictable manifestations of Indians' participation in a Bakhtinian discursive world. They enhance Indians' effectiveness and, because they are incorporated in distinctly indigenous ways, they constitute unique cultural products. Like Indians' creative use of indigenous representational forms such as bodily adornment (Conklin 1997) and new representational technologies such as cassette tape-recorders and video, creative language use represents the vitality and assertiveness that have long characterized traditional Indian culture (see Turner, this volume).

Insofar as Indians participate in global public arenas, we can expect their creative adoption—and unique adaptation—of new discursive and representational forms in their expressive practices. As long as Western romanticizations and fascination with Indians as static exotics persist, however, we can expect certain outsider audiences to interpret such usages as problematic, mistaking them for conscious deracinated exploitation or counterfeit manipulation.

CONCLUSIONS

In the autumn of 2000 Chagnon again found himself embroiled in an immense public controversy, one that raged nationally and internationally in email debates and print media. This time the controversy was over allegations that his methods of anthropological research incited violence among the Yanomami and that he and other North American scientists (a team led by geneticist James Neel) were spreading disease as part of an Atomic Energy Commission–funded research project. These allegations were published in journalist Patrick Tierney's book *Darkness in El Dorado: How Scientists and Journalists Devastated the Amazon* (2000).

In preparing to formulate an official public response to the allegations and issues raised by the book, the executive committee of the American Anthropological Association convened a panel of experts to speak at the association's ninety-ninth annual meeting in San Francisco. Hundreds of anthropologists were joined by members of the press to hear expert opinions, including that of Tierney himself. Chagnon declined the invitation to speak, wishing to avoid a "feeding frenzy" by his opponents. Instead, he was represented by Professor William Irons of Northwestern University.

Among the invited panelists was Noeli Pocaterra, a Venezuelan Indian and congressional representative, who is president of the Permanent Commission of Indigenous Peoples to the Venezuelan National Assembly. Congresswoman Pocaterra represented the concerns of Venezuela's indigenous population, who called for an investigation of the accusations. As she approached the elevated podium, her translator stepped up to a microphone that was proffered below. She then began her address, commencing with a greeting in her native language, Wayuunaiki, a language spoken by the Wayúu people who live in the Venezuelan state of Zulia. Her translator rendered her words simply as "a greeting in the native language." Pocaterra then proceeded to give her speech in fluent Spanish. In closing, she returned to Wayuunaiki, which her translator roughly rendered as "a closing in her native language."

This example beautifully illustrates indigenous creative use of language as a symbolic medium with which to assert identity. Noeli Pocaterra rhetorically used her native language to validate her voice, as a native voice, even though her credentials as an indigenous woman were not in question and she was speaking to a Western audience that was particularly appreciative of her indigenous point of view. To emphasize her indigenous perspective she uttered only two phrases in the native language. Yet these two utterances framed the entire speech; they signaled her Indianness and made her voice stand out from those of the other panelists. The utterances were indeed "greetings" and "closings," yet the language choice said something more to the Western audience. It pragmatically stated, "I am speaking to you as an Indian. Listen to what I have to say as an Indian." It is also significant that the translator did not (could not?) translate the "words" of her greeting, in that the propositional message content was clearly subordinate to the symbolic message, which had ideological intent.

Such creative blendings are as characteristic of ways that Indians use language within communities, when facing local indigenous publics, as they are of indigenous discourse that faces outward, toward Western audiences. An example that neatly parallels Noeli Pocaterra's rhetorical mix of languages is a speech delivered in 1982 by the elder Xavante leader Warodi to a group of young local men. The men were about to begin harvesting a large mechanized rice plantation that was part of a government-sponsored economic development project. The community had a great deal of pride in this project, and the occasion's mood was celebratory. Warodi began his speech in Portuguese, saying, "Bom Dia Rapazes (Good morning, young men)." He proceeded to give the body of his address in Xavante, sprinkled with an occasional Portuguese word. Warodi punctuated the end of his speech with the Portuguese expression "Pronto! (Done, it is finished!)" (Graham 1995: 45).

Both Warodi and Noeli Pocaterra used greetings and closings in languages that are distinct from the body of their speech to underscore aspects of their identity. Pocaterra highlighted her indigenous identity to outsiders and framed her Spanish language as the "speech of an Indian." Warodi used short Portuguese expressions oratorically to emphasize his position as an interlocutor with the outside—with FUNAI, which sponsored the project. Warodi's Portuguese greeting and closing pragmatically stated, "I am an effective mediator with the outside world." These examples, which inversely mirror each other, illustrate the creativity with which indigenous leaders deploy language when facing both local and global publics.

All indigenous representatives make choices about language use, as well as about message content and other forms of signification, when addressing Western audiences *and* indigenous publics. Based on experience, they gauge audience expectations and attempt to package their messages using the forms and ideas that they anticipate will be most effective. When facing outsiders, they may speak in the native language, through translators, or may mix languages. They may adopt culturally specific oratorical forms and insert culturally specific content, and they may adopt Western language and terminology as they see fit, in order to communicate message content and ideological position most effectively. All of these strategies are "authentic," for authenticity is a concept that must be seen within the global context as a reiteration or defense of boundaries of identity. Equally, identities within the global context are inevitably constructed in a dialectic between the local and global, between performer and observer.

Challenging the "authenticity" of a speaker (or singer or performer), as Chagnon did with Davi Yanomami, is a political statement. It is a challenge of boundaries and presupposes asymmetrical relations of power. Such challenges cannot be grounded in an evaluation of the performance as "indigenous" or not, because, in the global context, indigenous performance is by nature decontextualized, reinvented, and hybrid. This does not make it any less "authentic." Any performance that takes place in a new arena, before new audiences, or about new topics challenges performers to invent novel ways of presenting. Facing new publics in national and global public spheres, indigenous representatives recontextualize indigenous forms of expression and draw on the forms that circulate therein. In doing so, they join the other participants in a public sphere, as performers in a dialogically choreographed Bakhtinian play.

Acknowledgments

This chapter grew out of a paper prepared for the conference "Language Communities, States, and Global Culture: The Discourse of Identity in the Americas," organized by Nora England, Mercedes Niño-Murcio, and myself and held at the University of Iowa in October 1996 with funding from a conference grant from the Wenner-Gren Foundation, the Obermann Center, and the Center for International and Comparative Studies at the University of Iowa. It has benefited from the comments of participants in that conference as well as from audience members at other places where I have presented it, including the Department of Anthropology at the University of Santa Cruz, Latin American Studies Association, and American Anthropological Association panel "Indigenous Movements: Sources and Strategies of Self-Representation," organized by Jean Jackson and Kay Warren. I am grateful for the helpful comments I have received from Jean and Kay, as well as those from Ana Alonzo and Lynn Stephen. A number of people provided immensely useful comments on earlier drafts; for these I thank Bruce Albert, Manuela Carneiro da Cunha, Gale Gomez, Catherine Howard, Cory Kratz, David Maybury-Lewis, T. M. Scruggs, Michael Silverstein, Tim Taylor, Anna Tsing, Terry Turner, Greg Urban, Jerry Wever, and especially Beth Conklin and Jenny White. I appreciate the assistance of Frank Salamone, who helped me understand some of the controversy surrounding Davi Yanomami. I am also grateful to Sylvia Yanagisako and the Department of Cultural Anthropology at Stanford University, where I spent the summer of 1999 revising an earlier version of the manuscript. Thanks also to Geoffrey O'Connor for generously granting permission to use video images.

Notes

1. Like others (see Conklin 1997: 729*n*2), I reluctantly use the term "Western" in the absence of a convenient alternative. Readers should keep in mind that this is a contextually determined, heterogeneous category.
2. The problem of legitimate representation for native Amazonians is a complex one. Many groups do not have overarching political structures that represent autonomous communities; nor do they have traditional leadership roles that enable individuals to speak for or represent an entire group. Increased interactions with outsiders are thus creating pressures on Indians to develop new forms of political interaction, representation, and leadership to act in outsiders' political arenas (see Gow and Rappaport, this volume). New organizational forms such as federations (for example, the Shuar Federation) are developing that do not reflect traditional models of organizing (see Jackson 1995a: 13, 1999).
3. See Chagnon (1992: 275–278); Chagnon and Brewer-Carías (1994); Monaghan (1994: 19); Salamone (1997: 15, 22).
4. According to anthropologist Frank Salamone, despite their differences and disagreements, anthropologists and missionaries have a great deal in common. The relationship, which has been and continues to be important in Latin American indigenous politics, merits serious anthropological study. See Salamone (1985) for discussion of anthropologists and missionaries in Africa.
5. The Venezuelan investigation took place forty days after a Brazilian one. An excellent summary can be found in Rocha (1999: 18–25).
6. Chagnon's criticism of Davi has close parallels with the public debate in New Zealand that followed the publication of Allan Hanson's (1989) article on the "invented" nature of Maori oral tradition (see Linnekin 1991). Journalists in New Zealand seized upon the scholarly discussion of the "invention" of Maori

culture and raised the specter of "inauthenticity" at a particularly inopportune time, as Maori land claims were being contested and Maori identity was an issue in the struggle (Linnekin 1991: 447).

7. See Salamone (1997: 2). For discussion of the biosphere preserve, see Chagnon (1993b, 1993c); also Bortoli (1997: 70–73).

8. See Ramos (1987); Chagnon (1988); Albert (1989); Booth (1989); also Ferguson (1995); Sponsel (1998). Also see correspondence in the *Anthropology Newsletter* (May 1994 and September 1994) and Chagnon (1993c).

9. See Brooke (1993a, 1993b); Chagnon (1993a, 1993b, 1997); also Cappelletti (1993, 1994); Chagnon and Brewer-Carías (1994); Fox (1994); Monaghan (1994); Turner (1994); Wolf (1994); Alcântara (1995); Salamone (1996, 1997). In the *Times Literary Supplement* (Chagnon 1993b), for example, Chagnon denounced the Salesians for "killing the Yanomami by kindness"—giving them guns which they used in their endemic warfare and, by encouraging them to move to or near mission posts, increasing mortality by exposing Yanomami to a high incidence of disease. Chagnon's critics responded by pointing out that Salesians gave out only seven guns and stopped this practice almost immediately. Illegal Brazilian miners continue to be a constant source of guns. Salesians also note that deaths are disproportionately higher near Salesian missions because severely sick and dying Yanomami seek refuge at mission posts (see Albert quoted in Monaghan 1994; also Turner 1994).

10. Warren (1998: 46) also observes that, during the resurgence of Pan-Mayanism in Guatemala, "wars of words" were waged against Indians in the popular media. In the Mayan case, educated Mayas directly entered debates through the medium of print.

11. The debate over the legitimacy of Rigoberta Menchú's testimony is the most recent and highly visible instance of such a polemic (see Stoll 1998; for critiques of Stoll's argument, see Rus 1999, especially the essays by Norma Chinchilla, Victoria Sanford, Carol Smith, Georg Gugelberger).

12. For other examples of this, see the chapters by Jackson and Gow and Rappaport in this volume; also Brown (1993); Conklin and Graham (1995).

13. See Turner's discussion of Payakan Kayapó in this volume; also Brown (1993); Conklin and Graham (1995); Graham (2000).

14. For discussions of "authenticity," see Handler (1984); Clifford (1988); also Wagner (1975); Linnekin (1983); Handler and Linnekin (1984); Taylor (1992); Bendix (1997). Bendix notes that seeds of European notions of authenticity can be found in the writings of Rousseau and Herder.

15. I thank Michael Silverstein for this observation. Merry similarly notes that consciousness is redefined as cultural repertoires are transformed within social fields of power (1998: 587).

16. In some contexts Indians express resentment toward such external definitions. For example, urban-born Indian activist Eliane Potiguara states: "We

spend most of our lives trying to reaffirm that we are Indians, and then we encounter statements like, 'But you wear jeans, a watch, sneakers, and speak Portuguese'" (1992: 46).

17. Social scientists have drawn analogically on John Austin's (1962) notion of linguistic performatives to describe ways that individuals enact or "perform" social roles and positions in embodied ways (see, for example, Butler 1990).

18. Joseph Errington's (1985) notion of "pragmatic salience" describes native speakers' awareness of the social significance of linguistic alternates.

19. The Western ideological construction that equates a people with a language is conventionally dated to late-eighteenth-century German Romanticism and Johann Herder's characterization of language as the genius of a people. The formulation can, as Kathryn Woolard (1998: 16–17) points out, be traced to the French Enlightenment and the French philosopher Etienne Bonnot de Condillac. This Herderian ideology of language has been exported through colonialism and is globally hegemonic today (Woolard 1998: 17; see also Silverstein 1998). In debates over the issue of Indian status and legal rights that took place in the early 1980s in Brazil, for example, it was suggested that language be an essential criterion for determining Indian legal status (see Carneiro da Cunha 1987).

20. Similarly, Indians who use video cameras may be accused of inauthenticity, as Turner points out (this volume). Western ideas about language and identity strongly parallel the Western fetishizations of representational media that Turner discusses in his chapter. The logic that representational media are inherently Western, which is used as a basis for denying authenticity to Indians who use video cameras, mirrors arguments that Indians who speak Western languages are not Indian.

21. Because most native Amazonian spokespersons are male, I use masculine pronouns throughout the majority of this chapter. There are exceptions to this general pattern, such as Eliane Potiguara and Noeli Pocaterra. Why males predominate in this arena remains an unexplored question at the present time.

22. The Bourdieuan notion of "symbolic value" which I use here describes positive social evaluations which are achieved through, in Piercean terminology, iconic and indexical semiotic processes. The Bourdieuan concept entails assumptions about market values, in this case the market value of "Indianness." In the late 1980s and early 1990s Amazonian Indians clearly had a positive market value in the environmentalist public sphere. The problematics of this value, which is built on outsiders' idealizations, are discussed in Ramos (1994, 1998); Conklin and Graham (1995); Conklin (1997); O'Connor (1997a, 1997b).

23. In semantic reference, the meaning of words derives from their relationships to other words, as in dictionary definitions. Michael Silverstein (1996) suggests that "denotational meaning" is the more precise term.

24. Oakdale (n.d.) discusses generational tensions and changes in leadership patterns that result from the acquisition of new skills among the Kayabi; for other discussions of this issue in native Amazonia, see Wagley (1977); Brown (1993); Ramos (1994); Graham (2000). Rus (1994) offers an analysis of generational tensions among indigenous communities in twentieth-century Chiapas; Fowler (1987) discusses these issues and differing notions of identity among the North American Gros Ventre.

    Xavante do not participate in any overarching political structures such as federations or the indigenous organizations discussed by Gow and Rappaport (this volume).

25. As this chapter moved into the final stages of publication, an issue of *Public Culture* devoted to "Translation in a Global Market" was released (Apter 2001). This issue deals with language translation in the strict sense, as I discuss it here, as well as more broadly, with the problematics of translation in art, media, and other cultural objects.

26. Alarcón (1989) uses this same wordplay in her discussion of La Malinche, the indigenous woman who betrayed her people because she translated for Hernán Cortés and his army. Alarcón draws upon Mexican novelist and poet José Emilio Pacheco's poem entitled "Traddutore, traditori" (1976). Pacheco's translators, according to Alarcón, "who use language as their mediating agent, have the ability, consciously or unconsciously, to distort or to convert the 'original' event, utterance, text, or experience, thus rendering them false, 'impure'" (1989: 68).

27. See Kaplan (1995) for a critique of the Body Shop's bourgeois image-making and entrepreneurial capitalism.

28. I am grateful to Catherine Howard for sharing this anecdote with me. These statements, recorded from her account of the event, are not exact quotations.

29. The CPI was founded in 1987 as a collaborative experiment involving UNI, several indigenous groups, the Catholic University of Goiás (UCG), and the state agricultural research agency, Embrapa (Empresa Brasileira de Pesquisa Agropecuária). One of CPI's primary objectives was to provide Brazil's indigenous peoples with Western knowledge and skills in applied biological sciences so that they could apply new technologies in their reserves. Between 1989 and 1992 CPI and the Catholic University offered a training program tailored to indigenous students. GAIA did come on board as one of the funding agencies for this project. Financial support also came from the Ford Foundation, the European Economic Community, NORAD (Norwegian Agency for Development Cooperation), and the Rainforest Action Network. For more on the CPI and the Xavante fruit-processing project, see Graham (2000).

30. For critiques of this position, see, for example, Rosaldo (1982); Keane (1991); Graham (1993); Urban (1996).

31. This biographical information is taken from Albert (1995: 7–8).

32. "Becoming Indian" is the phrase Jackson (1991) uses to describe the ways that Tukanoans of Colombia are changing their notions of their history and culture to conform to outsiders' ideas about Indianness. Maybury-Lewis (1991) describes this as a pattern for lowland South American Indians.

33. In discussing the complex dialectic that has been emerging in the mutual construction of strategic alliances between NGOs and indigenous leaders, Albert (1997) notes that indigenous leaders employ various symbolic "ethnopolitical" discursive resources, including mythic and cosmological themes.

34. The notion of "strategic essentialism" is associated with the work of Gayatri Spivak (1989, 1990, 1993). Jackson (1999: 293) notes the problematic use of strategic essentialism or "strategic practice" in the Colombian Vaupés, where an indigenous organization doing the "strategic" representing does so in ways that are at odds with local realities. Warren (1998) discusses the complexity of "strategic essentialism" in the Guatemalan Mayan case.

35. For discussions of Altamira, see O'Connor (1997a, 1997b); also CEDI (1991); Turner (1991a); Conklin and Graham (1995); Conklin (1997); Rabben (1998).

36. Four Brazilian Guaraní communities recently produced the CD *Ñande Reko Arandu: Memória viva Guaraní* (Comunidade Solidária, ca. 1999). The CD *O canto das montanhas* features Krenak, Maxakali, and Pataxó musics (Núcleo de Cultura Indígena 1999). In 1999 Kàpey, an organization of Krahò communities, produced the CD *Krahò: Ampó-Hu, todas as sementes*. Marlui Miranda (1995, also 1997) released a CD that features her musical interpretations of Brazilian indigenous musics. In using indigenous musics as the basis for compositions, she follows an established pattern whereby outsiders claim inspiration from native musics (Carlos Gomes's opera *Il Guarany* written in 1870 and many compositions by Heitor Villa-Lobos—such as *Uirapuru* [1917], *Tres poemas indígenas* [1926], and *Tres canções indígenas* [1930]—are outstanding Brazilian examples). Outsiders' use of indigenous musics raises issues of copyright and intellectual property. For discussion of copyright issues related to recording and distribution of indigenous musics, see Seeger (1991, 1997).

37. Hugh-Jones (1988: 148–149) and Townsley (1988: 151–153) make similar points about mythological innovation.

References

Ação pela Cidania. 1990. *Yanomami: A todos os povos da terra*. São Paulo: CCPY, CEDI, NDI.

Alarcón, Norma. 1989. Traddutora, Traditora: A Paradigmatic Figure of Chicana Feminism. *Cultural Critique* 13: 57–87.

Albert, Bruce. 1989. On Yanomami "Violence": Inclusive Fitness or Ethnographers' Representation? *Current Anthropologist* 30 (5): 637–640.

————. 1995. O ouro canibal e a queda do céu: Uma crítica xamânica da econo-mia política da natureza. *Serie Antropologia* 174: 2–29. Reprinted from 1993: L'or cannibal e la chute du ciel: Une critique chamanique de l'économie poli-tique de la nature. *L'Homme* 126–128: 353–382.

————. 1997. Territorialité, ethnopolitique et développement: A propos du mouvement Indien en Amazonie Brésilienne. *Cahiers des Amériques Latines* 23: 177–210.

Alcântara, Euripedes. 1995. Indio também é gente [Indians Are People Too]. *Véjà*, December 6, 1995, 7–10.

Anderson, Benedict. 1991 [1983]. *Imagined Communities: Reflections on the Origin and Spread of Nationalism*. London: Verso.

Apter, Emily, ed. 2001. Translation in a Global Market. *Public Culture* 13 (1).

Austin, John. 1962. *How to Do Things with Words*. Oxford: Clarendon Press.

Bakhtin, Mikhail M. 1981. Discourse in the Novel. In Michael Holquist, ed., *The Dialogic Imagination: Four Essays by M. M. Bakhtin*, trans. C. Emerson and M. Holquist, 259–422. Austin: University of Texas Press.

Bauman, Richard, and Charles Briggs. 1990. Poetics and Performance as Critical Perspectives on Language and Social Life. *Annual Review of Anthropology* 19: 59–88.

Bendix, Regina. 1997. *In Search of Authenticity: The Formation of Folklore Studies*. Madison: University of Wisconsin Press.

Berkhofer, Robert E., Jr. 1978. *The White Man's Indian*. New York: Random House.

————. 1988. White Conceptions of Indians. In Wilcomb E. Washburn, ed., *Handbook of North American Indians: 4*, 522–547. Washington, D.C.: Smith-sonian Institution.

Booth, William. 1989. Warfare over Yanomamö Indians. *Science* 243: 1138–1140.

Bortoli, José. 1997. The Missionary Effort to Help the Yanomami Speak for Themselves. In Frank A. Salamone, ed., *The Yanomami and Their Interpret-ers: Fierce People or Fierce Interpreters*, 67–74. Lanham: University Press of America.

Bourdieu, Pierre. 1977 [1972]. *Outline of a Theory of Practice*. Trans. Richard Nice. New York: Cambridge University Press.

————. 1984 [1979]. *Distinction: A Social Critique of Judgement and Taste*. Trans. Richard Nice. Cambridge, Mass.: Harvard University Press.

Brooke, James. 1993a. Brazilians Reduce Indian Death Toll. *New York Times*, Sep-tember 1, 6.

————. 1993b. Raids on Miners Follow Killings in Amazon. *New York Times*, Sep-tember 19, 10.

Brown, Michael F. 1993. Facing the State, Facing the World: Amazonia's Native Leaders and the New Politics of Identity. *L'Homme* 33 (2–4): 307–326.

Brysk, Alison. 1994. Acting Globally: Indian Rights and International Politics in Latin America. In Donna Lee Van Cott, ed., *Indigenous Peoples and Democracy in Latin America*, 29–51. New York: St. Martin's Press.

Butler, Judith. 1990. *Gender Trouble: Feminism and the Subversion of Identity*. New York: Routledge.

Cappelletti, Rev. E. J. 1993. Venezuela Mine Scheme Targets Salesians. Letter. *New York Times*, January 18, 22.

———. 1994. Fighting the Common Enemy in the Amazon. Letter in Correspondence. *Anthropology Newsletter*, May 1994, 2.

Carneiro da Cunha, Manuela. 1987. *Os diretos do índio: Ensaios e documentos*. São Paulo: Editora Brasiliense.

CEDI (Centro Ecumênico de Documentação e Informação). 1991. O encontro de Altamira. In *Povos Indígenas no Brasil 1987/1988/1989/1990*, 329–336. Aconteceu Especial 18. São Paulo: Centro Ecumênico de Documentação e Informação.

Chagnon, Napoleon. 1988. Life Histories, Blood Revenge, and Warfare in a Tribal Population. *Science* 239: 985–992.

———. 1992a. *Yanomamö*. 4th ed. Fort Worth: Harcourt Brace Jovanovich College Publishers.

———. 1992b. *Yanomamö: The Last Days of Eden*. San Diego: Harcourt Brace, Jovanovich.

———. 1993a. Covering Up the Yanomamo Massacre. *New York Times* OP-ED, Saturday, October 23, 21.

———. 1993b. Killed by Kindness? The Dubious Influence of the Salesian Missions in Amazonas. *London Times Literary Supplement*, July–December, 11–12.

———. 1993c. The View from the President's Window: Anti-Science and Native Rights: Genocide of the Yanomamö. *Human Behavior and Evolution Society Newsletter* 2 (3): 1–4.

———. 1996. Transcript of Remarks at the AAA Session on Anthropology and Theology, Frank A. Salamone, Napoleon Chagnon, José Bortoli, and Teo Marcano. In Frank A. Salamone, ed., *Who Speaks for the Yanomami?* 33–70. Studies in Third World Societies. Williamsburg, Va.: College of William and Mary.

———. 1997. *Yanomamö*. 5th ed. New York: Harcourt Brace College Publishers.

Chagnon, Napoleon, and Charles Brewer-Carías. 1994. Response to Cappelletti and Turner. Letter in Correspondence. *Anthropology Newsletter*, September, 2.

Chinchilla, Norma. 1999. Of Straw Men and Stereotypes: Why Guatemalan Rocks Don't Talk. *Latin American Perspectives* 26 (6): 29–37.

Clifford, James. 1988. *The Predicament of Culture*. Cambridge, Mass.: Harvard University Press.

Conklin, Beth A. 1997. Body Paint, Feathers, and VCRs: Aesthetics and Authenticity in Amazonian Activism. *American Ethnologist* 24 (4): 711–737.

Conklin, Beth A., and Laura R. Graham. 1995. The Shifting Middle Ground: Amazonian Indians and Eco-Politics. *American Anthropologist* 97 (4): 695–710.

Duranti, Alessandro. 1988. Intentions, Language, and Social Action in a Samoan Context. *Journal of Pragmatics* 12: 13–33.

Errington, Joseph. 1985. On the Nature of the Sociolinguistic Sign: Describing the Javanese Speech Levels. In Elizabeth Mertz and Richard J. Parmentier, eds., *Semiotic Mediation*, 287–310. Orlando: Academic Press.

Ferguson, Brian R. 1995. *Yanomami Warfare: A Political History*. Santa Fe, N.M.: School of American Research Press.

Fowler, Loretta. 1987. *Shared Symbols, Contested Meanings: Gros Ventre Culture and History, 1778–1984.* Ithaca: Cornell University Press.

Fox, Robin. 1994. Evil Wrought in the Name of Good. Letter in Correspondence. *Anthropology Newsletter,* March, 2.

Gallois, Dominique T. 1993. *Mari revisitada: A reintegração da fortaleza de Macapá na tradição oral dos Waiãpi.* São Paulo: Núcleo de História Indígena e do Indigenismo/Universidade de São Paulo/Fundação Amparo a Pesquisa do Estado de São Paulo.

———. 1996. Controle territorial e diversificação do extrativismo na área indígena Waiãpi. In *Povos indígenas no Brasil 1991–1995,* 263–271. São Paulo: Instituto SocioAmbiental.

Garfield, Seth. 2001. Beholding the Miracle: Xavante Indian Community Development Projects under Brazilian Military Rule. *Americas* 54 (7): 551–580.

Giron, Luis Antônio. 1994. Indios querem pacificar brancos com CD. *Folha de São Paulo,* September 15.

Graham, Laura. 1993. A Public Sphere in Amazonia: The Depersonalized Collaborative Construction of Discourse in Xavante. *American Ethnologist* 20 (4): 717–741.

———. 1995. *Performing Dreams: Discourses of Immortality among the Xavante of Central Brazil.* Austin: University of Texas Press.

———. 2000. Lessons in Collaboration: Xavante Wildlife Management. In Ron Weber, John Butler, and Patty Larson, eds., *Indigenous Peoples and Conservation Organizations: Experiences in Collaboration,* 47–71. Washington D.C.: World Wildlife Fund.

Gugelberger, Georg. 1999. Stollwerk or Bulwark? David Meets Goliath and the Continuum of the Testimonio Debate. *Latin American Perspectives* 26 (6): 47–52.

Handler, Richard. 1984. On Sociocultural Discontinuity: Nationalism and Cultural Objectification in Quebec. *Current Anthropology* 25 (1): 55–71.

Handler, Richard, and Jocelyn Linnekin. 1984. Tradition, Genuine or Spurious. *Journal of American Folklore* 97: 273–290.

Hanson, Allan. 1989. The Making of the Maori: Culture, Invention and Its Logic. *American Anthropologist* 91: 890–902.

Hecht, Susanna, and Alexander Cockburn. 1990. *The Fate of the Forest: Developers, Destroyers, and Defenders of the Amazon.* New York: Harper.

Holquist, Michael. 1983. The Politics of Representation. *Quarterly Newsletter of the Laboratory of Comparative Human Cognition* 5 (1): 2–9.

Hugh-Jones, Stephen. 1988. The Gun and the Bow: Myths of White Men and Indians. *L'Homme* 106/107: 138–155.

Hymes, Dell. 1962. Introduction: Toward Ethnographies of Communication. In Dell Hymes and John Gumperz, eds., *The Ethnography of Communication,* 1–34. Special publication, *American Anthropologist* 66, part 2.

———. 1975. The Pre-War Prague School and Post-War American Anthropological Linguistics. In E. K. F. Koerner, ed., *Transformational Generative Paradigm and Modern Linguistic Theory,* 359–381. Amsterdam: John Benjamins.

Jackson, Jean. 1991. Being and Becoming an Indian in the Vaupés, Colombia. In

Greg Urban and Joel Sherzer, eds., *Nation States and Indians in Latin America*, 131–155. Austin: University of Texas Press.

——. 1995a. Culture, Genuine and Spurious: The Politics of Indianness in the Vaupés, Colombia. *American Ethnologist* 22 (1): 3–27.

——. 1995b. Preserving Indian Culture: Shaman Schools and Ethno-Education in the Vaupés, Colombia. *Cultural Anthropology* 10 (3): 302–329.

——. 1999. The Politics of Ethnographic Practice in the Colombian Vaupés. Special issue on Unintended Consequences: On the Practice of Transnational Cultural Critique (J. Peter Brosius, guest editor). *Identities: Global Studies in Culture and Power* 6 (2–3): 281–317.

Jakobson, Roman. 1960. Closing Statement: Linguistics and Poetics. In T. Sebeok, ed., *Style in Language*, 350–377. Cambridge, Mass.: MIT Press.

Kane, Joe. 1995. *Savages.* New York: Vintage.

Kaplan, Caren. 1995. "A World without Boundaries": The Body Shop's Trans/national Geographics. *Social Text* 43: 45–66.

Karttunen, Frances. 1994. *Between Worlds: Interpreters, Guides, and Survivors.* New Brunswick, N.J.: Rutgers University Press.

Keane, Webb. 1991. Delegated Voice: Ritual Speech, Risk, and the Making of Marriage Alliances in Anakalang. *American Ethnologist* 18: 311–330.

Linnekin, Jocelyn. 1983. Defining Tradition: Variations on the Hawaiian Identity. *American Ethnologist* 10: 241–252.

——. 1991. Cultural Invention and the Dilemma of Authenticity. *American Anthropologist* 93 (2): 446–449.

Mato, Daniel. 1977. On Global and Local Agents and the Social Making of Transnational Identities and Related Agendas in "Latin" America. *Identities* 4 (2): 167–212.

Maybury-Lewis, David. 1991. Becoming an Indian in Lowland South America. In Greg Urban and Joel Sherzer, eds., *Nation-States and Indians: Latin America*, 207–235. Austin: University of Texas Press.

Meintjes, Louise. 1990. Paul Simon's *Graceland*, South Africa, and the Mediation of Musical Meaning. *Ethnomusicology* 34 (1): 37–73.

Merry, Sally E. 1998. Law, Culture, and Cultural Appropriation. *Yale Journal of Law and the Humanities* 10 (2): 575–603.

Monaghan, Peter. 1994. Bitter Warfare in Anthropology. *Chronicle of Higher Education*, October 26, 10–11, 18–19.

Oakdale, Suzanne. n.d. The Culture Conscious Brazilian Indian: The 1992 Earth Summit and the Formation of the Xingu Indigenous Park in Kayabi Political Discourse. Unpublished MS.

O'Connor, Geoffrey. 1997a. *Amazon Journal: Dispatches from a Vanishing Frontier.* New York: Dutton.

Pacheco, José Emilio. 1976. Traddutore, traditori. In *Islas a la Deriva*, 27–28. Mexico City: Siglo XXI.

Potiguara, Eliane. 1992. Harvesting What We Plant. *Cultural Survival Quarterly* 16: 46–48.

Rabben, Linda. 1998. *Unnatural Selection: The Yanomami, the Kayapó, and the Onslaught of Civilisation.* Seattle: University of Washington Press.

Ramos, Alcida. 1987. Reflecting on the Yanomami: Ethnographic Images and the Pursuit of the Exotic. *Cultural Anthropology* 2 (3): 284–304.

———. 1988. Indian Voices: Contact Experienced and Expressed. In J. Hill, ed., *Rethinking History and Myth: Indigenous South American Perspectives on the Past*, 214–234. Urbana: University of Illinois Press.

———. 1994. The Hyperreal Indian. *Critique of Anthropology* 14: 153–171.

———. 1995. *Sanumá Memories: Yanomami Ethnography in Times of Crisis*. Madison: University of Wisconsin Press.

———. 1998. *Indigenism: Ethnic Politics in Brazil*. Madison: University of Wisconsin Press.

Rocha, Jan. 1999. *Murder in the Rainforest: The Yanomami, the Gold Miners and the Amazon*. London: Latin American Bureau.

Rosaldo, Michelle. 1982. The Things We Do with Words: Ilongot Speech Acts and Speech Act Theory in Philosophy. *Language in Society* 11: 203–237.

Rosaldo, Renato. 1989. *Culture and Truth: The Remaking of Social Analysis*. Boston: Beacon Press.

Rus, Jan. 1994. The "Comunidad Revolucionaria Institucional": The Subversion of Native Government in Highland Chiapas, 1936–1968. In Gilbert Joseph and Daniel Nugent, eds., *Everyday Forms of State Formation: Revolution and the Negotiation of Rule in Modern Mexico*, 265–300. Durham: Duke University Press.

———, ed. 1999. If the Truth Be Told: A Forum on David Stoll's *Rigoberta Menchú and the Story of All Poor Guatemalans*. *Latin American Perspectives* 26 (6): 5–14.

Salamone, Frank A. 1985. *Missionaries and Anthropologists: Case Studies*. Studies in Third World Societies. Williamsburg, Va.: College of William and Mary.

———. 1996. *Who Speaks for the Yanomami?* Studies in Third World Societies No. 57. Williamsburg: College of William and Mary.

———. 1997. *The Yanomami and Their Interpreters: Fierce People or Fierce Interpreters*. Lanham: University Press of America.

Sanford, Greg. 1997. Who Speaks for the Yanomami? A New Tribe's Perspective. In Frank A. Salamone, ed., *The Yanomami and Their Interpreters: Fierce People or Fierce Interpreters*, 67–74. Lanham: University Press of America.

Sanford, Victoria. 1999. Between Rigoberta Menchú and La Violencia: Deconstructing David Stoll's History of Guatemala. *Latin American Perspectives* 26 (6): 38–46.

Scott, David. 1999. *Refashioning Futures: Criticism after Postcoloniality*. Princeton: Princeton University Press.

Seeger, Anthony. 1991. Singing Other Peoples' Songs. *Cultural Survival Quarterly* 15 (3): 36–39.

———. 1997. Ethnomusicology and Music Law. In Bruce Ziff and Pratima V. Rao, eds., *Borrowed Power: Essays on Cultural Appropriation*, 52–67. New Brunswick: Rutgers University Press.

Silverstein, Michael. 1976. Shifters, Linguistic Categories, and Cultural Description. In K. Basso and H. Selby, eds., *Meaning in Anthropology*, 11–56. Albuquerque: University of New Mexico Press.

————. 1993. Metapragmatic Discourse and Metapragmatic Function. In John Lucy, ed., *Reflexive Language*, 33–58. Cambridge: Cambridge University Press.

————. 1996. Indexical Order and the Dialectics of Sociolinguistic Life. In Risako Ide, Rebecca Parker, and Yukako Sunaoshi, eds., *Proceedings of the Third Annual Symposium about Language and Society, Austin, Texas*, 266–295. Texas Linguistic Forum, Vol. 36. Austin: University of Texas Department of Linguistics.

————. 1998. The Uses and Utility of Ideology: A Commentary. In B. B. Schieffelin, K. A. Woolard, and Paul Kroskrity, eds., *Language Ideologies: Practice and Theory*, 123–145. New York: Oxford University Press.

Smith, Carol. 1999. Why Write an Exposé? *Latin American Perspectives* 26 (6): 15–28.

Spivak, Gayatri C. 1989. In a Word: An Interview. *Differences* 1: 124–56.

————. 1990. *Postcolonial Critic: Interviews, Strategies, Dialogues*. New York: Routledge.

————. 1993. *Inside the Teaching Machine*. New York: Routledge.

Sponsel, Leslie E. 1998. Yanomami: An Arena of Conflict and Aggression in the Amazon. *Aggressive Behavior* 24: 97–122.

Sting, and Jean-Pierre Dutilleux. 1989. *Jungle Stories: The Fight for the Amazon*. London: Barrie and Jenkins.

Stoll, David. 1998. *Rigoberta Menchú and the Story of All Poor Guatemalans*. Boulder: Westview Press.

Taylor, Charles. 1992. The Politics of Recognition. In Amy Gutmann, ed., *Multiculturalism and the Politics of "Recognition,"* 25–73. Princeton: Princeton University Press.

Thomas, Nicolas. 1994. *Colonialism's Culture: Anthropology, Travel and Government*. Cambridge: Polity Press.

Tierney, Patrick. 2000. *Darkness in El Dorado: How Scientists and Journalists Devastated the Amazon*. New York: W. W. Norton.

Townsley, G. 1988. Ideas of Order and Patterns of Change in Yaminahua Society. Ph.D. dissertation, University of Cambridge.

Turner, Terence. 1988. History, Myth, and Social Consciousness among the Kayapó of Central Brazil. In J. Hill, ed., *Rethinking History and Myth: Indigenous South American Perspectives on the Past*, 195–213. Urbana: University of Illinois Press.

————. 1991a. Baridjumoko em Altamira. In *Povos indígenas no Brasil 1987/1988/ 1989/1990*, 337–338. Aconteceu Especial 18. São Paulo: Centro Ecumênico de Documentação e Informação.

————. 1991b. Representing, Resisting, Rethinking: Historical Transformations of Kayapo Culture and Anthropological Consciousness. In George Stocking, ed., *Colonial Situations: Essays on the Contextualization of Ethnographic Knowledge*, 285–313. Madison: University of Wisconsin Press.

————. 1992. Defiant Images: The Kayapó Appropriation of Video. *Anthropology Today* 8 (6): 5–16.

————. 1994. The Yanomami: Truth and Consequences. Commentary. *Anthropology Newsletter*, May, 48.

Turner, Terence, and Davi Kopenawa Yanomami. 1991. "I Fight Because I Am Alive": An Interview with Davi Kopenawa Yanomami. *Cultural Survival Quarterly* 15 (3): 59–64.

Urban, Greg. 1991. *A Discourse-Centered Approach to Culture: Native South American Myths and Rituals.* Austin: University of Texas Press.

———. 1996. *Metaphysical Community: The Interplay of the Senses and the Intellect.* Austin: University of Texas Press.

Vološinov, V. N. 1979. *Marxism and the Philosophy of Language.* Trans. L. Matejka and I. R. Titunik. Cambridge: Harvard University Press.

Wagley, Charles. 1977. *Welcome of Tears: The Tapirapé Indians of Central Brazil.* New York: Oxford University Press.

Wagner, Roy. 1975. *The Invention of Culture.* Englewood Cliffs, N.J.: Prentice-Hall.

Warren, Kay B. 1998. *Indigenous Movements and Their Critics: Pan-Maya Activism in Guatemala.* Princeton: Princeton University Press.

Whittemore, Hank. 1992. A Man Who Would Save the World. *Parade*, April 12, 4–7.

Wolf, Eric R. 1994. Demonization of Anthropologists in the Amazon. Letter in Correspondence. *Anthropology Newsletter*, March, 2.

Woolard, Kathryn. 1998. Introduction: Language Ideology as a Field of Inquiry. In B. B. Schieffelin, K. A. Woolard, and Paul Kroskrity, eds., *Language Ideologies: Practice and Theory*, 3–47. New York: Oxford University Press.

Yanomami, Davi. 1993. Año Internacional de los Pueblos Indígenas del Mundo: Davi Yanomami discursa na ONU na abertura. *Anuário Indigenista* 32 (December): 161–163.

Audio-Video References

Beckman, Michael. 1989. *Kayapó II: Out of the Forest.* Produced and directed by Michael Beckman in collaboration with anthropological consultant Terence Turner. Grenada Films.

Communidade Solidária. ca. 1999. *Ñande Reko Arandu: Memória viva Guaraní.* São Paulo: Interlocução São Paulo.

Kàpey. 1999. *Krahò: Ampó-Hu, todas as sementes.* Itacajá, TO: Kàpey—União das Aldeias Krahò (with Fundação de Apoio a Pesquisa da Universidade Federal de Goiás, Goiânia, GO).

Miranda, Marlui. 1995. *Ihu: Todos os sons.* São Paulo: Pau Brasil Som Imagem e Editora Ltda.

———. 1997. *Ihu 2, Kewere: Rezar: Prayer.* São Paulo: Pau Brasil Som Imagem e Editora Ltda.

Nascimento, Milton. 1990. *Txai.* São Paulo: Sony Music Entertainment (Brasil) ICI.

Núcleo de Cultura Indígena (with Associação dos Xavante de Pimentel Barbosa). 1994. *Etenhiritipa.* São Paulo: Warner Music/Quilombo.

Núcleo de Cultura Indígena (with Krenak, Maxakali, Pataxó). 1999. *O canto das montanhas: Festival de dança e cultura indígena da Serra do Cipó.* São Paulo: Estúdios de Sonhos e Sons.

O'Connor, Geoffrey. 1991. *At the Edge of Conquest: The Journey of Chief Wai-Wai*. Produced and directed by Geoffrey O'Connor in collaboration with anthropological consultant Dominique Gallois. New York: Realis Pictures, Inc.

———. 1997b. *Amazon Journal*. New York: Realis Pictures, Inc.

Sepultura. 1996. *Roots*. São Paulo/New York: UNI/Roadrunner Records.

7. REPRESENTATION, POLYPHONY, AND THE CONSTRUCTION OF POWER IN A KAYAPÓ VIDEO

Terence Turner

The interplay of indigenous and Western cultural perspectives in the production of hybrid representations has become a major focus of theoretical, political, and ethical concern in anthropology. This concern has animated much of the recent anthropological discussion about the construction of written ethnographic texts; but it has been more central to both theory and practice in the field of visual anthropology, where various modes of intercultural mediation, consultation, and collaboration between anthropological filmmakers and documentarists and indigenous communities have been developed within the past two decades (Turner 1990a, 1990c, 1995; MacDougall 1992; Ginsburg 1994). Contemporary with these developments within anthropology, indigenous peoples themselves were increasingly producing their own videos and TV broadcasts. These indigenous media products present different analytical, theoretical, and evaluative problems than do anthropological documentaries, although there are varying degrees of overlap with collaborative anthropological approaches (Ginsburg 1995a, 1995b; Turner 1995).

The relation between Western and indigenous cultural elements in indigenous media productions has also been a subject of much debate among anthropologists and cultural theorists concerned with the nature and value of these productions as cultural documents. Like Western anthropologists and documentarists who make media representations of indigenous and other non-Western peoples and cultures, indigenous videomakers also include elements drawn from Western forms, conventions, and techniques of audiovisual representation as well as their own cultural traditions of representation and categories of meaning. Critical discussion has focused on the extent to which indigenous self-representations of their own cultures can themselves be considered "authentically" indigenous cultural products (this essay is intended, among other things, to demonstrate the vacuousness of the notion of authenticity as a critical standard in discussions of hybrid cultural forms). The most vociferous critics tend to define the key issue as whether indigenous cultures or cultural forms can employ Western techniques of representation, such as video cameras, without assimilating the Western cultural traditions of representation associated with them and thereby losing their own cultural integrity, authenticity, or simply their own cultures *tout court*. The main critics who have taken this position with specific reference to indigenous video are James Faris and James Wiener (Faris 1992; Wiener 1997; cf. Turner 1992, 1997).

The underlying assumption of these critiques is that non-Western cultures are so radically incommensurate with Western culture—and, in particular, Western forms of representation—that contact between them can produce only the destruction and replacement of the non-Western culture by the Western. Certain postmodern critics seem to be most concerned to deny the possibility that intercultural communication, conflict, and collaboration might give rise to viable and vital hybrid forms in which indigenous cultural perspectives, categories, and concepts of representation might frame, inform, or otherwise productively combine with Western cultural elements—in some cases on what appear to be political and ethical as much as theoretical and philosophical grounds.

The critics to whom I refer draw upon the postmodern critique of representation derived, via Michel Foucault and Jacques Derrida, from Martin Heidegger and Friedrich Nietzsche (Foucault 1970, 1980). For theorists of this orientation, representation is an "effect of power" and therefore an instrumentality of domination. The Foucauldian extrapolation of the Nietzschean idea of power as a natural force or universal demiurge, however, has the effect of making "power" into a self-existing essence without social sources or agents; it thus becomes both unitary, as an internally noncontradictory essence, and irresistible, as a naturalized condition of existence (for a cogent critique of Foucauldian notions of power along these lines, see Sangren 2000: 119–152). Power, in these terms, cannot be used against itself; it follows that its effects (in the case in question, representations) cannot be used to oppose or resist the exercise of power. The employment by subordinated non-Western "Others" of Western means of representation, supposedly the very means of their domination and deauthentication by the hegemonic imperial power of the West, to resist domination by Western societies and to assert their own political agency and cultural values thus appears to be a contradiction in terms. Theoretically, it seems, either the so-called crisis of representation or the phenomenon of indigenous representation using the new audiovisual media cannot be what they have been claimed to be by their respective authors, advocates, and producers. The theoretical stakes, not to mention political/ethical postures, at risk in this confrontation doubtless account for the intensity of the attempts by anthropological critics such as Faris and Wiener to question, discredit, and even deny the possibility of indigenous media.

Indigenous media-makers and anthropologists who have studied their work, to the extent that they have responded to these attacks, have tended to emphasize the continuity of indigenous media productions with indigenous social and political perspectives and cultural orientations (Turner 1992; Ginsburg 1994). Much indigenous video, for example, tends to focus on those aspects of the life of contemporary indigenous communities most directly continuous with their cultural past. It is often undertaken by indigenous video-makers for the purpose of documenting that past to preserve it for future generations of their own peoples. A mere emphasis on the continuity of indigenous culture or "tradition," however, runs the risk of slipping into uncritical cultural essentialism. It tends to ignore or obscure the extent to which the production of representations is a socially contested process involving the conjunction of differing voices, perspectives, and values on the part of different groups and individuals within indigenous communities. The production of social and political reality— as well as the representations through which it is mediated by and to its producers—is a multivocal process in which the participants draw in different ways upon their common cultural stock of ideas, symbols, tropes, and values, thereby altering the form and content of the elements of their stock of representations. Even when indigenous actors employ a reified, homogeneous representation of their own "culture" to present a common ideological front in defending it against assimilative pressures from non-indigenous social or political-economic agents, a close examination of the social process of *creating* and asserting such representations of common culture reveals the complexity and conflict among the structural perspectives, views, and objectives of the actors involved. This point has been made cogently by Susan Wright in a recent comment on the political use of representations of their own "culture" by the Kayapó (Wright 1998).

The polyphonic nature of social processes of producing "culture" is evident even in the most fully traditional aspects of the life of indigenous communities, such as the collective ceremonial performances that have been the preferred subjects of Kayapó video-makers. It is more vividly apparent, however, when indigenous video-makers turn to the representation of unscripted interethnic encounters such as the one that is the subject of *Peace between Chiefs*, the video that I discuss in this chapter. In such cases, the indigenous cultural perspectives and categories that inform the camerawork and editing decisions of the video-makers are highlighted by juxtaposition with novel, nonindigenous contexts; the ways that indigenous video-makers employ them to order the new material and impose their own meanings upon it can reveal more about the resilience and adaptability of indigenous cultures in interaction and coexistence with national and global social and cultural systems than can any number of faithful representations of traditional ceremonies or techniques. Such videos compel anthropological analysts to deal directly with the ways members of non-Western indigenous cultures frame and interpret nonindigenous aspects of their social and cultural worlds. Close attention to the ways such representations are constructed at the levels of camerawork and editing may do more than any amount of abstract theorizing about the oppressiveness and alienness of Western technologies of representation to reveal how the indigenous cultures that produce the videos in question succeed in maintaining their own relative cultural autonomy as a basis for dealing with national and global systems and pressures.

These remarks are even more apposite when the events related in such a video constitute successful resistance or a victory for the indigenous side in a confrontation with the nonindigenous society or state, and still more when the actual making of the video in question has played an integral part in the event and its outcome. Cases of this kind in which indigenous societies succeed in imposing their own meanings and cultural forms of representation upon Western attempts to enforce cultural and social-political domination—not only at the level of representation but at the level of material political action—help to expose the gratuitous Western triumphalism and ethnocentrism implicit in much of what currently passes for the critique of representation in anthropology and cultural studies. By inverting the terms of the fashionable critique of transcultural representation as an effect of Western power over Third and Fourth World cultures, they help to clear away some of the gratuitous confusion that has accumulated around a series of fundamental theoretical issues concerning cultural representation and empowerment that are posed by indigenous media more generally.

Peace between Chiefs is a case of the type to which I refer. It was filmed in 1991 and edited the following year by Mokuka, a skilled video cameraperson and editor who at that time had been working with me for two years in the Kayapó Video Project.[1]

7.1 The arrival of the leaders for the A'ukre meeting. Photo by Mokuka Kayapó.

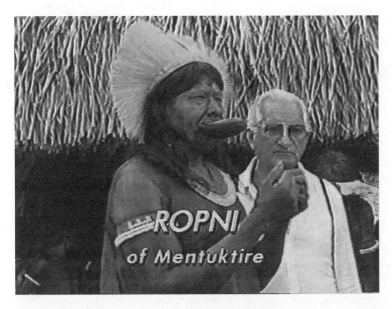

7.2 Ropni of Mentuktire greeting the president of FUNAI. Photo by Mokuka Kayapó.

7.3 Leaders of the different communities dance together before beginning the meeting. Photo by Mokuka Kayapó.

7.4 We have come to talk together … Ropni's victory speech. Photo by Mokuka Kayapó.

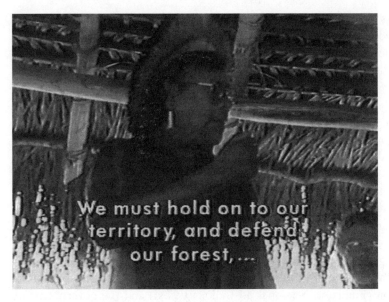

7.5 We must hold on to our territories ... Pombo delivering his concession speech. Photo by Mokuka Kayapó.

A KAYAPÓ SOCIAL DRAMA: KAYAPÓ CHIEFS
AND BRAZILIAN BUREAUCRATS IN DUBIOUS BATTLE

In 1991 Ropni, a Western Kayapó chief[2] generally referred to in the media as "Rauni," went on a fund-raising concert tour with the rock singer Sting. This unlikely duo succeeded in raising a large sum of money to be used to pay for the demarcation of an extensive territorial reserve for the Kayapó communities of Mentuktire, Menkrangnotire, Pukanu, and Baú, located on the west side of the Xingú River in central Brazil. One of Ropni's main goals in thus securing these communities' control over their land was to enable them to prevent the exploitation of its rich gold and timber resources by Brazilian miners and loggers. Miners and loggers had already penetrated the Kayapó area to the east of the Xingú, with the collaboration of certain Kayapó leaders. The most flagrant exponent of such collaboration was the late Tut, better known by his Portuguese name of Pombo, chief of the village of Kikretum. Pombo had permitted extensive gold mining and logging on Kikretum land in exchange for kickbacks from Brazilian mining and logging contractors. He had become a millionaire and owned an airplane, town houses, and a hotel in the Brazilian town of Tucumãn just outside the eastern Kayapó reserve.

As a Kayapó leader, Pombo represented everything that Ropni opposed. The two chiefs were the most famous and influential senior Kayapó leaders, not only among the fourteen Kayapó communities but among the Brazilian (and in Ropni's case international) public as well. Ropni's successful money-raising tour with Sting was a direct challenge to Pombo's style of collaboration in ecologically destructive extractivism for personal enrichment (with some "trickle-down" benefits for his community). Ropni had raised large sums of money, equal to or greater than those collected by Pombo from his corrupt deals with Brazilian contractors, but saved the entire sum to pay the costs of demarcating the promised new intercommunal reserve. He intransigently opposed granting concessions to Brazilian miners and loggers, both because of the destruction of forests and rivers caused by their activities and because of the social and cultural damage he claimed would inevitably follow from the influx of money brought in by payoffs to leaders like Pombo.

Ropni's success was also a stinging rebuke to the National Indian Foundation (Fundação Nacional do Indio: FUNAI) and the government of President José Sarney, which had failed to create the Western Kayapó reserve, alleging lack of funds. FUNAI itself was (and remains) implicated in the collusion of Kayapó leaders like Pombo with regional Brazilian loggers and miners and was generally hostile to any projects tending to empower Kayapó communities in ways that would make them independent of FUNAI. This was precisely the effect of Ropni's successful fundraising tour. Backed up by the nongovernmental organization that Sting and Ropni had jointly founded and funded, the Rainforest Foundation, Ropni was now demanding that the Brazilian government take the money he had raised and fulfill its promise to demarcate the huge area that had been allotted for the new reserve without further delay. This was not a step Sarney and his government—in which mining and logging interests carried a great deal of clout—wanted to take, especially on Ropni's terms. The pressure was on to find some way of discrediting Ropni, neutralizing his political influence, and thereby stalling the demarcation of the new reserve for the indefinite future.

A scheme to accomplish these ends was duly cooked up by FUNAI apparatchiks, with the willing cooperation of Pombo and elements of the Brazilian media. Pombo, in a well-attended press conference, announced that he had overthrown Ropni as paramount chief of all Kayapó (a position which did not exist and which Ropni had never claimed) and himself assumed the role. He had been driven to carry out this revolutionary coup, Pombo declared, by Ropni's selfish refusal to share the money he had collected on his European tour with Pombo and other eastern Kayapó leaders. In a well-coordinated media blitz, reporters, editorial writers, and cartoonists from major newspapers, magazines, and television rushed to cover the story in fulsome detail, most of them credulously accepting Pombo's claims at face value and gleefully celebrating the supposed downfall of the troublesome Ropni.

The irony of Pombo's polemics against Ropni's "selfishness" was not lost on the Kayapó, who recognized the whole performance as the Brazilian-instigated political smear campaign that it was. It swiftly became apparent that no Kayapó were willing to support Pombo against Ropni and that Ropni's downfall was not at hand. Ropni came to Brasilia and took up residence in the humble Indian shelter provided by FUNAI for visiting Indians, announcing that he was planning to stay there until Pombo and the government publicly withdrew their preposterous claims and charges and apologized to him. After several months of steadily deepening embarrassment over the obvious failure of their anti-Ropni campaign, Pombo and FUNAI were obliged to do precisely this.

A relatively face-saving way out for Pombo and the government agency was found by a third Kayapó leader, Payakan. Payakan had gained national and international renown as the leader of the Kayapó-led demonstration against the Brazilian government's Xingú River hydroelectric dam scheme at Altamira in 1989 but had quickly lost his Kayapó following amid rumors that he had embezzled funds contributed to the movement by foreign supporters. These rumors, however, had circulated only among the Kayapó; Payakan, ironically, continued to enjoy great prestige as a Kayapó leader among whites after having lost his support among the Kayapó themselves. He was able to convert this reputation into a series of lucrative associations with environmentalist NGOs, green capitalist companies, and FUNAI, all eager to associate themselves with the militant Kayapó leader of the Altamira demonstration. Thus it happened that, at the time of the dispute between Pombo and Ropni, Payakan had accepted a salaried position as "advisor for indigenous affairs" to the head of FUNAI. His role was essentially that of mediator between FUNAI and the Kayapó. In the Pombo-Ropni crisis he thus found himself in the delicate position of having to obtain a resolution satisfactory to his employer, FUNAI, while persuading the rival Kayapó leaders to go along.

With his own position at stake, Payakan proposed a compromise that met the needs of both sides while highlighting the centrality of his own role as mediator: a peace-making meeting to end the dispute, to be held on the neutral ground of Payakan's home village of A'ukre. Both Ropni and Pombo were willing to accept Payakan's suggestion. The scenario, worked out among the two Kayapó leaders and Payakan, called for the meeting to be attended by leaders from all fourteen Kayapó communities (with their air taxi expenses to be paid by FUNAI). At the meeting Ropni would be discreetly but unambiguously recognized as the winner and Pombo as the loser in the dispute, with FUNAI officials present to witness the outcome and publicly renew their respectful and supportive relationship with Ropni.

PEACE BETWEEN CHIEFS: A POLYPHONIC
REPRESENTATION OF A CACOPHONOUS EVENT

The meeting at A'ukre was videotaped by Mokuka, an accomplished Kayapó video cameraperson and editor; it is the subject of his edited video *Peace between Chiefs*. Mokuka made this video as a political and historical document of and for the Kayapó and supplied it with a running Kayapó narration. I was not at the meeting and played no part in the actual shooting. Later, in consultation with Mokuka, I made a shot record and acted as assistant editor, keeping the record for Mokuka to refer to as he edited the video. Mokuka made all the editing decisions and did the actual cutting and inserting. After he had finished editing the Kayapó version of the video, I suggested that we might produce a version that would be accessible to non-Kayapó audiences, with English subtitles and a short introductory section with English narration explaining the context of the event for foreign viewers. For the visual part of this introduction, I prepared a collage of Brazilian editorial cartoons, news stories, and photographs about the dispute between Pombo and Ropni. I wrote and narrated this introductory section and translated the subtitles. I translated my introductory narration into Kayapó for Mokuka, who approved of it and of the visual collage of Brazilian press clippings.

Like other Kayapó, Mokuka conceives of Kayapó-made videos as a way of reaching non-Kayapó publics with information about the Kayapó. The Kayapó in general feel that it is to their advantage to become better known to the outside world; they feel that this will make outsiders more disposed to support them against the Brazilian state and to provide other forms of aid. They conceive of their videos as potentially serving such an "outreach" function (Turner 1990a, 1992). The hybrid version of *Peace between Chiefs* composed of Mokuka's edited video with my introduction and subtitles thus exemplifies and fulfills one of the uses envisioned by Kayapó video-makers like Mokuka for their products: extending the accessibility of their work to an international audience of potential supporters.

As a moment in the struggle between the Kayapó, the Brazilian government, and regional economic interests over control of Kayapó land and resources and the extent of Kayapó local autonomy, the meeting of chiefs at A'ukre was a paradigmatic intercultural "social drama" that condensed many of the most important aspects of contemporary Kayapó social, cultural, and political reality. Overtly framed in traditional Kayapó political forms of oratory and conflict resolution, it was a polyphonic dialogue of different voices,[3] including those of Kayapó and non-Kayapó others.

Mokuka's video representation of this hybrid event employs a number of indigenous cultural forms as schemas for the construction of his visual representation of the event they helped to constitute. These include collective ritual performance, rhetorical tropes of political oratory and chiefly power, symbolically charged movements in social space, the organization of social discourse by age-grade hierarchy, and the formal Kayapó etiquette of public conflict resolution. He begins the video by showing the arrival of the main Kayapó chiefs in a sequence indexing their relative importance. Next he shows the arrival of the FUNAI officials, including an episode of horseplay with Ropni in which they act like old friends: the scene is cut on the sentence uttered by a FUNAI official: "The most important thing in life is friends." The irony is not lost on Kayapó audiences, fully aware that the whole attack on Ropni had been instigated by FUNAI to begin with.

The deft framing of the event by these two opening sequences is immediately followed by an interlude of collective ceremonial dancing, in which representatives of the communities of the disputing leaders join with members of the host community and the villages of the other leaders attending the meeting. This collaborative ritual performance prefigures the reaffirmation of the collective peace and solidarity the meeting was intended to confirm. In the video, it constitutes the visual bridge from the initial scenes focused on the arrivals of individual participants to the collective assembly to come.

It also represents a pivotal transition in the symbolic terms of Kayapó social space. Kayapó villages like A'ukre are laid out in concentric zones: a ring of houses surrounds a central plaza focused on a central men's house, which is the spatial setting of collective men's social and political activities and the site of the meeting of leaders that is about to take place. Ceremonial performances like the one in Mokuka's video take the form of massed columns of dancers circling the plaza just inside the ring of houses, as if rotating on the central hub of the men's house. Outside the houses is a circular zone associated with transitions between the social space of the village and extrasocial states or phenomena like death, ritual liminality, and the natural world of the forest.

This transitional zone is the location of the village graveyard, the seclusion camps of boys undergoing initiation, and the airstrip on which travelers from the outside world arrive. This is where Mokuka's video begins, with the arrival by air taxi of the Kayapó chiefs and Brazilian FUNAI officials who will attend the meeting. After filming the arrivals of the most important leaders, the camera follows the last group to arrive through the circle of houses constituting the village proper to the central plaza with its circling column of dancers. Only after pausing in this medial area does it move inward again to the central men's house. At first it pans into the men's house from a point outside it in the plaza: the men within gathered for the meeting appear darkly silhouetted against the brightness of the sunny plaza seen through the open walls. Then the camera moves inside and down to the center of the men's house floor, panning upward on the faces of the speakers to avoid the contrastive back-lighting of the open sides. For the Kayapó, the men's house—called "the center"— is not only the focus of social space but a dynamic source of power that holds peripheral elements like natural forces, households, and individuals around itself with a force potent enough to overcome the centrifugal force of petty conflicts that might otherwise threaten to disrupt community solidarity. The spatial movement of Mokuka's camera iconically embodies these fundamental cultural ideas and values and frames the narrative organization of the video with the cosmological significance of the concentric zones of social space.

Mokuka starts his representation of the meeting itself with a cut from Payakan's opening speech. In this speech Payakan adopts a patronizing tone toward his fellow Kayapó leaders, upbraiding them for having quarreled with one another while he was away in the city for FUNAI and calling upon them to bring their squabble to a satisfactory end so that he can report this outcome to the president of FUNAI. Payakan's rhetoric serves simultaneously to emphasize the importance of his role as spokesman and interpreter of the Kayapó to Brazilian officialdom and to evoke the authority he draws from this role over his Kayapó colleagues. The cut selected by Mokuka precisely captures the character of Payakan's ambiguous role as intercultural middleman and political broker, while epitomizing, in his condescending tone, the qualities that have made Payakan disliked and distrusted by many of his fellow Kayapó.

The ensuing sequence of speeches is organized according to Kayapó ideas of the hierarchy of age-set relations. As Mokuka emphasizes in his spoken voice-over, the senior men assume the active role of speakers and political leaders, while younger men and youths sit in deferential silence to listen and learn from their elders. Mokuka explains in his Kayapó voice-over that these younger men respectfully listened and later repeated to one another and others not present what was said by their elders. Mokuka selectively cuts to foreground the speeches of only the more senior chiefs. These are intercut with inserts showing the continual arrival of new leaders from outlying communities and younger men sitting attentively at the feet of the orators. Other inserts show blankly staring FUNAI officials scattered among the Kayapó audience, unable to understand a word of the long discourses they are obliged to listen to.

Mokuka cuts most of the content of the speeches but is careful to preserve the introductory passages in which the speakers assert their claims to the trust and attention of their hearers by itemizing and affirming their kinship relations with one another. Consistent with this theme, important Kayapó metaphors of solidarity and community are retained—as when one leader exclaims, with an inclusive sweep of his arms, "I like all of you, I want to sit together with you all"; or when the senior chief of A'ukre, the host village, assures the representatives of other communities located on the frontiers of the reserve that the men of A'ukre are ready to come to their support in any fight with Brazilian invaders. An account by an aged leader, Kromare of Mentuktire, of chiefly power as a kind of magic that is able to impose mutual solidarity upon members of a community, thus constraining them to stay together, is kept in its entirety.

After the other leaders speak, it is the turn of the two main protagonists, Ropni and Pombo. Never once making explicit reference to the actual dispute that occasioned the meeting, they code their respective victory and concession through metaphors of sexual potency, self-control, and fertility. Ropni proclaims that although he is old, he has great strength: the young men of distant Kayapó communities should not think that because they are far from his village they can get away with antisocial behavior, because his power is capable of projection over a great distance. At this point, Ropni's discourse recalls the aged Kromare's evocation of chiefly power as a kind of social magic. Ropni, however, goes on to suggest the source of this power of leadership: his controlled sexual potency. He proclaims that he is not like those weak chiefs who have sexual liaisons with their followers' wives, thus disrupting the social peace. On the contrary, at the end of a day of hunting in the forest, he says, he comes home and "I just fuck my own wife" (the term for sexual intercourse he chooses has the vulgar connotations of the English term I have used here to translate it). The effect of macho bonhomie is echoed by chuckles among the listening men. Ropni thus simultaneously asserts his sexual power and his power to restrain and control it for social good. These, he implies, are the complementary aspects of effective chiefly power.[4]

Pombo, in contrast, laments his own sexual impotence, associating it metaphorically with inability to go hunting: "I no longer take my dog out to the forest [to hunt], because I am afraid I would trip and not be able to get up. You young men know what I'm talking about." He is no longer directly involved in procreation, he explains, but is interested only in the doings of his children and grandchildren. In contrast to Ropni's claims to vigorous sexual power and the ability to project his authority over long distances in social space, Pombo thus proclaims his loss of power. In place of personal potency, he can now only indirectly participate in the potency of his offspring, as represented by the birth of his grandson.

Following the Kayapó leaders' speeches, the president of FUNAI brings them together in an embrace, proclaiming the end of their dispute even as he acclaims their "national and even international recognition," thus unwittingly extending the spatial metaphor of Ropni's claims for the spatial extension of his potency. The video closes with a shot of an air taxi flying over the village, carrying the departing leaders back to their home villages. The shot complements the opening shot of an air taxi coming in for a landing at the village airstrip. Taken together, the two shots also underscore the spatial metaphor of power central to the discourses of the chiefs and the FUNAI representative. Ropni's power has shown its potency by compelling this coming together and subsequent redispersion of the key political leaders of the Kayapó social world, including even Brazilian government officials. Mokuka's vignette of Ropni welcoming the arriving president of FUNAI with the words "Always we have had to come to you; now you have come to us" is clearly fraught with the metaphorical significance of the spatial projection of social power carried out in the structure of the video as a whole. In this context, Ropni's words clearly carry the meaning not merely of "coming to us" but "coming to me."

Mokuka's filming was itself a meaningfully charged part of the event he filmed. As I have written elsewhere, the Kayapó think of representation as in itself a contribution to the reality of the thing or event represented.

To produce a permanent, independently existing representation of an event, such as a video, has the effect of giving that event an added dimension of objective facticity (Turner 1992). Such "facticity," of course, is seldom disinterested, and the case of the A'ukre meeting was no exception. It was very much in Ropni's interest, and very much not in Pombo's, for Mokuka to have made this video record of the public recognition and collective confirmation of Ropni's triumph. It was also in the general interest of the Kayapó leaders (Pombo excepted) to have their own documentary record of what was in effect a smashing Kayapó victory over the machinations of FUNAI and the Brazilian government.

Nor was Mokuka's own role simply that of a disinterested objective recorder. At the time of the meeting, Mokuka was Payakan's main challenger for leadership in A'ukre. Payakan was still in control, and Mokuka had been temporarily obliged to leave the community after a particularly bitter confrontation. His role as official cameraperson for the meeting gave him a pretext to return in an important but ostensibly neutral role, in an event Payakan had organized in a way calculated to dramatize his own exclusive importance as a leader in his home community. Mokuka told me before the meeting that he had hopes that the assembled chiefs, after witnessing the settlement of the dispute between Ropni and Pombo, would undertake to mediate the dispute between him and Payakan and give at least some support to his claims. In the event, this did not happen; but Mokuka's hopes gave him an incentive to make the video and in the process to give even-handed treatment to all the leaders present.

The "voices" that make up the polyphonic dialogue of Mokuka's video include those of Mokuka as narrator, the Kayapó leaders (notably Ropni, Pombo, and Payakan), and the Brazilian president of FUNAI. My introduction and subtitles add the voices of the Brazilian media and my own voice, as both commentator and translator. The present essay may perhaps be regarded as a further dialogical addition to Mokuka's original text in yet another modality of my own voice, this time as anthropological interpreter. All of these voices carry distinctive representations of the event—representations that are at times complementary and at times divergent or contradictory. Perhaps the most powerful and pervasive representations, however, are carried by no single identifiable voice. The Kayapó cultural representations of social space and chiefly power that frame and encode the action of the event as a whole are conveyed in large part not by the voices of individual personages or narrators but by the movement of the camera and subsequent cutting of the audiovisual text. It is thus ironically the most untraditional component of the hybrid cultural product that is *Peace between Chiefs*, the camera, that serves as the vehicle of the most traditional aspects of its structure and meaning.

HYBRID REPRESENTATIONS, INDIGENOUS MEDIA, AND THE POLITICS OF CULTURAL EMPOWERMENT

Hybrid indigenous representations of interethnic encounters like the A'ukre meeting that is the subject of *Peace between Chiefs* provide unique insights into the dynamics of intercultural interactions.[5] They also challenge theoretical assumptions and ideological positions currently held by some anthropologists on questions of representation and the anthropological use and interpretation of visual materials. These challenges have stimulated intense critical reactions in certain anthropological quarters that have ranged from attacks on the authenticity of the indigenous cultural perspectives embodied in such videos to denials on *a priori* grounds that authentically indigenous representations in such media could exist. It is ironic that just as indigenous people themselves are learning to use media in ever more varied, creative, and culturally empowering ways, some anthropologists have become intensely invested in denying the ethnographic validity, political significance, and anthropological value of this contemporary cultural phenomenon (Faris 1992; Wiener 1997).

The effect of the postmodern critique of representation is to separate: to deconstruct the connections between sign and referent, signifier and signified, signification and meaning, discourse and reality, text and context, subject and power, culture and material social process, and cultural critic and politics, at least of the consequential kinds rooted in social issues, organized movements, and "master narratives" like the dynamics of class. This is the effect of the importation of politics into representation itself, as a relation of power between dominant signifier and subordinate signified.

The situation of the Kayapó, like that of most contemporary indigenous peoples, differs profoundly in political, social, and cultural terms from that of the Western intellectuals and academics engaged in the postmodern discourse on representation. For indigenous peoples struggling to redefine the terms of their relations to the national and transnational systems in which they are embedded, representational media such as video have been useful primarily as means of *connection* in time and space: connecting their present situations with their pasts and futures in historical time, and linking their communities in social space with their ambient local contexts as well as establishing connections with more distant indigenous groups and nonindigenous publics, organizations, and government agencies able to offer protection, support, and alliance. The exploitation of national and transnational communications networks and the employment of new representational media and informational technologies by indigenous peoples have played a central role in making these connections.

The purpose of such temporal and spatial connections for indigenous groups like the Kayapó has not been to insulate themselves from contact or engagement with the outside world but to engage more effectively with their ambient national and global systems, draw upon their resources, and take part in their politics in order to increase their power to control their own resources and determine the social and cultural terms of their own lives. Representation in this context appears not as a relation of power in and of itself but as a mediator of social relations of political struggle, in which power is produced and mobilized by both parties through the pragmatic manipulation of representations in contexts of use. Empowerment, not the inertial continuity of "tradition"; engagement, not separation; and hybridity, not cultural purity, are the values informing the vitality and assertiveness of renascent indigenous peoples and cultures all over the world, including the Kayapó.

The approach to representation manifested by the media productions of indigenous groups like the Kayapó proceeds from these values and the social and political activities they inform, and is itself instrumental in shaping them. The intrusion of nonindigenous voices, categories, and perspectives in the construction of these complex polyphonic representations does not detract from their value or effectiveness as cultural documents; nor is it inconsistent with a decisive indigenous cultural contribution to the total representational product. In the case of *Peace between Chiefs*, close analysis of the audiovisual text reveals that the perspectives and ideas through which the orchestration of indigenous and nonindigenous voices is effected are themselves drawn from the indigenous cultural stock of notions and values, albeit in different ways and for different purposes by the various (and opposing) Kayapó performers.

In one sense, at least, postmodern critics of indigenous media are correct: indigenous media—and above all hybrid indigenous media representations of intercultural events like the one considered here—do pose fundamental theoretical challenges to these critics' whole approach to representation. For one thing, by putting representation to creative political and social use, indigenous people demonstrate that representation as such, including representation produced with the use of contemporary

Western technologies like video, can be made the vehicle of emancipatory politics and creative cultural expression, accommodation, and change. By employing representation critically as part of political struggles, indigenous media-makers demonstrate that politics consists in the way representation is used to mediate processes of social action and conflict, not in the critique of properties of representation in the abstract. The troubling implication of this for the postmodern critique of representation is clear: the effects of representation cannot be assumed on *a priori* theoretical grounds but can only be understood—and their political implications appreciated—by analyzing the production and use of representation in pragmatic social contexts.

Indigenous videos that deal with the generation and use of power, like the Kayapó example discussed here, have valuable general lessons to teach about the relations of representation and power, the issue that lies at the heart of the postmodern "crisis of representation." Inverting the terms of the Foucauldian proposition that representation is an effect of power, they show, on the contrary, that power is an effect of representation. Specifically, power is the representation by individuals or groups of some form of effective force they claim to possess and threaten to use, coupled with the acceptance of those representations, claims, and threats by other members of the relevant social field. Power, in short, is not an agent that produces social subjects but a representational medium produced, circulated, and received by social agents. Ropni's victory over Pombo and FUNAI and his rhetorical representations of that victory are not depicted in *Peace between Chiefs* as produced by some pre-representational, intrinsic "power" of which Ropni happens to be the vehicle; rather, Ropni is shown producing his power—that is, his ability to compel the deference and support of his Kayapó listeners and colleagues—through the rhetorical representation of his libidinal force and potency. Pombo, for his part, is shown acquiescing in and thus confirming Ropni's idiom of power. Power, in other words, is depicted in the video as the social production, circulation, and acceptance of representations of intrinsically effective force of a culturally specific kind, possessed by a specific individual backed by a specific faction and occupying a specific social role in which the exercise of that power is legitimate and expected: that of *benhadjuòrò* or chief.

As a final point, it should be noted that *Peace between Chiefs* employs a contemporary Western technology of representation, video, as a vehicle for the decidedly non-Western Kayapó conception of representation as an act that contributes to the material social reality of the thing represented rather than merely reflecting a preexisting objective reality separate from the act of representation. This conception is already implicit in the way the actual process of representation, in this case the shooting of the video, becomes an integral part of the event being recorded. Mokuka's making of the video of the A'ukre meeting not only fixed the meaning of the event and its outcome for its contemporary and future Kayapó audience but was itself a contributory part of that event and its meaning. With Kayapó and other indigenous media productions, we thus move beyond Participatory Cinema in David MacDougall's sense—and beyond representation conceived as an abstracted image problematically separated from its context of social production and use—to representational activity as one connected element in complexly interrelated episodes of social praxis (MacDougall 1992).

Acknowledgment

I am indebted to Davydd Greenwood for an insightful critique of an earlier draft of this essay.

Notes

1. I founded the Kayapó Video Project (Projeto de Video Kaiapó) in June 1990, funded by a Spencer Foundation Grant. The project provided video cameras to Kayapó camerapersons in five villages and made available training in video editing, access to editing facilities, and technical assistance at the editing studio of the Centro de Trabalho Indigenista, São Paulo. The Kayapó Video Project also established the Kayapó Video Archive/Arquivo de Video Kaiapó (KVA/AVK) at the Centro de Trabalho Indigenista. This is a video editing and storage facility where original Kayapó video rushes and edited video masters are stored and recopied to prevent deterioration and where copies of masters can be produced and distributed to Kayapó communities and other interested viewers in Brazil and abroad. Mokuka had previously filmed the Kayapó rally at Altamira against a hydroelectric dam scheme promulgated by the Brazilian government and provisionally supported by the World Bank (Turner 1990a, 1990b, 1990c, 1991, 1992, 1995).

2. The Kayapó office of *benhadjuòrò*, which I translate as "chief," is a traditional status that combines ritual authority and political leadership. It is not hereditary but instead relies on consensual recognition by a man's age-set mates. Other factors, however, may be involved. Both the main protagonists of the social drama that ended in the A'ukre meeting, Pombo and Ropni, were propelled to chiefly office as a result of learning Portuguese and other Brazilian ways from, respectively, a missionary and a Brazilian administrative head of the

National Xingú Park (in its former incarnation as the Central Brazilian Foundation). Both thus began their chiefly careers as mediators between their communities and the Brazilian power structure. The two men went on to become relatively independent leaders, using their intercultural skills to achieve personal and communal ends.

3. On the concept of "polyphony" as used here, see Bakhtin (1981, 1984). Bakhtin emphasizes the different voices of class and status groups within the same society. In the present case, the voices of different ethnic groups involved in the interethnic situation and different groups and players within Kayapó society that define their distinctive voices in terms of contrasting relations to the Brazilian power structure—as well as different statuses and roles within Kayapó society itself—are represented.

4. There is not, to my knowledge, any conventional cultural association of chieftainship and sexual potency or behavior. The metaphorical linkage of sexual power with chiefly efficacy in the rhetoric of both protagonists was, as far as I know, an improvisation for this occasion.

5. On "hybridity," see Hall (1990) and García Canclini (1995). The event represented by the video, with the complex political, economic, cultural, and ideological processes that led up to it, and the video itself are good examples of the interplay of global, state-level, and local factors and forces—and the resulting creation of composite forms with elements drawn from different social and cultural strata—that García Canclini attempts to subsume in his formulation of the concept. The video, for example, can be seen as an exemplary representation of the construction of what García Canclini calls an "oblique" power relationship between the Kayapó and the state, in place of the "vertical" hierarchy between the state and its constituent groups that is the aim of the modernization process (García Canclini 1995: 3). The Kayapó case, at the same time, helps to clarify aspects of "hybridity" that García Canclini treats as "paradoxical" and in some respects challenges the basic presuppositions of his formulation: namely that "hybridization," as the essential process of cultural postmodernism, consists of a paradoxical combination of decentralization and dissemination in the cultural sphere with centralization and concentration of power in the political and economic sphere (García Canclini 1995: 103, 271). The Kayapó achievement of relative economic and political autonomy—against the opposition of the Brazilian state—through the global leverage of Ropni's successful international tour with Sting shows that hybridization may involve significant decentralization and redistribution of political and economic power.

At the same time, the careful construction of the A'ukre meeting as a symbolic event to show the confirmation and legitimation of this political loosening of state control over the defiant Kayapó minority by the representative of the state—through his literal embrace of the triumphant Ropni and his verbal recognition of Ropni's international as well as national renown—constitutes an important affirmation of cultural and ideological centralization (the state is reaffirmed as the essential source of legitimizing authority as it encompasses the relative autonomy of dissident groups). The Kayapó use of video in this and other instances, moreover, demonstrates forcefully that the creation of hybrid cultural forms does not necessarily entail the submergence or disappearance of "traditional" cultural categories and principles (cf. García Canclini 1995: 36–37). The assimilation of Brazilian and Kayapó elements, notably including the use of the video medium of representation as an integral part of the event represented, exemplifies García Canclini's perspective on hybridity as a juxtaposition of elements drawn from different cultural and social "strata" brought about within a field of conflicting power relations precipitated by the impact of the global concentration of capital on state and local relations.

References

Bakhtin, Mikhail. 1981. *The Dialogic Imagination.* Austin: University of Texas Press.

———. 1984. *Rabelais and His World.* Bloomington: Indiana University Press.

Faris, James C. 1992. Anthropological Transparency: Film, Representation, and Politics. In Peter Ian Crawford and David Turton, eds., *Film as Ethnography,* 171–182. Manchester: Manchester University Press.

———. 1993. A Response to Terence Turner. *Anthropology Today* 9: 12–13.

Foucault, Michel. 1970. *The Order of Things: An Archaeology of the Human Sciences.* New York: Vintage.

———. 1980. *Power/Knowledge.* Ed. C. Gordon. Trans. C. Gordon, I. Marshall, J. Mepham, and K. Soper. New York: Pantheon Books.

García Canclini, Néstor. 1995. *Hybrid Cultures: Strategies for Entering and Leaving Modernity.* Minneapolis: University of Minnesota Press.

Ginsburg, Faye. 1991. Indigenous Media: Faustian Contract or Global Village? *Cultural Anthropology* 6 (1).

———. 1994. Culture and Media: A (Mild) Polemic. *Anthropology Today* 10 (2): 5–15.

———. 1995a. Mediating Culture: Indigenous Media, Ethnographic Film, and the Production of Identity. In Leslie Deveraux and Roger Hillman, eds., *Fields of Vision: Essays in Film Studies, Visual Anthropology, and Photography.* Berkeley: University of California Press.

———. 1995b. The Parallax Effect: The Impact of Aboriginal Media on Ethnographic Film. *Visual Anthropology Review* 11 (2).

Hall, Stuart. 1990. Cultural Identity and Diaspora. In J. Rutherford, ed., *Identity, Community, Culture, Difference,* 222–237. London: Lawrence and Wishart.

———. 1992. Cultural Studies and Its Theoretical Legacies. In Lawrence Grossberg, Cary Nelson, and Paula Treichler, eds., *Cultural Studies,* 277–285. New York: Routledge.

MacDougall, David. 1992. Complicities of Style. In Peter Crawford and David Turton, eds., *Film as Ethnography,* 90–98. Manchester: Manchester University Press.

Sangren, P. Steven. 2000. "Power" against Ideology: A Critique of Foucauldian Usage. In P. Steven Sangren, *Chinese Sociologics: An Anthropological Account of the Role of Alienation in Social Reproduction*, 119–152. London School of Economics Monographs on Social Anthropology, Vol. 72. London and New Brunswick, N.J.: Athlone Press.

Turner, Terence. 1990a. The Kayapo Video Project: A Progress Report. *CVA Review* (Commission on Visual Anthropology, Montreal) (Fall): 7–10. Reprinted in *Independent* (January–February 1991): 34–40.

———. 1990b. A significativa política e cultural de usos recentes de video pelos Kaiapó. In *O indio ontem, hoje e manhã*, 110–122. São Paulo: Editora Memorial da America Latina.

———. 1990c. Visual Media, Cultural Politics, and Anthropological Practice: Some Implications of Recent Uses of Film and Video among the Kayapo of Brazil. *CVA Review* (Spring): 8–13. Reprinted in *Independent* (January–February 1991): 34–40.

———. 1991. The Social Dynamics and Personal Politics of Video Making in an Indigenous Community. *Visual Anthropology Review* 7 (2) (Fall): 68–76.

———. 1992. Defiant Images: The Kayapo Appropriation of Video. *Anthropology Today* 8 (6) (December): 5–15.

———. 1995. Representation, Collaboration, and Mediation in Contemporary Ethnographic and Indigenous Media. *Visual Anthropology Review* 11 (2) (Fall): 1–5.

———. 1997. Comment on J. Wiener, "Televisualist Anthropology." *Current Anthropology* 38 (2): 226–232.

Wiener, James F. 1997. Televisualist Anthropology: Representation, Aesthetics, Politics. *Current Anthropology* 38 (2): 197–211.

Wright, Susan. 1998. The Politicization of "Culture." *Anthropology Today* 14 (1): 7–15.

8. CUTTING THROUGH STATE AND CLASS

Sources and Strategies of Self-Representation in Latin America

Alcida Rita Ramos

[L]a idea de nación en la América Latina contemporánea está basada en la negación de las culturas indígenas.—Rodolfo Stavenhagen

SHORTCUTS

One of the most striking features of contemporary indigenous movements in Latin America and elsewhere is the rapidity with which they were organized and propelled into international arenas as legitimate and widely visible political actors. From the vantage point of the beginning of the twenty-first century, one tends to regard this brisk pace of worldwide native self-affirmation less as a genuine prowess and more as the sign of the times, which since World War II has taken a vertiginous turn. However, anthropologists and other observers seemed to lag behind these events. As late as 1977, we find passages such as the following: "In this day and time, . . . nothing has changed regarding the disgraceful treatment of the peoples and ethnic minorities in the Third World" (Binder 1977: 52). Even John Bodley, who later assessed the international achievements of the indigenous cause, in 1977 still argued in favor of "cultural autonomy" as if it were an issue yet to be posed (1977: 43–44).

In short, nearly a decade after debate on the indigenous issue had taken place in supranational forums such as the United Nations and the International Labor Organization, its effects, as pointed out by Andrea Muehlebach (2001: 415), had not trickled down to the anthropological community, to say nothing of the public at large.

It is thus worth tracing, albeit succinctly, the steps taken by the indigenous cause through international landscapes of human rights, if for no other reason than to show how observers of indigenous life can lag behind indigenous initiatives. The first timid steps toward internationalization of the indigenous cause escalated to a sweeping wave of liberalization on the part of national states with regard to legislation affecting indigenous peoples in the Americas. It is not a coincidence that this liberal trend in official policies occurs simultaneously with the neoliberal policies to minimize state powers and responsibilities as discerned in their drift toward privatization. This essay is about the repercussions of internationalization and state liberalism for the restyling of ethnic politics, here exemplified by Colombia and Brazil, and the consequences of all this for the relationship between ethnic groups and the state and for indigenous organizing at the beginning of this century.

In order to demonstrate that the pace of modern indigenous movements has been quick but that the phenomenon is not so recent as to allow characterizing it as brand new, I begin with a concise chronology of the most significant events that led to the international recognition of indigenous rights from immediately after World War II to the early 1980s. The following summary draws primarily on the work by Françoise Morin (1992) and Morin and Bernard Saladin D'Anglure (1994). A brief chronology of the main events attests to the rapidity with which the indigenous cause became internationalized. The first registered attempt to take indigenous claims to international forums was the frustrated appeal in the 1920s to the League of Nations by the Iroquois Confederacy against the Canadian government (Tauli-Corpuz 1999: 4). But it was the end of World War II that brought about the recognition of the need to establish safeguards against abuses such as those exposed in Nazi concentration camps. The modern version of the Universal Declaration of Human Rights celebrated in 1948 is the most finished product of these efforts. But before the declaration was ratified there was a long discussion of minority rights, a forerunner of indigenous rights.

In 1945, under the umbrella of the United Nations General Assembly, a Commission for the Rights of Mankind was created in the wake of the Holocaust with the purpose of preventing state atrocities against populations within or outside the state's boundaries. It met with the resistance of countries like Great Britain, which feared the disclosure of its own performance in India; the United States, which feared the disclosure of its internal problems with blacks; and Russia, which feared for the maintenance of its national sovereignty (Morin and Saladin D'Anglure 1994: 191).

In 1946 a Human Rights Sub-commission for the Eradication of Discriminatory Measures against Minorities presented a series of propositions and recommendations regarding "the protection of minorities and prevention of any distinctions based on race, sex, language or religion" (Morin 1992: 494).

In 1947, as a result, the International Pact for Civil and Political Rights, in Article 27, determined that persons belonging to any ethnic, religious, or linguistic minorities within any state should not be prevented from exercising their right of membership in these minority groups or from leading their own cultural life, professing and practicing their own religion, or speaking their own language. Although the pact's object was individual rather than collective rights, its insistence on preserving differences within nation-states irritated countries like France, where republican ideals were based on the uniformity of rights of citizenship.

In 1948 the Universal Declaration of Human Rights was celebrated under protest from the Soviet Union, which argued against its overemphasis on the individual to the detriment of social and economic collective rights (for the situation of a specific ethnic group, the Nivki, under Soviet rule, see Grant 1995). The declaration's philosophical conception was clearly based on European beliefs about "a universal human nature grasped through reason, and a natural right inherent to human nature" (Morin and Saladin D'Anglure 1994: 193).

In 1950 the need to define "minority" led the Human Rights Subcommission to declare: "The term 'minority' is only applicable to groups of non-dominant populations who possess and desire to preserve stable ethnic, religious or linguistic traditions or characteristics that are clearly different from those of the rest of the population." Nevertheless, "minorities must be loyal to the state of which they are a part" (Morin 1992: 495). The contradiction inherent in this definition—for loyalty to the state and loyalty to one's tradition are rarely in harmony—raised so many problems and objections that the subcommission abandoned the quest for an all-encompassing definition of "minority" and concentrated on protective measures.

In 1966 the U.N. International Charter for the Rights of Mankind declared in its first article that all peoples have the right to freely determine themselves politically and freely secure their cultural, social, and economic development. Catering to the "politics of decolonization advanced by the United Nations," this article turned out to be a useful instrument for the Indians to express their grievances (Morin and Saladin D'Anglure 1994: 193).

The 1960s was a dramatic decade for indigenous peoples, especially in Latin America, where nation-states were vigorously implementing large-scale development projects at the expense of indigenous lives and territories (Davis 1977; Bourne 1978). As denunciations of atrocities in Brazil, Colombia, Bolivia, and Guatemala filled mass-media news reports, both indigenous and nonindigenous organizations began to appear on the international scene. The first European NGOs dedicated to the Indian cause (the Danish International Work Group for Indigenous Affairs [IWGIA] and the British Survival International) began to pressure European governments to take action in defense of indigenous peoples against Latin American states. The result was an increasing visibility of the struggle of indigenous peoples qua ethnic collectivities, distinct from the minorities that had inspired the post–World War II international policies.

In 1971, "[f]or the first time, the Sub-commission distinguished the cases of native peoples from those of other minorities" and recommended that a work group dedicated exclusively to native populations be created to draw up a declaration of rights of native peoples (Morin and Saladin D'Anglure 1994: 194).

In 1974 for the first time an indigenous organization—the National Fraternity of Canadian Indians—was given official voice at the U.N., inaugurating a series of conferences about discrimination against native peoples in the Americas.

In 1977 about one hundred indigenous and Inuit delegates convened in Geneva to reject their inclusion in the statute of minorities, demanding to be classified as "peoples." They also required that Convention 107 of the International Labor Organization be revised to abolish its "assimilationist and paternalist" bias toward indigenous groups (Stavenhagen 1989: 91). In 1989 Convention 169 replaced Convention 107. This new statute no longer referred to Indians as populations but as "peoples," which led countries like Brazil[1] and the United States to refuse to sign it, using arguments that hinged on threats to national sovereignty. In September of that year an International Conference of NGOs on discrimination against indigenous peoples in the Americas declared the right of "indigenous nations to submit to international law if these peoples wish to be recognized as nations so long as they observe the fundamental conditions of every nation, as follows: (a) have a permanent population; (b) possess a defined territory; (c) have the capacity to relate to other nations" (Alcina Franch 1990: 14).

In 1978, during a U.N. conference dedicated to fighting racism and racial discrimination, thirty-three states signed a motion recognizing the territorial, economic, cultural, and linguistic rights of native peoples.

In 1981 that year's conference on native peoples and their relation to land proposed a U.N. Work Group for Indigenous Populations, which was created in 1982 and whose ultimate task is to draw up and gain approval for a Declaration of Indigenous Rights (Stavenhagen 1989: 91).

The first draft of this declaration had to wait until 1989 (Warren 1998: 7) and was finalized in 1993 (Muehlebach 2001: 443n1).

From then on indigenous participation in U.N. activities increased steadily (Tauli-Corpuz 1999), and many cases of state abuse against indigenous peoples were taken to U.N. forums. Australian Aborigines presented their case in 1988, the Inuit in 1989, peoples from the Philippines in 1990, and the Brazilian Yanomami in 1991. "After ten years of participating in this work group, one can say that the main indigenous groups in the world have developed a very sharp awareness that they are despoiled and threatened peoples and that they must reconquer their rights" (Morin and Saladin D'Anglure 1994: 197–198).

In short, if we take the year 1974, when the National Fraternity of Canadian Indians was accredited by the U.N., as the most significant landmark, we realize how quickly the indigenous issue was propelled to the supranational arena of ethnic politics. In less than twenty-five years "the natives of the West and then of other parts of world have accomplished an extraordinary feat of organization and structuring" (Morin and Saladin D'Anglure 1994: 198).

At the same time, on another front—no longer in Europe, but in the Americas—a number of initiatives brought the Indian issue to the world stage of interethnic politics. In 1940 the Interamerican Indigenist Institute was created in Mexico under the banner of the integrationist policies of the times (Stavenhagen 1989: 88). Thirty years later, in 1971, the first Declaration of Barbados was signed by eleven extremely committed, but all-white, anthropologists and indigenists, mostly from Latin America. For the first time, an international forum focused on the need for the Indians themselves to take on the struggle for self-government, development, and defense of their own rights (Alcina Franch 1990: 13). In 1975 the World Council of Indigenous Peoples was created. In 1977 Barbados II brought together equal numbers of Indians and whites. That same year indigenous representatives from Central America created the Regional Congress of Indigenous Peoples of Central America. In what is truly record time, indigenous peoples of the Americas replaced their white spokespersons with their own voices, while the trend continues to move from assimilationist state policies to indigenous demands for autonomy and self-representation.

These gains in international arenas did not, of course, come about as a sudden and spontaneous act of volition on the part of those involved, Indians and non-Indians. Rather, they were the outcome of decisive postwar historical conjunctures in which East-West power disputes, the quest for decolonization, and the involvement of Christian sectors in political issues, among other factors, at last opened the space indigenous peoples needed to raise their voices and be heard.

At the same time, these gains stirred up with renewed strength the contradictions that inhere in the coexistence of different ethnic minorities within a single nation-state. A clear and tragic example of the destructive force these contradictions can unleash was the prolonged civil war in Guatemala in the 1970s and 1980s that killed 200,000 Mayas and created conditions for the subsequent rise of antagonistic positions within the indigenous movement (Warren 1998).

A DOUBLE-EDGED SWORD

Part of the success in catapulting the Indian issue into the realm of international law is due to the cracks in the very constitution of modern Western ideology. If, on the one hand, the humanist quest for universalism has come to be the hegemonic idiom in which human rights are expressed everywhere regardless of cultural differences, on the other hand, universalism coexists with the equally humanist quest for relativism, according to which values are not universal but culture-bound and as such should not be submitted to universal principles. This contradiction is the immediate result of yet another contradiction, between the logic of nationality and the logic of ethnicity. In other words, the mismatch between the principles that rule a nation-state and the canons that orient ethnic identity produces a social vacuum that is open to a great deal of interpretation and experimentation.

Elsewhere I have attempted to make some sense of the ideological cacophony that results from the discrepant voices of universalism, nationalism, and ethnicity in making themselves heard at the same time and often in the same place (Ramos 1998a: Chapter 3). There I proposed to take Tzvetan Todorov's cue about a "well-tempered universalism" (1989: 421–437) and adopt the notions of universalism and relativism, not as "the fixed content of a theory about human beings," but as strategies for action supplying a "need to postulate a common horizon for interlocutors in a debate" (427). Therefore, we would have not only Todorov's idea of a *universalisme de parcours* (universalism in flux) but also a *relativisme de parcours* (relativism in flux). Seen in this light, the decades-long debates mentioned above at the United Nations and other forums make perfectly good sense. Indeed, they are extraordinary exercises in universalism and relativism of *parcours* on the part of both indigenous peoples and supranational powers.

Now, regarding the interaction between ethnic groups and their encompassing nation-states, these strategies meet with particularly tenacious resistance that goes well beyond matters of procedure and persuasion commonly found in international contexts. This resistance has been generated in the course of long historical trajectories that, in the New World, led to the emergence of creole societies in search of distinctive national identities different from both those of the aboriginal peoples of the land and those of the original colonial powers in Europe. Wars of independence, perhaps more than "print capitalism" (Anderson 1983), did much to crystallize the newly independent states. In these wars the "winners were obviously not those who continued their lives as 'Indians'" (Klor de Alva 1995: 270). Indeed, the newly constituted nations of the Americas proceeded to conquer their native populations by extermination policies to clear their precious lands, as in the United States and Argentina; by expropriation of their labor forces, as in the Andes and Central America; or by the pacification tactics of disingenuous "friendly persuasion" to surrender indigenous lands for national colonization, as in Brazil (Ramos 1998a: Chapter 5). Having conquered their Indians, the new states shoved them away to marginal areas of the national territory, as in the United States; pretended they did not exist, as in Argentina; merged them with peasants, as in Venezuela; tried to fragment indigenous states by resettling their populations in dispersed rural municipalities (*reducciones*) away from creoles, as in Guatemala; or infantilized them as "relatively incapable" under direct state wardship, as in Brazil. The net result of 500 years of forced coexistence with their conquerors, whether facing guns, forced labor, or alluring trinkets, is too well known to be exhaustively repeated: severe depopulation, loss of traditional lands, crippling dependence on national societies, demoralizing prejudice, and, for the survivors, a portentous will to live—and to live qua Indians. Through the centuries, insurgencies, revolts, uprisings, messianic movements, and other forms of protest against so much destruction did little more for indigenous peoples all over the American continent than deepen their submission to the national powers.

Perhaps the novelty of the twentieth century resides not in a qualitative difference in the treatment of indigenous peoples but in the new weapons with which the Indians can now defend themselves against the abuses of the nation-state. With some notable exceptions (such as the counterinsurgency wars in Guatemala and Chiapas), interethnic battlefields have been relocated to news media, courtrooms, and parliaments. Ironically it was the carnage of World War II that basically precipitated the production of these peaceful weapons now available to indigenous peoples.

In this modern arena of confrontation between ethnicity and the state one cannot overemphasize the crucial role of a new actor: nongovernmental organizations (NGOs). As we have seen, the first NGOs to take on the defense of indigenous rights were created in the mid-1960s; the effect of their actions was immediately felt, especially in Europe, in the form of public denunciations, motions, declarations, and other strategies that led to the results described earlier. NGOs have been instrumental in opening channels for indigenous peoples to vent their grievances at the national level but especially at the international level. Their singular usefulness is precisely in their role as political switchboards between the local and the global. As such they empower the Indians to bypass state resistance and launch their cause into international arenas. Supranational forums like the United Nations, the Organization of American States, the International Labor Organization, and the Russell Tribunal have upheld numerous complaints concerning state abuses against Indian peoples and censured many a transgressing country thanks to the joint effort of Indians and non-Indian NGOs. History has told a long story of the state against the Indians, but now we witness a more balanced contest where the Indians strike back against the state (Ramos 1998a: Chapter 3). Universal human rights—this double-edged sword—have in actual practice been more beneficial than detrimental to the Indians.

THE CUTTING EDGE OF ETHNICITY

Nongovernmental organizations have added a new twist to the dialectical spiral that involves the various actors in the scenario of interethnic relations. In face of the mistreatment Latin American indigenous peoples have suffered in both government and private hands, the more actors that enter the scene, the better the chances that conditions are created to reverse a centuries-long process. NGOs are one of the new agents that came in to fill the gap of communication between Indians and non-Indian powers. In fact, they often replace the state not only as conductors of indigenist policies but also as Indians' guardians (Ramos 1994). They represent crucial pieces in the complex chess game of interethnic politics by creating conditions leading to possible Indian checkmate. The logical chain in this game seems to follow a fairly predictable pattern: the nation-state violates indigenous human rights, Indians react, NGOs intervene by submitting the Indians' case to international forums, international forums censure the nation-state, and the nation-state takes measures to ease the pressure, cosmetic as these measures may be. Very often national and international public opinion provides additional support in favor of the Indians. Frequently the international agency in question is a development bank which sets conditions for loans pending a given state's assurances to treat its Indians better.

This is a twentieth-century phenomenon, unavailable to the numerous indigenous peoples who over the centuries disappeared altogether despite the efforts of some devoted defenders like Bartolomé de las Casas. One can only imagine how different the destiny of peoples like the extinct Tupinambá of the Brazilian coast would be if NGOs had already existed in the sixteenth and seventeenth centuries. The coming into being of NGOs and their steady growth in financial resources, power, and numbers are also a sign of this fin-de-siècle, an example of national governments' increasingly privatizing state responsibilities, including the management of indigenous affairs (Favre 1996; Ramos 1998a: Chapter 6).

The dialectical spiral of contemporary interethnic politics has culminated in constitutional provisions for indigenous rights in several Latin American countries. Stavenhagen puts it in a nutshell:

> Due to the political awakening of indigenous peoples some national laws have also been modified. In the past few years, for example, the constitutions of Panama, Guatemala, and Nicaragua have granted certain rights to their indigenous communities. Argentina has approved an indigenous law. Peru and Ecuador recognize indigenous languages . . . Although changes are slow . . . Latin American governments are responding to the demands of indigenous peoples and beginning to recognize, albeit reluctantly, certain collective rights one might call ethnic or indigenous rights that complement the individual human rights conferred—even when only on paper—to all persons, including the Indians. (1989: 90–91)

By the year 2000 Canada and sixteen Latin American countries had undergone constitutional reforms that incorporated provisions to guarantee fundamental rights to indigenous peoples (Padilla 1996: 96n1; Marés 1996; Van Cott 2000). In September 1999 representatives of various indigenous peoples in Venezuela marched on the National Congress in Caracas to pressure the Constitutional Assembly for the inclusion of important pro-Indian provisions in the new constitution, such as the right to ownership, free transit across international borders, free choice of nationality, and land demarcation within two years (*El Nacional*, September 8, 1999, p. 1).

Although the spirit and the letter of the law are not always followed in practice, the fact that nonindigenous legislators incorporated pro-Indian articles in their most fundamental law is in itself worthy of attention. Credit for this lies not so much with these legislators but rather with strong indigenist lobbies, sometimes through armed conflicts, that for decades amassed sufficient bargaining power to influence legislators and other state representatives. In this process the role of international forums is far from negligible, as explicitly acknowledged in the case of Colombia (Sánchez, Roldán, and Sánchez 1993: 30–31; Padilla 1996: 88).

In these cases where the new constitutions addressed the Indian issue at the national level, one might say that the complex pressures, national and international, that resulted in these constitutions exemplify what Veena Das has called "critical events," that is, milestones that triggered "new modes of action . . . which redefined traditional categories" (Das 1995: 6). Although the Latin American contexts of constitutional reform are not comparable to the tragic occurrences that Das exposes in India, the idea that an event or series of events can change the course of life for human populations is equally applicable to the dilemmas now facing indigenous peoples under liberal constitutions. Indeed, their newly acquired rights do not eliminate their mixed-blessing character or the ambiguous potential of constitutions to become Trojan horses (Padilla 1996).

By comparing Colombia and Brazil I hope to acquire a better sense of the underlying trends that led to the pro-Indian measures included in the constitutions of Colombia in 1991 and Brazil in 1988. This is my attempt to understand why national states have lately shown themselves to be so "magnanimous" toward their Indians, if I may be excused for the irony. I must emphasize that my purpose here is not to treat indigenous movements in general but to focus on two countries where the indigenous population is a very small minority whose influence in the wider affairs of those nations is virtually negligible. Unlike countries such as Ecuador, Peru, Bolivia, Mexico, and Guatemala where the weight of indigenous presence can sometimes depose presidents, affect state policies, and even lead to civil wars, in countries such as Brazil and Colombia, with Indians representing less than 2 percent of the population, the impact of indigenous political pressures necessarily has a different character and raises a different set of analytical issues. In these contexts one is faced with a distinct kind of indigenous power. It is a power that affects those countries' image rather than their *Realpolitik*.

The Colombian Case

In the 1960s newspapers carried the hideous story of Colombian men who, having brutally tortured and killed an Indian family, were judged and acquitted with the argument that they did not know it was a crime to kill Indians (Bodley 1975: 28). Thirty years later Colombia ratified what is perhaps the most progressive constitution in Latin America regarding native peoples. Three decades is indeed a short time for such a drastic change. What happened in the interim was a combination of armed conflicts, international attention, and the motivation of a weak state to hand over much of its responsibility toward its indigenous population to the Indians themselves. The iron hand of the church, to whom the state had delegated the management of indigenous communities; the continuous encroachment by landgrabbers; armed assaults on villages; and organized resistance on the part of the Indians were constant, with roots in colonial and republican eras (Jimeno and Triana 1985; Jimeno 1996).

In 1970, 80 percent of coffee-growing lands of the Cauca region were in non-Indian hands. The Indians responded by creating the Consejo Regional Indígena del Cauca (CRIC) in 1971, whose main agenda was to recover lost lands. The founding of CRIC marked a new phase in the ongoing land repossession campaigns in the region. Retaliatory action from both landowners and government resulted in the repression of indigenous assemblies and the militarization of the region. By 1979, 30 CRIC leaders had been killed and 40 more imprisoned (IWGIA 1986: 34). For a while CRIC was associated with the Marxist-oriented ANUC (National Association of Peasant Users) until it became clear to the Indians that their ethnic cause was being overpowered by the class struggle that guided the peasant movement. CRIC also issued a public denunciation of the Colombian Armed Revolutionary Forces (FARC), which was "not prepared to accept our autonomy" (IWGIA 1983: 35). In 1982 FARC claimed responsibility for the murder of seven CRIC members the previous year, arguing that the Indians were counterrevolutionaries. By July 1986 it was estimated that over 100 people had been killed in indigenous communities by members of FARC (IWGIA 1986: 37). The government in turn, claiming to find guerrillas among the Indians, proceeded to kill them as well. Caught in the right-left crossfire, CRIC lost many members. But, at the same time, the Indians reclaimed much of their lost land, while their organization gained international support and visibility (Rappaport 1994: 16).

In the early 1980s two nationwide indigenous organizations were created in Colombia: ONIC (National Indigenous Organization of Colombia) and AICO (Indigenous Authorities of Colombia). Heavily supported by NGOs, especially from abroad, both indigenous organizations were instrumental in preparing the way for the gains the Indians achieved in the 1991 Constitution (Jimeno Santoyo 1998: 126).

According to the new constitution, written by delegates directly elected by the people, Colombia is now defined as a "culturally and ethnically plural and diverse" nation where indigenous peoples enjoy the long-claimed right to have "their normative systems considered not simply as *usos y costumbres* [customary law], but as true systems of law distinct from the general legislation of the Republic" (Jimeno Santoyo 1998: 72–73). This constitution considers Indians to be Colombian citizens like the rest, with equal rights and duties, although as Indians they are assigned special rights. Furthermore, Indians now have their collective rights fully recognized. Is this a success story like that of the Kuna in Panama (Bartolomé and Barabas 1999)? Or are there other layers of political complexity in this apparently enlightened democratic turn?

Nearly a decade after the ratification of the 1991 Constitution, the outcome of self-government for Colombian Indians is still an uncertain blessing. Commentators are unanimous in praising the advancement of the new constitution when compared to previous laws (Padilla 1996; Jackson 1996; Jimeno 1998). But they also point out its risks. One is related to the sharp decline of indigenous political mobilization. Since the state "has imposed its own agenda on the Indians" by having them elected to government positions for the management of indigenous affairs, these new Indian officials can find themselves drowned in things non-Indian: "nowadays one needs a lot of time to be able to be an Indian" (Padilla 1996: 87). Getting the Indians busy with administrative chores and responsibilities where they incarnate the state within their own territory has produced a political vacuum, the effect of which is to dampen "what used to be the object of their criticisms and resistance" (Padilla 1996: 88). Entangling the Indians in bureaucratic labyrinths is one way of defusing political energy and shifting their attention away from structural problems inherent in the relation between ethnic minorities and the nation-state not contemplated in the new constitution, such as indigenous autonomy to manage natural resources in their territories. The new constitution, enlightened as it may be, leaves open the real possibility of turning indigenous lands into the object of both state and private development projects (Myriam Jimeno, personal communication, 1999).

The Colombian state has invaded indigenous spaces in a fashion similar to what was reported for Mexico during the Partido Revolucionario Institucional (PRI) era, when that all-powerful political party seized the statute of *usos y costumbres* (customary law) as its own in order to obtain indigenous support (Barabas 1998: 357–359). The result in Colombia has been a growing generational rift favoring young people who speak Spanish, are fluent in national affairs, and are thus more apt to carry out the new provisions of the 1991 Constitution. This occurs to the detriment of old, traditional leaders who stand for the very diversity the new constitution aims to protect and whose interethnic political tactics have become obsolete (Jimeno 1996). Behind state preservation of traditions and ethnic diversity, bureaucratic processes are dislodging the guardians of those traditions. In short, the state operational model may quite likely be incompatible with traditional management procedures.

When the affirmative principle of indigenous collective rights is put into practice, it runs the risk of falling into good old individualism: the new and inexperienced agents of indigenous affairs, in complying with the country's laws rather than relying on traditional modes of decision-making such as those, for instance, based on shamanic knowledge, end up depending on "professionals who most often are not attuned to the wisdom of indigenous thinking" (Padilla 1996: 80). Lack of indigenous expertise in Western-style management carries yet another risk: that of aggravating the centuries-old disdain for indigenous knowledge and modes of thought. Racism, intolerance, and greed are not automatically soluble into the text of a constitution. Furthermore, there is the very real danger of indigenous communities' being swallowed by national power structures (Hildebrand 1993: 20). If, as Padilla asks, "the constitutional text is not mere rhetoric . . . how should the relations between state and Indigenous Peoples be organized so as to allow for an equitable participation with mutual respect for diverse values and cosmovisions?" (Padilla 1996: 89).

The new constitution has in fact created what is perhaps an insolvable contradiction when it affirms the rights of indigenous peoples to their traditions and cultures and charges them with government-style management, while demanding from them a cultural authenticity that would justify these rights. After centuries of pressure for the Indians to assimilate into Colombian society, the inevitable question is asked: what is an authentic culture (Jackson 1991)? How can the Indians be both "authentic" and "state managers"?

At the bottom of this true aporia there is yet another contradiction at the heart of the Colombian pluralist nation-state: on the one hand, the legal rhetoric of preservation of authenticity and, on the other, the developmentalist impetus of both the government and economic groups such as oil companies (Myriam Jimeno, personal communication, 1999). Torn between the illusion of safeguarding the Indians' authenticity and incorporating them into the national economy and society, the Colombian state goes on generating layers of contradictions in a schizophrenic process that in the end transfers to the Indians the burden of a stifling collective double bind.

Seen from another angle, this state ambiguity discloses yet another chain of issues. Under the guise of reorganizing state powers in territories that were historically the province of other powers like the church, the new Colombian constitution reinforces the trend toward decentralization. Whereas indigenous affairs were previously part of the state's responsibilities—if not *de facto*, at least *de jure*—now, with the creation of Indigenous Territorial Entities, the state almost entirely delegates those responsibilities to the Indians themselves. What the 1991 Constitution seems to have done is ratify the image of Colombia as a weak state, as manifested in its incapacity, or unwillingness, to control missionary action, guerrilla activities, the illegal drug industry, or the undeclared civil war that has been undermining Colombian citizenship. In fact, this debility of the Colombian state has been expertly used by indigenous peoples and organizations in their self-empowering tactics. This is a vivid illustration of what we may call "ethnicity in flux," transforming concepts, laws, and precepts into fluid political tools (as Jull [1999] points out for the peoples of the Arctic), better regarded as mutating strategies than as fixed essences. As artifacts of the "white man," state constitutions tend to unveil the perhaps inevitable failure at the "fusion of horizons" (Gadamer 1975) whenever the logic of the West attempts to encompass other logics for its own purposes. They also reveal how the cracks in Western legal logic—and they are not small—can become the privileged territory of ethnic contestation and self-affirmation, as the following case demonstrates.

The Brazilian Case

The 1988 Constitution of Brazil, even without the enlightenment of its Colombian counterpart in ethnic matters, can nevertheless be viewed as a sort of watershed for indigenous affairs. We might well consider the order of things Indian as divided into B.C. (before the constitution) and A.C. (after the constitution). But, as we did with the Colombian case, let us go back to the 1960s in order to appreciate the importance of the new constitution for Brazilian Indians.

It was in the early 1960s that the country mostly ignored the last throes of the Xetá, a Guaraní-speaking people who lived in the southern state of Paraná. Relentlessly besieged by megacolonization projects, the Xetá were literally ambushed to death in their own shrinking territory under the absentminded inattention of the Brazilian state and society. Their total extinction, apart from eight survivors who were kidnapped in childhood by the invaders, put an end to a life of constant fear, daily flights through the forest, food poisoning, lethal epidemics, famine, the affliction of having their children abducted, and the interminable harassment of approaching tractors, chainsaws, pastures, farms, and mass colonization (Silva 1998). State "protection" in the Xetá case amounted to a few quick and timid attempts to locate the Indians in their desperate flight from site to site in the forest. The Indian Protection Service at the time could not or would not face up to the orders of the governor of Paraná, the major promoter of mass colonization. Disregarding the information provided by kidnapped Xetá youngsters used as guides, "attraction teams" decided that the area was clear of Indians, despite recent photographs taken in some camps by a team of researchers. When at last the state could no longer deny the existence of the Xetá, it morosely tried to set aside a piece of land for them. But before any bureaucratic steps were taken, the Xetá no longer existed. Ironically, the reserve allotted to them was in the region of the Sete Quedas Falls, later wiped out by the Itaipu dam. It is not hard to imagine how many times the Xetá kind of tragedy has been repeated for the last 500 years of Brazil's existence.

Well, times have changed since the 1960s. The political visibility of the indigenous cause has grown so much both in Brazil and in the world that indigenous peoples are not so easily, quickly, and inattentively extinguished. Largely guided by the new actors on the interethnic scene, the NGOs, the world's eye has been sufficiently focused on high-risk peoples like the Yanomami to prevent crimes against collectivities such as the Xetá from being committed with impunity and in silence.

The indigenous movement in modern Brazil began timidly in the early 1970s with a series of "indigenous assemblies" sponsored by the Catholic church. Just as the Salesians assisted the Ecuadorian Shuar in their organizing efforts that culminated in the creation of the Shuar Federation in 1962–1963 (Salazar 1977), the Brazilian Catholic CIMI (Indigenist Missionary Council) was highly instrumental in indigenous consciousness-raising. In 1980 the Union of Indian Nations (UNI) was created, in part as a direct response to some drastic measures the state was preparing aimed at ending the special status of the Indians (Ramos 1998a: Chapter 6). In 1978 Rangel Reis, President Ernesto Geisel's minister of the interior and at the time the immediate superior of the National Indian Foundation (FUNAI), drafted the infamous "emancipation decree" allowing the state to wash its hands of indigenous peoples as its wards. The undeclared reason behind this seemingly progressive move was to release indigenous lands from the exclusive usufruct rights held by the Indians and open them for development. As long as Indian peoples are under the wardship of the state, the lands they occupy remain inalienable as state property. The Indians are not the collective owners of their territories but have permanent and exclusive access to their natural resources, excluding the subsoil. The minister's move was meant to be a further—perhaps final—step toward the total integration of the Indians, in conformity with the assimilationist policy of the country since colonial times.

The result was a strong protest on the part of non-Indian supporters who actively contributed to the growth of the indigenous movement. In practically every state capital in Brazil a pro-Indian association cropped up, determined to pressure the government into shelving the emancipation decree. All over the country indigenous leaders sprang up as if by magic, engaging non-Indian audiences, often in flawed Portuguese but with an enthusiasm that urban society needed in times of military repression.

This sudden burst of indigenous indignation and clamor for justice, together with the prompt receptivity of non-Indian supporters, can be traced to at least two powerful motives: one was the centuries-old misery to which the Indians had been submitted, which was strongly expressed in the CIMI-organized indigenous assemblies, an efficient training ground for potential leaders. The other motive, on the part of non-Indians, was the severe censorship imposed by the military after the 1962 coup. In those circumstances, the Indian issue was practically the only subject-matter with political overtones that was somewhat safe to discuss openly, particularly when expressed by the Indians themselves, due to their definition as relatively incapable and therefore protected by legal impunity. Between the lines of indigenous protest discourses non-Indian sympathizers often found enough space to attack the military without overexposing themselves to harassment and arrest. While the labor movement in the 1960s was heavily repressed, the Indian movement survived the last ten years of dictatorship relatively unscathed apart from attempts by government agents to disrupt meetings and to dilute its political importance with the ban on the phrase "Indian nations" (Ramos 1998: Chapter 6). Thus, in the late 1970s and early 1980s the Indians were ready to speak out and their allies ready to listen.

The creation of UNI caused great discomfort in the jittery government. Military leaders even tried to declare it illegal on grounds of national security as the movement was, they said, infiltrated by undesirable alien influences. They argued that wards (*tutelados*) cannot create organizations outside their guardian's jurisdiction (Ramos 1998a: Chapter 6). Unlike the Colombian case, where open conflicts defined a situation of warfare engulfing the indigenous population, in Brazil the Indians' official status as "relatively incapable" members of Brazilian society continued to undermine their capacity to act as full agents in interethnic conflicts. Repression took the form of piecemeal, insidious murders of key leaders rather than clashes between whole communities and their assailants. In 1983 alone eleven Indians were assassinated in various parts of the country, mostly in situations of land disputes. All these crimes went unpunished.

The 1980s was a decisive decade for indigenous peoples. While state and private repression soared, the growing strength of the indigenous and indigenist movements began to make itself visible in the press, among lawyers, and in the National Congress. Although no indigenous candidate was elected to the House of Representatives prior to the Constitutional Assembly, the Indian cause gained the sympathy and support of large sectors of Brazilian civil society, including the Brazilian Anthropological Association (ABA), the Brazilian Bar Association (OAB), the Brazilian Association of Geologists (CONAGE), and a number of NGOs as major players. Public demonstrations by Indians and non-Indians outside the National Congress in Brasília filled prime-time news programs and made many a newspaper cover story. Large groups of Kayapó, Xavante, and various northeastern Indians—fully clad in feathers, black and red paint, and bright necklaces, singing, dancing, or simply seating themselves in Congress rooms facing the politicians in charge of the new constitution—generated a symbolic power that greatly contributed to the legal advances ratified in 1988. The political effervescence of those exhilarating days made it quite clear that, small as the indigenous population may be in Brazil (about 300 thousand people or less than 0.2 percent of the total population), their presence in the national scene is anything but negligible.

A major improvement in the 1988 Brazilian Constitution is the elimination of assimilationist clauses that were written in previous constitutions. The new law no longer refers to respecting indigenous traditions until the Indians are "harmoniously integrated into the national communion." It simply states the Indians' rights to their own "social organization, customs, languages, beliefs and traditions, and their original rights to the lands they traditionally occupy." This in fact changes the status of Indianness from a temporary condition to a permanent state, thus implying the obsolescence of the wardship (*tutela*) regime according to which the state is responsible for the Indians until they come of age as citizens.

Another step in the same direction of eliminating direct state intervention in the lives of indigenous peoples is Article 232 of Chapter 8, Title 8, which declares that the Indians, their communities, and their organizations are legitimate parties in court appeals defending their rights and interests. In such cases the Public Ministry is charged with the supervision of all legal acts. As we will see below, this provision has had the effect of changing the character of the Indian movement in ways that are reminiscent of what is happening in Colombia.

But, unlike Colombia, the postconstitution Brazilian state has not renounced its control of Indian lands, which continue to be state property. As before, the Indians have the right to permanent possession and exclusive usufruct of the natural resources of their territories, except the subsoil, but the lands are not the collective property of the Indians. The state is still responsible for demarcation and protection, and the necessary legislation to implement the text of the constitution has yet to be passed.

As a result, an increasingly weak and outmoded National Indian Foundation continues the feeble exercise of its powers of guardianship wherever there is a void of indigenous organizing. Proposed new legislation has been waiting for years in Congress for approval. One of these, the Statute of Indigenous Societies, should replace the 1973 Indian Statute. Notice that the word chosen is "Societies," not "Nations" or "Peoples," for both words have been banned from the official vocabulary for reasons that echo the disputes surrounding ILO Conventions 107 and 169. Another law awaiting presidential approval is the new Civil Code that is to replace the old Code of 1916 according to which the Indians are declared "relatively incapable." This new Civil Code removes the Indians from that category and adds the following paragraph: "The capacity of the forest dwellers [*silvícolas*] will be regulated by special legislation." While the new code deals with the transformation of indigenous status by simply suppressing any reference to the issue, it maintains the anachronistic characterization of the Indians as "forest dwellers." The Portuguese word *silvícola* carries a strong connotation of primitiveness.

Meanwhile, before wardship is definitely revoked, many indigenous peoples are acting as if it is already a thing of the past. Replacing the defunct UNI, which as a centralized body was far removed from the attention and interests of the country's highly dispersed and diverse indigenous population, myriad indigenous organizations cropped up in the late 1980s and 1990s. In the Amazon alone there are over 200 Indian NGOs, each with its own legal status, agendas, directive bodies, and non-Indian allies. Most of these new organizations are concerned with amassing funds (usually from abroad) to carry out local projects of health, education, or development. They are heavily supported by environmentalist NGOs that bet on the great potential of the indigenous sector to establish sustainable development (Albert 1997: 193–199).

The effect has been, as in Colombia, a numbing of the Indian movement as a political force. Whereas in Colombia, according to Colombian analysts, it is the state itself that undermines indigenous mobilization by placing state responsibilities in the Indians' hands, in Brazil the state has not explicitly delegated its custody of the Indians to the Indians themselves but has permitted other actors, especially NGOs, slowly to fill in spaces the state is unable or unwilling to occupy. Notice how President Fernando Henrique Cardoso reacted to the NGO protest against the unpopular Decree 1775 (establishing new procedures for land demarcation) during one of his visits to Europe: he made an appeal for them to turn into "neo-governmental organizations" (*Folha de S. Paulo*, September 9, 1995). What passed as a joke to change an uncomfortable subject has proved to be the prognosis of a tacit course of action. Almost imperceptibly the contemporary processes of signification and resignification of ethnicity as acted out by indigenous peoples in Brazil have been framed by national and international nongovernmental organizations (Ramos 1994). Privatization of indigenous affairs has come to Brazil as it has elsewhere in Latin America.

BOOMERANGING

State *tutela* having been severely undermined, the stage is now set for some interesting experiments in the field of indigenous rights. An illustration is the case of the Panará Indians, a Je-speaking group of Central Brazil who, under the name Krenakarore, became known in the early

1970s for the harassment they suffered from FUNAI's pacification teams. In 1967 the Panará saw for the first time a sample of white power in the form of airplanes flying low over their villages, which they tried to repel with bows and arrows. The pacification team under the leadership of *sertanista* (backwoodsman or, more freely translated, Indian tamer) Orlando Villas-Bôas was charged with the job of removing the Panará from the course of the Cuiabá-Santarém road under construction, which would cut through their territory. In 1974, in full view of photographers, naked Panará women and children were begging food from passengers in buses on that road. They were some of the few survivors of a series of epidemics that devastated their people. Between 1973 and 1975, 176 Panará died of contagious diseases (Araújo 1995: 316–319).

Certain of his humane intuitions, and after FUNAI's approval, Villas-Bôas decided to remove the Panará to the Xingú Park, some 250 miles to the east. Two planes were enough to remove the 79 surviving Panará, estimated to have been between 300 and 600 in the late 1960s. Not fully realizing what was happening, the Panará suddenly found themselves without a home base, with no relation to the new land, dropped on enemy ground, being greeted by a leader of their traditional foes, the Kayapó chief Raoni. For the next twenty-five years the Panará led a life of frustrations, embarrassments, and discomfort amidst other indigenous groups with whom they were obliged to interact and intermarry. In their Xingú saga, a reduced version of the North American trail of tears, the Panará were transferred seven times within the park, always hoping to find a place that would resemble the home they had been forced to abandon.

In the meantime, the state was handing Panará lands over to colonization and development. It gave 400,000 hectares to squatters ejected from indigenous lands in southern states. Occupation was frantic. "In the place of the largest village there is now the town of Matupá." Out of the traditional Panará area "23 towns and hamlets cropped up . . . Alta Floresta is the largest town, the hub of hundreds of gold prospectors and big landowners . . ." (Arnt et al. 1998: 100).

In October 1991 six Panará men went on a bus trip to their old area. Petrified, they saw the effects of twenty years of chaotic deforestation, cattle ranching, and gold prospecting. However, the northeastern portion of their old territory was still intact. The Panará began to nourish the hope of returning home. During the 1990s, with the legal support of two associated NGOs (one Brazilian, the other North American), they succeeded in retrieving about 500,000 hectares of still-preserved area. Over a two-year period the now 174 Panará began to leave the Xingú—some on foot, others by bus, still others by airplane—until, in March 1997, they all gathered together in the new Nacypotire village. They met again with their past and, most importantly, with a promising future (Arnt et al. 1998: 125). Then a boomerang effect against the Brazilian state began.

In 1994, with the help of two lawyers from the Instituto Socioambiental (former Núcleo de Direitos Indígenas), the Panará filed a lawsuit against the state seeking compensation for material and moral damages suffered during their removal to the Xingú. Three years later they won the case. The judge in charge (the same judge who had interdicted the Yanomami area in 1989 during the gold rush and whose son participated in the burning to death of a Pataxó Indian in the streets of Brasília in 1997) ruled in favor of a substantial monetary compensation for every one of the 176 Indians who died between March 31, 1973, and October 31, 1975. Although he argued that "one cannot pay for pain suffered," the judge found the Brazilian state responsible for the trauma inflicted on an indigenous people by disastrous actions on the part of one of its agencies, in this case FUNAI. The judge ordered that compensation of nearly half a million dollars be paid to the Panará, saying that the state "must pay the price of its own indecision or inefficiency" (Brasil 2001: C3). As Ricardo Arnt et al. remind us, this is the first time in 500 years, and after the extinction of 900 indigenous peoples, that a legal suit in favor of an Indian community so clearly recognizes that the shock produced by brutal interethnic contact facilitates crimes against indigenous peoples and abuses by the state, the self-proclaimed defender of the Indians.

With their quarter-century bitter exile in mostly unfriendly Xingú lands and their exultant homecoming, the Panará gave rise to a new interethnic status. Like all other Indians, the Panará had been mere objects of government (Michel Foucault, quoted in Thomas 1994: 71) or, worse, objects of nature who needed to be ferreted out of their jungle dens, in Villas-Bôas parlance (Ramos 1998b: 6). But with their successful court appeal, the Panará broke away from a debasing condition as objects of nature before their "pacification," then as objects of government, dependent on the state following pacification, finally emerging as subjects of their own will, able to choose allies and courses of action, agents of their present and their future. Without undue optimism, one can say that, as a direct outcome of the 1988 Constitution, the Panará, like any other indigenous people in the country, are, at least in principle, legitimate parties capable of representing themselves vis-à-vis the nation and the world. They too can now act against the state.

TO CUT A (NOT SO) LONG STORY SHORT

From the above discussion and from the essays in this volume, we can make some final points. One has to do with the issue raised by Padilla as to the reasons behind the recent dissemination of state concern in Latin America over indigenous rights, in stark contrast to the historical trend toward extinction, serfdom, or assimilation. Padilla interprets this trend as a consequence of the world's new interest in sustainable development. This "environmentally wise" approach validates non-Western systems of knowledge, such as those prevalent in indigenous cultures, because their treatment of nature and humans as sacred entities suits sustainable development discourses. Padilla fears that this validation may simply be a strategy to integrate indigenous populations and their territories into the world economy (1996: 92). It would, in other words, be the same developmentalist bias cloaked in a green robe.

This perfectly reasonable interpretation does not, however, preclude the motivations for the liberalization of indigenist policies in the continent. Closely associated with the economic component of contemporary logic is the equally perceptible trend toward the reduction of the state. Privatizations are the order of the day in Latin America; the IMF is unfailingly successful in persuading governments to cut back on social programs, and responsibilities formerly charged to the state are consistently being handed over to the private sector. Even traditionally strong states such as Brazil are quickly getting into step with this all-encompassing policy of "de-statetizing" the nation. This is a major feature of today's conceptual vision of how the world is being managed (Jimeno Santoyo 1998: 121). Like everybody else, indigenous peoples cannot avoid being pulled into this gravitational force, whether by means of explicit agendas like the 1991 Colombian Constitution, which delegates to Indians the management of their own Indigenous Territorial Entities, or by more subtle devices like the provision of the 1988 Brazilian Constitution that undermines state wardship to allow indigenous peoples to organize themselves as fund-raising entities for their own benefit.

Now allied with entrepreneurial NGOs, indigenous societies seem to be shifting their priorities: rather than joining forces for the advancement of a nationwide "Indian cause," they are rallying around mostly economic issues such as community development, which require a great deal of energy and money (Albert 1997). It is not surprising to find a perceptible reduction in contestatory activities on the part of the Indians, particularly in Brazil, where the indigenous population represents a very small minority. As stressed before—unlike the situation in nations with a majority or very high indigenous population—in Brazil, Colombia, Venezuela, and Argentina the influence of indigenous minority groups on the content and direction of state policies on a sustained basis is virtually null. If the majority—whether indigenous or not—has shown itself rather powerless to reverse the trend toward a "minimal state," what is to be expected of the minorities? Having obtained certain constitutional gains (some of which are peripheral to the nation's "real" concerns) and realizing that this means diminished official attention and sense of responsibility toward them, indigenous minorities are now channeling their energy less into pressuring the government to do what it was obliged to do and more into amassing funds to supply their communities with the basic services they once expected from the state (Albert 1997: 189). In such a context, it is apparent that political mobilization does not go well with self-management.

A second point I would like to make, which is especially relevant in cases such as Guatemala (Warren 1998 and this volume), is about class versus *ethnie*,[2] an issue that once mobilized heated debates and today, although much less absorbing, is still on the table. Even in the new economic and political context where indigenous peoples are summoned to participate in arenas historically alien to them, and thereby increasingly occupying spaces previously the dominion of national segments, ethnic logic and class logic do not merge easily into one another. We have seen in the case of the Colombian CRIC organization how the Indians detached themselves from the peasant and urban revolutionary movements the moment their common cause was superseded by considerations of class, on the one hand, and of ethnic identity, on the other. An analogous situation involved the Brazilian UNI (Union of Indigenous Nations) and the congregation of Amazonian workers in the extractive industry, particularly rubber tappers, under the banner of the Forest Peoples Alliance. Even though rubber tappers in Amazonia do not, strictly speaking, constitute a class, no doubt they aspire to be recognized as such. Indians and non-Indians were together during the time it took for their demands to be expressed in national and international forums. But the alliance did not survive the cleavage of ethnic and class interests. Although at times these interests may coincide, the "'ethnic line' . . . persists, cutting across occupational categories, neighborhoods, and even companionship" (Cardoso de Oliveira 1976: 65).

Ethnic awareness, like class awareness, emerges from specific historical processes which can, in fact, initially converge with class. But once created, ethnicity follows a path of its own; that is, "once objectified as a 'principle' by which the division of labor is organized, ethnicity assumes the autonomous character of a prime mover in the unequal destinies of persons and populations" (Comaroff and Comaroff 1992: 59). To subsume the logic of ethnicity under the logic of class is to miss its most significant attributes as a social, cultural, and political phenomenon. There is, among other things, a major difference in the ideologies that inform class and ethnicity: in one case, a quest for a uniformity of interests of the "workers of the world, unite!" type; in the other case, the quest for legitimate diversity. "Nor," say John Comaroff and Jean Comaroff, is this ethnic quest "confined to any particular sociological category. It applies as much to those for whom ethnic ideologies legitimize dominance as it does to those for whom ethnic labels are signs of subordination" (Comaroff and Comaroff 1992: 59).

One obvious difference between class and *ethnie* is the linguistic factor. Whereas language—important as it is—is not a major distinctive feature of class membership, among the profusion of traits that make up an *ethnie* (see, for instance, Smith [1981] for an extensive treatment of the subject) language stands out as a beacon of human diversity. Like everything else in matters of ethnicity, language becomes a political artifact whenever is it used as a measure of ethnic identity. Graham (this volume) demonstrates this by exposing the intricacies of the politics of language in the Brazilian interethnic context. The linguistic issue is particularly intense in Europe, where the demands of minorities, ethnic or otherwise, for full recognition collide with the notion of a European Union. In the last two decades linguistic rights have gained as much space in international arenas as human rights have over the past fifty years (Giordan 1992: 33–36). This quest for linguistic legitimacy goes hand in hand with the dissemination of armed conflicts the world over. In 1988 alone, 99 out of a total of 111 clashes in the world involved ethnic or regional minorities confronting governments for autonomy or secession (Giordan 1992: 9). It is evident that whereas *ethnie* and class, despite some points in common, espouse separate political projects with separate constituencies and agendas, *ethnie* and language are often associated in demands for self-representation vis-à-vis the nation-state, particularly in the case of indigenous peoples.

A third and final point refers to the ambiguity of the state toward its ethnic diversity. Here I am referring to that aspect of the state not as a hypostasized machine but as an organization run by individuals. Naturally, government affairs and objectives are not the same as those of its representatives. As a concept the state is, obviously, not an agent. As an institution it takes on a tangibility that goes well beyond its human agents. But there is undeniably a subjective side to the state. After all, institutional solutions arise from the subjectivity of human beings. Practices, norms, and laws are produced by people with their own personalities, ideological preferences, and political interests (Ramos 1998b).

A case in point is the removal of the Panará to the Xingú Park. It was the emotional arguments of Orlando Villas-Bôas, disturbed by the wretched scene of Panará beggars on the road, that prompted the president of FUNAI in 1975 to order: "Orlando, go ahead and transfer them!" (Arnt et al. 1998: 95). That was how Panará lands were cleared for large-scale occupation. Correspondingly, it was the absence of action or, to put it in less generous terms, criminal omission on the part of the Brazilian government that led to the demise of the Xetá in 1964. This voluntaristic aspect of the state deserves greater anthropological attention for its potential to unveil dimensions akin to the stuff of which "Orientalisms" (Said 1979) are made.

Indeed, the subjective face of the state is an important component in the construction of what I call Indigenism, an Americas-style, amplified form of Orientalism. It amounts to a permanently unfinished ideological edifice built upon ethnic differences. Indigenism is a Babel of conjunctions and disjunctions erected with a great variety of materials that include such disparate things as official policies, religious and lay agents, anthropological constructs, journalistic representations of the Indians, and regional and urban imagery as well as indigenous attitudes toward the dominant society. Both in the heart of darkness where the Xetá were exterminated and in the open stage of Panará deportation, it is hard to sort out state from nation from society. Xetá and Panará, like so many other indigenous peoples, are icons of the intricate game of interethnic politics that involves both private and public subjects. Entangled in this Babel of interethnic cross-purposes, Indigenism offers anthropology what Bruno Latour (1993) has described as a quasi-object, a hybrid hatched in the nest of interethnic misunderstandings.

The inability of virtually all national states to respect the interests of their indigenous peoples is in part responsible for the modern phenomenon of indigenist NGOs and the transit of the Indian issue through international forums. At the present conjuncture, ethnic groups have found the most comfortable alliance to be not with social classes, not with the state, not with the church, but with supranational powers and private managers of ethnicity. As apt instruments for the empowerment of indigenous peoples by means of substantial funding and the quest for autonomy—be it cultural, economic, or territorial—suprastate organisms like the U.N. and extranational entities like NGOs are equipping the Indians with the tools they need to reshape twenty-first-century ethnicity.

Acknowledgments

I thank Jean Jackson and Kay Warren for their kindness and fruitful comments; Myriam Jimeno and Wilson Trajano Filho for their perceptive observations; Dominique Buchillet, Silvia Vidal, and Paul Little for their generous assistance.

Notes

1. In early 1999 the Brazilian National Congress reluctantly approved Brazil's endorsement of Convention 169.
2. The difficulty of conveying in English the notion of "ethnic" in noun form leads me to follow Anthony Smith's option of using the French form (1983: 187). I could equally use the Portuguese and Spanish versions, etnia, but my choice is motivated by the precedent in the relevant literature in English.

References

Albert, Bruce. 1997. Territorialité, ethnopolitique et développement: A propos du mouvement indien en Amazonie Brésilienne. Cahiers des Ameriques Latines 23: 177–210.

Alcina Franch, José. 1990. Introducción. In José Alcina Franch, ed., Indianismo e indigenismo en América, 11–17. Madrid: Alianza Editorial.

Anderson, Benedict. 1983. Imagined Communities. London: Verso.

Araújo, Ana Valéria, ed. 1995. A defesa dos direitos indígenas no judiciário: Ações propostas pelo Núcleo de Direitos Indígenas. São Paulo: Instituto Socioambiental.

Arnt, Ricardo, Lúcio F. Pinto, Raimundo Pinto, and Pedro Martinelli. 1998. Panará: A volta dos índios gigantes. São Paulo: Instituto Socioambiental.

Barabas, Alicia. 1998. Reorganización etnopolítica y territorial: Caminos oaxaqueños para la autonomía. In Miguel Bartolomé and Alicia Barabas, eds., Autonomías étnicas y estados nacionales, 343–366. Mexico City: Conaculta/INAH.

Bartolomé, Miguel, and Alicia Barabas. 1999. Recursos culturales y autonomia étnica: La democracia participativa de los Kuna de Panamá. Anuário Antropológico/97: 197–223.

Binder, Teodoro. 1977. The Right of the Third World to Develop in Its Own Way and Remarks on the Idea of "Change." In Elías Sevilla-Casas, ed., Western Expansion and Indigenous Peoples: The Heritage of Las Casas, 51–56. The Hague: Mouton.

Bodley, John H. 1975. Victims of Progress. Menlo Park, Calif.: Benjamin/Cummings.

———. 1977. Alternatives to Ethnocide: Human Zoos, Living Museums, and

Real People. In Elías Sevilla-Casas, ed., *Western Expansion and Indigenous Peoples: The Heritage of Las Casas*, 31–50. The Hague: Mouton.

Bourne, Richard. 1978. *Assault on the Amazon*. London: Victor Gollancz.

Brasil, Sandra. 2001. Decisão inédita da' indenização a índios. *Folha de São Paulo*, November 18, C3.

Cardoso de Oliveira, Roberto. 1976. *Identidade, etnia e estrutura social*. São Paulo: Pioneira.

Comaroff, John, and Jean Comaroff. 1992. *Ethnography and the Historical Imagination*. Boulder, Colo.: Westview Press.

Das, Veena. 1995. *Critical Events: An Anthropological Perspective on Contemporary India*. Delhi: Oxford University Press.

Davis, Shelton. 1977. *Victims of the Miracle*. Cambridge: Cambridge University Press.

Favre, Henri. 1996. *L'Indigénisme*. Paris: Presses Universitaires de France.

Gadamer, Hans-Georg. 1975. *Truth and Method*. New York: Crossroad.

Giordan, Henri, ed. 1992. *Les minorités en Europe: Droits linguistiques et droits de l'homme*. Paris: Editions Kimé.

Grant, Bruce. 1995. *In the Soviet House of Culture: A Century of Perestroikas*. Princeton: Princeton University Press.

Hildebrand, Martin von. 1993. Presentación. In Enrique Sánchez, Roque Roldán, and María Fernanda Sánchez, eds., *Derechos e identidad: Los pueblos indígenas y negros en la constitución política de Colombia de 1991*, 17–24. Bogotá: Disloque Editores.

IWGIA (International Work Group for Indigenous Affairs). 1983. Colombia: CRIC Disassociates Itself from Guerrillas. *Newsletter* 33: 35.

———. 1986. Colombia: Indigenous Communities Caught in Web of Warfare. *Newsletter* 46: 33–38.

Jackson, Jean. 1991. Being and Becoming an Indian in the Vaupés. In Greg Urban and Joel Sherzer, eds., *Nation-States and Indians in Latin America*, 131–155. Austin: University of Texas Press.

———. 1996. The Impact of Recent National Legislation in the Vaupés Region of Colombia. *Journal of Latin American Anthropology* 1 (2): 120–144. Special issue on Ethnicity Reconfigured: Indigenous Legislators and the Colombian Constitution of 1991 (Joanne Rappaport, ed.).

Jimeno, Myriam. 1996. Juan Gregorio Palechor: Tierra, identidad y recreación étnica. *Journal of Latin American Anthropology* 1 (2): 46–77. Special issue on Ethnicity Reconfigured: Indigenous Legislators and the Colombian Constitution of 1991 (Joanne Rappaport, ed.).

———. 1998. A questão indígena na Colombia pós-Constituição. Paper delivered at the seminar "Indigenismo na América Latina: O estado da arte" organized by Alcida Rita Ramos, Departamento de Antropologia, Universidade de Brasília, November 23–24.

Jimeno, Myriam, and Adolfo Triana. 1985. *Estado y minorías étnicas en Colombia*. Bogotá: Cuadernos del Jaguar/Fundación para las Comunidades Colombianas.

Jimeno Santoyo, Gladys. 1998. *Los pueblos indígenas en el país y en América: Elementos de política colombiana e internacional*. Bogotá: Dirección General de Asuntos Indígenas del Ministerio del Interior.

Jull, Peter. 1999. Internacionalismo indígena: ¿Cuál es el próximo paso? *IWGIA Asuntos Indígenas* 1: 12–17.

Klor de Alva, Jorge. 1995. The Postcolonization of the (Latin) American Experience: A Reconsideration of "Colonialism," "Postcolonialism," and "Mestizaje." In Gyan Prakash, ed., *After Colonialism: Imperial Histories and Postcolonial Displacements*, 241–275. Princeton: Princeton University Press.

Latour, Bruno. 1993. *We Have Never Been Modern*. Cambridge, Mass.: Harvard University Press.

Marés, Carlos Frederico. 1996. As constituições americanas e os povos indígenas. In *Povos indígenas no Brasil 1991/1995*, 29–33. São Paulo: Instituto Socioambiental.

Morin, Françoise. 1992. Vers une déclaration universelle des droits des peuples autochtones. In Henri Giordan, ed., *Les minorités en Europe: Droits linguistiques et droits de l'homme*, 493–507. Paris: Editions Kimé.

Morin, Françoise, and Bernard Saladin D'Anglure. 1994. Le développement politique des peuples autochtones dans les Etats-Nations. In Gabriel Gosselin and Anne Van Haecht, eds., *La réinvention de la démocratie: Ethnicité et nationalismes en Europe et dans les pays du Sud*, 189–204. Paris: L'Harmattan.

Muehlebach, Andrea. 2001. "Making Place" at the United Nations: Indigenous Cultural Politics at the U.N. Working Group on Indigenous Populations. *Cultural Anthropology* 16 (3): 415–448.

Padilla, Guillermo. 1996. La ley y los pueblos indígenas en Colombia. *Journal of Latin American Anthropology* 1 (2): 78–97. Special issue on Ethnicity Reconfigured: Indigenous Legislators and the Colombian Constitution of 1991 (Joanne Rappaport, ed.).

Ramos, Alcida Rita. 1994. The Hyperreal Indian. *Critique of Anthropology* 14 (2): 153–171.

———. 1998a. *Indigenism: Ethnic Politics in Brazil*. Madison: University of Wisconsin Press.

———. 1998b. *Uma crítica da desrazão indigenista*. Série Antropologia No. 243. Brasília: Department of Anthropology, Universidade de Brasília.

Rappaport, Joanne. 1994. *Cumbe Reborn: An Andean Ethnography of History*. Chicago: University of Chicago Press.

Said, Edward. 1979. *Orientalism*. New York: Vintage Books.

Salazar, Ernesto. 1977. *An Indian Federation in Lowland Ecuador*. IWGIA Document 28. Copenhagen: International Work Group for Indigenous Affairs.

Sánchez, Enrique, Roque Roldán, and María Fernanda Sánchez, eds. 1993. *Derechos e identidad: Los pueblos indígenas y negros en la constitución política de Colombia de 1991*. Bogotá: Disloque Editores.

Silva, Carmen Lucia da. 1998. Sobreviventes do extermínio: Uma etnografia das narrativas e lembranças da sociedade Xetá. Florianópolis: M.A. thesis, Universidade Federal de Santa Catarina.

Smith, Anthony D. 1981. *The Ethnic Revival in the Modern World*. Cambridge: Cambridge University Press.

———. 1983. *Theories of Nationalism*. New York: Holmes and Meier.

Stavenhagen, Rodolfo. 1989. Los derechos humanos de los pueblos indios. In

Adolfo Colombres, ed., *1492–1992: A los 500 años del choque de dos mundos: Balance y prospectiva*, 85–92. Buenos Aires: Ediciones del Sol—CEHASS.

Tauli-Corpuz, Victoria. 1999. Treinta años de trabajo de "lobby" y abogacía por parte de los pueblos indígenas en el ámbito internacional. *IWGIA Asuntos Indígenas* 1: 4–11.

Thomas, Nicholas. 1994. *Colonialism's Culture: Anthropology, Travel and Government*. Princeton: Princeton University Press.

Todorov, Tzvetan. 1989. *Nous et les autres: La réflexion française sur la diversité humaine*. Paris: Seuil.

Van Cott, Donna Lee. 2000. *The Friendly Liquidation of the Past: The Politics of Diversity in Latin America*. Pittsburgh: University of Pittsburgh Press.

Warren, Kay. 1998. *Indigenous Movements and Their Critics: Pan-Maya Activism in Guatemala*. Princeton: Princeton University Press.

CONTRIBUTORS

DAVID D. GOW is the Baker Professor of Anthropology and International Affairs and holds a joint appointment in the Elliott School of International Affairs and the Department of Anthropology at George Washington University. His present research interests are indigenous models of development; the cultural politics of development; and the problematics of development anthropology. His publications include "Can the Subaltern Plan? Ethnicity and Development in Cauca, Colombia" (*Urban Anthropology*); "The Anthropology of Development: Discourse, Agency, and Culture" (*Anthropological Quarterly*); "Doubly Damned: Dealing with Power and Praxis in Development Anthropology" (*Human Organization*); and the coedited book *Implementing Rural Development Projects*.

LAURA R. GRAHAM is Associate Professor of Anthropology at the University of Iowa. Graham has conducted extensive linguistic and anthropological fieldwork among the Xavante Indians of central Brazil. Her research and published works focus on the ways in which social actors use discourse and forms of expressive performance, including music and narrative, to create identity, social organization, and social memory. Her current research focuses on Brazilian Indians in national and international public spheres. Graham's publications include the book *Performing Dreams: Discourses of Immortality* (Texas), which has won awards in anthropology and the humanities, and such articles as "A Public Sphere in Amazonia? The Depersonalized Collaborative Construction of Discourse in Xavante" (*American Ethnologist*); "Dialogic Dreams: Creative Selves Coming into Life in the Flow of Time" (*American Ethnologist*); and "The Shifting Middle Ground: Amazonian Indians and Eco-Politics" (with Beth A. Conklin; *American Ethnologist*).

JEAN E. JACKSON is Professor of Anthropology at Massachusetts Institute of Technology (MIT). She has carried out fieldwork in Mexico, Guatemala, and Colombia, mainly in the Vaupés region in southeastern Colombia. Her research interests include small-scale societies, ethnic nationalism, the indigenous movement, fieldwork methodology, and medical anthropology. She has published many articles and a book, *The Fish People: Linguistic Exogamy and Tukanoan Identity in Northwest Amazonia* (Cambridge), on indigenous issues.

VICTOR MONTEJO is Professor of Native American Studies at the University of California at Davis. He is one of Guatemala's foremost Mayan public intellectuals and writers. His work centers on Mayan cultural revitalization, the impact of Guatemala's civil war on Mayan communities, and the transnational Mayan diaspora as a consequence of the war. His books include *El Q'anil: Man of Lightning* (Arizona); *Testimony: Death of a Guatemalan Village* (Curbstone); *The Bird Who Cleans the World and Other Mayan Fables* (Curbstone); *Brevísima relación testimonial de la continua destrucción de Mayab'* (Guatemala Scholars Network); and *Voices from Exile: Violence and Survival in Modern Maya History* (Oklahoma).

ALCIDA RITA RAMOS is Professor of Anthropology at the University of Brasilia. She has done prolonged research among the Yanomami of Brazil and is investigating the politics of inter-ethnic relations in Brazil and other South American countries. She is the author of numerous articles and five books, two of which are in English—*Indigenism: Ethnic Politics in Brazil* (Wisconsin) and *Sanumá Memories: Yanomami Ethnography in Times of Crisis* (Wisconsin). She is currently President of the Brazilian NGO Pro-Yanomami Commission.

JOANNE RAPPAPORT is Professor of Spanish in the Department of Spanish and Portuguese at Georgetown University. Her research interests include contemporary indigenous cultural planning and the rise of indigenous public intellectuals, on the one hand, and indigenous literacy practices in the colonial period, on the other. Her research is based in highland Colombia. Her publications include *The Politics of Memory: Native Historical Interpretation in the Colombian Andes* (Duke); *Cumbe Reborn: An Andean Ethnography of History* (Chicago); and "Between Images and Writing: The Ritual of the King's Quillca" (with Tom Cummins; *Colonial Latin American Review*).

TERENCE TURNER is Professor of Anthropology at Cornell University after many years at the University of Chicago. He has done extensive field research among the Kayapó of central Brazil. His numerous writings cover their social organization, myth, ritual, history, politics, inter-ethnic contact and aspects of cultural, social, political, and ideological change. Since 1990, Turner has been a consultant to Kayapó videographers who have filmed and edited their own works for their communities' viewing. Turner has also made ethnographic films about the Kayapó with the BBC and Granada Television.

KAY B. WARREN is Professor of Anthropology at Harvard University. Her research focuses on multiculturalism and public intellectuals, social movements and ethnic nationalism, violence and peace processes, media issues, and Latin America's foreign aid donors. Her books include *Indigenous Movements and Their Critics: Pan-Maya Activism in Guatemala* (Princeton); *The Symbolism of Subordination: Indian Identity in a Guatemalan Town* (Texas); *Women of the Andes: Patriarchy and Social Change in Two Peruvian Towns* (with Susan Bourque; Michigan); and the edited volumes *The Violence Within: Cultural and Political Opposition in Divided Nations* (Westview) and *Ethnography in Unstable Places: Everyday Life in Contexts of Dramatic Political Change* (with Carol Greenhouse and Beth Mertz; Duke).

INDEX